Being for Beauty

Dominic McIver Lopes FRSC is Professor of Philosophy at the University of British Columbia and author of six books and a series of papers that examine the meaning and values of images, technology in the arts, and the nature of art and the arts. His current work looks beyond the arts to understand the human importance of our aesthetic practices.

Praise for *Being for Beauty*

"*Being for Beauty* is an immensely rich book.... It presents a distinctive and provocative account, one of the only thoroughgoing meta-aesthetic views currently on offer. It raises long overdue worries about received views like hedonism and response-dependence theories and hopes to shift some of the burden of proof onto them. In doing all this, it also eschews over-intellectual and over-noble depictions of aesthetic experts as always acting for the sake of the Fine, preferring realistic examples from an impressively wide range of cultures and aesthetic phenomena. The book aims at nothing less than setting a new agenda for aesthetics."

Alex King, *British Journal of Aesthetics*

"This tremendously rich book is required reading for, frankly, anyone interested on normativity at all, aesthetic or otherwise."

Robbie Kubala, *Estetika: European Journal of Aesthetics*

"a rich and wonderful book which not only develops a new account of aesthetic reasons, but does so in a way that engages with many different aspects of aesthetic normativity. This book is certainly of interest to those working in aesthetics, and is a must read, but it also is of interest to those working in normativity more generally."

Julia Driver, *Philosophy and Phenomenological Research*

"a monumental achievement—a wholesale reorientation of our thinking about aesthetic value, elegantly written, rigorous, and erudite. You have to read it if you're working in aesthetics. You should even if you aren't."

James Shelley, *Philosophy and Phenomenological Research*

Being for Beauty

Aesthetic Agency and Value

Dominic McIver Lopes

Great Clarendon Street, Oxford, OX2 6DP,
United Kingdom

Oxford University Press is a department of the University of Oxford.
It furthers the University's objective of excellence in research, scholarship,
and education by publishing worldwide. Oxford is a registered trade mark of
Oxford University Press in the UK and in certain other countries

© Dominic McIver Lopes 2018

The moral rights of the author have been asserted

First published 2018
First published in paperback 2021

All rights reserved. No part of this publication may be reproduced, stored in
a retrieval system, or transmitted, in any form or by any means, without the
prior permission in writing of Oxford University Press, or as expressly permitted
by law, by licence or under terms agreed with the appropriate reprographics
rights organization. Enquiries concerning reproduction outside the scope of the
above should be sent to the Rights Department, Oxford University Press, at the
address above

You must not circulate this work in any other form
and you must impose this same condition on any acquirer

Published in the United States of America by Oxford University Press
198 Madison Avenue, New York, NY 10016, United States of America

British Library Cataloguing in Publication Data
Data available

Library of Congress Cataloging in Publication Data
Data available

ISBN 978-0-19-882721-4 (Hbk.)
ISBN 978-0-19-285572-5 (Pbk.)

Links to third party websites are provided by Oxford in good faith and
for information only. Oxford disclaims any responsibility for the materials
contained in any third party website referenced in this work.

For Kristen Lopes
In memory of Maria Alexandra Clementina D'Souza Lopes

Preface

Being for Beauty: the words map three paths into this book's topic, aesthetic value. Putting the stress on "beauty" contrasts aesthetic value with other goods—social justice, insightful scholarship, friendship, or the Toronto Maple Leafs. We ask, how does aesthetic value differ from these other goods, and how does it fare in competition with them? Putting the stress on the "for" highlights the attitudes we take to aesthetic value. What is it to be for or against aesthetic value? Is it to like it, or promote it, or assent to its goodness? Both paths are worth mapping: a theory of aesthetic value should say what makes it unique, and also how we orient ourselves towards it. This book presents a theory of aesthetic value by putting the stress on *being* for beauty. Being for beauty is a configuration of human agency oriented on aesthetic values.

My secret plan, or hope, for twenty years has been to build up from a detailed examination of one art form towards a general theory of aesthetic value. *Understanding Pictures* (1996) treats images as blending language-like and perceptual elements, in a merger of the two most important information-processing systems of the brain, yielding the amazing diversity of depictive styles that thrive in different pragmatic and cultural contexts. A sequel, *Sight and Sensibility: Evaluating Pictures* (2005), locates the values of images in their extending the powers of perception, including the power to express emotions. However, a key move of the book distinguished the values images have as images from their aesthetic value, and I was disappointed that the distinction failed to impress, despite its touching on heated debates about ethicism (esp. Carroll 1996; Jacobson 1997; Devereaux 1998; Kieran 2001; Devereaux 2004; Stecker 2005; Gaut 2007).

Resolved to one day revisit the failure, I meanwhile turned to computer art, which I saw as an opportunity to investigate how materials and technologies generate artistic and aesthetic possibilities. *A Philosophy of Computer Art* (2009) also assembled the components of a comprehensive philosophy of an art form—that is, a theory of the nature of the art form, an ontology of works in the art form, a framework for criticism and appreciation, plus a defence of its status as an art. It would have been madness to attempt this with any of the well-established arts, but getting a big picture of an art form proved crucial to understanding the arts and aesthetic domains in general.

Generalizing from the special cases of depiction and computer art, *Beyond Art* (2014a) sets out a framework for building theories of any of the arts. The framework pairs the materials and technologies of each art form with a set of practice-constitutive norms, the cultural side of the story. In proof of concept, *Four Arts of Photography* (2016b) uses the framework from *Beyond Art* to rig out a new theory of photographic art practices, and to tie that theory into the history of photography.

In *Sight and Sensibility*, I had underestimated how hard it has become for philosophers to see past an assumed equation of artistic and aesthetic value. The framework set out in *Beyond Art* puts the specificities of the arts at the centre of theory-building, and it implies that an item's artistic value is just its value as a work of painting, music, dance, or one of the other arts (cf. Huddleston 2012; Stecker 2012; Hanson 2013). Since there is no more general artistic value, it seems like a good idea to retain a conception of aesthetic value alongside the values of the specific arts. Only aesthetic value resides in all the arts, and in much else besides.

A "Plea for Aesthetics" opened *Sight and Sensibility* and the "diversity constraint" of *Understanding Pictures* already allies aesthetics to the philosophy of culture, so this book about aesthetic agency and value has been a long time coming. From the beginning, I have been committed to methods that coordinate the explanatory power of generalization with close attention to lived reality—for details, see *Aesthetics on the Edge: Where Philosophy Meets the Human Sciences* (Lopes 2018). Hence the bottom-up trajectory of the books described above. The challenge has always been to know where to look for lived aesthetic reality.

While imagination kits us out to travel to unfamiliar territory, nothing beats first-hand experience, and the breakthrough insight came from a time of immersion in Japanese aesthetic culture. For several months, meeting weekly in a seminar with young artists and scholars, interacting with friends and neighbours, just greedily watching and listening, I was blown away by the texture of aesthetic activity in Japan, by the fine details of what people do in order to give expression to their aesthetic commitments. In that context, it dawned on me that philosophy has struggled to come to terms with aesthetic value because it has relied upon an attenuated portrait of aesthetic agency as consisting in the making of judgements. The remedy is to foreground rich and robust expressions of aesthetic agency that involve more than judging. Of course aesthetic agency belongs to no single people—we are all aesthetic agents—but what is hard for us to see in ourselves is very often obvious when we observe others active in a different culture.

Some astonishing confessions mark key moments of Derek Parfit's *On What Matters* (2011). Parfit thought that his life would not have been worth living were the main ideas of his book to turn out false. Philosophy lets us down when it hardens us against such personal appeals as Parfit's. We must respect how deeply important philosophy can be in the life of a philosopher. I do not say that the main ideas of this book must be true. We are only beginning to think about aesthetic value, and what we need above all is to lay a varied and enticing menu of options and arguments on the table. All the same, I do admit that I cannot imagine my career having amounted to much without my having attempted to take a fresh approach to beauty, rooting for its importance as a topic of philosophy.

A postscript for fellow style geeks, given the book's theme that aesthetic agency must be understood as thriving in local social niches. I routinely compose in British and U.S. English, though I am as much Canadian as anything else, so I have put this volume in Canadian English. I trust that's skookum.

D. M. L.

Vancouver
January 2018

Acknowledgements

Contrary to philosophy's pernicious self-image, there is no solo achievement. We each stand upon the shoulders of many others, relying upon their insights, skill and judgement, advice and generosity. Many hands deserve credit for anything in this book that has turned out well.

To begin with, all the authors I have cited. I have tried to read and cite everything pertinent, initially out of a concern about biases that skew admissions to the philosophy citation club. As it turned out, I learned far more than I expected from what I ended up reading, making the extra work worthwhile. My fellow philosophers, please try this. Cite like scientists.

The writings of Philippa Foot and Judith Jarvis Thomson most deeply influenced me. They insisted that the central cases for the study of value should be ground-level cases—being a good umbrella or being a good tiger. Philosophy has not paid nearly enough attention to relatively trivial aesthetic values and the mundane acts that engage those values. In allowing ourselves to be dazzled by grand values, we have ended up with a stunted understanding of aesthetic value across the board.

Many other philosophers have inspired the thinking in this book in more subtle yet crucial respects. A footnote to the whole book, rather than a sentence, would salute Sally Haslanger and Brian Epstein on social practices, Jerrold Levinson on aesthetic normativity, Joseph Raz on practices of value, Ernie Sosa on achievement, and Susan Wolf on value and meaning. Among philosophers writing on beauty, Mary Mothersill holds a special place. Although I completely disagree with her at the level of theory, she gets right so many of the details, and I quote from her more than anyone else. My own theory of aesthetic value develops a tradition that begins with Frank Sibley and is modified by Kendall Walton in his classic, "Categories of Art" (1970). I very much doubt I would have found a way to carry this tradition forward were it not for the intellectual companionship of James Shelley. He will not agree with all, or much, of what I have come up with, but my perception of where he might agree and where he might demur has spurred my thinking.

I also depend on attentive audiences and wise colleagues to push back with friendly skepticism. Hearty thanks go to Murat Aydede, Alan Goldman, Keren Gorodeisky, James Grant, Rob Hopkins, Robbie Kubala, Bence Nanay, Nick Riggle, James Shelley, Robert Stecker, and the Press's referees for their comments on (parts of) the first draft. Also to members of my 2017 graduate seminar, especially Aleksey Balotskiy, Jack Beaulieu, Bianca Crewe, Jeremy Dawson, Ian Heckman, Matt Kinakin, Phyllis Pearson, Sophia Sideris, Rodrigo Valencia, Servaas Van der Berg, and Juhan Yoon. Thanks to Abu Kamat for research assistance. And thanks to audiences at the University of Louisville, the University of Vienna, Paris–Sorbonne University, the 2016 annual meeting of the Canadian Philosophical Association, the International Congress of Aesthetics in Seoul, the University of Toronto conference on Art, History, and Perception, the Salt Lake City conference on Aesthetic Normativity, the 2017 meeting of the Nordic Society of Aesthetics, and Hunter College, New York.

Susan Herrington's generous read through the penultimate draft gave me the gumption to stop tinkering and get the text to press.

Finally, let me record how keenly I feel the loss of Peter Goldie and Peter Kivy, two friends whose reactions to this book would have meant a great deal to me.

Philosophers need time as historians need archives, archaeologists need pottery shards, and physicists need particle accelerators. I am deeply grateful to the institutions that materially supported the writing of this book: the John Solomon Guggenheim Foundation, the Social Sciences and Humanities Research Council of Canada, the Killam Foundation through the Canada Council for the Arts, and the University of British Columbia.

The main idea of this book was floated in "Aesthetic Experts, Guides to Value," given as a presidential address to the American Society for Aesthetics and published in the *Journal of Aesthetics and Art Criticism* (Lopes 2015). Passages of Chapters 5 and 6 rework bits of "Beauty, the Social Network," published in the *Canadian Journal of Philosophy* (Lopes 2017a), and some passages of Chapter 9 echo the text of "Disputing Taste," which was written for James O. Young's *Semantics of Aesthetic Judgement* (Lopes 2017b).

Anticipating Chapter 1, a thanks in closing to all those responsible for making a book out of a manuscript—the copy editor, designers, typesetters, printers and binders, slingers of xml, distributors, marketers, and Peter Momtchiloff, my intrepid editor, who is also a musician.

Contents

Introduction	1

Part I
1. Beings for Beauty	15
2. Getting Practical	32

Part II
3. To Seize upon the Applause of the Heart	53
4. Six Degrees of Separation	71

Part III
5. Strength and Warranties of Skill	91
6. Infrastructures of Aesthetic Agency	109
7. Hundred Mile Aesthetics	126

Part IV
8. By Happy Alchemy of Mind	147
9. Endless to Dispute	164
10. Beauty, Naturally	181

Part V
11. Getting Personal	201
12. Building Better Aesthetic Agents	217

List of Theses   235
References   237
Index   263

Nor custom stale her infinite variety.
—William Shakespeare

Introduction

What goes into dozens of decisions we take pretty much daily? What has fired the ambitions of many of our most gifted conspecifics for thousands of years? What consumes a hefty share of the world's wealth, galvanizing the efforts of national governments and local communities? What fills the temples we erect in witness to the marvellous diversity of our customs and traditions? Steve Jobs was called the CEO of what?

Beauty, of course.

The first signs of the modern mind are pieces of jewelry dating back a hundred thousand years, and the remains of fine architecture on a grand scale pepper the globe. More art is now made than ever before, using new technologies to yield new forms. A few taps or clicks open access to billions of songs, pictures, stories, and performances. Design is ubiquitous, adding value to mass manufactures. Civic events are dressed in aesthetic trappings. Natural beauty lies within easy reach. Ours is an era of unrivalled aesthetic opportunities, filling most every niche.

Yet these facts tell only half the story behind *Being for Beauty*. Putting "beauty" and (same thing) "aesthetic value" in the title of an academic book, with no hint of irony or censure, will raise eyebrows. Aesthetic value has had to endure indifference or suspicion from the scholars and thinkers to whom we have entrusted the task of helping us to make sense of ourselves and what we care about. So bad is the situation that champions of aesthetic value stand out as exceptions. A vast abyss has come to separate our best understanding of aesthetic value from the plain fact of its place in our lives. The time has come to close the gap.

The Primitive Question

Frustrated with interminable drawing-room jawing about matters of taste, Henry James's Countess Gemini declares, "I don't care anything about reasons, but I know what I like." And when Dave Hickey reminds us that "beauty is and always has been blue skies and open highways," he means that we should stop thinking and keep on driving (2009: 119). George Santayana opened *The Sense of Beauty* by confessing that nothing is so unfitting as disquisitions on the topic (1896: 6). However, the lesson is not that scholars must get out of the way of the rest of us—we ordinary folk who are innocent and unreflective receptors of aesthetic value. Worries about aesthetic value are not only academic.

Modest aesthetic endeavours that make up the fabric of everyday life need no patrons, whereas big ticket items—masterpieces of the fine arts—have needed bankrolling and protection, initially from palace and church and, more recently, from the state. Allocating state resources to the arts sparks sometimes heated debate on public patronage, its rationale and limits. Why should taxpayers fund the Bunka Cho, the Canada Council, or Conaculta? Must public arts spending be justified on the Bilbao Model, as boosting tourist revenues? Why single out the highbrow fine arts for subsidies? Only nuanced answers to these questions guide us in deciding how much support is warranted, if any. Even downright hostility to public arts spending invites thinking about aesthetic value.

Similar worries recur in the domestic sphere. Access to aesthetic value often requires learning. Much aesthetic education comes through informal channels: knowledge and skills are absorbed from exposure to the wide world and built up through play and by mimicking peers. At the same time, some aesthetic education is formal, requiring lessons taught by experts, and schooling is costly. Should it be a priority? Why? And how much? For several decades, parents have been assured that formal arts education benefits learning in the core curriculum. Many parents found this comforting, even if they already wished their children to be involved in the arts for other reasons. Alas, a comprehensive suite of meta-studies edited by Lois Hetland and Ellen Winner (2000) finds no evidence of the promised benefits. Arts education does not boost performance in math, language, science, history, or geography. Yet, as Winner cautions with Monica Cooper,

the failure to find evidence of a causal relationship between arts study and academic achievement should never be used as a justification for cutting arts programs. The arts deserve a justification on their own grounds, and advocates should refrain from making utilitarian arguments in favor of the arts. (Winner and Cooper 2000: 36)

The non-utilitarian justification the arts deserve is one we have yet to articulate.

On a personal level, almost everyone makes aesthetic commitments that impose personal costs. The costs are often easy to overlook because we are initiated into aesthetic life at an early age, without much awareness of what is happening, and we gradually grow more involved, taking for granted the price we pay as just another part of the cost of living. Only rarely are we compelled to decide whether or not to sacrifice some more tangible goods for what suddenly appear to be rather elusive and hard-to-quantify aesthetic goods. Paul Gaugin left his family to fend for themselves while he took off for Tahiti to make art. Each of us will recall how, at important moments in our own lives, aesthetic considerations have pulled uncomfortably against other considerations—in deciding on career or romantic partner, for instance. When the choice is more than a little uncomfortable, we wonder how aesthetic considerations come to have any weight at all.

Many inquiries get their first push from what Mary Mothersill called "primitive questions" (1984: 71–2). Primitive questions precede theorizing, they grip those who know nothing of theory, and they are often the questions that lead into philosophy. When one does launch a philosophical project, we keep the project on track by keeping in mind the primitive question with which it originated.

For Mothersill, the primitive question of aesthetics is, why does this item move me? Undoubtedly the question is a good one, it arises in advance of theory, and it is answerable to theory. But another question is truly the primitive question of aesthetics.

Socrates asked, how should we live? He did not mean to ask what the moral law permits us and demands of us (Williams 1985: 5). Rather, he burned to know what ingredients go into a life lived well. If, in his own life, Socrates seemed indifferent to beauty, he certainly talked it up a good deal, and Plato presents the great man's indifference as a charming oddity—perhaps a whiff of something otherworldly. Nowadays, only those gripped by some dour ideology or sour humour wish to banish beauty from their lives. (Few succeed. It is easier to live free of plastic bags.)

Since primitive questions come in advance of philosophy, we should not try to give them such definitive and rigorous statement as would entail their having gone through some philosophy. They serve us best when they are suggestive, so that we always wonder whether our theoretical achievements are true to our primitive instincts.

The primitive question of aesthetics is something like this: what is the place of aesthetic value in the good life? Or, what do aesthetic goods bring to my life, to make it a life that goes well? Or, how does beauty deserve the place we have evidently made for it in our lives?

Knowing what it is in an item that moves me leaves it open why my life goes better when it includes these things that move me. Mothersill's question is not Socrates' question, and Socrates' question is the primitive question of aesthetics. Part V returns in earnest to the primitive question, equipped to address it with the philosophy that is worked out in Parts I to IV.

Primitive questions need not be the most important questions, nor are they ones we are obliged to answer, or even ask. We must feel the tug of them. The tug is most firm during episodes of self-reflection. Listen, for example, to Monroe Beardsley in his 1968 Presidential Address to the American Society for Aesthetics:

> discoursing on aesthetic theory... ought to be done with quietness and patience. But a quiet voice is all too easily drowned out by the cries of anguish and of anger we hear around us, and patience is a virtue that only those who live in a less terrified society can afford to cultivate. Even hardened aestheticians (an obvious oxymoron) may suffer from doubts that beauty or significant form is what the world needs most right now, when quite different goods—intelligence and charity, for instance—are more likely to restore our sense of community and stop us from creating a society whose answer to all problems—aesthetic and otherwise—will be violent repression. When so many of us in this troubled land do not seem to care very much even for one another—much less for the ravaged nature and crumbling cities our descendants will inherit—the aesthetic point of view becomes difficult to sustain. It may even seem absurd. (1969: 3)

Events in the years since 1968 make Beardsley's plight all the more vivid. We cannot shut our eyes to the reality of so much suffering. How dare we waste precious energy in thinking about aesthetic value? How, in answering this question, can we guard against finding aesthetic value in only the grandest cultural monuments, monuments that might live up to Isaiah's offer of "beauty for ashes" (61:3)?

Beauty in Art

Once moved to reflect on aesthetic value, we naturally turn to arts scholars for insight, though, until recently, they have viewed beauty with suspicion, even scorn. As Arthur Danto put it in *The Abuse of Beauty*, "beauty rarely came up in art periodicals from the 1960s on without a deconstructionist snicker" (2003: 25). The arts scholars' snickers echoed the pronouncements of avant-garde artists, for whom denigrating aesthetic value was a ticket to being taken seriously. For example, John Cage admonished Juilliard students in 1952 that "the highest responsibility of the artist is to hide beauty" (2010[1952]: 98). Pushback finally came in 1999, when the Hirshhorn Museum put on a show, 'Regarding Beauty', to celebrate the persistence of aesthetic value in high-octane visual art of the late twentieth century. Ensuing years saw a smattering of provocative monographs in defence of beauty (e.g. Scarry 2001; Steiner 2001; Prettejohn 2005; Nehamas 2007; Hickey 2009; Gardner 2011; Konstan 2014).

Danto neatly sums up the charges against aesthetic value (see also Prettejohn 2005). First, aesthetic value trades in appearances. Beautification is aesthetic sophistry, "making the worse appear better," as we find in "cosmetics, fashion, interior decoration, and the like, where we are not dealing with natural but enhanced beauty" (2003: 83). Second, aesthetic value has to do with pleasure, especially sensual pleasure. For some, that is already cause for grave concern. Third, and perhaps in consequence of the first two counts of the indictment, aesthetic value is easy. The sensuous thrill comes, as Danto explains, "without benefit of argument or analysis" (2003: 93). By contrast, art makes us work hard to extract what it has to offer (Danto 2003: 89).

A fraud is a con when its victim is unaware that the crime ever occurred, and the allure of aesthetic value provides perfect cover for a con. Many arts scholars signed up for the anti-fraud squad, whose mission was to unmask hidden agendas, revealing to us, in the words of the critic A. O. Scott, that "what we have taken for beauty is really the afterimage of cruelty, inequality, intolerance, sexism, and greed" (2016: 99).

Like most things, beauty is dangerous in the wrong hands, and of course it falls to arts scholars to unmask nefarious agendas, but is it true that aesthetic value is non-contingently shallow, sensuous, and easy? Consider Titian's *Flaying of Marsyas*. We must work hard to overcome our immediate reaction and find our way to its deeper beauty. The painting scarcely brings sensuous pleasure. It is sickening to look at, utterly gut-wrenching. Nor does it indulge aesthetic sophistry, prettying up the cruelty. Titian yields not one drop of easy solace.

Acknowledging the point, Danto distinguishes aesthetic value outside art from aesthetic value that contributes to an item's value as a work of art (2003: 92–7). Whereas the former is shallow, sensuous, and easy, the latter demands "critical intelligence," imbues thought with feeling, and escapes being "shallow and false to the reality of the world" (2003: 97). For Danto, art redeems beauty.

Again: is it true that, except in art, aesthetic value is non-contingently shallow, sensuous, and easy? Does aesthetic value found outside art never demand hard work, never reward on an intellectual plane, prettify nothing? Euler's identity ($e^{i\pi} + 1 = 0$) is beautiful but hard as all heck, super-intellectual, and in no way misleading (Gallagher 2014; Inglis and Aberdein 2014). So why think that art owns a monopoly on the okay kind of beauty? Perhaps our aesthetic value concepts have acquired associations that bias our choice of paradigm cases towards beautification, while our concepts of artistic value have more hygienic associations?

Philosophers are fond of remarking that "aesthetic" was coined as a bit of technical vocabulary in the eighteenth century, though they rarely get the significance of the factoid. If "aesthetic" was introduced by stipulation for theoretical purposes, then the point of using the word is to reduce confusion and the chance of running inferences afoul of equivocation.

"Beauty" and "aesthetic value" can refer broadly to aesthetic goodness or narrowly to one species of aesthetic goodness. In the narrow sense, the beauty of some of Eric Clapton's renditions of blues numbers costs them some of their aesthetic gusto. In the broad sense, *Guernica* is beautiful because it is shocking—that is, it is aesthetically good because shocking. When Joseph Addison (1712) found passages of Milton that are "beautiful by being Sublime," he was not thinking of beauty as a complement of the sublime; he was thinking of the sublime as a variety of aesthetic value.

Let a habit of thought be a tendency to fall into patterns of reasoning under the influence of an idea that might be repudiated when made explicit. Two habits of thought lure us into bad faith about aesthetic value. The first is to overlook aesthetic value in its broad sense. Beautification happens, but only sometimes, and it is inevitable only if there is no beauty in the broad sense. In the broad sense, aesthetic value need not be shallow, sensuous, or easy. Compounding the first habit of thought is another, a tendency to look to the arts as the sites where aesthetic value comes into its own (Shiner 2001; Mothersill 2004; Forsey 2013; Wolterstorff 2015; Rose 2017). Steven Connor puts it a little more strongly when he reports that the aesthetic is commonly accepted as "having to do with the qualities that are specific to art" (2011: 55).

Sadly, the two habits of thought have hobbled recent defences of beauty in reaction to the anti-aesthetic climate. In its anti-aesthetic mode, art succeeds when it hides shallow, easy, sensuous beauty. Champions of beauty reply that beauty is integral to its artistic value when it is harnessed, through the power of art, to get us thinking hard. As Danto concluded, art redeems aesthetic value because it alone can provide difficult beauty a home.

At one time, beauty in art could be treated as a continuation of beauty outside art. After 1999, extra-artistic beauty remains beyond redemption—shallow, easy, and sensuous. Critics and champions of aesthetic value share in common the same bad habits of thought.

Decisively breaking the habit means paying attention to aesthetic value in the broad sense, wherever it may be found, not only in art. We ask, how does aesthetic value deserve the place we have made for it in our lives? In asking this, we keep in mind that some human beings have little room for art in their lives, and most have considerably more aesthetic value in their lives than they get from art. In overlooking what we find in a perennial border, a champion Komondor, the tapered leg of a table, or the economy of a mathematical proof, we cannot do justice to the primitive question.

Aesthetic Value in Aesthetics

Robert Nozick once named aesthetics the branch of philosophy that "speaks most frequently and articulately of value" (1981: 415). He was plumb wrong. Surveying the state of the field in his presidential address to the American Society for Aesthetics, Kendall Walton reported that "it would be a serious distortion, now, to characterize aesthetics as a species of value theory" (2007: 148). Only two recent books on aesthetic value have made the canon (Mothersill 1984; Goldman 1995). In a recent, five-year period, 95 percent of the pages of the field's flagship journals concerned art, while 3 percent went to nature (Irvin 2008b: 29). The aesthetics volume in the New Waves book series, which spotlights work by rising stars in each branch of philosophy, contains no chapter on aesthetic value (Stock and Thomson-Jones 2008). One might infer by induction that the topic is hopeless. Happily, the inference is defeated by an explanation of what has been happening in the field.

To begin with, art has taken a top spot on the agenda. Although many arts are ancient and found in every human culture, they only came to be grouped together as fine arts in early modern Europe (Kristeller 1951–2; Shiner 2001; Lopes 2014a: ch. 2; Pollock 2016: 1–3). Thus Chambers's *Cyclopaedia* of 1727 diagrams human activities in relation to one another as branches of a tree, and the arts are scattered across the tree. Painting goes with optics, music with applied mathematics, gardening with agriculture, and poetry with rhetoric and grammar... and heraldry. A few decades later, Diderot and d'Alembert drew a very different tree for their *Encyclopédie,* clustering the fine arts together as a single branch (Kristeller 1951–2: 520). With the new grouping came the thought that the arts share some common feature that bespeaks their special importance and distinguishes them from the sciences and the applied arts and crafts.

Kant (2000[1790]) was arguably the last in a line of philosophers who came to aesthetic value directly, not by way of art. Hegel (1975[1832]) viewed aesthetic value as belonging to the fine arts, justifying their lofty status. According to Jean-Marie Schaeffer (2000), a major project of the nineteenth century was to endow the arts with a power to reveal a special kind of knowledge, putting them on a footing with philosophy and the sciences. In Charles Taylor's history, the work of art was viewed as inspiring an awe that placed it "on the border of the numinous," where it held "the highest moral or spiritual significance" and promised us a chance to "recover wholeness, or at least escape degradation and fragmentation" (1989: 376, 419, 439).

Twentieth-century anglophone philosophy toned down the exaltation but retained the focus on art (e.g. Bell 1914). As R. G. Collingwood put it, "aesthetic theory is the theory not of beauty but of art" (1938: 41). The trend carries into postwar analytic aesthetics, notably in the work of Beardsley (1981[1958]; 1969; 1970b; 1979), Goodman (1976), and Richard Wollheim (1980). Ultimately Danto (1964; 1981) and George Dickie (1974; 1984) took the final step, theorizing art without any appeal to a notion of aesthetic value.

In the meantime, philosophers not paying dues to the aesthetics guild were writing insightfully on aesthetic value without having art primarily in mind, though, curiously, their work is unknown in aesthetics. Shining examples are G. E. Moore in *Principia Ethica* (1903) and C. I. Lewis in *An Analysis of Knowledge and Valuation* (1946). Both do more than gesture towards aesthetic value; they give it centre stage, without fussing over art. By contrast, in professional aesthetics, art has hogged the limelight.

Aesthetics has often made progress by incorporating insights from the history of philosophy and adapting tools from other areas of philosophy. Wollheim's *Art and Its Objects*, first published in 1968, tied problems in aesthetics to ideas in analytic metaphysics. That same year, Goodman's *Languages of Art* approached aesthetics as applied philosophy of language, thereby opening the door to studies of our responses to art works as implicating cognitive information processing (Lopes 2000). Perhaps it is no coincidence that the year when Beardsley expressed his despair about the wisdom of spending time on aesthetics was also the year when the field stepped closer to the rest of philosophy. Since 1968, rich work has been done on literary fiction, metaphor, art emotion, pictorial representation, and dozens of other topics (see Levinson 2003 or Gaut and Lopes 2013). The boom in productivity has been electrifying. To some extent, value got left behind in the excitement (Davies forthcoming).

Admittedly, some questions tangential to aesthetic value have been on the agenda. For example, are aesthetic evaluations objective or subjective (e.g. Goldman 1993; Schellekens 2006)? Are they ever justified by means of inferences (e.g. Hopkins 2006a; Dorsch 2013; Cavedon-Taylor 2017)? What are we to make of aesthetic disagreement (e.g. Kivy 2015; Young 2017)? How do aesthetic properties relate to non-aesthetic properties (e.g. Levinson 2005; Benovsky 2012)? You might concur with an anonymous referee who wrote that these are the questions that matter, while questions about aesthetic value per se are "irrelevant." The three chapters making up Part IV demonstrate how to make progress on the tangential questions with help from a new account of aesthetic value.

More importantly, though, no answers to the tangential questions come close to answering the primitive question of aesthetics. Suppose that aesthetic properties supervene on our responses and that aesthetic evaluations are subjective and never justified by inferences, so that there are no genuine aesthetic disagreements. Or suppose the contrary on each point. Either way, what does this tell us about why aesthetic value deserves the place we have made for it in our lives?

The Party Line

Addressing the primitive question of aesthetics requires a theory of aesthetic value. Until we know what aesthetic value is, we can hardly come to terms with its role in a life lived well. The situation is that philosophers have neglected aesthetic value, though they have a theory of aesthetic value. The inconsistency is only apparent, for there are two ways to neglect a topic. One is to say nothing on the topic. Another is to whip to a party line, taking an answer to be obvious, never engaging in genuine discussion. (Of course, that is precisely what tends to happen when attention lies elsewhere, on art or fiction or the ontology of musical works.)

Philosophers neglect aesthetic value because, when it does come up for discussion, it is so firmly whipped to a party line that little trouble is taken to do more than state what is taken to be obvious. Stated with maximal breadth, the party line is that aesthetic values are properties of worldly items that have to do with finally valuable experiences on the part of those who appreciate the items. Since a finally valuable experience is a pleasure, the party line amounts to a hedonic theory of aesthetic value. According to

AESTHETIC HEDONISM: an aesthetic value is a property of an item that stands in constitutive relation to finally valuable experiences of subjects who correctly understand the item.

So formulated, aesthetic hedonism is a template for any of a number of variants. Its main elements are unpacked in Part II. (The above formulation of aesthetic hedonism is included, along with the book's other main claims, in the List of Theses, which follows Chapter 12.)

Bibliographic note. Aesthetic hedonists include Lewis 1946; Beardsley 1969; Beardsley 1970b; Slote 1971; Dickie 1974: 40–1; Beardsley 1979; Beardsley 1982; Mothersill 1984; Dickie 1988; Eaton 1989; Goldman 1990; Levinson 1992; Walton 1993; Budd 1995: 4–8; Stecker 1997: 254–7; Miller 1998; Levinson 2002; Iseminger 2004: ch. 3; Goldman 2006; Stecker 2006; Budd 2008; Egan 2010; Levinson 2011; Strandberg 2011; Moran 2012; Pratt 2012; Stang 2012; Matthen 2015; Schaeffer 2015: 115–25; Kölbel 2016; Levinson 2016; Dammann and Schellekens 2017; and Matthen 2017. An opposition exists: Knight 1967; Zangwill 1999; Sharpe 2000; Carroll 2002: 154–63; Davies 2006; Shelley 2010; Wolf 2011; Lopes 2015.

The Main Argument and Bonus Arguments

Part III introduces the network theory of aesthetic value as an alternative to aesthetic hedonism. A theory of aesthetic value is a proposition that indicates the nature of aesthetic value. What says the network theory? Sorry, you must remain in suspense for a few more pages, and make do with an outline of three sets of arguments in favour of the theory.

The main argument is a limited, contrastive argument to the best explanation. A full abductive argument for the network theory would start with a set of facts about aesthetic value that competent inquirers accept as needing to be explained. Next would come a demonstration that the network theory better explains the facts than all contenders. These steps completed, an inference to the truth of the network theory would be warranted. Alas, a full argument to the best explanation is not yet in the cards.

To begin with, aesthetic hedonism and the network theory might not exhaust the options, and a full abductive argument must compare all the options. For now, there are reasons to proceed with less than a full set of alternative theories. Arguing for the network theory is a way to shake aesthetic hedonism from its dogmatic slumbers, so that its proponents are brought round to argue for it. At the same time, crafting and defending just one alternative to aesethetic hedonism is a way to inspire philosophers to invent fresh alternatives (e.g. Feinberg 1994: 114; Shelley 2010: 715–19; Shelley 2011: 217–21; McGonigal 2017). In as much as the network theory significantly differs from aesthetic hedonism, it can hint at a menu of features to include in new theories of aesthetic value.

A contrastive argument to the best explanation draws the conclusion that a theory is true because it better explains the relevant facts than does a competing theory, at a time when the two theories are the only serious contenders. Contrastive arguments are conclusive when the available theories ultimately turn out to be the only contenders, and they are promising when treated in a heuristic spirit—as the best we can do for now, a necessary step towards a full argument that takes all contenders into account.

A second fact calls for an abductive argument that is limited. As the party line, not much effort has been put into producing arguments for aesthetic hedonism. Scanning the literature yields neither a set of facts that competent inquirers accept as needing to be explained, nor even a set of contentious explananda around which disagreement is focussed. Some explananda must be assembled from scratch.

Limited abductive arguments proceed by proposing some explananda, when there are no prior, agreed explananda. The risk is that aesthetic hedonists will be tempted to reject any proposed explananda that their theory does not explain. The risk is worth taking. In a heuristic spirit, limited abductive arguments are a first step to bringing parties round to eventual agreement on explananda. They press their case as hard as possible in conditions that are, for the time being, less than ideal.

Part I launches the main argument by describing in concrete detail six scenarios where we see aesthetic value at work. From these scenarios, six explananda are extracted. Part II sings the attractions of aesthetic hedonism and then goes on to argue that the theory nonetheless does a poor job of explaining what needs to be explained. Part III follows up by setting out the network theory of aesthetic value and making a case for its explaining what needs to be explained. So concludes the main argument.

Supplementing the main argument are five bonus arguments, grouped in two sets, that enhance the network theory's appeal.

Questions sometimes arise, in the course of theorizing, upon which we find we require satisfaction. Philosophers have puzzled over the nature of the attitudes that we characteristically take to aesthetic goods, the significance of aesthetic disagreement, and how to accommodate aesthetic value facts in a natural world. Each topic is especially puzzling because we lack, and find it hard to get, a clear understanding of what problem needs to be solved. The three chapters of Part IV deploy the network theory first to clarify what problems we face and then to devise solutions. So we have three bonus arguments: the network theory clarifies and adequately addresses three philosophical problems. The background assumption is that it is a mark in favour of the truth of any theory that it solves philosophical problems.

With Part V, the book returns full circle by calling on the network theory to come to grips with the primitive question. Chapter 11 takes a personal perspective, sketching out how personal aesthetic pursuits contribute to personal well-being. Chapter 12 switches to the collective perspective, laying out an entirely new justification for aesthetic education and the aesthetic policies of groups, especially states. In other words, the book closes with two bonus arguments, both assuming that a theory of aesthetic value is fit for purpose when it sheds light on how aesthetic activity enriches our lives, as individuals and as members of communities.

In sum, the network theory beats aesthetic hedonism in explaining the facts that need explaining (Parts I to III). It articulates and then allays worries about aesthetic attitudes, aesthetic disagreement, and the metaphysics of aesthetic value (Part IV). Finally, it articulates insightful answers to the primitive question (Part V). Ergo the network theory is true.

Please do not be misled by a conclusion expressed so boldly, not tricked out with qualifications. Operating in a heuristic spirit means proceeding as if a conclusive case is in the making. Committed aesthetic hedonists are invited to regard the arguments for the network theory as foils to use in defending their own view. (Nothing focusses the mind like vigorous yet generous disagreement. Should aesthetic hedonists turn out to have been right all along, it will have been worthwhile to prove it.) Meanwhile, anyone unimpressed with the network theory is free to cherry-pick ideas for inventing new theories, and anyone impressed with the theory is invited to improve upon the clumsy start made here. Abductive arguments always invite alternative explanations of the same explananda, as well as proposals of alternative explananda. A new perspective on motivation, disagreement, the metaphysics of aesthetic value, and the place of aesthetic value in the good life is bound to open up some space within which we can locate a range of new views.

PART I

1
Beings for Beauty

Morality touts its saints (Urmson 1958; Wolf 1982). Aesthetics has its exemplary figures, too, who thrive in their aesthetic pursuits. Call them "experts." Experts do not rise heroically above the call of duty, but their capability, dedication, and effectiveness adorn them, and for this we rightly esteem them. Whereas you and I muddle through our aesthetic lives, hoping for the best, experts have what it takes to get it right. They do well because they tune in aesthetic value. In their agency, we see the difference aesthetic value makes.

Six Snapshots

Who are these experts? One search strategy is to make a list of admirable traits and then find out who has them. Aesthetic vocabulary abounds with adjectives of character assessment. People are aesthetically phoney or sincere, obtuse or insightful, baffling or clear, crude or perceptive, boringly obvious or intriguing. Maybe an aesthetic expert is one who matches all and only right-hand disjuncts. Another strategy is to comb the record for the big names, festooned with laurels, boasting the longest entries in the Who's Who of aesthetics, so as to assemble a gallery of great men of aesthetic eminence (given the method, they will be men). A serious concern speaks against both strategies. Outlier bias is an occupational hazard of aesthetics. Inspiring as they may be, outliers eclipse the less anomalous data points that need explaining. To remedy outlier bias, we sample widely and generously. Therefore, here are six mostly unsung types from many walks of life whose aesthetic endeavours merit admiration.

The Gardener and the Restorer. In 1925, the 53-year-old Elsie Reford was urged by her physician to take it easy after a bout of appendicitis. He thought that gardening might make a suitable pastime for a "convalescent woman of a certain age" (Reford 2001: 23). Reford had certainly lived energetically (Reford 2004). She was a skilled caribou hunter and salmon fisher, who enjoyed horseback excursions hundreds of kilometres into the Gaspé. When at home in Montréal, she chaired the management committee of a hospital for unwed and indigent mothers, founded the first women's club in Canada, helped to organize the women's vote after suffrage, and campaigned to improve relations between her city's anglophone and francophone communities (Hébert 2009: 284–90). Gardening was never going to be a few hydrangeas in the back yard.

Not yet knowing a daisy from a dandelion, Reford was nevertheless reputed in her family to combine the "enthusiasm of an amateur and the conviction of the convert" (Reford 2001: 9). The summer of 1926 saw her embark on what would turn out to be a decades-long scheme to transform the site of her fishing lodge at Grand-Métis into an elaborate suite of English gardens (Reford 2004). Grand-Métis lies far down the St Lawrence River, 600 kilometres northeast of Montréal, in rugged and inhospitable terrain. There were no nurseries nearby and, upon clearing the spruce forest, Reford learned that the soil was unfit for horticulture, so she had to make her own. Thirty years later, she had cultivated more than fifty thousand plants in a dozen gardens covering 15 hectares. Botanists admired her collection of more than sixty varieties of lily, the only gentian garden in the world, and her spectacular drifts of the rare and uncooperative Himalayan blue poppy (*Meconopsis betonicifolia*). None of this was imagined to be possible in Grand-Métis. The landscape architect Susan Herrington credits Reford with hitting upon a principle—one now widely adopted—to site plants according to microclimatic fit (2004: 48).

When she was unable to tend the garden any longer, Reford sold it as a park to the province of Québec, and it slowly declined, until 1994, when it was named a national historical site in trust of a non-profit foundation headed by Reford's grandson, Alexander Reford.

Agents have problems to solve. Elsie Reford set out to grow tender plants in brutal boreal conditions. Alexander Reford set out to restore the garden to its glory and puts its operations on a sound and sustainable footing. Elsie Reford had kept meticulous notes and her husband, Robert Reford, was an amateur photographer who also documented the gardens. However, funding the restoration and making the garden a going concern meant attracting repeat visitors from great distances—Grand-Métis is a long day's drive from Montréal and dense forests separate it from the northeastern United States.

Reford refurbished the lodge as an inn with conference facilities, a restaurant, and the inevitable gift shop. He added a museum and programs for school visits and educational holidays. He commissioned a blue poppy logo for the garden and marketed the plant's seeds with reliable advice on its cultivation. You can become a Friend of the Garden, and major donors are solicited. So far, these are the basic efforts, not enough to guarantee success.

Among the first sights to greet visitors to the Reford Gardens is an art work by Francine Larivée, a sculpture of moss, entitled *Un Paysage dans le paysage— Le Paysage comme tableau vivant*. Reford's genius move was to counterpoint the historical gardens with contemporary responses to them. In 2000, he opened the first garden festival in North America to serve as a landscape lab dedicated to "playful and provocative" installations by young landscape architects that "redefine our conception of a garden" (Reford 2004: 70). That first year there were six installations; by 2015, 309 teams from thirty-four countries competed for thirty spots. Many festival projects have reshaped thinking about landscape design (Johnstone 2007).

Visitors to the festival in its inaugural year would have had a chance to experience Claude Cormier's Blue Stick Garden. Cormier painted closely packed planting stakes poppy blue on three sides and orange-red on the remaining side. Moving through the space induces delightfully visceral op-art effects. Yet, according to the citation for an award from the Canadian Society of Landscape Architects, the garden is "firmly anchored in the context of traditional gardening practices" (CSLA 2001). Herrington explains that Cormier's work alludes to Elsie Reford's use, in her perennial plantings, of the colour theory propounded by Gertrude Jekyll (2009: 15–16). Cormier transposes Reford's soft blends of analogous colours into brash, pixellated complementaries. And whereas Reford's colours change with the seasons, Cormier's change with the visitor's movement. In place of her live plants needing tending, we have plainly artificial stakes, ones used for planting, that underscore Reford's own artifice as a designer and hybridizer. Reford acknowledges that while his forebear might not have appreciated installations like Cormier's, the garden festival updates, reflects upon, and enriches her accomplishment, keeping alive the adventure she embarked upon in 1926 (2004: 70).

Tens of thousands now travel annually to Grand-Métis to stroll Elsie Reford's gardens and delight in, or puzzle over, the festival installations. The Refords' joint accomplishment is now listed among the twenty-five *Great Gardens of America*, in company with Monticello and the Huntington (Richardson 2009).

The American Picker. A year after Elsie Reford took up gardening, Berenice Abbott met Eugène Atget. Abbott had quit college in the United States and moved to Paris, where she learned photography as an assistant in the studio of Man Ray and gained a reputation for her portraits of the likes of Janet Flanner and James Joyce. By 1928, she was showing her work alongside Ray and André Kertész and had enlisted Peggy Guggenheim as a patron. Returning to the United States, she was funded during the 1930s by the Federal Art Project of the Works Progress Administration (WPA) to photograph New York City, producing a book of three hundred images with supplementary historical documents (Abbott 1939). She also founded the photography program at the New School, where she taught until 1958, and wrote a successful how-to book (Abbott 1941). In 1939, she turned to photographing scientific phenomena—soap bubbles, magnetic fields, standing waves, refractions, motion—and she considered these photographs to represent the purest photographic realism (Abbott 1969). By the 1980s, she was recognized as one of the most important photographers of the modernist tradition, and of the century. She was the first photographer elected to the American Academy of Arts and Letters, in 1983.

Agents are often double agents, operating on behalf of many causes. Abbott certainly deserves to be celebrated as one of the most interesting and important photographers of her time. At the same time, she chose to direct some of her energies not towards her own work but to that of Atget.

At the time Abbott met him, Atget was an unknown. Around 1890 he had opened a studio selling photographs as materials for "designers, illustrators, amateurs of Old Paris, architects, tapestry makers, couturiers, theater directors, sign painters, sculptors, and painters" (Abbott 1964: xx). His clients included Braque, Vlaminck, Matisse, and Ray. By the late 1890s he had obtained commissions to document the urban fabric of Paris for six archives and libraries, though he kept up his trade plying images to artists (Worswick 2002: 26). His friend, André Calmettes, noted Atget's "intransigence of taste and process" (quoted in Abbott 1964: xxx). He used an $8 \times 10''$ view camera with a primitive, uncoated lens and no filters, from which he rendered contact prints using the albumen process with gold chloride tints. There was no dodging or burning or cropping. Yet something caught Abbott's eye. When he died in 1927, she purchased what was not in the national institutions—1,400 glass plate negatives and 7,800 prints of 4,218 subjects (Morel 2012: 14). By 1967, Abbott was able to lodge the collection with MoMA, in what was then the museum's single largest expenditure for art (Morel 2012: 18). By the 1980s, Atget had entered the textbooks, which played up both his quirky surrealism and his proto-modernist style and subject matter (e.g. Lifson 1980). Without Abbott, Atget would have ended up another unknown commercial photographer (Solomon-Godeau 1991).

The route from Abbott's 1927 purchase to the 1967 MoMA coup was anything but straight and easy: Abbott promoted Atget tirelessly and imaginatively. She exhibited him, first at the important Film und Photo show in Berlin in 1929, then at the Photography show at Harvard in 1930, where Atget headlined with Abbott, Walker Evans, Alfred Stieglitz, and Paul Strand (Morel 2012: 17). The breakthrough show was at the Limelight Gallery in New York in 1956. She also printed his plates, bringing to them the skill of one of the finest printers of the era, and her use of the silver gelatin process gave Atget a contemporary look. Since photographs are displayed in books as well as galleries, she orchestrated three volumes, including one pairing Atget with Proust (Abbott 1930; Trottenberg 1963; Abbott 1964).

Her 1964 *World of Atget* is a classic that confronts the toughest aesthetic problem that Atget posed. The problem had already been stated in her 1930 book, in an essay by Pierre MacOrlan. Atget had left behind a mountain of unedited work, and the problem was to extract a "personality" from "innumerable anonymous prints" (Abbott 1930: 23; see also Solomon-Godeau 1991: 30). Later commentators complain about her "aestheticization" of Atget (Baldwin 2000: 8). What was the alternative? Indeed, compounding Abbott's challenge was the perceived insecurity of photography as an art, or as a legitimate aesthetic medium (Abbott 1951; Abbott 1964: xxi). Every art photographer of the era had to build their career partly by making a case for taking the medium seriously.

As portrayed by Abbott, Atget is a quintessential modernist or "straight" photographer (Solomon-Godeau 1991: 37). Photographers in the pictorialist tradition had sought to secure the art status of photography by borrowing the thematics, atmospherics, and techniques of painting. The modernists rejected the pictorialist strategy as untrue to the essential power of photography to depict things as they simply are. However, the modernists' own strategy generates a dilemma (Lopes 2016a). What need the photographic artist, if the mechanical camera ensures photographic objectivity? And if the camera does not ensure objectivity, then how is the photographer any different from a painter, without the painter's freedom?

Abbott ingeniously squared the circle: apparent reasons to doubt Atget's artistry actually confirm it. His commercial practice insulated him from the aesthetic fashions that swept Paris and that might have steered him to pictorialism. Moreover, he made images to which others were to add the art. Not that he was some primitive or naive. He worked strenuously, trudging heavy equipment and glass plates around the city, making contact prints with exposures up to an hour long, then cataloguing them for multiple clienteles. Like a figure from Balzac, he was poor, a working stiff, and a social outsider (cf. Worswick 2002: 28). Even the gripping story of Abbott's discovering him dramatizes his specialness. She saw in him the rare ability to see photographically, to see what his camera could capture as true and hence enable us to see too. In this way, he opened our eyes to what painting cannot show—our everyday lives (Abbott 1964: xxvi; see also Trottenberg 1963: 22). In sum, Abbott's Atget was born to exploit photography's objectivity.

The portrait of Atget in *The World of Atget* snaps to life in Abbott's graceful editing of the images. His world is a world of manual labourers, carriages, shopfronts, domestic interiors, fairgrounds, streetscapes, industrial sites, canals, parks, and trees. As a result, "to see the work of Atget, one has to see the world from Berenice Abbott's point of view" (Worswick 2002: 9–10).

The Networker. Oprah Winfrey is a prizewinning actress, movie producer, writer, publisher, and entrepreneur. Her talk show has won thirty-four Emmy Awards, including nine for best in format and nine for best host. In 1996 Winfrey added a book club segment to the show, and three years later she was honoured at the National Book Awards for contributions to reading and books. While mere mention of the Oprah Book Club (OBC) occasions groans and snickers in some quarters, the hecklers are wrong.

According to its mission statement, the *Oprah Winfrey Show* aimed "to use television to transform people's lives, to make viewers see themselves differently, and to bring happiness and a sense of fulfillment into every home" (quoted in Rooney 2005: 13). Having observed that "our society values...swiftness of experience," Winfrey wondered whether "the slow, sensual art of reading—and its difficult pleasures—survive," and she set out to "reintroduce reading to people who've forgotten it exists" (quoted in Rooney 2005: 120, 187). However, as she knew, discussing books on TV cannot build audiences: it drives them away, because they lose interest unless they have already read the book and can follow the story. Agents have problems to solve, and the problem Winfrey faced was of the pump-priming variety.

Agents solve problems using means actually at their disposal. Winfrey is intelligent and articulate, affable and empathetic. In *Reading with Oprah: The Book Club That Changed America*, Kathleen Rooney describes her as "effusive, inclusive, enthusiastic, hellbent on personal betterment, and fun, fun, fun" (2005: 203). She was all this and more on television, a platform with huge reach, whose powers Winfrey had mastered.

She succeeded on several counts. First, she managed to retain her audience. Second, she massively pumped up readership, in a phenomenon that came to be called the "Oprah Effect." OBC selections sold out print runs in the hundreds of thousands, sometimes boosting sales by two orders of magnitude. The club drove more sales of Toni Morrison than the Nobel Prize for Literature (Rooney 2005: 123). Meanwhile, booksellers reported that 75 percent of those buying her book club selections also bought another title (Rooney 2005: 121–2). Within a few years, the number of small book clubs in the United States doubled to five hundred thousand, with five to ten million members (Rooney 2005: 14). Third,

Winfrey's choices siphoned sales from pulp fiction: readers hunkered down with more difficult texts (Garthwaite 2014). OBC selections included Jonathan Franzen and Barbara Kingsolver as well as *Anna Karenina* and *One Hundred Years of Solitude*. The first thirty-one selections, all new titles, included only three with negative reviews in the *New York Times* (Rooney 2005: 78). By Rooney's reckoning, the book club "put us through our paces of moral awareness, affiliation, and disaffiliation" (2005: 76). Finally, Winfrey's eclectic choice of authors and topics cut across and helped to dissolve the traditional divide between "high" and "low" literary culture in the United States (cf. Radway 1997).

Measurable successes such as these will hardly convince Winfrey's more thoughtful critics. Acknowledging her success, they deplore her means. One complaint is that the format of the show and its self-help philosophy encouraged superficial and sentimental treatments of books that had far more to offer than simplistic stories of triumph over adversity (Rooney 2005: ch. 4). Readers were asked to focus on how they felt about characters and their stories, and to always relate what they read to their own lives. According to another complaint, Winfrey missed the chance to get meta—to acknowledge and question her power as an arbiter of taste, to entertain some self-consciousness and irony about the process, and hence to encourage multiple readings (Rooney 2005: 26–7, 52, 134–5). As Rooney puts it, Winfrey made "communal and familiar what should be an individual and unsettling experience" (2005: 110).

Both complaints share a mistaken assumption, namely that the club was a vehicle for reviewing and criticism—practices that run from the bestseller list, at the most basic level, to the seminar room, at the more sophisticated end of the spectrum. Critical reflection can be done on TV: if you want the BBC's *Talking Books*, then there is always the BBC's *Talking Books*. The OBC was exactly what Rooney says, a space for a community of readers to share experiences (2005: xii). That is not what happens in a seminar room. Winfrey created a space for community sharing by understanding her audience, finding the books that would speak to what they had been through and what they cared about, and helping them to witness to that. Wally Lamb, an Oprah author interviewed by Rooney, makes the point that the club

> mirrors what goes on in the thousands of living rooms across the country where book discussion groups proliferated: a general discussion during which people relate their questions, observations, and reasons why they did or didn't relate to the characters. We both filter fiction through our own lives and use it to go beyond our lives. That ... is more purposeful than the performance of critical autopsies. (2005: 112)

To pooh-pooh the communal mode of reading that Winfrey fostered is to impose on all readers a set of standards associated with "high" literary culture.

Bollywood audiences sing along with musical sequences, having the projectionist replay them over and over; audiences at predominantly African-American cinemas shout out advice to the characters and josh with each other as they comment on the action. Many are the ways we profitably engage with stories.

As it happens, some book club enthusiasts were drawn into more reflective, detached, and individualistic reading styles. Rooney found audience hopefuls in line at the studio with marked-up books, disagreeing about points of interpretation, pondering the challenges faced by Canadian writers in the US book market (2005: 130–1). Modes of reading can complement and even support each other, either synchronically or sequentially.

Winfrey's successes with her book club came not despite but, on the contrary, because of the features of her show that her more thoughtful critics dislike. She destabilized traditional hierarchies because she knew her audience wanted "richly drawn, fully realized characters, moving purposively and plot-fully through sophisticatedly rendered and vividly described worlds" (Rooney 2005: 73) and she understood how to get her audience to find these qualities in difficult books. Sales of *Anna Karenina* went through the roof because she led her audience in relating to it. That made for great TV to boot. Discussing books can tie them into our personal histories so as to connect us to each other. Winfrey breathed new life into the ancient institution of the neighbourhood book club by bringing it into living rooms across the continent.

The Reverse Engineer. Medieval Romans mined their city's antiquities for building materials, apparently without giving their pillaging a moment's thought. Nowadays tremendous resources are devoted to cultural preservation, from UNESCO to local museums and archives. A few years ago I found myself in conversation with Sam, a colleague's teenage child, who told me that she contributes to an international fan base of video game conservers. Whether or not any video games are works of art, many appeal aesthetically (Lopes 2009; Tavinor 2009; Gaut 2010). Sam's contributions are aesthetic acts.

Brick-and-mortar institutions archive video games. By 2007, the Library of Congress outpost in Culpepper, Virginia, had collected three thousand games. Each game is represented by a written description, a printout of fifty pages of source code, and a video clip of game play (Bernstein 2014). The International Center for the History of Electronic Games at the Strong National Museum of Play in Rochester does better. It exhibits video games, publishes blogs, and sponsors research. It also archives the personal papers of important game designers, such as Will Wright, and it stores game consoles and platforms as well as software. The Strong is the Getty Institute of video games.

What the fan base does is importantly different. Sam and her peers aim to keep classic games alive. They are conservation ecologists rather than archivists. The problem they face is that video games are acutely vulnerable to two kinds of obsolescence. Obsolete physical media—consoles and hardware—make games impossible to run. Obsolete data formats make them impossible to maintain. So the fan base looks out for "abandonware," proprietary applications that are no longer supported by their manufacturers, and they try to get their hands on the source code. With source code, it is much easier to fix bugs and distribute patches, and a game can be ported to new platforms, breaking dependencies on specific physical platforms.

Since source code also reveals how a game works, inspecting it affords understanding and creativity. Documentation embedded in the code is directly informative. For example, engineers' comments provide a peek behind the scenes of the creative process, as in this very human example from the code for *Donkey Kong*:

;; HISTORY: ;;
;; Nov '82—IDS, initial coding ;;
;; Dec '82—more coding, hair pulling, general cruftiness ;;
;; Jan '83—schedule screaming, rampant insanity, accusations ;;
;; Feb '83—semi-winnage, accompanied by cries of anguish and threats ;;
;; Mar '83—Lucifer announces a cooling trend ;; (Tempest 2008)

Anyone who writes for living will appreciate that. In addition, appreciation is deepened when a peak beneath the hood reveals design challenges (Baxandall 1985). Here a hacker announces the release of the *SimCity* source code:

The key thing here is to peek inside the mind of the original Maxis programmers when they built it. Remember, this was back in the day when games had to fit inside of 640k so some "creative" programming techniques were employed. *SimCity* has been long a model used for urban planning and while it's just a game, there are a lot of business rules, ecosystem modeling, social dependencies, and other cool stuff going on in this codebase. It may not be pretty code but its content sure is interesting to see. (Simser 2008)

An Atari 2600 game called *E.T. The Extra-Terrestrial* is reputed to be one of the worst games ever. A devotee's blog makes a case for the game's virtues by stepping readers through the code, inviting them to modify bits of code so that they can see for themselves how the game works (Anonymous 2013).

Some manufacturers now release the source code of unsupported applications into the care of their fans (e.g. Crowd 2015). However, when manufacturers cannot or do not cooperate and release source code, fans go it alone. They monitor eBay for sales of old disks, they launch crowdfunding campaigns to raise funds to buy materials, they engineer "leaks" from the inside, and sometimes they dumpster dive in search of discarded disks (Good 2014). Another approach is technical. Executables can be disassembled and decompiled. However, since brute force decompiling is often unreliable, aficionados learn the techniques and styles of early coders, track down snippets of original code, and use their experience of the game to refine the decompiled code, much as you might reverse engineer some English translated by Google into Japanese and then back into English. Websites document individual experiences with the task and pass on tricks (e.g. Slangard 2014). As should be obvious, members of the community copiously document and share their sleuthing and what they uncover.

The Dance School Director. Aesthetic agents operate upon items of aesthetic interest, but they also operate upon each other. Indeed, they operate on items by operating on each other, and they operate upon each other by operating on items (a theme of Chapter 6). Take aesthetic education, for example. Experts spread their knowledge and skills to raise the general level of aesthetic proficiency. Typically they do this by guiding our encounters with items of aesthetic interest. So any aesthetic agent who has an impact on other aesthetic agents contributes to aesthetic education. Some make it their business.

A few years ago Hannah inherited a dance school in a tiny village. Dance schools in well-populated areas can count on a ready clientele of little girls who are keen on ballet, but this school must draw students from some distance. Therefore it must keep up a reputation for offering something special. High standards are set for instructors and students. Challenges must be keyed to ability, so that students are neither bored nor frustrated. Not every instructor has the judgement to reliably attune what students are dancing to what they can dance, so judgement is needed in hiring decisions. Meanwhile, public performances motivate. They motivate intellectually by bringing together elements learned in isolation. They also motivate by affording pride in success through effort and capability. The school calendar features performances of interesting and well-produced dances. Finally, in a setting like this, considerable sensitivity to social externalities is an asset, if not an absolute necessity. Asked for an example, Hannah reported that boys are easily spooked. She never mentions leotards. In just a few years she has sent an unusually high number of dancers to the national ballet school.

Aesthetic agents are made, not born; they follow lifelong trajectories, not calling it a day once they have mastered finger painting or Harry Potter; and they welcome new things. What aesthetic agents do depends on what they are trained up to do, as a result of their interactions with each other.

Sam, Winfrey, Abbott, Hannah, and the Refords are some of my favourite aesthetic experts. None are world-historically important for the accomplishments credited to them here. And perhaps their accomplishments are not as they appear. Perhaps the festival is no good for the Reford Gardens, Winfrey has hastened the demise of reading, and classic video games are not worth keeping in play. Whether or not my examples are good ones, there are some aesthetic experts, and you are free to assemble your own album. Our albums will not match, and they should not match. Local aesthetic experts do not light up large stretches of terrain, so they are rarely known outside their orbits. Still, they light up small spaces and we gauge their power as long as we are willing to inhabit or travel to those spaces.

Six Explananda

Howard Becker, the dean of American sociology of art, emphasizes that "the people who do the mundane work are as important to an understanding of art as the better-known players" (2008: xxiii). By enriching his data set, his mundane arts workers pointed him to viable hypotheses that he would have missed otherwise. While raw data points are not yet explananda, a good sample of aesthetic experts does suggest six facts that need to be explained.

1. Aesthetic experts disperse into almost all demographic niches. Folk from the walks of life represented by our sample of experts have not won starring roles in writing on aesthetics since the eighteenth century. Shaftesbury echoed the commonplace of his time that "the taste of beauty...perfects the character of the gentleman" (1999[1711]: 407). A gentleman is a white male, ethnically European, socially privileged, at leisure, and highly educated (Shusterman 1989; Jones 1998). Mothersill warns that "one of the impediments to progress in aesthetics has been the resolve on the part of theorists to find a system capable to underwriting what they take to be their own impeccable taste" (1984: 349). We must attend to the dispersion of aesthetic experts across demographic niches.

The early modern demographics of taste are no accident. Economic changes in western Europe had vastly expanded the leisured classes, opening up a market for the newly emerging fine arts and hence a consumer class in need of aesthetic guidance. In his history of the coalescence of the concept of the fine arts, P. O. Kristeller (1951–2) gives a prominent role to the emergence of criticism, or advice on what to experience and how. Men of taste were imagined to survey and select the best of human culture, especially the best in art (Townsend 2003: 341).

Bourdieu explains how philosophy is ensnared in the social dynamic. Since competition for cultural prestige requires resources, it interacts with competitions for economic and educational resources. In each zone of competition, agents take advantage of various ploys in order to make and cement their gains. One ploy on the part of the aesthetic establishment has been to sponsor philosophical theories of aesthetic value that cement the establishment's competitive advantage (Bourdieu 1984: 1–8). Kant is fingered for complicity in the culture wars, by having elevated collusion between taste and fine art to the level of conceptual necessity.

The antidote is to acknowledge aesthetic experts who hail from all walks of life and to take seriously how local aesthetic expertise is shaped by social dependencies. The Refords could not have achieved what they did without taking advantage of their privileged wealth, property, eduction, and social connections. Intense competition among members of the avant-garde art world spurred Abbott's campaign on behalf of Atget. Winfrey's approach to her book club was coloured by her African-American heritage and her upbringing in a poor family in rural Mississippi. Sam perfectly represents a subculture of young, geeky game players. Hannah blends her dance skill with a middle-class, Thatcherite entrepreneurial spirit.

Our experts are not all gentlemen, not all European, not all "highbrow." All the brows are in the lineup. Allied to every social niche are aesthetic niches where experts flourish, and a theory of aesthetic value must explain why that is the case.

2. Aesthetic experts jointly inhabit the whole aesthetic universe. Aesthetic demographics pair with genre hierarchies, as Bourdieu (1983) also stressed. Tradition promoted the man of taste partly by privileging some aesthetic domains, the highbrow ends of the fine arts. For operational purposes, the man of taste was the man who went in for just these things. Classical music, art house cinema, the kind of poetry collected in the Norton anthologies. Not so much country music, *chanbara*, or the kind of poetry inscribed in greeting cards. Also not swap meets, tattooing, or science fiction.

Contemporary analytic aesthetics aspires to repel any bias towards high art and the fine arts (Cohen 1993; Cohen 1999; Saito 2007; Fisher 2013; Saito 2015; Wolterstorff 2015). It honours our aesthetic interest in our dwellings and their arrangements, in urban and agrarian landscapes, in clothes, automobiles, and bicycles, in food, our bodily states, our pets, our companions and lovers—every element of our personal aesthetic lives (e.g. Hanson 1990; Korsmeyer 1999; Brady 2006; Irvin 2008a; Irvin 2008b; Parsons and Carlson 2008; Parsons 2015). Nobody denies that a complete aesthetics must accommodate unbuilt nature too (e.g. Carlson 2000; Budd 2002; Brady 2003; Parsons 2008). John Dewey observed that what has "most vitality for the average person are things he does not take to be arts:

the movies, jazz music, the comic strip, ... and newspaper accounts of love-nests, murder, and exploits of bandits" (1934: 4). A theory of aesthetic value is not up to its job if it cannot explain what has vitality for anyone.

The point is not that every region of the universe of aesthetic activity has equal value. Maybe all or some genre hierarchies are justified at the end of the day. Maybe they are not, or there is no way to settle the question, or the question turns out not to matter (Chapter 11). The claim that some aesthetic pursuits are better than others is not one on which there is much agreement, so it is not a fact to begin an inquiry by trying to explain. Even were it true that the fine arts are special, explaining what is special about them fails to explain the larger phenomenon of which they are a special part. It is liable to sabotage explanations of the larger phenomenon.

Taken jointly, our experts sweep the great world of the aesthetic, from popular art to the fine arts, from mainstream to the fringe, from nature to design, from private life to the public sphere. A theory of aesthetic value should account for agents operating in all contexts of aesthetic activity. Local experts jointly cover more than high culture and more than just those aesthetic domains that we call the arts.

Great art is an occupational hazard for philosophy. Bedazzling us, it veils less anomalous aesthetic goods. As Joseph Raz nicely remarks, "small goods are small but good nonetheless" and they need not be "trivial instances of big values" (1999a: 30). Outlier bias wrecks theories. To remedy outlier bias, we sample widely and generously.

3. Aesthetic experts specialize by aesthetic domain. No individual in our parade pretends expertise in any more than one or perhaps a few local aesthetic domains. None are generalists; all specialize. A theory of aesthetic value should explain specialized aesthetic agency.

An agent's specialization is rarely a matter of free preference. Browsing iTunes, I may choose to listen to some Yo La Tengo or to watch *The Mary Tyler Moore Show*. Nothing about me forces the choice but what I want, granted that what I want has been shaped by my history. I am prepared to act in many, many aesthetic domains—domains in which I am no expert. This is not how it is for our local experts. The praise Elsie Reford won for her gardens did not make her a ceramicist, Alexander Reford's subsequent stewardship of the gardens does not qualify him to run the Alvar Aalto Museum, Hannah probably should not be put in charge of the school orchestra, Oprah's Dance Club is at best an amusing thought, Sam's video game conservation work does nothing on behalf of early computer music, and Abbott would have been a poor advocate for Navajo textiles. Agents channel their expertise into specific aesthetic domains.

Aesthetic agents do not inhabit silos, of course. To begin with, some have multiple areas of specialization. Collectors with universal aesthetic expertise do not exist, but someone might collect *netsuke* and also George Nakashima tables. Sometimes expertise implies a level of acquaintance, falling short of full-fledged expertise, in a nearby domain. Just as philosophers of art need more than passing familiarity with logic, experts in nineteenth-century symphonic music need some grounding in eighteenth-century chamber music and nineteenth-century poetry. Finally, specialists can leverage their non-aesthetic expertise. Alexander Reford built on his background in history, and Winfrey on her command of the television talk-show format.

Rich ties between domains of aesthetic specialization add up to a rich set of facts for a theory of aesthetic value to explain, provided that the ties are systematic. Terrific springboard divers make lousy shot putters, and a master plumber would not be much good at training horses. Yet terrific springboard divers would probably make pretty good gymnasts, and dance teachers would have a leg up on horse training. This tells us something about springboard divers and dance teachers. Likewise, what makes a new music critic a decent critic of contemporary poetry potentially indicates something about what they are attuned to in those aesthetic domains. By the same token, it takes more to make a movie expert into an expert on architecture. To explain this, we cite facts about aesthetic values for those domains.

Aesthetic agency channels into categories of art, design, and nature appreciation. A theory of aesthetic value should explain the disunity of aesthetic agency and the systematic ties of affinity between agency in some domains, as contrasted with others.

4. Aesthetic experts specialize by activity. Local experts are specialists in different kinds of activity. They contribute to their domains of expertise by editing, curating, collecting, conserving, exhibiting, teaching, and connecting audiences. A theory of aesthetic value should explain aesthetic agents' specialized undertakings.

Specialization by type of activity is not the same as domain specialization. Agents specialize by domain in the sense that an expert literary editor is not an expert photographic editor. The same type of action can be done in different aesthetic domains, and domain specialization means that expertise in acting in one domain does not amount to expertise in acting in all domains. To see the difference domains make, hold act-types constant. Conversely, to see the difference different act-types make, hold domain constant. One and the same aesthetic domain sees agents busy at different tasks, and specialization by act-type means that being good at one task in a domain does not ensure expertise in other tasks in the same domain. Agents specialize in an act-type when an expert literary editor is not an expert book jacket designer.

A good sample of local experts represents this dimension of variation. Alexander Reford is not the gardener his grandmother was. Sam's cleverness at conserving video games is consistent with her being an obtuse critic and a clumsy player. Again, the idea is not to house agents in silos. Some multi-task within a domain. Abbott edited Atget's photographs even as she made groundbreaking photographs. Winfrey is a successful publisher and writer. A theory of aesthetic value that does full justice to the intricacies of aesthetic agency will explain the overlaps between different types of activity, when they do overlap.

Aesthetic agents act in a huge variety of ways, even within one aesthetic domain. Philosophy pretty much runs out at what we think of as the big three—creating, performing, and appreciating. An exception is Dickie, who sees art worlds as social systems made up of agents playing socially defined roles (1984: 72–5). The roles of creator, performer, and appreciator are primary roles, which are constitutive of the system. Secondary roles support but do not constitute art worlds. Within the art world of dance, choreographers, dancers, and ticket-buying members of the public play primary roles. Secondary roles are played by impresarios and program directors, advertisers, critics, and many others. Whether or not Dickie is right that only some roles are constitutive of art world systems, many of these roles are played by agents who act aesthetically. For the purposes of theorizing about the aesthetic values realized in wine, for example, there is no reason to ignore some roles (Burnham and Skilleås 2012).

Dickie really is the exception; philosophy's conception of aesthetic agency excludes everything but creating, performing, and appreciating. Downplaying the big three is a good heuristic to counteract a long-standing neglect of the full range of aesthetic action. That is why this chapter de-emphasizes the traditional triad. For the record: creating, performing, and appreciating are important. A theory of aesthetic value must explain them too. Possibly, however, we can learn something about them by looking at a wider range of actions (see Chapter 8).

5. *Specialization by activity and domain interact.* Aesthetic act-types and domains interact. Suppose a two-dimensional space with columns for high-level act-types (creating, performing, appreciating, editing, and so on) and rows for aesthetic domains (architecture, dance, fashion, the human body, birds, sunsets, and so on). Figure 1.1 shows how the specifics of an act are a function of both the aesthetic act-type and the aesthetic domain.

Wollheim emphasized the differences between creative acts in different arts. What he called the "painter's stance" must be characterized as a stance before the

	Φ_1	Φ_2	...	Φ_j
K_1	$\varphi_{1,1}$	$\varphi_{1,2}$	...	$\varphi_{1,j}$
K_2	$\varphi_{2,1}$	$\varphi_{2,2}$	...	$\varphi_{2,j}$
...	...	...	...	...
K_i	$\varphi_{i,1}$	$\varphi_{i,2}$	...	$\varphi_{i,j}$

Figure 1.1 Interaction of aesthetic domains by aesthetic act-types

materials of painting, so that it is not the same as the composer's stance before their different set of materials (1987: 19–23). Ditto for other act-types. Someone editing a poem is performing the same type of act as someone editing an album of photographs, but there are differences between what they do that trace to the specificities of poetry and photography. Likewise, Abbott, Reford, and Sam all conserve, but the details of what they do vary to fit the domains where they operate.

Now we see how our experts are "local." They are specialists. Each operates with a kit of tools tailored to what they are doing and where they are doing it. The specificities give us something grippy to explain. Aesthetic values figure in the doings of agents who are specialized by aesthetic domain and act-type. Taken individually, each expert illuminates a small space. Taken jointly, they illuminate the aesthetic universe. We gain the advantages of specific explanation without abandoning all hope of general explanation.

6. Aesthetic expertise is relatively stable. Finally, beginner's luck does not open the door to the guild of aesthetic experts. Admiring an agent for a one-off success is not the same as admiring her for her relatively stable traits, and many words of praise and blame target stable traits. Thinking morally and epistemically, we call people self-indulgent or brave, closed-minded or curious. In matters aesthetic, we rate agents by commending their energy, nuance, and ingenuity, or by putting them down as tame, obvious, ham-fisted. A theory of aesthetic value should predict that agents have traits that enable them to act well time and again.

The very idea of expertise needs some defence. Contemporary virtue ethics grapples with skeptics who cite empirical evidence indicating that stable psychological traits are at best a minor factor in explaining moral behaviour (e.g. Harman 1999; Doris 2002). If the empirical evidence is correct, and if moral virtues are stable traits that explain behaviour, then nobody has any moral virtue. So why think stable psychological traits make some of us aesthetic experts?

Skepticism about moral virtue does not warrant skepticism about all forms of expertise. The empirical evidence is that there are some genuine experts. According to one charming list, they include "livestock judges, astronomers, test pilots, soil judges, chess masters, physicists, mathematicians, accountants, grain inspectors, photo interpreters, and insurance analysts" (Kahneman and Klein 2009: 521).

If the skeptics are right, moral "experts" belong with those who have been shown not to have genuine expertise. According to one alarming list, they include "stockbrokers, clinical psychologists, psychiatrists, college admissions officers, court judges, personnel selectors, and intelligence analysts" (Kahneman and Klein 2009: 521). The case against moral virtue attends to empirical reality, given a theory of moral action. Likewise, the reality of aesthetic expertise is an empirical matter that cannot be settled without an account of aesthetic agency. As we shall see, aesthetic hedonism and the network theory of aesthetic value pair with different pictures of stable aesthetic agency.

Aesthetic experts are anything but sphexish. To have a stable psychological trait is not invariably to output one behaviour when presented with a given stimulus. Stable psychological traits are generally flexible. Moreover, the trait itself can change, though normally at a gradual pace. Local experts are nimble in their responses and can adapt to changing circumstances. A full account of their performance will explain how aesthetic expertise is relatively stable.

Take the explananda in reverse. Local aesthetic experts possess relatively stable traits that enable them to excel aesthetically. Since there are many types of aesthetic acts and many domains of aesthetic activity, they are specialists. No fair sample singles out those who have invested themselves in the fine arts alone: they represent all social niches. They operate in the fields of Bollywood movies, first-person shooter games, Parisian gypsy jazz, gentian drifts, step dance, concrete poetry, architectural photography, dog breeding, and the fashion industry. In relaying the texture, grit, and grip of what they respond to, they snap the spell of conventional beauty and act upon a million beauties everywhere.

2

Getting Practical

A theory of aesthetic value should explain facts about the doings of aesthetic agents, and Chapter 1 teased out six explananda. The main argument for the network theory of aesthetic value is just about ready to roll. But not quite. After all, the argument is that the network theory beats aesthetic hedonism at explaining what needs explaining, but since we see what needs explaining only by examining a sample of data, abductive arguments fail when they are keyed to biassed samples. Limited arguments to the best explanation are extra-risky. Anyone touched by aesthetic hedonism will have been taken aback, at least a little, by the parade of figures in Chapter 1, who hardly fit our preconceptions. Committed aesthetic hedonists might be tempted to challenge the sample and explananda extracted from it (and maybe the principle that "a theory of aesthetic value should explain facts about aesthetic agency"). The challenge must be met with caution, as any intuitive qualms we have in reaction to Chapter 1 might simply echo the party whip around aesthetic hedonism. What we need is some neutral, common ground that gives everyone reason to accept the explananda and the sample from which the explananda are drawn.

Aesthetic Acts

A key piece of neutral, common ground concerns what counts as an aesthetic act.

At first glance, the examples of aesthetic acts presented in Chapter 1 are contentious, not at all common ground. Having announced its aim to portray some "exemplary aesthetic figures," the chapter went on to nominate some folk who are not the types who spring immediately to mind as exemplary aesthetic figures. No doubt some sociology drives the reaction, but some philosophy is implicated too. Alexander Reford commissions a logo, Abbott sequences some shots by Atget, Winfrey leads her audience in sharing about *The Corrections*, Sam patches *E.T. The Extra-Terrestrial*, and Hannah selects a number for the curriculum. Each has a goal and a practical problem to solve along the way, and each uses what they have to solve their problem and reach their goal. Each is totally mixed up in practical affairs. The trouble is that we are accustomed to equate aesthetic action with appreciation.

C. I. Lewis submits that "aesthetic values are not the goods of action;" they are "pay-day goods, not work-day goods" (1946: 437: 454). After wondering "what action is called for by a true judgement of aesthetic value," Mothersill throws up her hands in perplexity (1984: 97). For Wollheim, aesthetic judgement has "no consequences for action" (1991: 38). Alan Goldman considers that art "removes us entirely from the real world of our practical affairs;" we "lose our ordinary, practically oriented selves in the world of the work" (1995: 8, 151).

Statements such as these evoke what might be called an "appreciation model" of aesthetic acts (see also Moore 1903; Miller 1998: 38–40; Archer 2013: 71; cf. King forthcoming). According to the appreciation model,

all aesthetic acts are acts of aesthetic appreciation.

The model says, first, that to appreciate is to act. Surely Lewis, Mothersill, Wollheim, and Goldman are not to be taken literally. After all, what is it to appreciate an item, if not to do something with it? Rather, the idea is to give acts of appreciation a monopoly on aesthetic agency. Consequently, the appreciation model predicts that it will seem odd to nominate the Refords, Abbott, Winfrey, Sam, and Hannah as exemplary aesthetic figures, because none are presented as exemplary appreciators. The model also predicts resistance to some proposed explananda, especially the proposition that aesthetic agents specialize in a number of activities.

Consider an alternative to the appreciation model that is clearly not up to scratch. Agents act or operate upon items. Opening the can operates on the can, kicking the ball operates on the game, and reading the third critique operates on that book. Making do with the intuitive grip we have on the concept, stipulate that an aesthetic act is an act that operates on an item of aesthetic concern. Jack shelves Dickens in the PR4000 stacks. Peg, a security guard, makes sure that Judy Chicago's *Dinner Party* remains in Brooklyn. Winfrey reads *The Corrections*. All act aesthetically because all operate on items of aesthetic concern.

The proposal's fatal flaw is an instructive one. Stipulating to a theory of aesthetic acts must serve the point of inquiry, which is to learn something about aesthetic value, but we can learn nothing about aesthetic value from the doings of Jack and Peg. We can learn something about aesthetic value from what Winfrey does because her take on the aesthetic value of *The Corrections* makes a difference to what she does. What we need is a theory of aesthetic acts that represents agents as guided in their performances by their assessments of aesthetic value.

Let an aesthetic evaluation be an occurrent or dispositional state of mind that attributes an aesthetic value to an item. In a nutshell,

EVALUATION: a state is an aesthetic evaluation = the state is a mental representation of some item as having some aesthetic value.

Some aesthetic evaluations are belief-like judgements, while others are perceptual or affective states; some are conscious, while others are tacit (Millar 2000; Stokes 2014; Lopes 2014a: ch. 9; Lopes 2016b; Tappolet 2016; Alvarez and Ridley 2017; Stokes 2018). Most of us make hundreds of aesthetic evaluations every day, with no inkling of having done so, and we are often unable to verbalize them on demand. What works so well in the mix of carrots sautéed in butter with toasted cumin seeds? Some can say, but many grope for words, even as they are in a state that vividly represents the very feature in question.

Running with this, let an act operating on an item be an aesthetic act just when it is sensitive, in the right way, to an aesthetic evaluation of the item. The act goes as it does because the agent attributes some aesthetic value to the item: all else being equal, the act would have gone differently were different values attributed to the item. In a formula,

ACT: A's φing is an aesthetic act = A's φing counterfactually depends on the content of A's aesthetic evaluation of x, where A's φing operates on x.

The idea is not to say what makes an aesthetic act an act; ACT merely distinguishes aesthetic acts from other acts.

Arriving home one evening you catch your roommate pinning a *Portlandia* poster to the wall, and you wonder whether her act is aesthetic. ACT answers thus. She forbears to act aesthetically if no aesthetic value she attributes to the poster makes any difference to how she proceeds. Suppose she would have pinned it to the wall whether she found it atrocious, stunning, lively, or deadening. She acts non-aesthetically. She acts aesthetically if she would have done otherwise, given a different aesthetic evaluation of the poster, all else being equal.

Does ACT collapse into the appreciation model, so that they render the same verdicts on which acts are aesthetic? Well, they are not equivalent unless aesthetic appreciation just is aesthetic evaluation, but there is more to aesthetic appreciation than aesthetic evaluation. An aesthetic evaluation of an item is a mental representation of its aesthetic value. Going on to appreciate the item involves more than representing its aesthetic value. Having consulted the folks at Lonely Planet, Nick judges that there is a Poussin worth looking at in the National Gallery. Only once he arrives at the gallery does he begin to appreciate the painting, inspecting it closely, bringing to bear his knowledge of the medium, the genre, and the historical context, searching for meaning, testing competing interpretations, responding emotionally. Not all aesthetic acts involve appreciation, but all involve aesthetic evaluation.

Loose talk muddies the waters. Philosophers use "aesthetic judgement" or "aesthetic experience" to speak sometimes of evaluation, and sometimes of appreciation. Stipulation eliminates ambiguity. An aesthetic evaluation is any mental representation—be it a judgement, experience, or feeling—of an item as having an aesthetic value. An aesthetic appreciation is a distinct aesthetic act, about which more needs to be said (Chapter 8; Lopes forthcoming).

The appreciation model and ACT render different verdicts on the aesthetic agency of Abbot, Winfrey, Sam, Hannah, and the Refords. The former has their claim to aesthetic agency hang on whether they are engaged in aesthetic appreciation. On the latter, it hangs only on whether their performances counterfactually depend on the contents of their aesthetic evaluations.

Meanwhile, the proposals are asymmetric. On one hand, ACT counts aesthetic appreciation as an aesthetic act. Nick's appreciating the Poussin is an aesthetic act if it counterfactually depends on the content of his aesthetic evaluation of the painting. (Indeed, it is consistent with ACT to maintain that acts of appreciation play a special role in aesthetic affairs.) On the other hand, the appreciation model is the stingy model, excluding much of what ACT includes while including nothing of its own.

Reasons are always needed to go stingy. In the context of a contrastive argument, those reasons cannot include a prior commitment to aesthetic hedonism. For example, it will not do to argue as follows: ACT is wrong because there is more to an aesthetic act than its sensitivity to the content of an aesthetic evaluation; aesthetic acts must yield finally valuable experiences. Only aesthetic hedonists need aesthetic acts to yield finally valuable experiences, and an aesthetic hedonist who reasons this way begs the question in favour of their theory. Absent an argument for the appreciation model that is independent of aesthetic hedonism, ACT should be staked out as neutral, common ground.

Another consideration also speaks against stinginess and in favour of ACT as neutral, common ground. The point of stipulating a theory of aesthetic acts is to gather a sample from which we will learn something about aesthetic value. The best strategy is to stand aesthetic acts in maximally inclusive relation to aesthetic values, so that anything is an aesthetic act, subject to the proviso that the content of a representation of aesthetic values makes a difference to how the act goes. The proviso rules that Jack and Peg are not aesthetic agents, and indeed their acts can tell us nothing about aesthetic value. Robert Stecker observed that it also rules out a chemist studying the material makeup of a painting and an art historian putting the painting into context without regard to its value (personal correspondence). Granted, both make important contributions to the aesthetic realm, but their doings cannot tell us anything about aesthetic value, for they would do the same no matter what the painting's aesthetic value. Nothing like the same reasoning favours the appreciation model and rules out, for example, Sam's sleuthing source code. Maybe the act of appreciating a game tells us something special about aesthetic value. It does not follow that the sleuthing tells us nothing. Looking at what Sam does, we see the difference aesthetic value makes. The stipulated theory is fit for purpose.

Raz had it right when he observed that "there is no specific action-type … which can constitute the practice of beauty" (2003: 38). Some types of act do come in aesthetic flavours; they are typically, though not invariably, done aesthetically. Examples include appreciating, curating, exhibiting, reviewing, editing, conserving, collecting, plating dishes, and romancing. At the same time, just about any act that is not typically done aesthetically can be spiced up aesthetically. Working, praying, protesting, hiking, buying, and philosophizing, for instance.

Aesthetic Reasons

Aesthetic values figure in aesthetic reasons: the claim carries us to another piece of neutral, common ground, the terrain of aesthetic normativity.

Start with a platitude of aesthetics:

> necessarily, V is an aesthetic value only if, for some x, the fact that x is V is an aesthetic reason.

Leave the domain of x unrestricted, since items of (just about) any kind can have aesthetic merits or demerits. Also, call the fact that x is V an "aesthetic value fact." Finally, note how the "only if" leaves it open whether all aesthetic reasons are aesthetic value facts (cf. Ziff 1966). In plain English, then, daintiness is not an aesthetic value unless the fact that Ping is dainty is an aesthetic reason, and dumpiness is not an aesthetic value unless the fact that Pong is dumpy is an aesthetic reason. Denying the platitude would mean that, possibly, daintiness is an aesthetic value, though the fact that Ping is dainty is not an aesthetic reason. Nobody denies a platitude.

Reasons come in two kinds. Theoretical reasons are facts that raise the probability that p. The fact that the sun is setting on the mountains in the west is a theoretical reason because it raises the probability that it is evening. Practical reasons bear on what an agent should do in the circumstances. The fact that it is evening in the wilderness is a practical reason because it favours the agent's gathering some fuel and building a fire. It counts towards or lends weight to the proposition that they should build a fire (Scanlon 1998b; Raz 1999a; alternatives are Hieronymi 2005; Skow 2016: ch. 6). Obviously, one and the same fact can raise the probability that p and also bear on what someone should do.

Philosophers habitually take aesthetic reasons to be critical reasons and critical reasons to be theoretical reasons. In his classic paper on "Critical Communication," Arnold Isenberg dissented from a "widely held" three-step model of criticism:

there is the value judgment or *verdict* (V): "This picture or poem is good—." There is a particular statement or *reason* (R): "—because it has such-and-such a quality—." And there is a general statement or *norm* (N): "and any work which has that quality is *pro tanto* good."   (1949: 330)

On this model, when the inference is sound, the critical statement, R, represents a fact that raises the probability that the picture or poem is good. Thus the fact that Ping is dainty is an aesthetic reason that raises probability that he is pretty, for example. (The point equally holds for particularists, who deny that N is needed to step from R to V.) In general, those for whom criticism always renders verdicts will tend to regard aesthetic reasons as theoretical.

Granted that aesthetic reasons are theoretical, they are also practical. Isenberg (1949) thought that critical reasons bear on what one should do, specifically, by way of aesthetically appreciating an item (Sibley 1965; Ziff 1966; Burnham and Skilleas 2012; Moran 2012: 304–5; Mole 2016; Cross 2017b; McGonigal 2017; McGonigal forthcoming). The following principle generalizes to aesthetic acts beyond aesthetic appreciation. For some item, x, some agent, A, some act, φ, and some circumstance, C,

> necessarily, the fact that x is V is an aesthetic reason only if the fact that x is V is a reason for A to φ in C.

The principle is not a platitude because some have (wrongly) tended to think of aesthetic reasons only as reasons for critical verdicts. All the same, the principle is as weak as it gets. What would it take to deny it? The fact that Ping is dainty might be an aesthetic reason and yet nobody ever has reason to appreciate him! No, matters are worse than that: possibly, Ping's daintiness is never reason for anyone to appreciate him, and yet his daintiness raises the probability that he is pretty!

Unite the platitude and the principle and it follows that aesthetic values are reason-giving, figuring in practical reasons or reasons to act (cf. Parfit 2011: 39–42). Minding the existential quantifiers, necessarily, V is an aesthetic value only if the fact that x is V is an aesthetic reason for A to φ in C.

As the point is often made, where there be values, there be reasons to promote, to cherish, to protect, to approve, and the like (e.g. Dancy 2004: 177). Characterize value generically, and you get reasons to perform generic acts; characterize it specifically and you get reasons to perform specific acts. Where a set of shots is haunting, Abbott has reason to sequence them together just so. Where this garden proposal is playful, Alexander Reford has reason to place it next to that more demanding installation. Where *The Bluest Eye* is poignant, Winfrey has reason to share it with her audience. Aesthetic values have fine-grained practical significance.

Practical reasons were introduced above as facts that count towards or lend weight to what an agent should do. They have practical normativity. Christine Korsgaard explains that practical questions arise "in the heat of action," where "we must do as we are obligated to do" and "we demand to know why" (1996: 91). So the question that presses upon an agent is, what should I do? In searching for an answer, agents suss out what they have reason to do. That a sequence of images brings out the unity of Atget's vision is an aesthetic reason for Abbott to publish it as part of her campaign on his behalf. It lends weight to the proposition that she should publish it as part of the campaign.

To underline the point that aesthetic reasons are practical reasons,

REASON: the fact that x is V is an aesthetic reason for A to φ in C = the fact that x is V lends weight to the proposition that A aesthetically should φ in C.

Given REASON and the offspring of the union of the platitude and the principle, namely the proposition that

necessarily, V is an aesthetic value only if the fact that x is V is an aesthetic reason for A to φ in C,

it follows that

VALUE: necessarily, V is an aesthetic value only if the fact that x is V lends weight to the proposition that A aesthetically should φ in C.

REASON and VALUE simply make explicit the practical normativity of aesthetic values and reasons. Neither ventures substantive claims about the nature or source of aesthetic normativity. (On that, aesthetic hedonism and the network theory will part ways.)

Here are answers to four questions of clarification about REASON and VALUE.

1. Why do aesthetic reasons lend weight to what an agent aesthetically should do? Many aesthetic reasons lend weight to what an agent aesthetically should do, but it is not the case that the agent aesthetically should do it. These reasons are not decisive. That is,

> necessarily, A aesthetically should φ in C if and only if A has decisive aesthetic reason to φ in C.

Often A has aesthetic reasons to φ in C that are not decisive. You have some aesthetic reason to listen to William Shatner's rendition of "Lucy in the Sky with Diamonds," but you aesthetically should not go there. You have aesthetic reason to watch a colourized version of *The Big Sleep*, but, again, you aesthetically should not go there. (The fact that black-and-white film contributes to the mood of the movie is reason to watch it as is, and it outweighs the reason to watch it in colour that is given by the fact that Lauren Bacall's eyes are a mesmerizing blue-green.) For present purposes, we need not settle the question of when aesthetic reasons are decisive. Perhaps aesthetic reasons to φ are decisive when they are not outweighed by aesthetic reasons to do any other act. Perhaps they are decisive when they outweigh aesthetic reasons to do any other act. Perhaps they are decisive when they surpass a threshold of weightiness.

2. What is it for φ to be what A aesthetically should do? Often, an agent should not do what they aesthetically should do. Suppose Gaugin had decisive aesthetic reason to traipse off to Tahiti. Put only aesthetic reasons in the balance and the pan tips down on the side of traipsing. Now put all kinds of reasons in the balance, and maybe his aesthetic reasons are outweighed by moral reasons, reasons of love, and other non-aesthetic reasons. A decisive aesthetic reason for me to crash on the couch and listen to Amy Winehouse is, sadly, outweighed by the reason I have to sit tight and do my taxes. I aesthetically should listen to Amy Winehouse but I really should do my taxes. The contrast is between what an agent should do all things considered and what an agent should do only weighing aesthetic reasons. What they should do all aesthetic reasons considered is what they aesthetically should do.

3. Aesthetic shoulds? Seriously? Talk of what agents aesthetically should or should not do, sounds off-key, too moralistic. Some set aesthetics apart from ethics by arguing that there are no aesthetic oughts, shoulds, or musts (e.g. Hampshire 1954). Moral dilemmas exist, but not aesthetic dilemmas: moral agents face situations where they are bound to act one way or another, but aesthetic agents' apparent dilemmas are "gratuitous"—they can simply walk away from them. Moreover, what appear to be aesthetic uses of "should" are nowhere near as serious as moral uses (Kivy 2015: 41). They only appear in "good form" recommendations on a par with "don't play polkas at funerals" (Hampshire 1954: 162). Finally, aesthetic choices do not trigger certain emotions. Martha Nussbaum reports:

> I can, visiting a museum, survey many fine objects with appropriate awe and tenderness. I can devote myself now to one, now to another without the sense that the objects make conflicting claims against my love and care. If one day I spend my entire museum visit gazing at Turners, I have not incurred a guilt against the Blakes in the next room. (1990: 132)

Only oughts, shoulds, and musts engage emotions such as these.

In response, Marcia Eaton (2008) offers nice cases of interpreters and museum curators who face serious aesthetic dilemmas that entrain painful emotional consequences. Others derive aesthetic obligations from the rights of art works (see Tormey 1973a; Goldblatt 1976; Hein 1978; Sparshott 1983). Alfred Archer and Lauren Ware (2017) argue that there are acts of aesthetic supererogation, but there is no supererogation without shoulds in a practical domain. Anthony Cross (2017a) sources aesthetic obligations in our love of works of art. We underestimate the seriousness and intensity of aesthetic reasons (see also Moran 2012).

Granting these replies, a more fundamental mistake is to assume that shoulds and oughts necessarily concern serious business, generating dilemmas and threatening the Furies' reprisal. G. E. M. Anscombe reminds us "that athletes should keep in training, pregnant women watch their weight, film stars their publicity, that one should brush one's teeth, that one should (not) be fastidious about one's pleasures" (1963: §35). Morality has no lock on normativity, and not all normativity is heavy-duty normativity (e.g. Raz 1999a; Wedgwood 2007; Thomson 2008; Parfit 2011; Wallace 2012; Scanlon 2014). We wonder what we should do, even when there is no dilemma in sight, nothing serious at stake, and no impending guilt or shame. We wonder what we should do whenever we have an aesthetic problem to solve.

4. How do REASON and VALUE bring us any closer to a theory of aesthetic value?

A brief detour leads to the answer. An aesthetic reason is a worldly fact, the fact that x is V. An aesthetic evaluation is a mental representation of x as V. When an agent's evaluating x as V explains why they act, their aesthetic evaluation is among their motives, where motives explain acts. The aesthetic value fact that is an aesthetic reason for an agent to act is not the same as the aesthetic evaluation that is the motivating reason that explains their acting. After all, A's evaluation of x as V explains A's φing only if A φs; however, the fact that x is V is reason for A to φ in C even though A does not φ. Your judgement that Ping is dainty explains your aesthetically appreciating him only if you appreciate him; but the fact that Ping is dainty is reason for you to aesthetically appreciate him, even if you fail to appreciate him. End of detour.

Expert agents routinely act from motives that represent the reasons they have. The Strada EP by La Marzocco is a very good espresso machine, so a barista at Timbertrain has reason to use it to fix me a caffè macchiato. (He does not act well if he nips round to the nearest Starbucks to pull the shot on their unholy contraption.) Maybe he is a temp, not trained to a level of expertise, and the explanation of why he pulls the shot on the Strada is not that he judges that the Strada is a good machine. Were he an expert, though, he would pull the shot on the Strada, having sized it up as a good machine. Expert agents routinely act on the basis of evaluations that accurately represent the reasons they have.

For experts, it is routine that

when the fact that x is V is reason to φ in C, experts φ in C, and their evaluation of x as V explains their φing in C.

In short, experts routinely act on the reasons they have. As a result, aesthetic value is on display in the doings of aesthetic experts. I have reasons to act, but I am no expert and I bumble: my sorry performances tell you little about the reasons I have to act. Only a correct picture of aesthetic expertise delivers a correct picture of the aesthetic values to which aesthetic experts routinely respond. In their agency, we see the difference aesthetic value makes.

This, too, is common ground between aesthetic hedonism and the network theory, as we shall see in Chapters 3 and 5. Both try to understand aesthetic value by inspecting its afterimage in the doings of those who act on the reasons they have.

Two Questions about Aesthetic Value

Hannah has reason to select a piece for the curriculum: it is edgy in a fun sort of way. Alexander Reford has reason to install an art work: it adds flair to Elsie Reford's garden. Winfrey has reason to feature *Anna Karenina* on the book club: it treats a familiar story with insight. Sam has reason not to work on the code for a game: it is derivative, a knock-off. Abbott has reason to edit Atget's work as she did: it brought out a unity of vision. Being unified, tawdry and derivative, insightful, richly textured, and entertainingly edgy are aesthetic values. Agents act aesthetically who act under the guidance of these and other aesthetic values (see ACT). The values feature in aesthetic value facts that lend weight to what they aesthetically should do (see REASON and VALUE). The task is to argue for a theory of aesthetic value, which answers the question, what is an aesthetic value? The question divides into two subsidiary questions (Beardsley 1979: 743).

Call the first question the "aesthetic question." Putting the emphasis on "aesthetic," it asks what makes a value an aesthetic one. Many values are non-aesthetic. An action's being cruel is a classic case of a moral demerit, a person's being curious is a prime example of an epistemic merit, an umbrella's being able to withstand gusts of wind is a design merit, and a market's inefficiency is a textbook economic demerit. None of these is typically an aesthetic value. The list propels us to the question of what makes some values—for example, being unified, complex, or tawdry—aesthetic values. A theory of aesthetic value answers the aesthetic question by completing the template:

a value, V, is an aesthetic value = ...

In completing this template, we do not say what makes V a value—we take that for granted. To make that obvious, the left-hand side of the identity stipulates that V is a value. The right-hand side calls only for conditions that must be met by any value for it to be an aesthetic value.

The second question is—no surprise—the "normative question." The normative question places the emphasis on the "value" in "aesthetic value," in light of the understanding of aesthetic normativity articulated in the previous section, "Aesthetic Reasons." In brief, aesthetic values are reason-giving, in the sense that the platitude and the principle imply that

necessarily, V is an aesthetic value only if the fact that x is V is an aesthetic reason for A to φ in C.

From this proposition plus the proposition that aesthetic reasons are practical (see REASON) it follows that

VALUE: necessarily, V is an aesthetic value only if the fact that x is V lends weight to the proposition that A aesthetically should φ in C.

In other words, aesthetic values are reason-giving in the sense that they source practical normativity.

The normative question is a question about VALUE. How do aesthetic values source practical normativity? More precisely, what is it about V that makes it the case that the fact that x is V lends weight to what an agent aesthetically should do? Answers to the normative question provide an informative analysis of the consequent of VALUE, completing the following template:

an aesthetic value, V, is reason-giving = the fact that x is V lends weight to the proposition that...

When complete, the template does not say what makes V aesthetic. That is already taken for granted. To make that obvious, the left-hand side of the identity stipulates that V is aesthetic. The right-hand side calls only for conditions that must be met by any aesthetic value in order for it to figure in facts that lend weight to what agents aesthetically should do. The task is to fill in the ellipses with a reductive account of why an agent aesthetically should act.

The normative question is best viewed as the question that is answered by any tenable completion of the template. For convenience, a shortcut version of the normative question is: what makes aesthetic values normative? For convenience, call an answer to this question that completes the template a "theory of the normativity of aesthetic value."

In sum, a theory of aesthetic value has two parts. One answers the aesthetic question of what makes some values distinctively aesthetic. The second is a theory of the normativity of aesthetic value, which answers the normative question—namely, what makes aesthetic values normative?

Here is a turn-up for the books. Both aesthetic hedonism and the network theory only attempt answers to the normative question—more in Chapters 3 and 5. Both are theories of the normativity of aesthetic value. We may lay claim to another chunk of neutral, common ground.

Some Answers to the Aesthetic Question

In principle, theories of aesthetic value fall into four categories. Some punt on the aesthetic question, some punt on the normative question, some give each a stand-alone answer, and some answer both in tandem, bagging two birds with one stone. Aesthetic hedonism and the network theory are theories of the normativity of aesthetic value. In their pure forms, they punt on the aesthetic question, so while either can be combined with a stand-alone answer to the aesthetic question, neither implies a tandem answer to both questions.

Beardsley sometimes thought that an aesthetic value is a capacity in an item to yield an experience with a distinctive phenomenal character. Experiences with this character have four of five features, always including the first. The diagnostic features are (1) a willing attention to features of an item, (2) a feeling of freedom from concerns beyond the experience itself, (3) a detached affect, (4) an awareness of mental effort and achieved intelligibility, and (5) a sense of personal integration or wholeness (Beardsley 1979: 741–2; 1982: 285–9; cf. 1981[1958]: 527–8). Since the fact that an item produces such an experience does not give agents any reason to act, Beardsley punts on the normative question.

More recently, Rafael De Clercq has argued that aesthetic values are values that are perceived, specifically by perceiving their bearer's non-aesthetic properties, and not vice versa (2002: 170–3). De Clercq makes constitutive what many regard as a merely necessary condition on being an aesthetic value, namely being presented in experience (e.g. Sibley 1965: 137; Tormey 1973b; Wollheim 1980: 233; Pettit 1983, 24–5; Zangwill 1998; Fudge 2005: 151–2; Levinson 2005; Hopkins 2005; Hopkins 2006b; Lopes 2014a: 179–84; Lopes 2016b). Again, that a value is primarily accessed in experience gives nobody any reason to act: the proposal punts on the normative question.

Theories, such as Beardsley's and De Clercq's, that punt on the normative question can be combined with aesthetic hedonism, thereby yielding stand-alone answers to the aesthetic and normative questions. For example, according to J. O. Urmson (1957), an item's aesthetic value is a feature that presents itself to the senses and thereby yields delight in how the item appears (see also Mothersill 1984: 338–41). If agents have reason to get themselves into states of pleasure, the pleasure supplies the normativity, while the sensory phenomenology specifies the value as aesthetic. Beardsley himself (1969; 1970b) floated a theory with the same two-part structure. An item's aesthetic value is its capacity to gratify when correctly and completely experienced. This answers the normative question. The second part of the theory answers the aesthetic question by restricting the content of the experience. For Beardsley, "gratification is aesthetic when it is obtained primarily from attention to the formal unity and/or the regional qualities of a complex whole, and when its magnitude is a function of the degree of formal unity and/or the intensity of regional quality" (1970b: 46).

Both of these theories imply aesthetic hedonism: they assert that aesthetic values stand in constitutive relation to finally valuable experiences. Since not all pleasures stand in constitutive relation to aesthetic value, a further condition is added. The pleasure must be a pleasure in an experience with a specified phenomenology or content. The pleasure component supplies the normativity; the restriction on the experience component answers the aesthetic question.

Put another way, stand-alone answers to the aesthetic question are consistent with aesthetic hedonism. Occasional skirmishes over the aesthetic question do nothing to perturb the consensus around aesthetic hedonism, which concerns itself only with the normative question. We may safely ignore what Beardsley, De Clercq, Urmson, and others have to say about what makes some values aesthetic.

The same does not go for any theory that bags two birds with one stone, answering the aesthetic and normative questions in tandem. Its answer to the aesthetic question cannot be set aside as we consider its answers to the normative question.

Only one known theory of aesthetic value fits the bill, but it may have ancient roots and it dominated philosophy until the mid-twentieth century (Konstan 2014). According to this theory, an aesthetic value is a property of an item that stands in constitutive relation to disinterested pleasure (e.g. Hutcheson 1738). The theory answers the aesthetic and normative questions in tandem. Disinterested pleasure sources the normativity of aesthetic value because any agent always has reason to act to get pleasure. Meanwhile, the pleasure's being disinterested distinguishes it from non-aesthetic pleasures, which in turn distinguishes aesthetic values from other values.

Were disinterested pleasure an ordinary pleasure taken in an item's aesthetic character, the proposal would provide stand-alone answers to the aesthetic and normative questions. In fact, however, disinterested pleasures are meant to source a distinctively aesthetic normativity. The idea is that, whereas any pleasure motivates agents to act, disinterested pleasure has a unique motivational profile. It motivates no act but appreciation, or "mere contemplation," in Kant's expression (2000[1790]: 90; see also Hutcheson 1738: 11–13). Hence, what is special about aesthetic values is that they figure only in reasons to perform acts of appreciation; they do not give agents reason to perform any other acts (Dickie 1988: 18–20; Zangwill 1992; Kemp 1999; Shelley 2013b: 6–7; Konstan 2014: 161–6; Riggle 2016: 2–3; Wolterstorff 2015).

Appeals to disinterested pleasure dominated philosophy partly because they suited new ideas about art. Until the modern period, works of art were regarded as instruments of social betterment, either bringing moral and spiritual edification or embodying civic and religious ideals. A growing middle class created a new market for art, which had become a reputable way of enlivening leisure time. As Noël Carroll puts it, "instead of serving objective social purposes, art began to be esteemed for the subjective pleasures it sustained" (2007: 152). These could not be pleasures motivating action for the social good; they were disinterested.

In effect, the disinterested pleasure theory marries aesthetic hedonism with the appreciation model, on which the only aesthetic acts are acts of appreciation. However, aesthetic hedonism does not imply the appreciation model, and, as we saw above, aesthetic hedonists should not accept the model. Contemporary aesthetic hedonists make no constitutive appeal to disinterested pleasure.

Some items surely do kindle disinterested pleasure (Schier 1986: 129; Levinson 1992; Parsons and Carlson 2008: 104). Aesthetic hedonism and the network theory do not deny the reality of the phenomenon, but they accept it as common ground that aesthetic values bear a non-constitutive relation to disinterested pleasure, so the disinterested pleasure theory is false. More generally, they also align in punting on the aesthetic question. Each is consistent with any stand-alone answer to the aesthetic question.

How to Punt on the Aesthetic Question

While aesthetic hedonism and the network theory punt on the aesthetic question, neither denies that the question deserves an answer. They simply set the aesthetic question aside, at least temporarily, and make do with a working conception of which values are aesthetic.

Often, in philosophy, theoretical disagreement echoes disagreement about paradigm cases. When this happens, theorizing is inevitable. Luckily, as much as philosophers might disagree about what makes some values aesthetic, they concur on paradigm cases of aesthetic value. In a proof of the utility of lists, Frank Sibley's list of aesthetic terms might be among the most cited in philosophy: "unified, balanced, integrated, lifeless, serene, somber, dynamic, powerful, vivid, delicate, moving, trite, sentimental, tragic" (1959: 421). He immediately adds a sampling of aesthetic phrases, such as "sets up a tension." De Clercq surveyed and tabulated all the aesthetic adjectives used as examples in ten of the more influential papers on aesthetic properties (2008: 895; see also Wilson 2017). The lists strongly overlap, and none seems outré (e.g. Carroll 1999: 190; Goldman 1995: 17).

So neat is the convergence upon paradigm cases that they are criterial. That is, no answer to the aesthetic question is adequate unless it counts the paradigm cases as genuine aesthetic values. In the circumstances, a good working conception is this:

a value is aesthetic when it is a paradigm aesthetic value.

The paradigm aesthetic values are those that either appear on Sibley's and De Clercq's lists or that nobody would object to including on their lists.

The working conception is a stopgap. A principled answer to the aesthetic question, which tells us what makes some values aesthetic, will equip us to deal with non-paradigm aesthetic values (Budd 1999: 300). In addition, paradigm aesthetic values vary from one cultural context to the next (Layton 2011: 210–12). An answer to the aesthetic question will explain why all are paradigms. It will also help with bits of discourse that contain no terms for paradigm aesthetic values (Kivy 1975; Eaton 1989: 13, 44–5; Sibley 2003b: 248). A *New York Times* critic once described Saul Bellow's sentences as "double-breasted" (Pahlka 2012). And here is Chef Mark Miller describing the taste of a raisin:

when you bite down, it is sweet in the beginning. It has a medium tempo and flavor—it becomes tannic on the edge, it gets a little bit juicier, and it gets highly accentuated sugars and a little bit dusty in the mid-palate over time. There's a certain intensity that goes up. And then the sweetness dies off, and then the tannin dies off, and what you're left with is a kind of seedy little bit of sweetness that follows through. What you have is this curve of experience—from a single raisin!   (quoted in Dornenburg and Page 1996: 25)

If we cannot look up all aesthetic values in an aesthetic lexicon, then the working conception is a stopgap that leaves to another day what we should say about how the critic's metaphor and the chef's homage to raisins count as aesthetic discourse (for a start, see McNally and Stojanovic 2017).

All the same, it is sensible to make do with the working conception, for two reasons.

Stopgap measures permit progress on the normative question, which might outfit us to one day return to the aesthetic question. For example, in answering the normative question, we might learn that the normativity of aesthetic reasons is not the same as the normativity of some other, non-aesthetic reasons—moral reasons perhaps. Making this discovery will whet our appetite for an answer to the aesthetic question, as we will want to know why aesthetic and moral reasons have different kinds of normativity. At the same time, the discovery will be a first step towards an answer to the aesthetic question: we will see that part of what makes some values aesthetic is their normativity.

Admittedly, promissory notes rarely set minds at ease. Another consideration speaks for the wisdom of putting the aesthetic question on ice. Recall that the quest for a theory of aesthetic value was born of a primitive question (see the Introduction). What is the place of aesthetic value in the good life? What do aesthetic goods bring to my life, to make it a life that goes well? How does beauty deserve the place we have evidently made for it in our lives? In asking these questions, we are in no quandary about which values are aesthetic. We know beauty when we see it. Visitors to the Guggenheim Bilbao might puzzle over whether its façade is graceful, and they might puzzle over whether its being graceful is a merit or a flaw, but none doubt that being graceful is an aesthetic value. Likewise, tasters of a muscat raisin might not agree that its flavour has a medium tempo, and they might wonder whether a medium tempo is a merit or a flaw in it, but we just feel sad for anyone who has no idea whether a medium flavour tempo is an aesthetic value.

The primitive question of aesthetics gives voice to puzzlement about why the fact that the façade is graceful and the fact that the raisin has a medium flavour tempo should have any call upon us. Why should they make any difference to the plans, priorities, and commitments by means of which we structure our lives? Answers to the normative question do bring us closer to answering the primitive question. To understand why the façade's grace means I aesthetically should do this act or why the raisin's medium tempo means you aesthetically should do that act helps to understand their place in how we should live. After all, how we should live is the sum total of what we should do. We live by doing. In a slogan, the normative question is what becomes of the primitive question once we get technical.

From the point of view of the primitive question, the normative question is mandatory while the aesthetic question is optional, maybe a distraction. The remedy is to put the aesthetic question on ice. The way to do that? Adopt the working conception. You know the refrain: aesthetic hedonism and the network theory share in common the working conception as a stopgap answer to the aesthetic question.

Plain Vanilla Normativity

Theories of the normativity of aesthetic value answer the normative question but offer nothing in answer to the aesthetic question. They are consistent with any stand-alone answer to the aesthetic question. Adopting the working conception is a way to operationalize a total shift of attention to the normative question. It also sends us in search of plain vanilla normativity.

Plain vanilla normativity is normativity that may well be found outside the aesthetic domain; it is not distinctively aesthetic. Think of it this way. A theory of the normativity of aesthetic value completes the following template:

> an aesthetic value, V, is reason-giving = the fact that x is V lends weight to the proposition that...

The task is to fill in the ellipses with a reductive account of why an agent aesthetically should act. When the normativity of aesthetic value is plain vanilla, the resources that we draw upon to complete the template are resources that might also cash out what agents should do non-aesthetically. So a theory that appeals to plain vanilla normativity identifies the normativity of aesthetic values with a more familiar form of normativity.

A perfect illustration is aesthetic hedonism, which understands aesthetic values to be reason-giving by reducing them to powers to please, where the fact that an item pleases inherently gives us reason to act. The network theory will appeal to a different kind of plain vanilla normativity.

Note that to identify the normativity of aesthetic reasons and values with plain vanilla normativity is not to reduce the aesthetic to the non-aesthetic. The aesthetic question remains!

Therefore, why not adopt a policy to always keep in mind that the aesthetic question remains? An honest and transparent policy is to include "aesthetic" on both sides of every assumption that frames our inquiry. For future reference:

> EVALUATION: a state is an aesthetic evaluation = the state is a mental representation of some item as having some aesthetic value.

ACT: A's φing is an aesthetic act = A's φing counterfactually depends on the content of A's aesthetic evaluation of x, where A's φing operates on x.

REASON: the fact that x is V is an aesthetic reason for A to φ in C = the fact that x is V lends weight to the proposition that A aesthetically should φ in C.

VALUE: necessarily, V is an aesthetic value only if the fact that x is V lends weight to the proposition that A aesthetically should φ in C.

An aesthetic act is one motivated by an aesthetic evaluation, which is a representation of aesthetic value. Aesthetic values figure in aesthetic reasons to act, which lend weight to what an agent aesthetically should do. Never is the aesthetic phenomenon on the left-hand side reduced on the right-hand side to some non-aesthetic phenomenon. The formulas above make this perfectly plain by mentioning the aesthetic on both sides.

The intention is not to provide a circular account of the aesthetic, not even one that is virtuously circular on the model of Dickie's "art circle" (1984). The aim is rather to signal that the aesthetic question remains open.

Given common acceptance of EVALUATION, ACT, REASON, VALUE, and the working conception, it is reasonable to proceed with the limited abductive argument. An abductive argument is limited when there are no prior, agreed explananda, and the argument may proceed when some explananda are proposed that all sides have reason to go along with, at least for the time being. The agents profiled in Chapter 1 act in accordance with ACT. Moreover, in accordance with REASON and VALUE, they do as they aesthetically should, acting on the aesthetic reasons they have, in which aesthetic values figure. Since all indications are that they represent a good sample of expert aesthetic agents, there can be no objection to the six explananda proposed in Chapter 1. The limited abductive argument may proceed. The next task is to get contrastive, by taking a closer look at the virtues of aesthetic hedonism.

PART II

3

To Seize upon the Applause of the Heart

With the aesthetic question on ice and a working conception of paradigm aesthetic values in hand, the normative question has the stage to itself. "The Erlking" is haunting, and the Gardner diesel engine epitomizes design with square-dealing, no-nonsense integrity. How can these facts make any practical difference—any difference to what anybody is to do? Philosophers default to aesthetic hedonism for the answer, and the network theory supplies a new answer. The main argument for the network theory is a contrastive abductive argument. In mounting a contrastive argument against aesthetic hedonism, every pain must be taken to sing its praises.

Aesthetic Hedonism

As it is formulated in the Introduction, most accept

> AESTHETIC HEDONISM: an aesthetic value is a property of an item that stands in constitutive relation to finally valuable experiences of subjects who correctly understand the item.

Nobody puts the theory in exactly this form, which is crafted to keep the theory's commitments to a minimum, while still pointing to an answer to the normative question. In this way, the formulation sidesteps occasional skirmishes, especially over answers to the aesthetic question (see Chapter 2). At the same time, the theory packs in several commitments.

1. What has aesthetic value? Aesthetic hedonism locates aesthetic values in items that are objects of experience, but it leaves open what kinds of items bear aesthetic value and how those kinds of items are experienced. Some items bearing aesthetic value are material objects represented in sense experience—it is Grace Kelly's face that is radiant. Others are events—the pizzazz is in the event that is the Italian entry to the Vancouver firework festival. Some are abstract entities not directly perceived by means of the senses—the compact elegance of Euler's identity, or of Joseph Kosuth's *One and Three Chairs*. Each of these values is a property of an experienced item; it is not a property of the experience itself.

2. Are finally good experiences pleasures? Yes, so long as we conceive pleasure broadly.

Philosophers seem to be reluctant to use the plain English "pleasure" in place of some jargonistic expression like "finally good experience." Since all pleasures are experiences with final value, the complaint is not that some pleasures do not fit the bill. Rather, the complaint is that some finally good experiences are not pleasures. Parfit takes pleasures to be sensations that we like having, and he distinguishes them from experiences of music that we also like having (2011: 1.52–4). Laurie Paul similarly distinguishes pleasure, which is a value in a qualitative sensory feel, from valuable experiences that "extend past the merely qualitative" and include "rich, complex...lived experiences resulting from our sensory as well as our non-sensory cognitive phenomenology" (2014: 12).

Granting the distinction between finally valuable experiences with sensory phenomenology and those that have no sensory phenomenology, it remains a lexical nicety what to call a "pleasure." The folk concept of pleasure is broad. When a student reports being pleased by the paradox of the surprise examination, their "pleasure" has no qualitative sensory feel. The same goes for the concept of pleasure deployed in the human sciences, which is just as broad (e.g. Schroeder 2004; Bloom 2010). Among the philosophers, Eaton highlights pleasures that "involve comparing, contrasting, fitting things into patterns, and figuring out meanings and connections" (1989: 123). Jerrold Levinson thinks of pleasure not "as a physiological occurrence, passively borne, but rather as more on the order of enjoyment, actively achieved" (1992: 295). Pleasure can arise, he writes,

because one's cognitive faculties are notably exercised or enlarged; because one's eyes or ears are opened to certain spatial and temporal possibilities; because one is enabled to explore unusual realms of emotion; because one's consciousness is integrated to a degree out of the ordinary; because one is afforded a distinctive feeling of freedom or transcendence; because certain moral truths are made manifest to one in concrete dress; or because one is provided insight, in one way or another, into human nature. (1992: 301)

Pleasure is broad, sometimes a product of sophisticated cognition (see also Ryle 1954; Walton 1993: 504–6; Budd 1995: 7; Goldman 2006: 334).

(Which is not to endorse puritanical attitudes toward sensory or sensual pleasures. According to Prettejohn's (2005) history, Alexander Baumgarten's aesthetics was initially met with accusations of "hedonism," and subsequent thinkers fretted over the accusations, especially in defensive response to homoerotic elements of Johann Winckelmann's writing. Let us put all that behind us.)

Obviously, not all pleasures stand in constitutive relation to aesthetic values. Consider the pleasures of slaked thirst, warm baths, sleep, horseplay, winning lotteries, and receiving praise. Nor are sophisticated pleasures the aesthetic ones. Consider the pleasures of scoring a philosophical point, concluding a productive meeting, helping someone in need, or learning something just for the heck of it. Aesthetic hedonism ventures no answer to the aesthetic question.

3. What is final value? Some clarity is needed here.

Chores are only good in as much as they bring about further goods. All the value of scrubbing the bathtub derives from its being a means to a sparkling clean washroom (or self-discipline). It has no value for its own sake. Unlike chores, some things are good as means and also good for their own sake. The taste of strawberry is good for its own sake, and that makes it additionally good as a means to eating a more balanced diet. Suppose strawberries are loaded with cholesterol but taste the same: their taste would have no instrumental value, but it would be good for its own sake. Or suppose eating them contributes to a healthy diet, they taste bland, but that taste is benignly addictive: their taste would retain its instrumental value, but it would not be good for its own sake. The lesson is that one cannot argue that an experience is not good for its own sake because it is good as a means to some end. By the same token, one cannot step from the claim that an experience is good for its own sake to the claim that it has no value as a means.

Let an item's final value be its value for its own sake. Aesthetic hedonists rarely characterize the value of good experiences as "final," preferring to talk of experiences that are "intrinsically valuable" (an exception is Stang 2012). However, we need to mark a pair of orthogonal distinctions: the distinction between final and non-final value versus the distinction between intrinsic and extrinsic value (Korsgaard 1983; O'Neill 1992).

A simple bracelet of braided paracord might have little value except that it was a gift from a loved one. Neither its design nor its materials have much intrinsic value. Its value is extrinsic, coming from its role in the relationship. So intrinsic values reside in items independent of the existence of anything else, or are fully characterized without reference to anything else (O'Neill 1992: 142; cf. Rosen 2010: 112). Probably there are very few purely intrinsic values. The pleasantness of a sensation taken in strict isolation might be intrinsically good, but only rarely. Even the goodness of the taste of strawberry has an extrinsic component, namely its coming from strawberries. (How good is the taste of a shot of strawberry-flavoured saliva?)

One common mistake is to conflate intrinsic and final value. Obviously, a bracelet presented as a gift from a loved one has a value that is extrinsic yet final. Its owner rightly cherishes it for its own sake, as something tied to someone they love. The danger in conflating final with intrinsic value is that it turns up the pressure to construe final values as intrinsic, and too few values are purely intrinsic.

Feeling the pressure, some aesthetic hedonists have located the final value of experiences in their intrinsic, qualitative feels or phenomenologies (e.g. Beardsley 1982). Contemporary aesthetic hedonists happily allow that part of what makes an experience of a Hiroshi Sugimoto Seascape finally good is its being an experience of the Seascape, not an experience of any vista that looks just like the Seascape. The value of experiencing the Seascape is extrinsic yet final. Put another way, Beardsley borrowed trouble when he invoked the conceit of a pill that induces finally valuable experiences (1970b: 49–51; see also Lewis 1946: 433). Dropping some acid could produce an experience qualitatively identical to skiing perfect powder in the British Columbia back country, but the experience got by skiing the BC back country has more final value than the experience got by dropping acid. How can this be? No worries, the final value of each experience is at least partly extrinsic: the final value of one, and only one, comes from its tie to the back country.

There is no great mystery here. Those who think there is should remember their box of keepsakes. Nobody thinks their keepsakes have only intrinsic or instrumental value, for their keepsakes often have little of each: their value is mostly extrinsic and final.

The good news is that disentangling final from intrinsic value means there is more final value around than we might have thought. Much of it is extrinsic. In particular, the final value of most pleasures is extrinsic.

4. How does the aesthetic value of an item stand in relation to the value of an experience of it? As officially formulated, aesthetic hedonism leaves open what constitutive relation holds between the aesthetic value borne by an item and the finally valuable experience of the item. Is it a disposition to cause the experience? A power or capacity? The metaphysical nuances need not detain us.

No matter what the details of the relation, quite a bit of ink is spilled over the worry that aesthetic hedonism construes aesthetic value as purely instrumental (Levinson 1992: 303–4; Budd 1995: 13–14; cf. Stecker 2006: 4–5; Shelley 2010). If the relation in which an item stands to an experience is a relation that makes it a mere means to the experience, then the item's aesthetic value is nothing but its instrumental value as a means to the experience. Presumably, the problem is that purely instrumental values are fully fungible. As we say, whatever gets the job done. Yet an item's aesthetic value is not fully fungible.

Disturbed by this reasoning, some have asserted the principle that an item has some final value if it is a necessary part of something with final value. Suppose the final value of a Seascape-experience is extrinsic, so that the Seascape itself contributes constitutively to the final value of the experience. Given the asserted principle, the Seascape's aesthetic value is partly final. Unfortunately, though, the asserted principle is false. In Nick Stang's example, a particularly dramatic rest in a Beethoven piano sonata might be a necessary constituent of the sonata, and an experience of the sonata might have final value, but the rest has no final value (2012: 273).

The reasoning need not disturb anyone, because aesthetic hedonism does not imply that an item's aesthetic value is purely instrumental and fully fungible. If an item contributes constitutively to the extrinsic final value of an experience of it, then it is not just a means to the experience, and its aesthetic value is not purely instrumental. Moreover, since a similar experience of a different item has a different extrinsic final value, the item's aesthetic value is not fully fungible. My sweetheart's gift to me is no substitute for your sweetheart's gift to you, because the final value of each lies in its tie to the right sweetheart. Likewise, dropping a hallucinogen will not get you an experience with the very same final value as an experience of skiing the BC back country. In general, an item's aesthetic value is neither fully fungible nor purely instrumental if it stands in relation to an experience whose final value derives at least in part from a constitutive tie to the item itself, and no other.

From this it does not follow that an item's aesthetic value is also a final value. Maybe some non-instrumental values are not final values. One might deny that anything can have final value in so far as it constitutively contributes to the extrinsic value of something else (e.g. Stang 2012: 273). Possibly, then, an item's aesthetic value is not a final value. Should aesthetic hedonists worry? Well, what would be the source of their worry? To repeat, the item's aesthetic value is not fungible and not instrumental.

Maybe the worry is a reaction to an offence against an intuition that an item's aesthetic value is a final value. In matters as abstruse as this, however, intuitions have scant claim to theoretical innocence. They must be interpreted in light of theory. Why not interpret any worries as stemming from intuitions to the effect that aesthetic value is neither fungible nor instrumental?

C. I. Lewis proposed that some things have inherent value, which is "resident in objects in such wise that they are realizable in experience through presentation of the object itself to which they are attributed" (1946: 391; see also Bishop 2015: 115ff.). Aesthetic value is inherent value in Lewis's sense. An item is essential to the realization of its aesthetic value in an experience of the object. But so what if inherent aesthetic value is not final value? What remains at stake that makes this question a threat to aesthetic hedonism?

Nowadays, nobody produces arguments for aesthetic hedonism, but Moore once reacted in an interesting way to an argument that he attributed to Henry Sidgwick (1884). According to Moore, Sidgwick reasoned that nobody has reason to produce beauty when there is no chance of its being experienced; therefore, any item's aesthetic value lies entirely in its relation to experience (1903: 92–3). Sidgwick's argument fails if there are extrinsic values. The fact that a bracelet has no value apart from its role in a romantic attachment does not show that it has no extrinsic value when it does serve as a token of love. Moore himself thought that beautiful items have only small intrinsic value, but they have great extrinsic value when they are experienced. Indeed, he thought the value of the experience of a beautiful item is greater than the sum of the value of the experience and the value of the item (1903: 94, 187–9).

Basic Normativity

"Let's watch *Die Hard* tonight," suggests Siobhan. Murat thinks about it, and then wonders, "Why should we do that?" Siobhan is ready: "But it's a hoot!" Convinced, Murat reaches for the remote. Clearly Siobhan gets that Murat gets that the fact that the movie will please them is eminently respectable reason to watch it. They understand the normativity of hedonic facts, which give them reasons to act, lending weight to what they aesthetically should do. If being a hoot is an aesthetic merit in *Die Hard*, then aesthetic hedonism answers the normative question. However, a wrinkle appears once we spell out the details.

A theory of aesthetic value answers the normative question by completing the following template:

> an aesthetic value, V, is reason-giving = the fact that x is V lends weight to the proposition that…

The idea is to fill in the dots to provide a substantive replacement for the proposition that A aesthetically should φ in C (as in VALUE). Aesthetic hedonism suggests a basic hedonic theory of the normativity of aesthetic value. For some x, some A, some φ, in some C,

> an aesthetic value, V, is reason-giving = the fact that x is V lends weight to the proposition that it would maximize A's pleasure were A to φ in C.

Call this the "basic theory" for short.

The step from aesthetic hedonism to the basic theory requires a very plausible claim,

MAX.   anyone has reason to act to maximize finally valuable experiences.

General value hedonists say that anyone has decisive reason to maximize pleasure, but general value hedonism is not very plausible, since it seems that we have many non-hedonic reasons to act (cf. Crisp 2006). Good thing that (MAX) does not imply general value hedonism. It says merely that anyone has reason—sometimes not decisive—to act to maximize pleasure. Only when conjoined with aesthetic hedonism does (MAX) imply that anyone has decisive aesthetic reason to maximize pleasure. Only then does (MAX) imply that anyone aesthetically should maximize pleasure.

So, start with the claim that an aesthetic value is a property of an item that stands in constitutive relation to pleasures of subjects who correctly understand the item. Now conjoin aesthetic hedonism with (MAX). The basic theory follows. Being a hoot is reason-giving because of the fact that *Die Hard* lends weight to the proposition that it would maximize Siobhan's and Murat's pleasure were they to watch it tonight. The basic theory reduces aesthetic normativity to plain vanilla hedonic normativity via (MAX). What could be easier? Time for a beer!

Except that only a tiny minority of aesthetic hedonists are content with the basic theory (Santayana 1896; Ducasse 1966[1929]; Melchionne 2010; Kölbel 2016). Few even consider it in order to dismiss it.

Distinguish responder-dependent from response-dependent values (cf. Kölbel 2016). A value is response-dependent just when it stands in constitutive relation to a response of standard observers in standard conditions. V is responder-dependent just when an item's being V for some A stands in constitutive relation to A's response to the item in favourable conditions. Being tasty is responder-dependent: the gelato's being tasty for Alex stands in constitutive relation to Alex's response to the gelato in favourable conditions. Responder-dependent values are perfectly normative. Alex goes wrong if conditions are favourable for her to taste the durian gelato and yet she chooses the less tasty treat. She gustatorily should taste the durian gelato. She owes herself a facepalm.

On the basic theory, aesthetic values are responder-dependent. *Die Hard* is a hoot for Siobhan and Murat in that it pleases them when they watch it in favourable conditions. They go wrong if conditions are favourable and they choose to watch the parliamentary channel instead. They aesthetically should watch *Die Hard*.

To put it another way, recall that an aesthetic expert is configured so as to routinely act on the aesthetic reasons they have. According to the basic theory, Siobhan and Murat are experts if they have what it takes to routinely get what they personally like. That is, if they accurately detect what pleases them and they have the wherewithal to put themselves in a position to get the pleasure, when conditions are favourable. Aesthetic experts are experts in themselves, in what they like, personally, and how to get it (Melchionne 2010; Kölbel 2016).

A few years ago, the *New Yorker* printed a cartoon of a couple exiting a theatre, the husband remarking to his wife, "I never said it wasn't good. I just said I didn't like it." Comparing two paintings, Diderot reported, "artists will prefer the first and they will be right. Personally, I prefer the second" (quoted in Fried 1980: 118). Bernard Williams once quipped, "I simply don't like staying in good hotels" (1985: 125).

Each bit of wit implies a distinction between aesthetic value and responder-dependent hedonic value. Armed with the basic theory, Williams will acknowledge that, for Alxan, the Banff Springs Hotel is elegant and she aesthetically should stay there because it will maximize her pleasure. He cannot, given the basic theory, regard its elegance as giving him any reason to act. Yet the Banff Springs is elegant. So his quip implies a response-dependent conception of aesthetic value: a hotel's elegance stands in constitutive relation to a response in standard observers in standard conditions. Williams simply confesses that he is not a standard observer. He is saying that the Banff Springs is elegant, even if he does not like staying there. If he does not stay there, he does not do as he aesthetically should do. He does not do as a standard observer has reason to do. He just does as he pleases.

In the end, any hedonic theory of the normativity of aesthetic value must be assessed for how well it predicts the six explananda laid out in Chapter 1. Leave the exercise to basic theorists. Most aesthetic hedonists assume that aesthetic values have a more robust normativity than the basic theory puts on the table.

True Judges

According to the basic theory, for an aesthetic value to be reason-giving is for it to maximize someone's pleasure when they φ in C. According to philosophers not content with the basic theory, what makes an aesthetic value reason-giving is that φing would maximize the pleasure of anyone who is like a standard or ideal aesthetic agent, Hume's "true judge." Admittedly, the reputation of true judges is yet more tarnished than beauty's: it evokes the image of the snob, sneering at his inferiors. Who does not wince as Kant empowers the man of taste to approve or condemn the judgements of others, insanely insisting that, when it comes to matters aesthetic, "we allow no one to be of a different opinion" (2000[1790]: 159, 123)? Otherwise gentle Hume disagreeably contends that we pronounce "without scruple" to be "absurd and ridiculous" the sentiments of those who prefer Ogilby to Milton or Bunyan to Addison (1777: 232). What can we say but, ease up, fellas? A less disagreeable picture paints true judges as setting a standard that we can eagerly embrace.

The first step is to replace the basic theory with "standardized aesthetic hedonism" or the "standardized theory." For any A, some φ, and some C,

> SAH: an aesthetic value, V, is reason-giving = the fact that x is V lends weight to the proposition that it would maximize A's pleasure were A to φ in C, were A's hedonic responses calibrated to those of true judges in joint verdict.

The elegance of the Banff Springs gives anyone aesthetic reason to take a room there. How so? Take Williams. The hotel's elegance would add to the pleasure he would get from a stay there were he much like the true judges in his hedonic responses. In fact, he does not like staying at the hotel, but that tells us nothing about its elegance; it only tells us something about him—namely that he is not much like the true judges.

True judges are aesthetic experts, agents configured so as to routinely act on the reasons they have. They routinely do as they aesthetically should: they routinely stay at the Banff Springs Hotel, enjoying its elegance; they routinely get pleasure from beauty.

The Puzzle of Standardized Normativity

All else being equal, Williams aesthetically should stay at the elegant Banff Springs, Diderot aesthetically should spend time with the more beautiful first painting, and husbands aesthetically should venture off Broadway with their wives. And why aesthetically should they do these things? The answer, according to the standardized theory, is that, by so acting, they maximize their pleasures, in as much as they are like true judges. That is what the standardized theory says, but it raises a puzzle.

Aesthetic hedonism plus (MAX) do not imply (SAH). Grant that an aesthetic value is a property of an item that stands in constitutive relation to pleasures of subjects who correctly understand the item. Now conjoin aesthetic hedonism with (MAX), the very plausible principle that anyone has reason to act to maximize pleasure. What follows is the basic theory, not the standardized theory.

The gap shows up intuitively. Being a hoot is reason-giving in the sense that *Die Hard's* being a hoot lends weight to the proposition that it would maximize

Siobhan's and Murat's pleasure were they to watch it tonight. All else being equal, that is what they aesthetically should do. After all, they aesthetically should maximize their pleasures. So says the basic theory. Meanwhile, the standardized theory says that they aesthetically should watch, say, *Seven Beauties*, because its unblinking eye would give them more pleasure were they like true judges. The problem is that they are not much like true judges, and the fact that they are not much like true judges is important when it comes to what they have reason to do. So the question is why aesthetically should they do as true judges do? Maybe true judges aesthetically should watch *Seven Beauties*, but Siobhan and Murat are not true judges and find Wertmüller too harsh. If they will get far more pleasure from watching *Die Hard*, why aesthetically should they forgo that pleasure and endure the Wertmüller?

Switch examples. The fact that Bunyan gives me pleasure is reason for me to read Bunyan, but the fact that Addison gives someone else pleasure is not much of a reason for me to read Addison. I might readily concede Addison's aesthetic superiority: Hume assures us that the true judges prefer Addison to Bunyan—and Hume's word is gold. Conceding that has no necessary impact on what pleases me, hence on what I have hedonic or aesthetic reason to do. The joint verdict of true judges exercises no command over my pleasures. So why read Addison? Why not do as I please?

Examples such as these illustrate how the standardized theory cannot rest upon aesthetic hedonism and (MAX) alone. Additional assumptions are needed, from which (SAH) follows. Presumably, those assumptions will capture the thought that Murat, Siobhan, and I will be aesthetically better off, overall, if we refashion ourselves to be more like the true judges. But why? What is so special about these true judges that makes us better off if we emulate them?

Levinson puts the problem vividly (2002: 230). Call those who rate Bunyan over Addison and *Die Hard* over *Seven Beauties* "middling judges." Why think that we middling judges are aesthetically better off becoming like true judges? The items that appeal to true judges will come to appeal to us. Equally, however, some items appeal to us and not true judges. Why not conclude that true judges should become middling judges? Then the items that appeal to us will come to appeal to them. In other words, why should we switch our gratifiers for the true judges' gratifiers? Why not invoke parity and say that true judges have equal reason to switch their gratifiers for ours?

Indeed, the situation is not even one of parity, because we middling judges have reason to retain our middling judge ways. Change takes time and eats up resources. Levinson asks, "What motivation does one have to change aesthetic programs, given the real cost of such change, in terms of education, training, effort, and the foregone pleasures of what one has already come to appreciate?" (2002: 231; see also Godlovitch 1990: 65).

The Levinhume Deduction

Mothersill (1989) and Levinson (2002) locate the answer in a brilliant reading of Hume's 1739 essay "On the Standard of Taste" (see also Lewis 1946: 459–61; Burnham and Skilleas 2012: 155–65; Ross 2012; alternate readings of Hume are Guyer 2005; Shelley 2013a). The portrait of the true judges sketched by Mothersill, filled in by Levinson, bespeaks the power of aesthetic hedonism to go beyond the basic theory in addressing the normative question.

Assume aesthetic hedonism, the theory that an item's aesthetic value is a property that stands in constitutive relation to finally valuable experiences of those who correctly understand the item. Next, stipulate that a masterwork is any item that in fact appeals across temporal, cultural, and socio-economic boundaries. Observation: there are some masterworks. Some items have in fact appealed across the boundaries of history, culture, and social group. The best explanation of this observation is that masterworks have high aesthetic value. By abduction, the masterworks have high aesthetic value. Now picture a true judge as someone who prefers masterworks to non-masterworks. By Mill's rule, given two experiences, E and E', E' is better than E if those who experience both prefer E' to E. Hence, experiences of masterworks are better than experiences of non-masterworks. Final assumption: we have reason to maximize pleasures. Consequently, anyone aesthetically should perform the acts that true judges perform. In doing so, they maximize their overall pleasures.

Written out plain and proper, the "Levinhume deduction" goes like this:

1. an aesthetic value is a property of an item that stands in constitutive relation to finally valuable experiences of subjects who correctly understand the item (AESTHETIC HEDONISM)

2. a masterwork is an item that appeals across temporal, cultural, and socio-economic boundaries (STIPULATED)

3. there are some masterworks (OBSERVATION)

4. the best explanation of (3) is that the masterworks have high aesthetic value

5. therefore, masterworks have high aesthetic value

6. true judges are those who prefer masterworks to non-masterworks (STIPULATED)

7. if those who have two experiences, E and E′, prefer E′ to E, then E′ has greater final value than E (MILL'S RULE)

8. therefore, experiences of masterworks have greater final value than experiences of non-masterworks

MAX. anyone has reason to maximize finally valuable experiences

SAH. therefore, for any A, some φ, and some C, an aesthetic value, V, is reason-giving = the fact that x is V lends weight to the proposition that it would maximize A's pleasure were A to φ in C, were A's hedonic responses calibrated to those of true judges in joint verdict.

One of the most inventive and richest pieces of reasoning in the field in the past twenty years, the Levinhume deduction distills and connects some influential ideas in aesthetics with ideas about practical reasons in general. It merits a closer look.

From Masterworks to True Judges

True judges gain considerable charm once knocked off the Throne of Aesthetic Judgement, stripped of any power to condemn others. In the Levinhume deduction, they model a standard that we all have reason to emulate. Their job description is articulated in the stretch of the deduction from premises (2) to (6). The bookend premises, (2) and (6), stipulate the meaning of two bits of technical jargon, (3) is an empirical observation, and the rest is logic.

The folk concept of a masterpiece comes wrapped in the same cloak of grandeur as the folk concept of genius, and, like the concept of genius, it is an early modern invention (Cahn 1979). One of its sources is the chef-d'œuvre that gained apprentices and journeymen full membership in the medieval guilds. Aspirants proved their competence by making a work meeting recognized, conventional standards of craftsmanship (the doctoral dissertation is a vestige of the practice). A second source of the masterpiece concept is ideas about the miraculous, divine creation of the world. Under the influence of these ideas, masterpieces came to be seen "not so much as the best of a given class as objects in a class by themselves" (Cahn 1979: xv). These masterpieces are so special that they earn wide, enduring attention.

Masterworks are not the same as masterpieces in the folk sense. Some items have aesthetic appeal over long stretches of time. Homer and the Mahākāvya come to mind, not to mention the balanced symmetrical tool designs of the Acheulean industry, which lasted over a million years. Some items have aesthetic appeal for members of many cultures: architecture in the International Style, perhaps, or the Harry Potter novels, which have been translated into more than seventy languages, from Scots to Sinhala. Finally, some items appeal to people young and old, rich and poor, more or less educated. Examples might include the music of the Beatles, blue jeans, and the Grand Canyon. Stipulate masterworks to be just those items that check all three boxes: they have enduring, wide, and broad appeal. Few masterworks in this sense are masterpieces in the jumped-up sense of being in a class beyond high quality. Not all masterworks have made the art canon, and not all canonical masterpieces are masterworks—Vermeer's paintings were virtually unknown until the late nineteenth century.

By themselves, (2) and (3) perform little philosophical work. They imagine a survey that picks out items with enduring, wide, and broad appeal, and then (2) simply attaches a label to what's in the dragnet, calling them "masterworks." More weight is carried by (4), which offers a hypothesis. The best explanation of why items appeal across time, across cultures, and across social groups is that they have high aesthetic value. By inference to the best explanation, it follows, in (5), that some items, the masterworks, have high aesthetic value.

The opening stretch of the Levinhume deduction concludes with a second stipulation. Let a true judge be whoever prefers the masterworks to everything else. In other words, the masterworks provide a litmus test for a certain kind of person. Whoever they are and whatever else they might be, call them "true judges" (see also Dickie 1988: 142–3; Goldman 1995: 173).

Granted, the possession of certain traits might explain why true judges prefer works with enduring, wide, and broad appeal. In Hume's famous breakdown, true judges have "strong sense, united to delicate sentiment, improved by practice, perfected by comparison, and cleared of all prejudice" (1777: 242). A delicate sentiment equips them to accurately perceive the features of an item that underlie its aesthetic value. Absence of prejudice enables them to set aside personal interests and focus all attention on what they are judging. With strong sense, they relate the formal and functional parts to the whole of an item. Practice in making comparisons ensures they know how to weigh an item's value in its genre and across different genres. Perhaps Hume's list is but a start and we can add to the traits of true judges (e.g. Ross 2008: 24). All the same, they are not defined as having these traits; they are defined as those who prefer the masterworks.

The role of the true judges is metaphysical, not cognitive or epistemic. Since none exist and none meet in Paris (or Tokyo) to render their joint verdicts, the proposal is not that we consult them to get the lowdown on aesthetic value. Nor is it that we may cite their joint verdicts to justify our aesthetic judgements. A judgement of an item's beauty is justified by pointing to more specific facts about the item, not by citing the authority of the true judges in joint verdict. The joint verdict of true judges functions as a normative standard that makes it the case that anyone aesthetically should act in certain ways—for example, by reading Addison instead of Bunyan when there is opportunity to read only one of them. True judges are the aesthetic counterparts of moral philosophy's ideal observers (Hospers 1962; Taliaferro 1990; Ross 2011; cf. Bonzon 1999).

Care must be taken to guard against identifying masterworks with masterpieces and against identifying true judges with members of cultural elites. The masterworks are not necessarily Mahler and Atwood, and the true judges are not necessarily Fraser and Niles Crane. Those who tend to be credited with "taste" are, as Carolyn Korsmeyer observes, "suspiciously coincident with people of wealth and social standing within a select group of European nations" (1998: 360). The Levinhume deduction is designed to bypass biased images of the masterworks and the true judges. True judges are just those who prefer those items whose high aesthetic value has secured their cross-border appeal.

The Problem Aesthetic Agents Face

In its final stretch, from (6) to SAH, the Levinhume deduction takes on the puzzle of standardized normativity. Why aesthetically should I read Addison rather than Bunyan, when Bunyan gives me more pleasure? Sure, the true judges get more pleasure reading Addison than Bunyan, but why is that fact any reason for me to act? Presumably, the thought is that I will be aesthetically better off, overall, if I refashion myself to be more like the true judges. But why is that the case? What is so special about the true judges that makes any of us better off if we emulate them? Steps (6) to SAH answer by appeal to nothing more than plain vanilla, hedonic, normativity.

True judges prefer masterworks to non-masterworks. According to Mill's rule, if those capable of undergoing two experiences prefer the first to the second, then the first has greater final value than the second. Hence, if true judges prefer reading Addison to reading Bunyan, then the experience of reading Addison has greater final value than the experience of reading Bunyan. In general, experiences of masterworks have greater final value than experiences of non-masterworks. Given these results plus aesthetic hedonism and (MAX), (SAH) follows.

How? Suppose that Addison's measured prose lends weight to the proposition that reading him would maximize the pleasures of the true judges. Since aesthetic values are hedonic values and since I have reason to get a lifetime of pleasure, I aesthetically should do as the true judges would do, as they are the gold standard of how to get a lifetime of pleasure. So Addison's measured prose lends weight to the proposition that reading him would maximize my pleasures, or yours, or anyone's, were we to refashion ourselves to get a lifetime of pleasure. Having measured prose is, in this sense, reason-giving. Aesthetic hedonism answers the normative question via the standardized theory.

To understand an agent as someone who has reasons to act, consider what problem they face. In effect, (MAX) represents an assumption about the problem that aesthetic agents face. Our problem is to locate what brings most pleasure (Schier 1986; Gracyk 1990; Brooks 1993; Goldman 1995: 21–2; Levinson 2002; Guyer 2005; Melchionne 2010). Hence Levinson describes true judges as our "best truffle pigs" and our "best barometers" (2002: 234). They root out what we have reason to go for. (So they are not the same as ideal critics. Critics draw attention to features of items that we otherwise overlook, but true judges need not do that.)

Yet the deep lesson of the Levinhume deduction is that the problem of how to get the most pleasure now, at this moment, naturally gives way to the problem of how to cultivate a capacity for hedonic response so as to get the most pleasure overall, not just now, this minute. True judges are more than truffle pigs. They model our best aesthetic selves—the versions of ourselves who get the most pleasure overall. As Lewis put it, the aesthetic ideal "holds an imperative for the good life, being that discrimination by which the purer, the more fecund, and the more desirable inherent goods [viz. pleasures] are selected" (1946: 437).

In a nutshell, (MAX) does not speak of the pleasures we have reason to maximize now; we have reason to maximize our pleasures overall.

By the way, the proposal is not that we aesthetically should fix our gaze on Cy Twombly, and erase all but Mahler from our playlist. Satiated on Mahler, one might have aesthetic reason to mix it up with a little Diana Ross. To get more out of Twombly, one might have aesthetic reason to get in the street and look at graffiti. The proposal is only that we aesthetically should act, in C, in a way that befits the ranking of items that corresponds to the joint verdict of true judges. Put in other words, we aesthetically should do exactly as true judges would do, all else being equal.

Motivational Hedonism

An expert agent is one so configured that they routinely act on the reasons they have to act. Muddlers have the same reasons to act, but they often enough fail to act on the reasons they have. The same goes for aesthetic experts and aesthetic muddlers. The aesthetic reasons anyone has to act are visible in the doings of true judges. Their agency is so configured that they routinely act on the reasons they have. A Humean picture of the configuration of agency nicely fits the aesthetic case.

What makes aesthetic values reason-giving? What is it about V that makes it the case that the fact that x is V lends weight to what an agent aesthetically should do? As it appears to Abbott, from her perspective as an agent, the normative question is why the fact that a sequence of images brings out a unity of vision lends any weight to the proposition that she aesthetically should publish the sequence as part of her campaign on Atget's behalf. Humeans hear the normative question as asking something more. They hear it as asking how aesthetic reasons can motivate agents to act (Williams 1981; Hampton 1998: 1–7). Elizabeth Anderson remarks that "any theory of the good must have normative force: we must be capable of being moved to action by the reasons it gives" (1993: 21). In Korsgaard's metaphor, to answer the normative question is partly to explain how "reasons get a grip on the agent" (1996: 240).

A classic piece of reasoning derives a Humean or desire-based theory of reasons from two principles. The first is reasons internalism, Williams's (1981) principle that no fact is a reason for someone to act unless she can be motivated to act by representing the fact to herself. The second principle is a Humean theory of motivation. Beliefs do not suffice to motivate action, desires are required, so motives are belief–desire pairs (e.g. Davidson 1963; Smith 1987). On the Humean theory of motivation, desires are mental states whose nature consists in the functional role they play in action, not in their phenomenology, and they need not be articulated linguistically or even brought to consciousness. So, assuming that an agent has a reason to act only if they can be motivated to act, and assuming that motives implicate desires, practical reasons implicate desires. With this result in hand, Humeans say this about the normativity of practical reasons: the authority of our desires explains why reasons lend weight to what we should do.

Cut the reasoning down to aesthetic size. Aesthetic reasons internalism plus the Humean theory of motivation yields a desire-based theory of aesthetic reasons. According to

AESTHETIC REASON INTERNALISM: necessarily, the fact p is an aesthetic reason for A to φ in C only if A can be motivated by a p-representing state to φ in C.

The "can" indicates rational possibility: either an agent's existing motivational make-up already includes the required motive or it is possible for them to acquire it just by correctly reasoning from their current motives. Aesthetic reason internalists deny that the splendour of the fireworks is a reason for you to go view them as long as an awareness of their splendour could not motivate you to go view them—as long as you were to be rigidly indifferent to the splendour (Strandberg 2011). When conjoined with a Humean theory of motivation, AESTHETIC REASON INTERNALISM implies a desire-based theory of aesthetic reasons.

Desire-based theories of aesthetic reasons can take many forms; here is one modelled on Mark Schroeder's (2007) proposal that for a fact to be a reason for someone to act is for the fact to explain why their performing the act would fulfill some desire of theirs. Weakened to a necessary condition and limited to aesthetic reasons,

>   DESIRE: necessarily, p is an aesthetic reason for A to φ in C only if A has a p-representing desire that would be satisfied by A's φing in C and the fact that p explains why the desire would be satisfied by A's φing in C.

A p-representing desire is an aesthetic desire. For example, the fact that Anne Carson's translation of fragment 31 of Sappho is direct is an aesthetic reason for me to read it now only if its being direct explains why an aesthetic desire I have would be satisfied by my reading it now. (A theory such as DESIRE is more plausible than desire-based theories of reasons in general—see Anderson 1993; Quinn 1993; Scanlon 1998b: 42, 44–9; Foot 2001).

Aesthetic hedonism fits DESIRE hand in glove. After all, pleasures are states of experience that we want to undergo or that we want to persist for their own sake (Beardsley 1973: 50). Our desiring experiences in this way just comes with their being pleasures. If this is correct, then the fact that a poem is direct implies that it stands in constitutive relation to states that we want to undergo or that we want to continue. On any plausible conception of the constitutive relation, the fact that the translation of fragment 31 is direct explains why an aesthetic desire would be satisfied by my reading it now. As long as desires have normative authority, because we cannot remain indifferent to them, weight is added to the proposition that aesthetically I should read it.

The poem is direct. Why does that lend any weight to the proposition that I aesthetically should read it here and now? Given DESIRE, the question becomes this: would my reading the poem now satisfy an aesthetic desire, where the explanation of the desire's being satisfied is that the poem is direct? According to aesthetic hedonism, the poem's directness stands in constitutive relation to a pleasure. But pleasures are states that we want to start up or go on. So, if the poem is direct, then my reading it now satisfies my desire for pleasure. That is why its being direct lends weight to the proposition that I aesthetically should read it now.

Alas, I seem to lack the least desire to read Sappho. Like most people nowadays, I am a muddler when it comes to poetry. Nevertheless, the directness of Carson's translation of the fragment is reason for me to read it. It lends weight to the proposition that I aesthetically should read it. But how can it be that I aesthetically should read the poem, given DESIRE and the wretched fact that I seem to lack the least desire to read it?

The answer is that I do want to read Sappho, though I am not aware of what I want under the description "wanting to read Sappho." Desires are dispositional states. I have a standing desire to maximize my pleasures, which is a standing desire to configure my hedonic capabilities so as to win the most pleasure. I want to read Sappho, if that is what the ideal aesthetic agent wants. In this respect, I am not peculiar. Just by virtue of wanting pleasure, we all want to be our best aesthetic selves and to live up to the standard set by the joint verdict of the true judges. Only by so doing can we get what we most want, aesthetically—to live the most pleasure-filled lives.

When combined with DESIRE, the standardized theory answers the normative question of how aesthetic values give reasons to act, but it also answers the Humean question of how aesthetic reasons can motivate us to act. True judges are so configured that they act on the aesthetic reasons they have. They are so configured that they act to get what they most want, aesthetically speaking. On this picture, true judges set a standard that we eagerly embrace.

Aesthetic hedonism does not imply a desire-based theory of reasons, but it fits a theory such as DESIRE hand in glove. One might wonder how much there is to like in aesthetic hedonism without DESIRE.

So concludes the song in praise of aesthetic hedonism. The standardized theory deftly answers the normative question via the Levinhume deduction, which starts out with a broad and flexible interpretation of aesthetic hedonism and then appeals to an empirically respectable conception of masterworks and an agreeable portrait of true judges.

4

Six Degrees of Separation

Aesthetic hedonism answers the normative question by way of the standardized theory:

> SAH: for any A, some φ, and some C, an aesthetic value, V, is reason-giving = the fact that x is V lends weight to the proposition that it would maximize A's pleasure were A to φ in C, where A's hedonic responses are calibrated to those of true judges in joint verdict.

Now the time has come to move on to the next step of the main (abductive) argument—to see why the standardized theory fails to explain the facts about expert aesthetic agency that were tendered in Chapter 1. The first section of this chapter sizes up the explanatory gap. The rest of the chapter offers an error theory, an account of why the standardized theory is attractive yet mistaken.

The Explanatory Gap

Recall the theoretical backstory. Aesthetic values give agents reasons to act, so any theory of aesthetic value must answer the normative question, by stating how aesthetic values are reason-giving. In as much as aesthetic reasons impact what agents do, we should be able to assess any theory for how well it explains general facts about the doings of aesthetic agents. Not all aesthetic agents, for many of us do not act on the reasons we have. Only for experts is it routinely true that

> when the fact that x is V is reason to φ in C, experts φ in C, and their evaluation of x as V explains their φing in C.

In expert agency, we see most vividly the difference that aesthetic value makes. Accordingly, a theory of the normativity of aesthetic value should explain general facts about expert aesthetic agents, and the task is now to assess how well the standardized theory explains general facts about aesthetic experts.

A limited argument to the best explanation, where there are no prior, agreed explananda, leaves us but one option. We must come up with some facts to be explained, ideally as generalizations of concrete empirical observations. Chapter 1 proposed six explananda:

1. aesthetic experts disperse into almost all demographic niches,
2. aesthetic experts jointly inhabit the whole aesthetic universe,
3. aesthetic experts specialize by aesthetic domain,
4. aesthetic experts specialize by activity, where
5. specialization by activity and domain interact, and
6. aesthetic expertise is relatively stable.

Does standardized aesthetic hedonism, elaborated through the Levinhume deduction, predict these facts about aesthetic experts? Does it predict that aesthetic experts are distributed across all demographic niches, that they jointly inhabit every aesthetic domain, that they individually specialize in some domains and activities, and that their expertise is relatively stable?

Since aesthetic experts exist, but not true judges, who represent a purely notional ideal or standard, it would be unfair to read the standardized theory as predicting that aesthetic experts literally are true judges (so as to go on to complain that nobody is a true judge!). Fairness demands some adjustment be made in the direction of a non-ideal theory.

Let aesthetic experts closely approximate true judges. Here "closely approximate" is technical. Aesthetic experts closely approximate true judges in the sense that no aesthetic expert falls short, in principle, of the title of true judge. When someone falls short of the title, it is only because they are human, hence limited in native ability, upbringing, and social support or capital. Such factors are ones that can be surmounted in principle. In this way, the core insight of the standardized theory is preserved: what you or I have reason to do is what an expert has reason to do, because the expert's responses closely track those of true judges in joint verdict. Aesthetic experts realistically model our best aesthetic selves.

1. Aesthetic experts disperse into almost all demographic niches. To answer the normative question, the Levinhume deduction installs the joint verdict of true judges as a normative standard. Setting aside some unfortunate connotations that attach to the designation of "true judge," the concept of true judges is stipulated in a way that carefully avoids ensconcing true judges among cultural elites. A true judge is just anyone who prefers masterworks to non-masterworks, where the masterworks are those items that have proven appeal across boundaries of time, culture, and socioeconomic status. Therefore we should predict that aesthetic experts, who closely approximate true judges, will have overcome their social backgrounds. They will not hail only from social elites.

While the true judge represents an advance, in this respect, on the early moderns' "man of taste," we are only halfway home. The Levinhume deduction allows that aesthetic experts might very well represent every walk of life, but to allow for a possibility is not yet to explain it. To explain why any aesthetic expert might hail from any social niche is not to explain why each social niche harbours and fosters its own experts. The question remains why the social world is saturated through and through with aesthetic experts.

Indeed, the task is to make robust sense of the social dependencies of aesthetic agency. Aesthetic agents conduct business by drawing upon larger social resources. The Refords could not have done what they did were they raised in the Montréal neighbourhood of La Petite-Bourgogne, Winfrey's background as an African-American from rural Mississippi is not irrelevant to her book club work, and Sam's sensibility non-accidentally represents a slice of contemporary youth culture. Yet aesthetic experts who closely approximate true judges abstract away and transcend social dependencies such as these. The Levinhume deduction lacks resources to explain why every social niche has its experts, who are especially adapted to thrive in just that social milieu.

2. Aesthetic experts jointly inhabit the whole aesthetic universe. Leaving social demographics to one side, take all the aesthetic domains, from dog breeding to installation art. A second fact to explain is this. The class of all aesthetic experts covers all aesthetic domains. Every aesthetic domain accommodates aesthetic expertise.

This the standardized theory would seem to explain with bells on. Aesthetic experts closely approximate true judges by leaving behind their personal baggage, sampling items from all aesthetic domains, understanding them correctly. Having done so, they each, individually, inhabit the whole aesthetic universe. That they individually inhabit the whole aesthetic universe implies that, together, they inhabit it jointly too.

Explanations with bells on should always raise an alarm, though. The claim that aesthetic experts individually inhabit the whole aesthetic universe is much stronger than the claim that they inhabit it jointly too. As a rule, we should be suspicious of accounts that explain a weaker fact by explaining a much stronger fact that implies the weaker fact. Explanans and explanandum should match each other in strength.

Whether the concern pans out depends on there being independent reason to doubt that aesthetic experts individually inhabit the whole aesthetic universe. For that, turn to the next pair of explananda.

3. Aesthetic experts specialize by aesthetic domain. Taken jointly, aesthetic experts populate every corner of the aesthetic universe, from contemporary dance to gamelan to *chanbara* and 1970s muscle cars. Taken individually, each specializes in only a handful of aesthetic domains, usually ones that tend to package together in a social context. Expertise in *chanbara* entrains a bit of expertise in spaghetti westerns, but no expertise in 1970s muscle cars or *khoomei*.

However, in order to explain how aesthetic experts inhabit the whole aesthetic universe, the standardized theory represents each as a generalist, equipped to appreciate *Zatoichi's Cane Sword* alongside a low rider with a flame hood, Mahler's Fifth, the unix operating system, and *Passerina ciris*.

It goes to the core of the standardized theory that it represents aesthetic experts as generalists rather than specialists. Through (MAX), the theory reduces the normativity of aesthetic value to plain vanilla hedonic normativity. If what I aesthetically should do just now is maximize my pleasure, then I should not take my cue from Felix, who knows only Mahler, because the best Mahler might not be best for me, now. If the question is how I should refashion myself to secure a lifetime of pleasure, I probably should not emulate Odette, the 1970s muscle car gal. The standardized theory predicts that aesthetic experts, who set the standard for pleasure maximizers, are generalists, not specialists.

4. Aesthetic experts specialize by activity. Aesthetic experts specialize by act-type: some collect, some document, some restore, some curate. All of these are aesthetic acts, complying with ACT. Moreover, we observe that expertise in one type of act does not imply expertise in arbitrarily any other act-type, even within the same domain. Sam's cleverness at conserving video games is no guarantee against her being a clumsy player, and Alexander Reford lacks his grandmother's green thumb. Transfer can happen, of course. Abbott's expertise as a photography editor complemented her own photographic artistry, and Winfrey successfully publishes and writes. An account that does full justice to the intricacies of aesthetic agency will explain how overlaps such as these can, but need not, occur.

Are such intricacies what the standardized theory tells us we should expect to see in aesthetic experts who closely approximate true judges? True judges themselves are experts in one aesthetic act, namely appreciation. What about experts who closely approximate them? Nothing in the standardized theory rules out that their expertise might channel into diverse act-types, but nothing predicts it either. Why do so many aesthetic experts, who closely approximate true judges in their appreciative prowess, also cultivate aesthetic expertise beyond appreciation? Is appreciative expertise necessary for any other aesthetic expertise? Why? Are there no experts who get little pleasure from the medieval tapestries that they conserve or the wedding playlists that they put together? The standardized theory explains the channelling of aesthetic expertise only if it has resources to answer questions such as these.

5. *Specialization by activity and domain interact.* Someone editing a poem is engaged in the same high-level activity as someone editing an album of photographs, but there are differences between what they do that trace to the specificities of poetry and photography. By the same token, agents who edit and appreciate photographs engage in different types of acts within the same aesthetic domain. Both domain and act-type need to be taken into account to characterize what it takes to perform as an expert. The standardized theory explains this fact only if it explains facts (3) and (4). Since it does not explain facts (3) and (4), it also fails to explain the interaction of activity and domain in specialized aesthetic expertise.

6. *Aesthetic expertise is relatively stable.* Neither beginner's luck nor pure guesswork make an agent an aesthetic expert. Experts routinely act on the reasons they have because they have relatively stable traits of character. Relative stability does not imply rigidity, though. Aesthetic experts are nimble enough to adapt as circumstances require, in pace with changing circumstances. The crank who thinks it is all downhill since Satyajit Ray is no more a cinema expert than the fan who adores the latest Spielberg, no matter what.

The Levinhume deduction serves to quell the concern, aroused by the basic theory, that aesthetic hedonism makes aesthetic value just as vulnerable to individual whim as are other hedonic values. The true judges standardize because they are as stable in aesthetic character as can be. In so far as aesthetic experts closely approximate true judges, their capacities to assess aesthetic value are also stable. So the theory predicts that aesthetic expertise is stable.

Does it also predict that aesthetic expertise is relatively, not absolutely, stable? Does it predict that aesthetic experts are nimble enough to change with changing circumstances? True judges, notional beings that they are, judge timelessly. Insisting that the same goes for aesthetic experts would be churlish, so grant that aesthetic experts learn to appreciate what appears on the scene. What they cannot learn is new standards of evaluation that apply to what appears on the scene. The standardized theory predicts stability of aesthetic expertise at the expense of making sense of other explananda, especially (3).

To sum up, since aesthetic values are reason-giving, we should be able to assess a theory of the normativity of aesthetic value for how well it explains general facts about the doing of aesthetic experts, who act on the aesthetic reasons they have. However, the standardized theory does a poor job at explaining the facts about aesthetic experts. At bottom, there is a gap between an image of aesthetic experts closely approximating true judges and more modest images of aesthetic expertise.

Truth be told, philosophers are not quick to give up on a theory that fails to explain what it should. Technical details are too easy to shrug off as chores for another day. To up the ante, the next four sections expose subtle flaws in the Levinhume deduction. The flaws point up inadequacies in the standardized theory, while their subtlety explains why the standardized theory has legs.

Perverse Pleasures

Pleasure is plastic: some pleasures can be more intense than the pleasures of those who closely approximate true judges. After all, true judges sniff out what appeals across boundaries of time, culture, and social group, and masterworks might not be the very best precisely because they cross these boundaries. Wide appeal can impose hedonic sacrifices. Yet, according to premise (8) of the Levinhume deduction, experiences of masterworks have greater final value than experiences of non-masterworks. As it turns out, the reasoning to (8) is invalid. Questioning (8), we have reason to doubt that (SAH) sets the normative standard that it purports to set.

Here is the reasoning spanning (5) to (8):

5. masterworks have high aesthetic value

6. true judges are those who prefer masterworks to non-masterworks

7. if those who have two experiences, E and E', prefer E' to E, then E' has greater final value than E

8. therefore, experiences of masterworks have greater final value than experiences of non-masterworks.

Premise (6) is stipulated, grant (7), and note that to get to (SAH) via (MAX), we really do need (8). The rub is that the inference running from (6) to (8) works only if the masterworks have the highest aesthetic value. That masterworks have high aesthetic value does not imply that they have highest aesthetic value. Premise (5) falls short.

We should confirm that the case for (5) does not warrant the stronger claim that masterworks have the highest aesthetic value. Premises (2) to (4) of the deduction go as follows. A masterwork is any item that appeals across the boundaries of time, culture, and socio-economic status. Some items do fit the bill. Moreover, the best explanation of this fact is that the masterworks have high aesthetic value. So masterworks have high aesthetic value.

Why not strengthen (5) to say that the best explanation of the appeal of masterworks is that they have the highest aesthetic value? Obviously, externalities can figure into masterwork status. Symbols of cultural identity persist as a culture spreads. Markets sometimes promote the second rate over the first rate. Societies with very efficient aesthetic distribution systems might have insipid aesthetic production, while some of the very best works are no doubt made in unstable cultures with crummy distribution networks. An item's appeal can take a dent if it is made by (or for) a person belonging to a stigmatized group—people who are female, queer, or indigenous, for example. These forces, and many more like them, make it a fluke that all and only masterworks will turn out to have the highest aesthetic value. At the same time, social forces with local effect tend not to have broad effect, so it is unlikely that the externalities are powerful enough to clinch masterwork status for what has low aesthetic value. The case is solid for (5) as it is stated in the deduction.

Therefore, we have room to question (8).

Pleasures are plastic, prone to be channelled in the most idiosyncratic ways. (Not persuaded? Try surfing the Internet.) Imagine a community whose members get a heart-pounding aesthetic thrill from manicured lawns. These Texans understand lawns perfectly; they know perfectly that lawns do not express themes from Haida lore or the Second Brandenburg Concerto. Yet suburban lawns ring their bells like no bell has been rung before. True judges, who also understand lawns correctly, rate them mighty low in aesthetic value. In this scenario, what aesthetic reason have Texans to make make themselves more like true judges? Surely they have every aesthetic reason to shrug off the joint verdict of true judges?

The plasticity of pleasure generates a well-known puzzle for general hedonism: it seems to imply that subjects should lower their pleasure threshold, so that they get pleasure from (just about) anything. Pure hedonists should warn us against being picky about our pleasures, because pickiness staunches the flow of pleasure. Suppose it is better to enjoy Addison and not *Friends* than to enjoy *Friends* and not Addison. As James Shelley (2011) points out, it does not follow that someone who enjoys *Friends* and not Addison should try to be someone who enjoys Addison at the expense of *Friends*. What they have stronger reason to do is enjoy both equally maximally. In Shelley's analogy, it is better to be a pitcher with a good fast ball and a bad curve ball than a pitcher with a bad fast ball and a good curve ball. However, it does not follow that pitchers with bad fast balls and good curve balls should try to be pitchers with good fast balls and bad curve balls. They should try to be pitchers with good fast balls and good curve balls.

Experiments with psychotropic compounds promise a world where it is possible to manipulate long-term pleasure response without mischief to correct cognition (e.g. Griffiths et al. 2008). Suppose that a super-psilocybin is perfected that induces character changes sufficient to take experiences to the final value maximum, leaving understanding completely intact. Drugged subjects score their experiences of *Friends*, Addison, and everything else perfect tens for final value, while correctly understanding each one. What aesthetic reason does anyone have to decline to pop the pill and thereby align with true judges in having less finally good experiences of *Friends* than Addison? (Do not reply that true judges will pop the pill! They, by definition, prefer masterworks to non-masterworks.)

Reasons to question (8) are reasons to question (SAH). True judges do not set the standard for ideal aesthetic agency across the board. Defined as those who prefer masterworks, they set a standard for one special kind of aesthetic agent, one who aims to appreciate what passes a test of reach and endurance. They are analysts in the bureau of aesthetic endurables. They seem to play a role that they might not play because masterworks seem to have a value ranking that they might not have.

Limited Aesthetic Agents

According to the home stretch of the Levinhume deduction,

> 8. experiences of masterworks have greater final value than experiences of non-masterworks
>
> MAX. anyone has reason to maximize finally valuable experiences
>
> SAH. therefore, for any A, some φ, and some C, an aesthetic value, V, is reason-giving = the fact that x is V lends weight to the proposition that it would maximize A's pleasure were A to φ in C, where A's hedonic responses are calibrated to those of true judges in joint verdict.

Grant the very plausible principle, (MAX), and, notwithstanding the "Perverse Pleasures" section, also grant (8). From these premises plus (1), we derive an answer to the question of what makes aesthetic values reason-giving. Anyone would maximize their pleasures were they to respond in line with true judges. Presumably, the step from (MAX) to (SAH) implies two claims. The first is a solid principle of prudence: anyone has reason to use the best means to their ends. The second is substantive: the best means for anyone to maximize pleasure is for them to calibrate their responses to those of true judges in joint verdict.

A key insight of Adam Morton's *Bounded Thinking: Intellectual Virtues for Limited Agents* is that an agent's best method is not always to do as the expert would do. Knowing that we are imperfect, we often believe the thing to do is to try to emulate the best agents. However, trying to emulate the best is sometimes suboptimal. Sometimes we do better by emulating exemplars who are not the best. In failing to see this, we succumb to the fallacy of approximation, which is to assume that an "attempt to approximate an ideal will lead to approximately ideal results" (Morton 2012: 25). Put comparatively, the fallacy is to assume that when one method is superior to another, an approximation to the superior method produces better results than an approximation to the inferior method.

Approximating the ideal need not return results that are either approximately ideal or even better than those obtained by approximating the nonideal. A student is struggling with her writing, which is clear but so soporific that readers miss her terrific ideas. I do not advise her to write like Nozick, though his literary flare makes long books seem short. Her attempts to write like Nozick would risk the merit of clarity that her writing already has. To be stylish and still clear is no mean feat. A better idea is for the two of us to sit down and thumb through some recent journals, looking over some engaging pieces by young philosophers. Their efforts are ones she can approximate to good effect. (The procedure was long ago codified in the Buddhist doctrine of *upāya*.)

Ordinary aesthetic agents are limited too (Burnham and Skilleås 2012: 145–6). Some of our limitations are part of the general lot—inadequate brainpower and incomplete information, for example. More specific limitations stem from the path dependence of what aesthetic options are available to any given agent. Suppose that Noh is beyond reach for those raised on Gilbert and Sullivan, but not kabuki. A Gilbert and Sullivan fan should not approximate true judges, who rate Noh over kabuki. Instead, she should emulate aesthetic experts specializing in popular musical theatre. The Oprah Book Club never claimed to select the greatest novels ever—the ones that would top the true judges' list. Winfrey's stated goal was to select very good works suited to her viewers, given their knowledge of and commitment to certain literary genres. Critics who gripe that the club did not go far enough in pushing highbrow literature either ignore prudential considerations or commit the fallacy of approximation, failing to take seriously enough the psychological and social dependencies of aesthetic agency. For most of us, there are no choices that we could make that would put us on a path to closely approximating true judges.

What an agent has reason to do must take account of their limited agency. Perhaps it is true that the fact that Addison's prose is measured lends weight to the proposition that it would maximize my pleasure to read Addison were I like a true judge. However, the fact that Patrick O'Brian is a good romp lends more weight to the proposition that it would maximize my pleasure to read the Aubrey–Maturin series were I more like the best I can be, given who I am. If that is correct, then the explanation of why some aesthetic values are reason-giving does not lie in the standardized theory.

A big assumption has been made so far, both in expounding the Levinhume deduction and in developing the concern about the fallacy of approximation. The assumption is that what anyone has aesthetic reason to do is what aesthetic experts have reason to do. In other words, we are to imitate them. However, aesthetic experts need not set a standard to imitate.

Some say that a fact is a reason for me to act if and only if it would motivate me were I fully rational. When I recognize the fact as a reason, I treat my fully rational self as an ideal to imitate (e.g. Korsgaard 1986: 15). A case described by Michael Smith dramatizes the pitfalls of this idea:

> Suppose I have just been defeated in a game of squash. The defeat has been so humiliating that, out of anger and frustration, I am consumed with a desire to smash my opponent in the face with my racket. But if I were fully rational... I wouldn't have any such desire at all. My desire to smash him in the face is wholly and solely the product of anger and frustration, something we can rightly imagine away when we imagine me in my cool and calm fully rational state. The consideration that would motivate me if I were fully rational is rather that I would show good sportsmanship by striding right over and shaking my opponent by the hand. In that case, does it follow that what I have reason to do in my uncalm and uncool state is stride right over and shake him by the hand?   (1995: 111)

Not if the anger and frustration would cause the blow to be struck! Instead, Smith observes, "what I have reason to do in my uncalm and uncool state is to smile politely and leave the scene as quickly as possible" (1995: 111). This is what Smith's fully rational self would advise his imperfect self to do in the circumstances. So what Smith has reason to do is what his fully rational self advises him to do. The advice model is an alternative to the imitation model (Railton 1986; Railton 2003; Morton 2012: 14).

The advice model of aesthetic expertise dodges the fallacy of approximation. On the advice model, aesthetic experts set the standard for what an agent is advised to do, where what the agent is advised to do need not be what experts would do themselves (Mason 2001). Creatures such as you and I aesthetically should not always do as the experts do, but we always have aesthetic reason to do as they advise us to do. They prefer the Noh play, but they advise those bred on Gilbert and Sullivan to try kabuki. Taking their advice is the best method for aesthetic agents to use in order to maximize their pleasures within their limitations. Put technically, the proposal is to amend the right-hand side of (SAH) to read that, for any A, it would maximize A's pleasure were A to φ in C, where A's hedonic responses are calibrated to those advised for A by true judges in joint verdict.

Alas, the dodge fails, because it betrays the conception of true judges that is key to the Levinhume deduction. Smith's fully rational counterpart is equipped to render advice that states what Smith has most reason to do because Smith's fully rational counterpart knows Smith about as well as Smith does. Smith's fully rational counterpart is an expert in Smith. By contrast, true judges are not experts in you, me, or any other specific aesthetic agent. They are defined as those who home in on the masterworks, so they will be those whose responses represent that

Aoi no Ue is aesthetically better than *Yoshitsune Senbon Zakura*, which is aesthetically better than *The Mikado*. Having no expertise in the psychological and sociological background of ordinary aesthetic agents, their responses set no standard for what to advise you and me to try, except the very best. As Matthew Kieran (2008) acutely argues, advice is personal and true judges are not equipped with personal knowledge.

Putting the point another way, we already have a theory that represents aesthetic experts as ideal counterparts of individual aesthetic agents. According to the basic theory, I may not know that I aesthetically should try kabuki, but I aesthetically should try it if so advised by a fully rational and fully informed version of myself (Kölbel 2016). Remember, however, that it was discontent with the basic theory that drew us towards the standardized theory in the first place.

If we stand by the imitation model, then the standardized theory fails to set a normative standard for limited aesthetic agents. If we amend the standardized theory to accommodate the advice model, then we give up on the Levinhume deduction and revert to the basic theory. The dilemma is as easy to miss as the difference between the imitation and advice models.

Aesthetic Personality

Imagine we all routinely acted on the aesthetic reasons we have, responding in sync with true judges in joint verdict. In this perfect world, Alexander Nehamas writes, "we would all find beauty in the very same places," and, he warns, "that dream is a nightmare" (2007: 83). Would it be a stretch to assume that no theory of the normativity of aesthetic value should quash our efforts to cultivate and indeed celebrate differences in aesthetic personality? Yet the standardized theory seems to leave little room for aesthetic personality.

To see how serious the problem is, consider an attempt to take it seriously. Levinson (2010) worries about an apparent tension between the normative ideal represented by the true judges and our sense of ourselves as expressing our personalities aesthetically. On one hand, it seems "we have a strong reason to improve ourselves as aesthetic appreciators;" on the other hand, "we have as well, it seems, a strong reason not to give up our individual aesthetic selves" (Levinson 2010: 229). Whether or not the tension is genuine depends on how we understand aesthetic personality.

Levinson defines an agent's aesthetic personality as consisting in their "personal preferences in matters aesthetic" (2010: 228). What makes me who I am, aesthetically speaking, is what I go for: raindrops on roses, bright copper kettles, and my other favourite things. Your aesthetic personality consists in your preference for whiskers on kittens, cream-coloured ponies, and your other favourite things. (True judges prefer none of our favourite things.)

As long as someone's aesthetic personality consists in their actual preferences, the tension that Levinson worries about is easy to relieve. You and I both have reason to calibrate to the joint verdict of true judges, but we happen to take pleasure in different things. We share the same aesthetic ideal, but we differ in aesthetic personality. Only as we closely approach it does the ideal threaten our aesthetic personalities, but we do not closely approach it. To put the point another way, we gain aesthetic personality at the expense of aesthetic perfection, and it is easy enough not to be perfect.

However, the tension returns if there is more to aesthetic personality than a mere pattern of preferences, which might be haphazardly or loosely associated. Ted Cohen (1998) claims that an aesthetic personality must exhibit a degree of coherence; it must come together in what we often call a style. As he remarks, it is no surprise when a chap—call him "Bill"—"who wears standard, conservative Brooks Brothers clothing to work and to evening affairs turns up wearing boat shoes when he is on an outdoor outing" (1998: 120). A haphazard collection of preferences is not yet an aesthetic personality.

Once their aesthetic personality is up and running, exhibiting a degree of coherence, an agent has reason to act with an eye to the coherence of their personal style. The coherence of their aesthetic personality gives them reasons to act, and they have reasons to act in ways that address—strengthen, or play with—the coherence of their aesthetic personality. Bill shops for shoes, and two pairs come in his size: a pair of Allen Edmonds toecap Oxfords and a pair of Fluevog wingtip brogues in blue and brown leather. Bill has more reason to buy the Allen Edmonds than the Fluevogs. The coherence of his style calls for the conservative pair and buying the conservative pair ups the coherence. So, aesthetic personality is more than a set of preferences; its coherence sources reasons to act.

With this result, the question is whether style-given reasons are aesthetic reasons. Does the standardized theory admit that they are?

Levinson makes a case for the affirmative (2010: 231–3). What we have aesthetic reason to do is set by the joint verdict of true judges, but that standard leaves wiggle room for expressions of coherent aesthetic personality. After all, we can have different experiences of items that please us equally. Moreover, we have a free choice between items equal in aesthetic value. Finally, our past preferences are part of our aesthetic personalities.

The case fails, however. As Nick Riggle points out, we cannot have hedonic (or aesthetic) reasons to act on past preferences, to choose between equally good items, or to have different experiences equal in final value (2013: 279–80). In addition, the wiggle room that Levinson offers is not enough. The fact that the Allen Edmonds fit Bill's style gives him reason to buy them even if Fluevogs are aesthetically better and even if he experiences the conservative shoes in just the same way as everyone else. The coherence of aesthetic personality is a source of reasons, but not aesthetic reasons, according to the standardized theory.

Biting the bullet, one might insist upon the standardized theory and concede that style-given reasons are not aesthetic. Bill has non-aesthetic reason to buy the Allen Edmonds that simply outweighs the aesthetic reason he has to buy the Fluevogs. To say he expresses his aesthetic personality in buying the conservative pair is to speak loosely, for he neither has nor acts upon aesthetic reasons. Facts about what coheres with his style are not aesthetic value facts. Were he to do as he aesthetically should, he would act out of character.

Should the bullet prove too hard to bite, the alternative is to concede that at least some aesthetic reasons are not hedonic reasons. In particular, facts about our aesthetic personalities give us aesthetic reason to act, independent of our preferences and the standard set by the joint verdict of true judges. The standardized theory fails because aesthetic hedonism, the first premise of the Levinhume deduction, is false. We must try for a new answer to the normative question.

No doubt it is hard to see why taking aesthetic personality seriously puts pressure on aesthetic hedonism. Pleasures are regarded as paradigmatically subjective states. Considerable reflection is needed to see how our aesthetic personalities give us reasons to act that go beyond the preferences we have.

Cool Customers

Aesthetic hedonism nicely accommodates a Humean picture of the configuration of agency. Humeans hear the normative question as asking not only how we have aesthetic reasons to act but also as asking how aesthetic reasons can motivate agents to act. To gist the answer, if aesthetic values are hedonic values and pleasure is inherently desired, then items with aesthetic value offer us what we want, so that, in acting upon the aesthetic reasons we have, we get what we want. Hedonic desires can always motivate aesthetic acts.

Ruby Meager distinguishes aesthetic experts from connoisseurs. Whereas experts have knowledge and perform well, connoisseurs are "motivated... by an original dedication to aesthetic value... such as to render the works which embody it objects of love," and so as to derive a satisfaction that is unknown to "the wretched expert... among his facts and attributes" (Meager 1985: 138). Can there be genuine aesthetic experts who are not connoisseurs, or does aesthetic expertise engender love and the promise of pleasure?

The Humean picture of aesthetic agency yokes some of the appeal of aesthetic hedonism to the internalist claim that an agent has reason to perform an act only if they can be motivated to do the act by representing that very reason to themselves. In the aesthetic case, we have,

AESTHETIC REASON INTERNALISM: necessarily, p is an aesthetic reason for A to φ in C only if A can be motivated by a p-representing state to φ in C.

With this assumption in place, we hear the normative question as asking how an aesthetic value fact can get a grip on an agent, putting them in gear to act.

Given AESTHETIC REASON INTERNALISM plus a Humean theory of motivation, according to which motives include desires, a Humean theory of aesthetic reasons follows. That is,

DESIRE: necessarily, p is an aesthetic reason for A to φ in C only if A has a p-representing desire that would be satisfied by A's φing in C and the fact that p explains why the desire would be satisfied by A's φing in C.

For example, the fact that Addison's prose is measured is aesthetic reason for Caroline to read Addison now only if Caroline would get what she wants by reading Addison now and the fact that Addison's prose is measured explains why that act would get her what she wants.

Conjoining DESIRE with aesthetic hedonism bears an interesting consequence. According to aesthetic hedonism, being measured is a hedonic value, and the fact that Addison's prose is measured is a hedonic value fact. So ask this: what desire would be one whose satisfaction is explained by a hedonic value fact? Surely a hedonic desire, a desire for pleasure. So, an agent has an aesthetic reason to act only when they could be motivated to act out of a desire for pleasure.

The consequence is not interesting because surprising. Aesthetic agents have a problem to solve and aesthetic hedonists readily admit that they regard aesthetic agents as constitutively seeking pleasure. Rather, what is interesting is how tight a package we can make of AESTHETIC REASON INTERNALISM, the Humean theory of motivation, DESIRE, and aesthetic hedonism in order to answer the normative question. The meadow is glorious. So what? If its glory means that it pleases and visiting it fulfills a want, then you aesthetically should visit the meadow because that gets you what you want. The Humean package answers the normative question by appeal to the practical authority of desires, as states to which we cannot be indifferent.

However, the conjunction of DESIRE and aesthetic hedonism implies that an agent has an aesthetic reason to act only when they could be motivated to act out of a hedonic desire that would be satisfied by their so acting. The implied claim seems almost self-evident, but it is arguably false. It is false if, as Jon Elster contends, some aesthetic pleasures are essential by-products of acts motivated by other considerations (1983: 77–85).

What are essential by-products? Take acting naturally and playing an entertaining game of hockey. Acting naturally occurs only as a by-product of going about business for the usual reasons. I render daft advice when I urge students preparing for job interviews to "be themselves." Trying to follow my advice makes it impossible to follow my advice. Going about business with the aim of acting naturally is not a way to act naturally (except for those poor creatures who make it a life goal to act naturally). Likewise, hockey players who play well in order to entertain their fans only end up disappointing. Fans take pleasure in watching team members playing out of an earnest and single-minded desire to vanquish their opponents. Any entertainment that the fans get from watching the game is an essential by-product of players not playing to entertain.

Elster diagnoses some aesthetic flops as the fallout of attempts to obtain aesthetic effects that are essential by-products of acts motivated by other aesthetic considerations. Conceptual art backfires when it caters to a public whose command is "Surprise me!" Inevitably, he writes, there is a "bored quality to the surprise it generates" (1983: 84). Victorian painting lets us down because it tries for certain delicious effects that can be achieved only as by-products of artists trying to get right what they aesthetically should get right. Elster writes that "making a work of art is an intentional act, a series of choices guided by a purpose.... To engage successfully in this activity is utterly satisfactory, and the result may be utterly impressive, but in both cases only and essentially as by-products" (1983: 77).

Sure, Elster is no expert in aesthetics. How about Michael Fried? He tells how a painting in eighteenth-century France "had to call to someone, bring him to a halt in front of itself, and hold him there as if spellbound and unable to move" (1980: 92). The minute the appreciator realizes how the picture makes a bid for their attention, offering them pleasure, the spell is broken. Even in an art gallery, where it would seem our presence is motivated by a desire for pleasure, the game is on: only by acting on other motives do we gain gratification as an essential by-product.

Conjoining DESIRE and aesthetic hedonism implies that an agent has an aesthetic reason to act only when they could be motivated to act out of a hedonic desire that would be satisfied by their so acting. If Elster is correct, the consequent is false. Sometimes an agent has an aesthetic reason to act and yet they could not be motivated to act out of a hedonic desire that would be satisfied by their so acting. To get any pleasure, they must act out of non-hedonic motives. Strolling through the Louvre, they happen upon the Chardins, and they look at them. So long as they do not look seeking pleasure, they get the pleasure that the paintings afford. We miss this because we fallaciously take the desirability of a state always to be a motive upon which we can act to bring it about.

Since the conjunction of DESIRE and aesthetic hedonism implies a false claim, at least one conjunct is false, by modus tollens. Assume aesthetic hedonism. Therefore, DESIRE is false. Since the conjunction of AESTHETIC REASON INTERNALISM and the Humean theory of motivations imply DESIRE, at least one conjunct is false, again by modus tollens. Some do oppose the Humean theory of motivation (e.g. McDowell 1979; Wiggins 1990; Foot 2001; see also Scanlon 1998b: 37–40). Be that as it may, it is better for now to grant any claim with general scope and to focus instead on claims whose scope is limited to aesthetic matters. Therefore grant the Humean theory of motivation. It follows that AESTHETIC REASON INTERNALISM is false.

In other words, aesthetic hedonism and AESTHETIC REASON INTERNALISM are inconsistent. Xavier is an expert poet, who, like any expert, routinely performs well in his area of expertise. He writes poems for the aesthetic reasons that he has. According to aesthetic hedonism, the aesthetic reason that he has to write today's sonnet is a hedonic reason. However, if the pleasure it yields comes as an essential by-product of his writing it, then he cannot be motivated to write it for that reason (he must has some other motive). Since the hedonic motive is the motive that AESTHETIC REASON INTERNALISM requires him to have, AESTHETIC REASON INTERNALISM is false if aesthetic hedonism is true.

As long as we regard the desirability of a state always to be a motive upon which an agent can act to bring the state about—as long as we regard aesthetic agents as acting from hedonic motives—we regard aesthetic experts as connoisseurs, in Meager's sense. However, if pleasure is sometimes an essential by-product of acting aesthetically, then aesthetic experts need not be connoisseurs. They simply perform their tasks well, whatever their motives, and they get pleasure as a bonus.

Logic permits aesthetic hedonists to cut AESTHETIC REASON INTERNALISM loose, but some of the appeal of aesthetic hedonism flows from its partnership with AESTHETIC REASON INTERNALISM. Why be so sure that aesthetic values stand in constitutive relation to pleasures as long as we no longer think of aesthetic agents as just those agents who are moved to seek pleasure?

In sum, the standardized theory does a poor job at explaining the facts about aesthetic experts. Added to that, subtle flaws in the Levinhume deduction raise issues about the standardized theory and also about the core aesthetic hedonist claim. The flaws are subtle enough to explain why aesthetic hedonism and the standardized theory seem so attractive.

Going forward, one option is to attempt a defence of aesthetic hedonism as elaborated in the Levinhume deduction. Another option is to revert to the basic theory, which is immune to concerns about the Levinhume deduction. How likely is it that the basic theory can account for the six proposed explananda? The exercise is left to interested parties. A third option is to concoct an entirely new variant of aesthetic hedonism as an alternative to the basic and standardized theories. Perhaps the six proposed explananda can be accommodated within aesthetic hedonism, given (MAX) and some further, new claims. All three options are worth pursuing.

Philosophy abhors a vacuum. Arguments against a theory rarely stick until plausible alternatives line up to fill the empty space. At this juncture, there can be no objection to sketching an alternative to aesthetic hedonism.

PART III

5

Strength and Warranties of Skill

Though they are well known to lovers as places of safe haven, art galleries perform a further service, fostering mutual exploration. It is "an easy slide from aesthetics to biography," remarks a protagonist of Ian McEwan's in recalling a courtship in the National Portrait Gallery (2012: 203). Wondering how a painting's clinical insightfulness or its calm elegance can make a difference to how we aesthetically should act, we are easily led to reflect upon ourselves. Aesthetic hedonism depicts us as aesthetic satisfaction seekers. This chapter and Chapters 6 and 7 develop an alternative to aesthetic hedonism, the network theory, that better fits the biographies of aesthetic agents.

Laying in a Course

To plot a course to a destination, we first locate where we are now. In philosophy we usually know where we are by dead reckoning. After a quick look round our surroundings, we retrace the intellectual course we took, noting changes of direction along the way. Having fixed our current position, we scope out what lies ahead.

The destination is a theory of aesthetic value, a statement of the nature of aesthetic value. Or, a bit more modestly, the destination is half a theory. One question a full theory answers is the question of what makes any value aesthetic. Setting the aesthetic question aside, another question is how aesthetic values source practical normativity. More precisely, what is it about V that makes it the case that the fact that x is V lends weight to what an agent aesthetically should do? This is the normative question.

In the background of the normative question are two principles. One is,

REASON: p is an aesthetic reason for A to φ in C = p lends weight to the proposition that A aesthetically should φ in C.

Take the fact that Vikram Seth's *The Golden Gate* is smartly cheerful. For that fact to be an aesthetic reason for Winfrey to select it for her book club is for that fact to lend weight to the proposition that she aesthetically should select it for the club. The fact that the novel is smartly cheerful is an aesthetic value fact wherein being smartly cheerful is an aesthetic value. Consequently, for some A, some φ, and some C,

> VALUE: necessarily, V is an aesthetic value only if the fact that x is V lends weight to the proposition that A aesthetically should φ in C.

With these principles under our belt, we can see that an answer to the normative question will fill in the following template:

> an aesthetic value, V, is reason-giving = the fact that x is V lends weight to the proposition that...

To ask the normative question is to ask how an aesthetic value can figure in a fact that lends any weight to what an agent aesthetically should do. Different theories of the normativity of aesthetic value complete the template in different ways.

Agents act aesthetically, so we require a conception of what makes an act aesthetic. According to

> ACT: A's φing is an aesthetic act = A's φing counterfactually depends on the content of A's aesthetic evaluation of x, where A's φing operates on x.

As mundane an act as buying a pair of socks is an aesthetic act just when the shopper would have done otherwise had they made a different aesthetic evaluation of the socks. What is an aesthetic evaluation? According to

> EVALUATION: a state is an aesthetic evaluation = the state is a mental representation of some item as having some aesthetic value.

Any mental state that attributes an aesthetic value is an aesthetic evaluation.

By making reference to the aesthetic on both their left- and right-hand sides, we signal that all four propositions sidestep the aesthetic question. None offers a reductive account of what makes a value, evaluation, reason, or act an aesthetic value, evaluation, reason, or act.

The standardized theory introduced and assessed in Part II answers the normative question by identifying what an agent aesthetically should do with what an aesthetic expert would do, where aesthetic experts closely approximate true judges in joint verdict. As it turns out, the network theory also understands the normativity of aesthetic value by appeal to expert aesthetic agency. The two theories share yet another piece of common ground.

Judith Jarvis Thomson offers a scheme for mounting perspicuous analyses of what an agent should do in terms of expert agency (2008: 209–14; see also

Foot 2001: 15–16). First, an agent should perform an act in C just when they belong to a specialized agent-kind and an agent of that kind is defective if they fail to perform the act in C. Mary should rotate my car's tires once a year. She is an automobile mechanic, and it is a defect in an automobile mechanic if they fail to rotate a car's tires once a year. Linda should flake her sheets. She is a sailor, and it is a defect in a sailor if she fails to flake her sheets. Obviously, there are defective agents of a kind only if agents can be more or less good exemplars of the kind. The second element of Thomson's scheme captures this by bringing in expertise. A specialized agent-kind is one such that an agent is as good as a member of the kind can be only when they have expertise. The kinds made up of automobile mechanics and sailors are specialized agent-kinds. Someone is as good a mechanic as a mechanic can be only if they are an expert mechanic, and they are as good a sailor as a sailor can be only if they are an expert sailor.

Summed up in a formula keyed to aesthetic normativity, Thomson's principle states that,

A aesthetically should φ in C = there is an agent-kind, S, such that (1) A is an S, (2) an S is as good as an S can be only if they have aesthetic expertise, and (3) if an S does not φ in C then it is a defective S.

That an agent aesthetically should φ in C comes down to its being a flaw in the relevant aesthetic expert were they not to φ in C. In other words, Thomson's principle is an invitation to answer the normative question by plugging in a substantive conception of an aesthetic expert.

The standardized theory plugs right in to Thomson's principle. Why aesthetically should I read some Addison this rainy Sunday afternoon, instead of flaking out with some Amy Winehouse? The answer is: (1) I belong to the pleasure-seeker agent-kind; (2) a pleasure-seeker is as good as a pleasure-seeker can be only if they closely approximate a true judge; and (3) if I do not read the Addison this afternoon then I do not cut it as a true judge. Notice how the Levinhume deduction puts meat on the bones of (1) to (3).

The network theory plugs another, rather different, conception of aesthetic expertise into Thomson's principle. The procedure is to seek a conception of aesthetic expertise that can explain the six facts that a theory of aesthetic value should explain. Aesthetic experts are sociologically diverse, representing most every social group. They jointly cover all aesthetic domains. Taken individually, they channel into relatively specific aesthetic domains and many specific act-types. Moreover, there is an interaction between their specialization by activity and domain. Finally, their expertise is stable yet dynamic.

Expert Performance

Aesthetic agents have many different problems to solve because they perform many different act-types, from appreciation and making to editing and conserving, in countless aesthetic domains, from chess and *chanbara* to religious ritual and architecture. Why not start with an all-purpose account of expert agency that applies to any agent with any problem to solve in any context? A family of views with roots in Aristotle is undergoing something of a revival, precisely because the views represent instances of normativity—epistemic normativity in particular—as instances of a familiar, almost unremarkable, genus (Sosa 2007; Greco 2010; Sosa 2011; Morton 2012). Simply put, performances evaluate along three dimensions—success, competence, and achievement—and agents' performances are defective if they fail along any of these dimensions. Accordingly, experts are those who perform well along all three dimensions. They ring all three bells. The same goes for aesthetic experts (Lopes 2015; Ransom 2017; Roberts 2018).

Success. A performance is good partly to the extent that it succeeds in its aim. As Heather Battaly bluntly puts it, to perform well, an agent "gets the goods" (2015: 31). An archer gets the goods when she hits a bull's eye and a barista gets the goods when he pulls a delicious shot of espresso, for a bull's eye counts as a success in archery and the barista succeeds by making tasty coffee. That its success makes an act good is no big surprise, of course. The point of acting is to nudge the world in the direction of a better one, so an action is good when it has that effect.

Performances are acts, and acts are behaviours done intentionally, but an agent need not intend to bring about the very aim whose realization makes for a successful performance. A philosopher might set out to write a paper that solves a technical problem in modal logic, and she might end up revolutionizing our thinking about the relationship between possibility and conceivability, though that was not what she expected or intended. It does not follow that her success is by accident: she does act intentionally because she deliberately engages in the activity of writing philosophy. However, the product that makes an act a success can be a by-product of the act as intended by the agent. (Where would we be without the occasional gift of unintended success?)

Ernie Sosa takes the good that is brought about in certain successful performances to be the fundamental value of some organized activities (2007: 77–8). An activity's fundamental value is one around which any other values are organized. Archers succeed when they hit the bull's eye, and getting a bull's eye is the fundamental value of archery. The sport is organized around the pursuit of the bull's eye, which determines the value of equipment, methods, training regimes, competitions, and all the other goods of archery. Likewise, for Sosa, truth is the aim of belief, and hence it is the fundamental epistemic value. Intellectual inquiry is organized around the pursuit of truth, which determines the value of methods, dispositions to believe, systems of memory and problem solving, understandings and explanations, and all the other epistemic goods.

Yet we need not think of all activities as organized around fundamental goods that are brought about by certain successful performances. Sometimes no privileged class of successful performances tops a hierarchy that organizes the activity. To take an example dear to us all, consider scholarship. What is its fundamental value? The acquisition of new and useful knowledge? Student learning? The initiation of citizens into liberal democratic culture? The preservation and propagation of the best of human achievement? Inventing solutions to pending social problems? Worker training? Well, successful acts of scholarship bring about all these goods, but none are fundamental, and our ancient and honourable society thrives when its members perform with success in different yet coordinate areas. Sometimes the good brought about by certain successful performances is an activity's fundamental, organizing value. Sometimes not.

Aesthetic agents do not share a single aim. Success for Sam is ensuring the continued playability of classic video games. For Hannah, it comes when her students make a deep and lasting commitment to dance. Winfrey's success has been to foster communities where people read more, and read more widely, and forge meaningful connections with each other. Abbott succeeded in shaping our conception of the life's work of a photographer who seemed to fit nowhere in the received history of the medium. For the Refords to succeed, they had to create a special garden and then transform it into a sustainable operation with a contemporary feel and impact. ACT represents all as aesthetic agents, even as they succeed in bringing about so many different goods.

According to aesthetic hedonism, pleasure is like the bull's eye in archery. Successful acts of appreciation hit the hedonic bull's eye, and the pleasure that appreciation brings about organizes the goods of all other aesthetic activities. Successful acts of conservation keep up a supply of future pleasures, and successful acts of editing improve appreciators' chances of getting pleasure where they find it. On this model, appreciation is the privileged aesthetic act whose successful performance brings about the fundamental value of the aesthetic sphere. That value is aesthetic value, understood to be what it is in an item that stands in constitutive relation to pleasure.

When leaving aesthetic hedonism behind, care must be taken not to lug along the baggage. ACT does not define aesthetic acts in terms of their aims or success conditions; it says instead that an aesthetic act is one that is sensitive to a representation of aesthetic value. As a result, ACT leaves it open whether aesthetic value comes into the picture as the good that is brought about by the successful performance of certain privileged aesthetic acts (e.g. acts of appreciation). Perhaps it is, and the bull's eye model applies. Perhaps not, and something closer to the scholarship model applies. We must keep an open mind on the question.

After all, the claim that a type of value is fundamental in an organized activity is a claim intended to do some work explaining facts about how the activity is organized; it is not a fact to be explained. The accumulated momentum of the long tradition of aesthetic hedonism can make what is really an explanatory claim seem like received wisdom that is in need of explaining.

Competence. An archer's shot, or a barista's, might succeed through dumb luck. With a bit of good luck, incompetents can succeed. The dissociation goes the other way, too, for success is not the inevitable result of competence. As the Teacher observed, the race is not to the swift nor yet favour to the skilled: chance happens to them all. Through bad luck competent archers, and baristas, sometimes fail.

Performances vary in value partly to the extent that they issue from competence. It is a merit in a performance that it is done out of the agent's competence, even if it fails in its aim. On the flip side, it counts against a performance that it manifests the agent's incompetence, whether or not it succeeds. The two dimensions of value vary independently. By implication, the value that accrues to performances is not all instrumental; performances have some measure of final value just in virtue of their being done out of competence on the part of the performer.

Sosa defines a competence as "a disposition, one with a basis resident in the competent agent, that would in appropriately normal conditions ensure (or make highly likely) the success of any relevant performance issued by it" (2007: 29; see also Greco 2010: 11). He later refers to competence in this sense as "constitutional competence," by contrast with fleeting conditions of the agent and their situation that impact their overall chance of performing with success (2010). An archer's skill and knowledge is their constitutional competence, but their overall ability to perform is impacted by such fleeting conditions as their alertness and the position of the sun in relation to the target. When such conditions as these are appropriately normal, the archer's constitutional competence raises their chances of success. Henceforth, let "competence" refer to constitutional competence.

Competence can be inborn or acquired. Memory is an inborn competence, as is the capacity to make basic perceptual discriminations. Some acquired competences consist in bodies of propositional knowledge. Others are skills, competences acquired through repeated effortful trying. As Mothersill explains, "what begins as a clumsy step-by-step maneuver evolves into an effortless habit that needs only to be monitored" (1984: 132). The archer's competence is a skill in this sense. Whether acquired or inborn, competences are seated in the agent, so not any regularity in performance is a competence. A regularity in performance that is a competence is a regularity explained by the physical and psychological traits of the agent.

Whereas the archer's competence is almost all skill, some competences blend innate ability, skill, and propositional knowledge. The competences of aesthetic agents are mostly blended. Abbott's editorial competence illustrates the typical mix (see also Mag Uidhir and Buckner 2014: 132–6). She stands over her light table, exercising her competence to sequence some prints for *The World of Atget*. A capacity for perceptual discrimination plays a role. So does some of what she knows—for example, that two prints represent scenes in Paris. Skills acquired through repeated effortful trying also come in—she can see that placing one print on the left and another print on the right makes for a strong composition on the spread. Probably this skill implicates the exercise of some special conceptual schemes (Augustin and Leder 2006).

As the aims of aesthetic agents vary, so do their competences. In as much as what it takes for Abbott to succeed differs from what it takes from Sam to succeed, each needs a different competence. Sam needs detailed knowledge of legacy programming techniques and an acquired knack for seeing how routines would have been coded. Ask her to sequence photographs for publication and she will be operating in the dark.

As should be evident, a performance is good when it manifests the agent's competence, even if the agent does not succeed. By the same token, a performance is flawed, even if successful, when it manifests incompetence.

Achievement. A performance is good when it succeeds and also when it is done from the agent's competence. Is it better still when both conditions are met? Only when they are met in a particular way. An archer lets fly with perfect skill. Unluckily for her, a seismic tremor jolts the target sideways just as the arrow leaves her bow. Luckily for her, a sudden gust of wind blows the arrow back on track in perfect compensation. She hits the bull's eye. But she has been Gettiered. Her performance is successful and competent, but she would have performed better were her shot successful as a result of her competence. Success is good and so is exercising competence but best of all is achievement, which is success out of competence. So we may ask of any successful performance whether it is an achievement: is its success caused by an exercise of competence?

Achievement does not ensure the safety of a performance (Sosa 2007: 28–9). A performance is safe just in case it could not easily have failed. Our archer hits a bull's eye because she lets fly with a consummate skill—a skill that nearly ensures her success in normal conditions. Her performance is an achievement. Nevertheless she might easily have missed, because conditions might easily have been abnormal. She is competing in the Rim of Fire Tournament and seismic activity is in a peak phase. Or the sake served at the opening reception might easily have landed her with a headache, impairing her eye–hand coordination. As it happens, conditions are normal—the earth is quiet and the front desk of the hotel had some ibuprofen. Her bull's eye is an achievement, though it might easily have turned out otherwise, so it is not safe. The gap between achievements and safe performances will come in handy below.

Aesthetic agents are no different from archers. Aiming for success, they bring their competence to bear, and their performances are achievements when they are successful because competent. Aesthetic achievement is success in an aesthetic act caused by competence. In other words,

> A's φing is an aesthetic achievement = A's φing is an aesthetic act and A successfully φs out of competence.

Thus Abbott succeeded in her campaign on behalf of Atget because she campaigned so skilfully, and we rightly admire her aesthetic achievement. Alexander Reford's aesthetic achievement was to combine his abilities as a historian, fundraiser, and curator to restore and update his grandmother's garden. For that we rightly admire him too. Combining her skills as a talk-show host and as a bookworm, Winfrey succeeded in broadening American reading practices. She deserves more credit for her achievement than she sometimes gets.

Experts are agents who routinely act well. Since acting well entails achieving, the next step is to set out an achievement model of aesthetic expertise. Before taking that step, we should pause to note that the theory of achievement articulated above is minimal—sufficient to characterize expertise. Some articulate a more robust conception of achievement (Hurka 2006; Pritchard 2010; Bradford 2015). On the more robust conception, a toddler's first steps are an achievement, Penny Oleksiak's Olympic gold swim is an achievement, and Cornelia Hahn Oberlander's design for Vancouver's Robson Square is an (aesthetic) achievement. In each of these cases, achievement involves effort in surmounting difficulty. The robust conception has its place, and sometimes aesthetic experts achieve robustly, but they need routinely achieve only in the modest sense.

Aesthetic Expertise. According to Thomson's principle, what someone aesthetically should do in C is what an aesthetic expert would do in C. An aesthetic expert is an agent who is as good as a kind of aesthetic agent as an aesthetic agent of that kind can be. In a slogan, aesthetic experts are aesthetic high achievers; they have what it takes to wring success out of competence in acting aesthetically.

Keeping in mind that achievement is success out of competence seated in the agent, for any A and some φ,

EXPERT: A has aesthetic expertise = A has competence for achievement in φing, where φing is an aesthetic act.

As it happens, EXPERT also states how psychologists think of expertise, as a relatively stable trait that explains consistently successful performance in normal conditions (e.g. Ericsson and Smith 1991; see also Burnham and Skilleås 2012: ch. 5; Mag Uidhir and Buckner 2014).

Plug EXPERT into Thomson's principle and it follows that what makes it the case that someone aesthetically should φ in C is that there is a relevant aesthetic expert, who has competence for aesthetic achievement, whose failure to φ in C would betray their expertise. Recall that Thomson's principle is a way to think about how to fill in the template for a theory of the normativity of aesthetic value. So we now have material for a first pass at the network theory. For some A, some φ, and some C,

an aesthetic value, V, is reason-giving = the fact that x is V lends weight to the proposition that it would be an aesthetic achievement for A to φ in C.

This first pass portrays a configuration of aesthetic agency where aesthetic values figure, but it is only a start. Two components are added in Chapters 6 and 7.

Two remarks in closing. First, the network theory models aesthetic normativity as plain vanilla normativity—or what Morton calls "down-to-earth normativity" (2012: 87). Any agent who has a reason to act at all, therein has reason to achieve. They should succeed by using the resources they have at their disposal, including their competence. Expert mechanics, sailors, archers, and baristas routinely ring all three bells, and that makes them as good as mechanics, sailors, archers, and baristas can be. Aesthetic experts are just the same. They are as good as aesthetic agents can be, because they have competence to routinely achieve when they act aesthetically.

Second, notice how the first pass at the network theory does not imply that only one kind of success counts as aesthetic success, that only one kind of competence counts as aesthetic competence, or that there is only one aesthetic agent-kind. The theory permits (but does not yet predict) diverse kinds of aesthetic agents, having a variety of aims, endowed with competences to suit.

Core Aesthetic Competence

EXPERT says what it is for any kind of aesthetic agent to be as good an agent of the kind as they can be. They have a competence for aesthetic achievement. Since competence befits aim, performances with diverse aims engage diverse competences. Expert editors and collectors have different skills. So do expert poetry editors versus expert editors of short stories. Figure 1.1 displays the interaction of aesthetic act-types and aesthetic domains in the form of an array. Now each cell of the array may be rewritten to represent a unique pair of success conditions and competences through which agents of each kind pull off their distinctive aesthetic achievements. By leaving open what competences go into aesthetic expertise, the model handily accommodates (but does not yet predict) the dizzying diversity of aesthetic acts and agents.

Yet differences are informative only against a backdrop of similarity. Is there no core aesthetic competence that must be shared in common by all aesthetic experts, engaged in any aesthetic enterprise in any aesthetic domain?

For philosophers, it is at most a pleasant diversion to enumerate the many competences aesthetic agents enlist to perform successfully. Serious empirical work lies in understanding what the competences are, what precise conditions are normal for their exercise, how they are seated in agents' more basic psychological traits, how they are acquired, how they interact with one another, why they diversify and change in a regular manner... and that is just for starters. Perceptual psychology and psychometrics have a place; so do affect studies, human kinetics, developmental and social psychology, linguistics, sociology, anthropology, and history. The empirical literature on aesthetic expertise is vast.

I happen to be an anomalous trichromat who fails some green–blue discrimination tests. Although I cannot see how garishly they clash, I nevertheless have aesthetic reason not to pair this green tie with that blue jacket. It would be a defect in my tailor were she to make the same match. Being an expert in clothing with well-calibrated colour vision, she would not pair the tie and jacket. Similar stories can be told about aesthetic reasons that lend weight to what agents aesthetically should do when they are music directors whose expertise implicates emotional intelligence, art journalists whose expertise implicates an understanding of post-conceptual art, industrial designers whose expertise implicates a capacity to intuit others' sense of embodiment, or cooks whose expertise implicates being imaginative with spices. Concrete empirical realities give root to many aesthetic reasons.

Enough with pleasant diversions into the tangled empirical roots of aesthetic agency. The common ground for the main, abductive argument includes a hook from which to hang a core aesthetic competence and core aesthetic achievement. According to,

ACT: A's φing is an aesthetic act = A's φing counterfactually depends on the content of A's aesthetic evaluation of x, where A's φing operates on x.

If no act is an aesthetic act unless it counterfactually depends on an aesthetic evaluation, then aesthetic agents have to make aesthetic evaluations. Since evaluators may or may not get right the aesthetic values of the items they evaluate, their evaluations have accuracy conditions. Do aesthetic evaluators also possess a competence, seated in their psychological makeup, that would ensure or make highly likely that they get items' aesthetic value right in relevant normal conditions? If the answer is yes, then we have a recipe for core aesthetic achievement. Core aesthetic achievement is success out of core competence in aesthetic evaluation.

Grant for the moment that there is a competence in aesthetic evaluation. The competence is core if it is a factor to be taken into account in assessing every aesthetic performance. To deny that competence in aesthetic evaluation is core to aesthetic agency is to commit to the possibility that an agent acts as well as possible—and deserves full credit—in cases where their aesthetic performance counterfactually depends on a correct aesthetic evaluation, even though the evaluation does not issue from any competence in aesthetic evaluation. Surely an editor's lucky success in getting right the aesthetic qualities of a poem counts against their achievement in editing it. The same goes for the curatorial performance of a blogger whose notes on perfumes happen to be correct, though they are in fact subliminal reactions to the perfumes' popularity or sales figures. It is hard to imagine any case of full aesthetic achievement without achievement in aesthetic evaluation.

A few observations refine our picture of core aesthetic competence. Virtue theorists often consider that the heart of virtuous agency is the capacity to recognize facts as reasons and to weigh them appropriately in choosing what to do (e.g. Foot 2001: 11–12). Following the same line, we might identify an agent's core aesthetic competence with the psychological infrastructure that explains their getting into the right relation to the aesthetic value facts. Nehamas might articulate the same idea when he writes that the competence is "what one exhibits when one focuses on the right features in the right way" (2007: 99). Core aesthetic competence is what enables agents to tune in the aesthetic values that items actually have.

Arguably, though, more is needed for core aesthetic competence than a competence in tuning in items' actual aesthetic values. Action often makes a difference because awareness of how the world is combines with awareness of how the world will come to be, should one act successfully. When agents aim to modify the aesthetic values that items have, they must envision how those items will come to be through their action. They must attribute aesthetic values counterfactually, so that how their performance goes depends on an attribution of aesthetic values that an item does not yet have (which is why making an item can be an aesthetic act).

Not all aesthetic performances modify items' aesthetic values, and an aesthetic act that leaves an item's aesthetic features unchanged can also implicate an awareness of how the item might have had different aesthetic values. Aesthetic experts make counterfactually rich aesthetic evaluations, taking into account how differences in an item's value-realizing properties would impact its aesthetic value. An expert music critic, for example, cannot get by with an aesthetic evaluation of a song in complete ignorance of how differences in instrumentation, voice, tuning, and rhythm would impact the song's aesthetic merits and demerits. Part of core aesthetic competence is competence in attributing counterfactual aesthetic values.

A final observation concerns the relevant normal conditions for aesthetic evaluation. The evaluations that aesthetic agents need to make are keyed to their practical contexts. A curator and a conservator characteristically tune in different values in the very same work, for example. Consequently, normal conditions are not generic conditions—they need not apply to all aesthetic agents alike. Aesthetic agents conduct their evaluations in conditions that are normal for their expertise—for conserving rather than curating, or for conserving netsuke rather than platform games.

With a more refined picture of aesthetic evaluation in hand, we can return to the question of whether anyone has core aesthetic competence. What speaks for our having traits that ensure or raise to a high probability successful acts of aesthetic evaluation in relevant normal conditions? The reasoning is this. Performance in aesthetic evaluation varies from agent to agent (Silvia 2011). Moreover, it has a developmental trajectory. Some perform well, others not so well, and we tend to improve with practice in similar conditions. The best explanation of these facts is that we have a competence seated in a cluster of more basic traits, at least some of which are acquired. Therefore, the competence is one we have.

How well the reasoning works comes down to the details of the traits that are thought to seat the competence. Here are some strong contenders: perceptual and affective discrimination, conceptual repertoire, attention, and counterfactual imagination. Experts are said to be those for whom a small difference makes a big difference. They also make exactly the kinds of classifications that are relevant to their expertise. They have learned where and how to look, to look selectively, with an eye to the practical context. Finally, in order to arrive at counterfactual evaluations, they richly imagine the effects on an item's value that would come with changes in the properties that realize its value (Ransom 2015). Empirical studies are needed to clinch the reasoning. The key finding will be that variance between subjects in successful aesthetic evaluation is largely predicted by variance in performance in perceptual and affective discrimination, classification, attention, and rich imagination.

Aficionados of recent aesthetics will no doubt catch, in this portrait of aesthetic competence, an echo of what Sibley called "taste" (which not the same taste for which the joint verdict of true judges is supposed to set a standard). Sibley held that an application of an aesthetic concept to an item requires an exercise of a faculty of perceptiveness, sensitivity, and discrimination exceeding "normal intelligence and good eyesight and hearing" (1959: 423). As he famously argued, no rules govern the application of an aesthetic concept to an item solely on the basis of non-aesthetic information about the item (1959: 424–31; see also Sibley 1974). However, the network theory makes no commitment either to the unruliness of aesthetic concepts or indeed to Sibley's assumption that aesthetic evaluations are judgements in which aesthetic concepts are applied (EVALUATION leaves open whether aesthetic evaluations can have non-conceptual contents). What about the thought that core aesthetic competence is seated in more than normal intelligence and perceptual abilities? Is it more than an acquired assemblage of these? An answer to this question must await Chapters 6 and 7.

Aesthetic Meta-Competence

Sosa contrasts the archer with the bow hunter (2011: 5–11). Whereas the archer's task is to hit the target, the hunter has a second task too. Some prey are easier to hit than others and some prey are more valuable than others, so she must select her targets with care. Her choice can be more or less successful, and an expert hunter is more likely to be successful because she lets fly only in conditions where it is likely enough that her archery skill will result in bagging sufficiently high-value prey. Competence in target selection is a meta-competence that consists in competently selecting occasions for first-order performance. Part of any aesthetic expert's competence is aesthetic meta-competence.

All the aesthetic experts paraded in Chapter 1 chose their targets well. Elsie Reford hybridized lilies rather than irises or roses, and Alexander Reford calculated that he was well positioned to revive his grandmother's gardens. Abbott chanced upon Atget's work, but she also saw the chance, and took it. In creating her book club, Winfrey had to take the measure of her own talents and the situation. When the situation changed, she adapted and brought in social media. Hannah makes monthly decisions about what goals to pursue, given the abilities and motivations of her student cohort, and what is happening in the larger dance culture. Sam takes on a new project when she completes what she is working on. How much of herself she throws into the new project is a function of her abilities and the project's value.

One side of target selection is evaluating the target. Is it a scrawny specimen or trophy material? The same goes for aesthetic target selection: it means getting right the target's aesthetic values. Nobody who is unreliable in aesthetic evaluation is likely to be all that successful in target selection. Offered a chance to buy the Atget collection, Abbott had to see Atget's distinctive quirkiness. So, one side of target selection is competent aesthetic evaluation.

However, target selection involves more than core aesthetic competence; its second side is the exercise of a meta-competence. Recall that an agent's competence raises their chances of success, taking into account any further conditions that impact their overall chances of success. For example, a bow hunter's chances of success are impacted by such fleeting conditions as her state of alertness and the position of the sun in relation to the target. Although she achieves when she hits the target by using her skill in normal conditions, sometimes abnormal conditions curtail her chances of success. Hence, she tends to achieve more when she is meta-competent, or competent in assessing the conditions for the exercise of her archery skill. Since experts tend to achieve more, an expert's competence for achievement will include meta-competence.

By the same token, aesthetic target selection calls upon aesthetic meta-competence in addition to core aesthetic competence. Aesthetic experts must be able to assess whether conditions are both normal and relevant for them to achieve by exercising their core aesthetic competence. Normal conditions are, at the very least, those that are normal for perception, attention, imagination, and the other more basic psychological competences that seat core aesthetic competence. For example, a conservator's meta-competence includes a capacity to tell whether a photograph of an artifact can be used to make an aesthetic evaluation of the artifact in the course of repairs. What about relevance? As is well known, an aesthetic evaluation of an item is accurate only when the item is evaluated in the aesthetic category to which it belongs (Walton 1970). An expert in classic film stills would misapply his competence, with sorry results, if asked to curate a collection of Cindy Sherman's pastiches. He would systematically misrepresent the aesthetic values of the Shermans.

Aesthetic meta-competence is not a core aesthetic competence because its exercise is not essential to performing an aesthetic act. An aesthetic agent can achieve without exercising aesthetic meta-competence (and they can exercise aesthetic meta-competence without achieving). Someone's skill in graphic design can open their eyes to the strong design qualities of Brillo boxes, yet they know nothing of pop art and might easily have gone wrong were they confronted with *Brillo Boxes*. (And someone's exercise of meta-competence to evaluate *Brillo Boxes* as pop art might nonetheless take the work to be so loaded with irony that they overlook the homage to Brillo boxes.) All the same, aesthetic meta-competence is a part of any kind of aesthetic expertise. As EXPERT says, an aesthetic expert is an aesthetic agent with a competence for aesthetic achievement, and any aesthetic agent tends to achieve more by having and using meta-competence.

Advanced aesthetic agents can reflect on the conditions in which they exercise their first-order competences. Their aesthetic meta-competence matters a great deal, as it boosts the safety of their aesthetic evaluations. This function of aesthetic meta-competence will play an important role in fleshing out the network theory over Chapters 6 and 7.

Evaluation Versus Appreciation

Nehamas writes that it has been "an article of faith that the end of our interaction with the arts comes when we are in a position to make a judgement of value" (2007: 15). If he is right (and if the point extends to all aesthetic domains), then the network theory breaks the faith. Our agency begins—it does not end—when we are in a position to make an aesthetic evaluation; it begins with competence in aesthetic evaluation. Articles of faith cry out for explanation. How could we have come to persist so long in error?

Part of the answer is that it is easy to blur the distinction between evaluation and appreciation. An evaluation is a mental attribution of aesthetic value (see EVALUATION). Aesthetic appreciation is more than aesthetic value attribution. Under aesthetic hedonism, aesthetic appreciation is a savouring of the value—feeling the pleasure to which the value stands in constitutive relation. Consider Nehamas's expression, "judgement of value." Is a judgement of aesthetic value an attribution of aesthetic value and hence an aesthetic evaluation? Not if the point of aesthetic engagement is appreciation. Talk of "judgement" blends evaluation with appreciation. Indeed, the raging debate on aesthetic testimony trades on the assumption that there is no room for an agent to make a judgement that is not an appreciation (e.g. Hopkins 2000a; Budd 2003; Livingston 2003; Meskin 2004; Laetz 2008; Hopkins 2011; Konigsberg 2012; Lopes 2014a: ch. 9).

Assume that aesthetic judgement is aesthetic appreciation and that competence in judgement is core. It follows that competence in appreciation is core. The appreciation model seems mandatory: all aesthetic acts are acts of aesthetic appreciation. Aesthetic appreciation is the result of an aesthetic encounter, when all goes well. We will think of the encounter as aiming at, and culminating in, aesthetic appreciation. Our submission to Nehamas's article of faith is complete.

The first stage of the cure is to police the distinction between aesthetic evaluation and aesthetic appreciation, acknowledging how much room there is to attribute aesthetic value without appreciating it. To deepen the distinction, consider that only aesthetic evaluations give agents access to aesthetic reasons. To evaluate x is to represent x as V. By contrast, each aesthetic act is performed under counterfactual guidance of a representation of some x as V. Aesthetic evaluations are inputs; aesthetic acts are outputs. The identification of evaluation with appreciation obscures this, if aesthetic appreciation is an aesthetic act.

Stage two of the cure is to recognize that aesthetic appreciation is an aesthetic act. In the example from Chapter 2, Nick has consulted a guidebook and judges that there is a Poussin worth looking at in the National Gallery. Only once he arrives at the gallery does he begin to appreciate the painting, inspecting it closely, bringing to bear his knowledge of the medium, the genre, and the historical context, searching for meaning, testing competing interpretations, responding emotionally.

To complete the cure, we take seriously that many types of aesthetic acts can be performed given an aesthetic evaluation, and not all of them involve appreciation. Nick might have consulted his guidebook, judged that there is a Poussin worth looking at in the National Gallery, and rewritten a passage of his essay on the importance of context in art appreciation. Yet he has never seen the Poussin. Not all aesthetic acts are acts of aesthetic appreciation.

When accurate, aesthetic evaluations give agents access to aesthetic reasons to act. Some go on to perform acts of appreciation (see Chapter 8). Some perform other aesthetic acts. All aesthetic acts implicate evaluation, not appreciation. The core competence for aesthetic agents is competence in aesthetic evaluation, not appreciation.

An Aesthetic Gerrymander

At a first pass,

> an aesthetic value, V, is reason-giving = the fact that x is V lends weight to the proposition that it would be an aesthetic achievement for A to φ in C.

A's performance is an achievement just when A succeeds out of competence in φing in C. Since an expert is someone equipped to routinely achieve by φing in C, the first pass says that what A has aesthetic reason to do is what A's expert counterpart has aesthetic reason to do. However, the first pass will not do as it stands. A second pass is needed to solve a gerrymandering problem.

I am tying a bell lanyard using a Matthew Walker knot, a diamond knot, and a footrope knot. It seems to come out wonky. Nevertheless, I administer myself a hearty pat on the back. I say: it is perfect, and my performance was an aesthetic achievement. Not an achievement for a beginner, but an achievement plain and simple. The lanyard came out that way because I φ'd, but its going that way lent no weight to the proposition that I aesthetically should not φ. Granted, Clifford Ashley would not have φ'd in the circumstances, and he is a knot expert with competence for achievement in knot tying. Indeed, he literally wrote the book on the subject (Ashley 1944). All the same, there are many, many aesthetic domains and many, many aesthetic action-types. I do knots Lopes-style—I call them "gnots"—and I have perfect competence for achievement in tying gnots. This lanyard is not a wonky knot; it is a gnot with *wabi-sabi*. Ashley's expertise is not normative for me, or for others who tie gnots (try it—gnots are much easier!)

My philosophy skills exceed my knot-tying skills: I rationalize by appeal to Thomson's principle and EXPERT. Thomson's principle states that

> A aesthetically should φ in C = there is an agent-kind, S, such that (1) A is an S, (2) an S is as good as an S can be only if they have aesthetic expertise, and (3) if an S does not φ in C then it is a defective S.

EXPERT just identifies aesthetic expertise with competence for achievement in an act-type. So the idea is that what makes it the case that someone aesthetically should φ in C is that there is a relevant aesthetic expert, who has competence for aesthetic achievement and whose failure to φ in C would betray their expertise. My rationalization exploits the fact that there are no constraints on what agent-kinds there are. I have asserted that I am an instance of the gnot-tying agent-kind. What I do is always exactly what the perfect example of that agent-kind does. What I aesthetically should do is always exactly what I do... no matter what I do!

One problem with my gerrymandering myself into aesthetic expertise is that it robs aesthetic expertise of the normativity it purports to supply. "Should" is empty if what I aesthetically should do is always exactly what I do, no matter what I do. A second problem is that there is nothing special about me. Too many aesthetic acts are successful out of the competence constitutive of aesthetic expertise, given some concocted, gerrymandered conception of the relevant expert.

Some people are experts at crooked nails, or burnt toast, or invalid arguments! Nobody fails to achieve anywhere near often enough. A third problem is that it seems that there are some genuine aesthetic domains and aesthetic act types. Ersatz expertise does not count as genuine. We need a way to capture what is genuine and what is not.

Confronted with similar problems concerning gerrymandered aesthetic domains, Walton gave aesthetic domains a social reality (1970: 357–8). Our six facts about aesthetic experts suggest the same thought. Ashley's expertise has a social reality that mine lacks. Chapter 6 solves the gerrymandering problem by locating aesthetic agents in the social networks that give the network theory its name.

6

Infrastructures of Aesthetic Agency

Sometimes the hardest trick in philosophy is to glom onto the obvious, and then make it count. How obvious it is that aesthetic agents rarely operate solo: they conduct their business as integral members of networks of other aesthetic agents. Anderson once lamented philosophy's "impatience with the pluralistic, contestable, historically contingent, socially informed evaluative practices in which people participate" (1993: 15). Seconding the complaint, Simon Blackburn pointed to aesthetics as the exception that takes seriously the social side of value (1998: 30–1). He is only half right, though. Some have represented the arts as social practices (esp. Olsen 1981; Dickie 1984; Lamarque 2008; Lamarque 2010; Abell 2012; Lopes 2014a). According to the second pass at the network theory, social practices configure aesthetic agency so as to give agents aesthetic reasons to act. The second pass tackles the gerrymandering problem by following the "social turn" of recent philosophy (e.g. Lewis 1969; Kitcher 1993; Searle 1995; Raz 1999a; Raz 2003; Bicchieri 2006; Haslanger 2012; Epstein 2015).

Scaffolds, Constraints, and Rational Explanation

So pervasively does aesthetic activity saturate daily life that it is often invisible. When aesthetic geniuses dominate the headlines, we overlook the vast resources disbursed in small amounts over great spans of time to secure the many aesthetic goods that we now take for granted. Piling detail upon detail, Fernand Braudel's monumental history of the *Structures of Everyday Life* documents the gradual and also precarious history of aesthetic improvement (1979: 183–333). Though he would never use the word, Braudel makes an effective case for a trajectory of aesthetic progress as momentous as the political and industrial transformations that shaped the modern world. Technology usually gets the credit, of course, but equally important was social organization, which spurs technical innovation while equipping us to take advantage of it. An agent's power to change the world is hugely amplified by their social arrangements, and their power to effect aesthetic improvements is no exception.

Three facts about the social configuration of agency pull in opposite directions, and so must be held in a balance that gives each some weight in our thinking.

Some of Sally Haslanger's recent work reminds us that "the terms of our action and interaction are not up to us as individuals. What is valuable, what is acceptable, even what we do, and want, and think, depends on cultural frameworks of meaning" (2014: 20). Haslanger speaks for a slightly pessimistic tradition that emphasizes the social constraints on action (and thought). Every choice is made within an architecture that determines what choices agents see as open to them, as well as the meaning or value of their choices. In this tradition, the emphasis is often on a critique of choice architectures that fail to serve, or that positively harm, their inhabitants.

Yet social arrangements also enable individuals to perform acts that would otherwise be impossible, or even unthinkable. To play off the metaphor of choice architecture, social arrangements scaffold agency. Ted Slingerland quotes some down-to-earth examples of non-social scaffolding from the *Xunzi*:

> I once stood on my tiptoes to look into the distance, but this is not as good as the broad view obtained by climbing a hill. Climbing a hill and waving your arms does not make your arms any longer, but they can be seen from farther away; shouting downwind does not make your voice any louder, but it can be heard more clearly; someone who borrows a carriage and horses does not improve the power of his feet, but he can travel a thousand miles.... The gentleman is not different from other people—he is simply good at borrowing external things. (2014: 58)

Social scaffolding is like the scaffolding of agents' powers by tools and by features of the natural environment.

The third fact is that social arrangements can emerge at the micro-level, where agents interact with each other on a one-to-one or few-to-few basis. At the same time, even at the micro-level, interactions between agents are usually supported by existing scaffolding. In view of the intricate interdependence of agency with its social scaffolding, the slightly pessimistic tradition gets right the social constraints on agency, while the more optimistic tradition gets right how social arrangements empower individual agents. Anyone who seeks to understand the micro-social foundations of social arrangements must do justice to the reality that "the creation of culture results from choices by parties to action" even as "agency is always shaped by externalities" (Fine and Fields 2008: 131).

The proximal task is not to explain social phenomena in full. After all, the distal task is to answer the normative question, what makes it the case that aesthetic value facts lend weight to what agents aesthetically should do? Accordingly, we ask, how do social arrangements impact the aesthetic reasons that lend weight to what agents aesthetically should do?

A rational explanation of a social arrangement points to some reasons that agents have to act anyway as reasons for them to act in ways that conform with and support the arrangement. What gets explained is not why agents do in fact behave in ways that conform with and support the arrangement. After all, agents often fail to act on the decisive reasons they have. Rather, what gets explained is why agents have reason to act in ways that turn out to conform with and support the arrangement. They have reason to act in ways that conform with and support the arrangement because they have other practical reasons. A rational explanation makes sense of what might be described as the arrangement's normative validity.

Not being causal explanations, rational explanations fall short of explaining how social arrangements come into existence. Social arrangements come into existence through agents' acts, but acts are causally explained by agents' motives, not their practical reasons. An agent who has decisive reason to φ might not φ; when they do φ, they might not be motivated by a belief or desire that represents the reason they have to φ. So we must appeal to facts about agents' motives, not their reasons, to explain how social arrangements come into existence. Rational explanations yield causal explanations of social arrangements only when experts, or enough non-experts, often enough act on the reasons they have.

The next section, "Out of the Aesthetic State of Nature," proposes some rational explanations of social arrangements that scaffold (and constrain) aesthetic agency. In as much as the explanations refer to aesthetic reasons agents have, they set up for a second pass at the network theory and a solution to the gerrymandering problem. The final section of the chapter, "Elements of Aesthetic Practices," takes a look at how to explain causally what is explained rationally; it sketches some self-sustaining elements of the social arrangements that provide infrastructures of aesthetic agency.

Out of the Aesthetic State of Nature

The state of nature is a tool for nosing out rational explanations of social arrangements. Imagine agents in an aesthetic state of nature, acting aesthetically, but without benefit of any social scaffolding that would modify their performance. We ask what aesthetic scaffolding they would have reason to erect, given the aesthetic competences they already have. Since rational explanations rapidly ratchet up in complexity as the competences of aesthetic agents come more and more to be shaped by the choice architectures in which they act, the aesthetic state of nature keeps things simple.

As useful as it might be in nosing out rational explanations, the aesthetic state of nature is no good for causal explanation or historical reconstruction.

The archaeological record contains no evidence of aesthetic activity in the absence of economic behaviour, "deep" planning, or symbolic representation (Mithen 1996; McBrearty and Brooks 2000). Advanced aesthetic competence seems to have appeared in tandem with complex social organization. An interesting hypothesis is that aesthetic activity, boosted by social organization, helped in turn to drive further social organization. At any rate, rational explanation is not to be confused with historical speculation.

Another mistake is to regard states of nature as Hobbesian. The poor blighters in Hobbes's state of nature compete for scarce resources, but not all resources are scarce. Auguste Comte's example is language, "a kind of wealth, which all can make use of at once without causing any diminution of the store, and which thus admits a complete community of enjoyment; for all, freely participating in the general treasure, unconsciously aid in its preservation" (quoted in Lessig 1995: 1000). Inspired by Comte, one might wonder whether it turns out, beautifully, that aesthetic value is a kind of wealth that grows with use, the store never running out of stock.

Once upon a time, out on the Serengeti, our distant ancestors were provisioned with plenty of low-level aesthetic goodness—charming sunsets, pungent flowers, washboard abs. In view of the goodness of these things, they had aesthetic reason to act in ways that turned out to enlarge their aesthetic inventory. To inject a dose of archaeological reality into the scenario, suppose that they had aesthetic reason to make cosmetics and symmetrically proportioned tools. Acting on their aesthetic reasons, they added aesthetic goodness to the world.

Knapping stone is not as easy as it looks, and neither is making and applying cosmetics. Since skill is acquired through repeated effortful trying, an agent who acts on an aesthetic reason to knapp symmetrical stones today gets better at knapping symmetrical stones tomorrow. As long as competence makes a difference to success, a reason to act is a reason to achieve, which is a reason to acquire and exercise competence. Having aesthetic reason to knapp these symmetrical stones today is reason to acquire competence in knapping stones.

Aesthetic meta-competence accelerates learning. Learning a skill is efficient to the extent that repeated effortful trying leads to competence for achievement. An agent with an ability to select just those opportunities for acting where achievement is likely, while keeping up a bit of a challenge, will learn the skill more efficiently. So a reason to acquire and exercise competence is a reason to acquire and exercise meta-competence.

Now for the bad news. Human performance is plastic, but limited. While learning can improve performance, there is a cap on how far we can get just by learning. Inevitably there comes a point where no individual can significantly improve their skill on their own. A sailor who learns to handle each sheet and halyard on a tall ship still cannot sail her single-handed.

A sound strategy for agents who reach the limit of personal performance is: divide and conquer. You and I have a fourteen-digit number to recall, but short-term memory tops out at seven digits, so you take half and I take the rest. In this case, it makes no difference whether we divide the numbers one way rather than another.

Take a case where we differ by competence. We have a 3-metre wall to scale, so one of us boosts and the other lifts. If I am stocky with a strong core and you are light with a strong arm, then we do better if I boost and you lift. Our having to routinely scale the wall means we do better if I do crunches and you do curls and dips. We do better if we develop those individual competences that can be combined to raise our joint chance of achievement.

Specialization is a division of labour where each specialist allocates more resources to their specialization and relies on others to cover their self-induced areas of incompetence. I take care of philosophical aesthetics, leaving modal metaphysics and philosophy of biology to others. You do the same in developing your AOS. Collectively, we cover more ground in more depth than could a population of generalists. Individually, we achieve far more by specializing and cooperating than we would as jacks of all trades.

Switch back to prehistoric cosmetics. An important occasion looms and every member of the group dresses up and paints their body. Each digs pigmented clay, pounds it on a stone into a powder, binds fine reed into a brush, conceptualizes a design, applies the pigment, and proudly displays it. Perfecting every element in the skill set demands time and resources, and performance limits are soon reached. Once the limits are reached, the way to get even better makeup is for members of the group to specialize, perfecting their specialized skills, with an eye to trading off with other specialists.

Agents have reason to use result-getting strategies. In suitable conditions, our all having reason to do philosophy is reason to specialize—to act in a way that conforms with and supports a cooperative division of philosophical labour. Hence, our having reason to act anyway rationally explains the social arrangement that is our cooperative division of labour. In general, when conditions are suitable, social arrangements wherein agents specialize are rationally explained by the fact that agents who have reason to act thereby have reason to specialize and cooperate. Social arrangements for specialization are rationally explained by a "specialization escalator."

An aesthetic specialization escalator operates under three conditions. First, agents face choices about how to act that impact how they develop their aesthetic competences. Second, the prospects for each, in terms of chances of aesthetic achievement, are affected by the acts of others. Finally, each does better, raising their prospects for aesthetic achievement, by acting in ways that lead to specialization and cooperation. In these conditions, agents who have reason to act thereby have reason to achieve and thereby have reason to act in ways that build specialized cooperation. The aesthetic specialization escalator is up and running. One more preliminary before looking at a range of scenarios.

Competence is a disposition, seated in the agent, that raises the agent's chance of success in performing a task. Aptitude is a special competence: a disposition, seated in the agent, for acquiring a competence for achievement. Aesthetic aptitude is a disposition, seated in the agent, for acquiring a competence for aesthetic achievement. Chances are high that any two aesthetic agents will differ in aesthetic aptitude. Aesthetic aptitude is sometimes part of an agent's natural-born endowment—maybe a lithe build gives a dancer an aptitude for ballet, for example. Sometimes, aesthetic aptitude is seated in traits acquired with non-aesthetic competences. Training in gymnastics can also produce an aptitude for ballet.

Suppose that two agents out in the Serengeti face a choice between acting in a way that either trains up their cosmetic design skills or their skills in making pigments. They bomb if they both choose the same specialization, of course. As it happens, one has some inborn aptitude for design, and the other, being an expert miller, has an aptitude for grinding pigments. The following payoff matrix represents the chances of achievement for each given how the other acts:

	design	pigment
design	0,0	2,2
pigment	1,1	0,0

Column aesthetically should work on her competence for grinding pigments and Row aesthetically should work on his design skills. That is, Column should repeatedly try to make pigments to suit Row's design ideas and Row should repeatedly try to concoct designs that work with Column's pigments. Their having reason to act anyway is reason for them to achieve and thereby to specialize, which rationally explains their division of labour.

Now suppose the nearby landscape sources two kinds of pigment. As it happens, one suits a softly shading style of cosmetics while the other is ideal for hard-edge tattoo-like makeup. The pigment grinder faces a choice. Her resources are limited, so she can consistently act in ways that will boost her competence in preparing the materials suited for only one style. The designer faces a parallel choice: should he consistently act in ways that work up skills suited to the soft style or the tattoo style? Both have reason to act in ways that will develop facility in the same style, as neither will achieve otherwise. Again, a payoff matrix represents the chances of achievement for each of them in every combination of acts:

		pigmenter	
		soft	hard
designer	soft	2,2	0,0
	hard	0,0	1,1

In this scenario, there is only one combination where each does as well as they can in raising their chances of achievement. Agents in this scenario, having reason to act, thereby have reason to achieve, which is reason to specialize. Their having reason to act anyway rationally explains their converging on the soft style.

A payoff matrix in standard game theory represents agents' preferences, which are motivations to act, and the payoffs are combined utilities. Here, each payoff matrix represents agents' acts, and the payoffs are combined chances of achievement.

Philosophers have a soft spot for agents with coordination problems (e.g. Lewis 1969; 8–24, following Schelling 1960; cf. Bicchieri 2006). In coordination problems, there is a set of payoffs with more than one member, such that nobody gains in any other combination. The following matrix represents agents who have better chances of achievement if they act in ways that develop competence in the same cosmetic genre, but who have the same chances of achievement whether they both go soft or both go hard:

		pigmenter	
		soft	hard
designer	soft	1,1	0,0
	hard	0,0	1,1

The fact that each has reason to achieve is not decisive reason for either to act in ways that develop competence in one style rather than the other. Agents in this scenario, having reason to act, thereby have reason to achieve, and thereby have reason to act in ways that conform to and support a social arrangement involving an exchange of promises, perhaps, or a convention.

Coordination problems are rather special, and rare, because they involve agents with equal aptitudes. Human beings have equal aptitude for learning to drive on the right and driving on the left, and they have equal aptitude for being native speakers of English and Tagalog. Only because driving and linguistic aptitudes match do conventions explain regularities in traffic control and language use. In most areas of human achievement, aptitudes range widely.

Great swaths of aesthetic culture organize around trends. Trends that grab the headlines are often trends in consumer choice, and the breakthrough study of imitative trends looked at the fashion for miniskirts in the early 1960s (see Bicchieri 2006: 31–3). However, there are also trends in skills acquisition—just consider cookbook trends (Julia Child is back).

Trends require a special two-way division of labour. A sizeable population of agents have an aptitude for learning to do what many others do. They are followers. Members of a smaller population have an aptitude for developing curricula that attract followers. Take a trend spreading an aesthetic competence in craft brewing. Since the craft brewery relies on agents with many aesthetic competences, focus on the brewmasters, and pretend that there are only two kinds of beer—hoppy and malty. Here is a payoff matrix:

| | | trendsetter | |
		hoppy	malty
follower	hoppy	1,2	0,1
	malty	0,1	3,1

As the matrix shows, a brewer who is a follower has the best shot at achievement if he acts in ways that perfect his skill at brewing malty ales, provided he falls in with trendsetters. Meanwhile, the trendsetting brewer has the best shot at achievement if she acts in ways that perfect her ability to brew American Pale Ales (APAs) and India Pale Ales (IPAs), provided that followers go along. So the achievement of each hangs on their brewing trendily. The trendsetter is more likely to achieve when she has followers, and the follower fails if he brews out of step with the trend. As a result, both have decisive aesthetic reason to brew hoppy. Agents who have reason to act thereby have reason to achieve, and hence to act in ways that conform to and support a pattern of social imitation, or a trend.

A final, rudely Hobbesian, scenario amounts to an aesthetic prisoner's dilemma. Architects and builders should acquire competences such that builders can do a good job building what architects design while architects can specify what is within the capabilities of builders. Being attuned to their familiar surroundings, builders have the best chance of success out of competence when using vernacular forms and materials (e.g. gabled roofs, shingle siding). Being concerned to offer themselves to clients as rendering some extraordinary service, architects have the best chance of achievement when specifying, say, brutalist forms and materials (e.g. flat roofs, poured concrete). Ideally, the dilemma is solved by a compromise, wherein they adopt a modified modernist style (Smiley 2001).

A payoff matrix shows their dilemma:

		architect	
		mod–mod	brutalist
builder	mod–mod	1,2	0,3
	vernacular	3,0	1,1

If both act in a way that gives them the best chance of individual achievement, they will develop competences that give them only modest chances of joint achievement. Both will do better by compromising, acting in ways that build competence in modified modernism. The trouble is that if only one compromises and the other defects to their comfort zone, then the one who compromises will face disaster. Since neither has decisive reason to act in a way that builds the compromise competence, they are condemned to modest achievement. Those flat roofs will leak.

Why squander the potential for joint gain that accrues when both act in ways that build mod–mod competence? Each avoids disaster and has substantial, though not maximal, chances of achievement. In scenarios like this, aesthetic agents, having reason to act anyway, have reason to achieve, hence to act in ways that conform to and support social arrangements that include external incentives to acquire the compromise competence. For example, they have reason to insist that mod–mod is obligatory, divinely ordained, or natural and inevitable, so that it becomes taboo to design or build anything else. They have reason to scorn peers who do not compromise and to reward peers who do.

A social arrangement is rationally explained just when some of the reasons agents have to act anyway are reasons for them to act in ways that conform with and support the arrangement. Divisions of aesthetic labour are rationally explained when agents have reason to act, and hence to escalate their prospects for aesthetic achievement, by fostering specialized competences in cooperation with each other. At the heart of the explanation is a picture of aesthetic agents as groups of individuals who "are in the middle of doing something that requires them to pay attention to each other, to take account consciously of the existence of others, and to shape what they do in the light of what others do" (Becker 2008: 375).

The Aesthetic Tower of Babel

Denizens of an aesthetic state of nature have reasons to act in ways that conform with and support social arrangements because they have reasons to act anyway, where their reasons to act anyway are not already scaffolded by existing social arrangements. In a state of nature, scaffolding only goes so high, but agents can build scaffolding on their scaffolding. As long as they have reason to exceed their current reach, they have reason to ride the escalator towards more specialization and cooperation.

Rational explanations of scaffolding in the state of aesthetic nature simplify in two ways. They abstract away from the temporal dimension, and they consider interactions of only two aesthetic agents with two choices each. Dropping the simplifications only intensifies the dynamics that give aesthetic agents reason to act in ways that ramp up specialization with cooperation.

A reference network comprises agents whose members must keep an eye on each other and act in light of how other members act (Bicchieri 2006). Aesthetic reference networks are almost always much larger than two kinds of agent. All else being equal, the larger the network, the stronger the reasons its members have to specialize and cooperate. The more specific the AOS, the larger the area of self-induced incompetence, therefore the greater the reliance on other specialists, and the more reason all have to converge on specific, interlocked competences.

Cultural transmission over time means that, as a rule, past gains in aesthetic competence are more readily acquired in the future. All else being equal, descendants of those who opted for the soft makeup style have stronger aesthetic reason to follow in their ancestors' footsteps: they will be more likely to acquire competence for achievement. In order to achieve further, they will likely have to craft sub-genres of the soft style.

Within an aesthetic reference network, further specialization is path-dependent. The specialization escalator goes up, never down. Agents in a reference network revert to less specialized competences only when some scaffolding collapses. When the dark ages come and aesthetic agents can no longer count on others to exercise their most refined competences, then all go back to basics. In fact, we observe in reality what the model predicts in theory: aesthetic specialization increases across generations of a reference network except when external forces disrupt cooperation.

The model also predicts that scaffolding constrains. Once a reference network is on the escalator up to the soft style, its members are all but cut off from the hard style. They might not even be able to imagine the possibility. If they can, they have overwhelming reason not to go there.

Recall the gerrymandering problem. I tie a lanyard and it looks wonky, yet I declare it to be *wabi-sabi*. The first pass at the network theory encourages a rationalization: the lanyard's aesthetic value is reason-giving because the fact that it is *wabi-sabi* lends weight to the proposition that it is an aesthetic achievement for a gnot tier to tie it that way. The trouble is that, without a way to set a high enough bar for aesthetic competence, performances too easily count as aesthetic achievements. I have perfect competence in doing it my way, and you have perfect competence in doing it your way.

Since what makes someone a member of an aesthetic reference network is the reasons they have to act, an aesthetic reference network is a notional construct. My gnot expertise is a node in a reference network made up of potential aesthetic agents who must keep an eye on each other and act in light of how other members act. I comfort myself with dreams of a network of gnot critics, conservers, collectors, and indeed appreciators. None of them exist, however. Nobody but me ever acts on gnot-based aesthetic reasons.

The solution to the gerrymandering problem is now obvious. My expertise is ersatz because genuine experts are specialists in reference networks that are not merely notional. Let an aesthetic practice be a social arrangement that implements an aesthetic reference network. A second pass at the network theory says that,

> an aesthetic value, V, is reason-giving = the fact that x is V lends weight to the proposition that it would be an aesthetic achievement for some A to φ in C, where x is an item in aesthetic practice, K, and A is a member of K.

The coordinated achievements of members of an aesthetic practice set the bar for aesthetic competence, but there is no aesthetic practice without social reality. Since I do not constitute an aesthetic practice all by myself, there is no practice of gnots. The only aesthetic practice in the vicinity is that of knots, where Ashley is an expert. He would not have tied the lanyard that way. Tied that way, it is wonky (not *wabi-sabi*), and its being wonky does not lend weight to its being an achievement to tie it that way.

One question, addressed in the next section, "Elements of Aesthetic Practices," is what goes into an aesthetic practice to implement an aesthetic reference network? Chapter 7 completes the network theory by saying what it is for an agent to be a member of an aesthetic practice.

Elements of Aesthetic Practices

Having reason to act upon items of aesthetic interest, aesthetic agents have reason to act upon each other, and, having reason to act upon each other, they have reason to act upon items of aesthetic interest. Not only that, aesthetic agents often enough do act upon items of aesthetic interest by acting upon each other, and they often enough do act upon each other by acting upon items of aesthetic interest. Some social practices are aesthetic practices.

Structures: schemas and resources. In its broadest sense, a social practice is a pattern or regularity of performance in a group of agents that is explained by reference to what social scientists call "structures" (e.g. Bourdieu 1977; Giddens 1984; Coleman 1990; Sewell 1992; see also Haslanger 2014). In William Sewell's (1992) synthesis of the idea, structures are constellations of cognitive schemas and pools of resources that both scaffold action and tend to be reproduced by scaffolded action. Resources are sources of power, mainly human capacities and the affordances of objects in the human environment. Cognitive schemas are beliefs, concepts, recognition capacities, propensities to affective response, and other habits of mind. As the list hints, cognitive schemas can be implicit, not represented in occurrent thoughts, even as agents act upon them (Lewis 1969: 63–4; Haslanger 2014: 21). Strategies for directing attention can be cognitive schemas that determine but do not enter into the content of representational states (Nanay 2016). The same goes for dispositions to acquire concepts (Sperber 1996: 69). Think of cognitive schemas and resources as the dry and wet ingredients that go into cooking up social practices.

On this model, aesthetic practices are regularities in the performance of aesthetic agents that are explained by cognitive schemas and resources. Specific cognitive schemas and resources are unique to certain aesthetic practices. Viewers of Mughal miniatures did not share the expectation of viewers of eighteenth-century French paintings that a painting hold them "as if spellbound and unable to move" (Fried 1980: 92). *Tintal* is a rhythmic resource of north Indian classical music, but not of rockabilly. That granted, some general types of structural elements are commonly found in aesthetic practices.

Schemas: norms. Whether or not norms are constitutive of all social practices, they are constitutive of aesthetic practices. For a group of agents to participate in an aesthetic practice is for them to display behavioural regularities that are due, at least in part, to their conforming to norms. Norms are cognitive schemas because they are rules of action that agents follow given expectations about the actions or attitudes of other agents. Philosophers haggle over the specifics (e.g. Bicchieri 2006: 11–42; Burge 2010: 311–15), but the following theory is fit for present purposes:

> a rule of action, R, for circumstances, C, is a norm in population, P, = (1) enough agents in P know that R applies in C and (2) conform to R in C on condition that (3) they expect enough others in P to conform to R in C and (4) they expect enough others in P to expect them to conform to R in C.

This theory is outfitted so that the fact that aesthetic agents conform to a norm can help explain the division and distribution of aesthetic competences in aesthetic practices.

Compliance with norms is not to be over-intellectualized. Becker portrays participants in art world practices as having a "mutual appreciation of the conventions they share and the support they mutually afford one another" that "produces a shared sense of the worth of what they collectively produce" and convinces them of the value of their contributions to the practice (2008: 39). Nevertheless, what agents know and expect is not always transparent to them. We often act without deliberation, on the basis of expectations that we are not prepared to verbalize or explicitly endorse. Indeed, attempts to verbalize aesthetic reasons can interfere with aesthetic performance (Wilson et al. 1984; Wilson et al. 1985; Wilson and Schooler 1991; Johansson 2005; Johansson et al. 2006; Hall et al. 2010; see also Irvin 2014; Lopes 2014b). Perhaps the same goes for expectations of compliance with aesthetic norms: how transparent are the mutual expectations of members of a musical ensemble in the flow of performance?

Chapter 7 gets specific about the norms constitutive of any aesthetic practice.

Schemas: sanctions. Norms come with minimal sanctions baked in (Lewis 1969). At a minimum, an act is sanctioned when it is conditioned on the agent's expectation that others expect them to conform to a rule of action (as in clause (4) above). The rule that professors have a sense of humour is sanctioned because my cultivating a sense of humour is conditional on my expectation that my students expect me to have a sense of humour. They will tend to be surprised if I present as humourless, and they will tend to explain my self-presentation discreditably: they will think me pathetic. Possibly their reaction will affect our future interactions. My knowing this helps explain my conforming to the rule. Minimal sanctions baked into norms consist in agents taking themselves to be accountable to others.

Aesthetic agents hold themselves accountable to others' criticism, advice-giving, and advice-taking (see Chapter 9). A book jacket designer who proposes a cover that cannot be taken in at a glance is going to hear from the folks in marketing, perhaps the author too, and she cannot brush off their concerns. Legibility is an aesthetic priority in the circumstances. Minimal sanctions often suffice to explain why agents comply with the norms of aesthetic practices.

Without stronger sanctions, aesthetic agents are sometimes doomed to fare poorly, as in the case of the architects and builders described earlier. Strong sanctions are those that are both costly to impose and impose significant costs on those who are sanctioned, so as to modify combined payoffs in ways that bring the most benefits all (Coleman 1990: 250–3). Social and institutional sanctions can erase the gains that our architects get by defecting while builders compromise, and vice versa.

Schemas: context recognition. When networked agents often enough act on the aesthetic reasons they have, then they participate in an aesthetic practice, and agents in a practice often enough act on the aesthetic reasons they have because they comply with norms, sometimes nudged by sanctions. Since norms are rules of action that apply in given circumstances, and since sanctions attach to norms, we cannot expect much compliance with norms in a practice unless agents can recognize the circumstances. Crucially, they have to be able to recognize when they are in circumstances where the norms of a practice kick in (Bicchieri 2006). For this reason, steps are sometimes taken to lay down cues that amplify agents' abilities to recognize what the context is. Recognizing the cues, agents know which competences to bring to bear when they take their seats in a concert hall—rather than take a stand in the mosh pit—or when to bang out a blog post about a new video game—rather than pen a review of the latest Whitney Biennial for the *Nation*.

Resources: technologies. Bits of the material world afford various acts. The Salish Sea affords swimming, for example, and the Alphonso mango affords devouring. Artifacts are sometimes designed to afford acts whose performance brings agents in compliance with norms. Canadians drive on the right by convention, but engineers have laid down tonnes of concrete and asphalt in configurations that make it easy to drive on the right and difficult to drive on the left, thereby scaffolding compliance with the rules of the road. In general, technologies build norms into the material circumstances of action (Becker 2008: 34).

Technologies can reach beyond acts deep into human competences. For instance, aesthetic practices of making and using images take advantage of human perception, but they also shape it (Gombrich 1960; Lopes 1996; Lopes 2005; Kulvicki 2013). Some go as far as to say that vision has a history (Nanay 2016: ch. 7). A recent and dramatic example is the discovery of tactile pictures, which has unlocked new perceptual and aesthetic opportunities for blind people (Kennedy 1993; Hopkins 2000b; Lopes 2002).

The social landscape is equally a product of technology. Presumably, the arts are social practices. According to one proposal, an art form is a social practice constituted by norms governing the appreciation of works in a medium, which is a technical resource (Lopes 2014a: chs 7–8; cf. Dickie 1984; Abell 2012; Wolterstorff 2015). Photography is an imaging technology, and different arts of photography lay down different rules that guide our appreciations of images as products of the technology (Lopes 2016a). Whereas modernist photography enjoined that we regard photographs as veridical records of surprising realities, more recent practices enjoin that we regard photographs as depictive articulations of ideas.

Through technologies, aesthetic practices reproduce and modify themselves. A technology affords aesthetic acts, which shapes new technologies, which come to afford further aesthetic acts. What aesthetic agents manipulate and the tools they use to manipulate it are engineered to suit the competences of past aesthetic agents and to scaffold and constrain the competences of future aesthetic agents.

Resources: education. Aesthetic practices could not have anything like the stability that they have without mechanisms for transmitting cognitive schemas, especially skills. Deepened aesthetic specialization entails that we must rely on collaborators with complementary competences, which means that we all need to be able to count on there being specialists to rely upon in the future.

Learning is not restricted to formal schooling. Mere exposure to items in the local environment is largely responsible for the formation of genre concepts, such as the concept of impressionist painting (Cutting 2003). Communication technologies of all kinds spread skills and knowledge. Perhaps there are aesthetic memes (Sperber 1996).

Nevertheless, formal schooling plays a special role in leveraging the plasticity of aesthetic competences. Orchestrated changes in competence can secure to agents the benefits of specialization with cooperation, but they also allow for lateral shifts in specialized competence. A good example is the transformation in the aesthetic practice of the visual arts, which was brought about by the campaign to establish "post-studio" art school pedagogy (Newall 2016). Such radical retraining could hardly happen without institutionalized systems to coordinate change across many specialized competences.

So important is the role of formal aesthetic education in aesthetic practices that a chunk of Chapter 12 is devoted to the topic.

Everybody knows that the stupendous aesthetic attainments of human beings around the world since the decoration of the caves at Chauvet could not have been the work of solo operators. Only some deeply entrenched ideas about aesthetic value could lull philosophers into giving the fact so little weight in their theorizing. Works of art and other aesthetically outstanding items are not only products of the human mind running at full throttle. Competent aesthetic performance also counts amongst the most impressive instances of human sociality working at full capacity.

Appendix: Structuralist Aesthetics

Having aesthetic reason to act, agents thereby have reason to act in ways that conform to and support social arrangements, and when enough of them often enough act upon the reasons they have, we see regularities that we can explain as products of social practices made up of cognitive schemas and resources. Our explanations balance three facts. Social arrangements constrain individual agency, yet they scaffold it, and they are products of interactions among individuals. For all that, micro-level explanations of macro-social phenomena remain controversial in some circles, though they are winning converts (e.g. Witkin and DeNora 1997; Acord and DeNora 2008; see DeNora 2003; Inglis 2005; and Layton 2011 for surveys; see Coleman 1990 and Fine and Fields 2008 for general theory). The competition is structuralism, but the message for structuralists is this: structuralism is not incompatible with micro-level explanation.

Structuralists view social phenomena as patterns that are homologues of each other, transposed from one part of a culture to another (e.g. Washburn 1983). The textbook example is Bourdieu's analysis of the architectural arrangement of the Kabyle house around opposing elements that are homologues of culturally dispersed oppositions that are homologues of each other. Bourdieu expresses the homologues as second-order relations between the oppositions, namely, "high : low :: light : dark :: day : night :: male : female :: *nif* : *h'urma* :: fertilizing : able to be fertilized" (1977: 275). The idea is then that an agent's aesthetic competence tunes into patterns of homologues of non-aesthetic cognitive schemas.

Patterns of aesthetic activity homologous to patterns in non-aesthetic culture are not inconsistent with micro-level explanations. A cognitive schema might be salient for agents who face a coordination problem, giving them reason to act, precisely because it has obvious homologues in their culture. Trends might echo homologues, as the fad for molecular cuisine echoed the fad for industrial chic. Aesthetic acts can be sanctioned by association with homologues with social power (e.g. the gender binary). Micro-level explanation can enhance the structuralist picture of what is happening at the macro level.

Meanwhile, structuralism cannot go it alone in answering the normative question, the question of what makes it the case that aesthetic value facts lend weight to what agents aesthetically should do. By itself, the fact that an item has features homologous to features of items in some other domain of culture sheds no light on why a given agent should do one act rather than another. This is a general problem with structuralist approaches. As James Coleman complained, "the absence of an explicit normative principle at the level of the individual...has denied sociological theory the possibility of making normative statements"

(1990: 41). If the rejoinder is that social theory is not in the normativity business, then that concedes that a pure structuralist approach does not suit present purposes.

Bourdieu (1984) is not himself a pure structuralist; he proposes a micro-level explanation of the organization of aesthetic "fields" in terms of competition rather than cooperation between agents. He regards popular musicians and their fans as locked in desperate competition for cash and glory with "highbrow" musicians and their clientele.

Again, the incompatibility is only apparent (Becker 2008: 373–81). Agents who compete with each other in performing the same act-type can simultaneously cooperate with agents performing different act-types. Indeed, cooperation between agents with different specializations can be more effective precisely because agents compete within a specialization. Curators in competition with one another up their game, which benefits artists whose work they represent. In return, artists who seek to outdo each other are more likely to create work that shows well, boosting the prospects for curatorial achievement.

Neither pure structuralists nor those mixed structuralists who follow Bourdieu have any reason in principle to oppose the network theory.

7

Hundred Mile Aesthetics

A theory of aesthetic value answers the normative question: what is it about beausage that makes it the case that the fact that this bicycle has beausage is a fact that lends weight to the proposition that A should φ in C? The first two passes at the network theory answer that what an agent aesthetically should do is the act that would be an achievement in the context of a social practice. The time has come to finalize the network theory, and then use it to explain our six facts about aesthetic expertise.

The Network Theory

According to the second pass at the network theory, beausage is reason-giving because a Rivendell's beausage lends weight to the proposition that it would be an aesthetic achievement for a bicycle aficionado to perform some act in the relevant aesthetic practice. Now the question is: what practice is that?

Two answers will not do. One is that the items on which its members operate make an aesthetic practice the one that it is. The answer does not pan out because members of two aesthetic practices sometimes operate on the same collection of items, and members of any aesthetic practice might have had different items to operate upon. Another answer is that its membership makes an aesthetic practice the one that it is. Again, however, the same population of agents is sometimes active in more than one aesthetic practice, and any aesthetic practice might easily have different members. What we really want is the idea that its members have certain features that make an aesthetic practice the one that it is.

An immediately plausible answer needs refining. Surely, if an aesthetic practice is a social practice, then its cognitive schemas and resources make it the aesthetic practice that it is. We now need to know what specific cognitive schemas and resources characterize an aesthetic practice, but refinement is not far off. Recall the scenarios presented in Chapter 6, where aesthetic agents, interacting with each other, have reason to develop specialized competences for achievement. In each scenario, agents must get on the same page, aesthetically; they must come to share a conception of the aesthetic good; they must converge on the soft style of makeup, hoppy beer, or architecture in a mod–mod mode. What counts as wonky, *wabi-sabi*, or having beausage varies from one aesthetic practice to the next precisely because aesthetic practices enable agents to develop specialized competence for achievement.

In its third and final pass, here is the

NETWORK THEORY: an aesthetic property, V, is reason-giving = the fact that x is V lends weight to the proposition that it would be an aesthetic achievement for some A to φ in C, where x is an item in an aesthetic practice, K, and A's competence to φ is aligned upon K's aesthetic profile.

The configuration of aesthetic agency that makes someone a member of K lies in their having an aesthetic competence that is "aligned" on K's "aesthetic profile." The scare-quoted jargon replaces the metaphor of agents getting on the same page, aesthetically, and it carries forward the thought that some features of its members make an aesthetic practice the one it is. The next two sections, "Sibleyan Shades of Value" and "Aesthetic Profiles," unpack the notion of an aesthetic profile. The idea of "aligning" in competence will be understood in terms of a pair of core aesthetic norms.

Sibleyan Shades of Value

Perhaps the deepest, yet least well appreciated, part of Sibley's legacy is an aesthetic value pluralism (1959; 1965, 2003b; see also Zangwill 1995). The notion of aesthetic profiles relies on Sibley's pluralism.

Aesthetic value monism holds that aesthetic value is exactly one value property—that exactly one way of being good is being good aesthetically. Aesthetic value monists acknowledge the panoply of paradigm aesthetic values. A shot by Atget of a Parisian street is haunting, and Claude Cormier's Blue Stick Garden is vibrant. Being haunting and being vibrant are aesthetic values. However, each combines the single property of being aesthetically good with some non-value properties. To simplify, the photograph's being haunting is its being aesthetically good plus its depicting the street as empty, and the garden's being vibrant is its being aesthetically good plus its having complementary hues. In other words, paradigm aesthetic value properties share a single property, which is what makes them aesthetic value properties.

Aesthetic hedonists are typically aesthetic value monists (e.g. Goldman 1990; Levinson 2001; Goldman 2006). They say that being haunting and being vibrant are different properties, but what makes them value properties is the same. Both are properties that stand in constitutive relation to finally valuable experiences. The photograph's being haunting is not the same as the garden's being vibrant only because the items differ with respect to some of their non-value properties.

What about aesthetic value pluralism? How can there be many properties of being aesthetically good? Sibley proposed that being aesthetically good is a determinable whose determinates include being haunting and being vibrant (Sibley 1974: 113–15). An item that has a determinate property also instantiates every determinable property that the determinate falls under: a haunting photograph is beautiful, and it is just plain good (if there is a property of plain goodness). Moreover, an item that has a determinable property must also instantiate some determinate that falls under the determinable: nothing is beautiful unless it is beautiful in some way—vibrant, for example. Most importantly, being vibrant does not combine being aesthetically good with having some further, independent feature. Compare: scarlet and crimson are determinates of red, but neither is a combination of red plus some further, independent feature. Scarlet and crimson items do not share redness and then differ in some further respect; rather, they differ in how they are red. Just so, being haunting and being vibrant do not share in being aesthetically good while differing in some further respect; they are different ways of being aesthetically good. They are determinates of the determinable, aesthetic goodness.

In this way, the determinable–determinate relation contrasts with other genus–species relations (Wilson 2017). PCs and smart phones are species of computers. They share the property constitutive of their genus—being electronic information-processing devices—and they differ in respect of further, independent properties—notably their physical dimensions and ergonomics. By contrast, no further, independent feature distinguishes a determinate from sibling determinates of the same determinable. What distinguishes scarlet from crimson as shades of red is the shade of each. What distinguishes being haunting from being vibrant is its "shade" of aesthetic value.

The network theory implies aesthetic value pluralism. Suppose that a photograph's being haunting gives A aesthetic reason to φ and the vibrancy of a garden gives A′ aesthetic reason to φ'. The monist claims that the image's being haunting is its depicting the street as empty plus its having some aesthetic value property, and the garden's being vibrant is its having complementary hues plus its having the very same aesthetic value property. In that case, what does the common, aesthetic value property contribute to explaining why A has aesthetic reason to φ, while A′ has aesthetic reason to φ'? Can we not make full sense of why they have reasons to perform different acts by referring to the fact that the image depicts an empty street while the garden has complementary hues? The network theory is genuinely a theory of the normativity of aesthetic value only given aesthetic value pluralism. On aesthetic value pluralism, the photograph's being haunting is a way of being aesthetically valuable that is reason for A to φ and the garden's being vibrant is a way of being aesthetically valuable that is reason for A′ to φ′. Being haunting and being vibrant do not share any independent aesthetic value property; they are ways of being beautiful.

Aesthetic value monism and pluralism are not to be confused with superficially similar claims about aesthetic value concepts. The concepts of being haunting and being vibrant are made up of evaluative and non-evaluative components. Some think that having these concepts implies having concepts of the non-evaluative features alone (e.g. Zangwill 1995; Levinson 2001). Others disagree, arguing that the concepts are "thick" in the sense that they do not enable their possessors to pick out the non-value features without making the evaluation (e.g. Bonzon 2009, after Williams 1985). Be that as it may, aesthetic value monism and pluralism are views about values, not views about evaluative concepts. Aesthetic value pluralists might well deny that aesthetic value concepts are thick (e.g. Sibley, according to Bonzon 2009).

Aesthetic Profiles

For Sibley, an item's being V is a way of its being aesthetically good or bad, independent of any social arrangement. Having forcefully critiqued Sibley on the point, Walton (1970) proposed a way to rectify the oversight (Laetz 2010). Aesthetic profiles abstract away from the details of Walton's proposal.

Take a dancer's movement, characterized in the vocabulary of human kinetics, as lowering their foot to the ground in a direction with force and velocity. Executed as a tap move by Savion Glover, the vector is emphatic. Yet the very same vector is heart-wrenching when made by a ballerina dancing a piece by Pina Bausch. Each dancer realizes an aesthetic value by making a movement, but the very same movement, as characterized in the vocabulary of human kinetics, realizes different aesthetic values. Clearly there is some relationship between the vector and the value, but executing the vector is not by itself sufficient for realizing the value.

By the same token, dancers in different traditions might have to make different movements in order to get the same aesthetic value. A ballerina for the Tanztheater Wuppertal executes a vector movement of her foot and the result is heart-wrenching. If Glover makes the very same movement, the result is emphatic, not heart-wrenching. Something different is required for his movement to be heart-wrenching.

Let the aesthetic profile of a practice be the pattern of correlations that obtains between the aesthetic value properties of items in the practice and some other properties they have. Alternatively, let it be a relationship between the distribution of aesthetic values over the items in the practice and the distribution of some other properties over the items.

One tap number includes a move that is emphatic, having a certain movement vector; another tap number includes a move that is heart-wrenching, having a different movement vector. These two correlations excerpt a wider pattern of correlations across all tap numbers. Meanwhile, works of ballet include moves that are heart-wrenching and emphatic when made by movements whose vectors are not the same as the ones that make for the same values in tap dance. Tap and ballet have two different patterns of correlation and hence two different aesthetic profiles.

Ascending a level, the properties that correlate with an emphatic dance move are different from the ones that correlate with the emphatic cadence in a line of verse, the emphatic rock formations in a landscape, the emphatic geometry of the 1967 Mustang hardtop, or an emphatic reductio ad absurdum.

Two questions will bestir those who know the literature. First, what are the other properties with which aesthetic value properties correlate? Are they items' intrinsic properties? Or do they include items' extrinsic, relational properties? Aesthetic formalists debate the answers with contextualists. Second, what is the relation between value properties and these other properties, whatever they are? Is it supervenience? Constitutive dependence? Determination? Identity? The question herds us towards a metaphysics of aesthetic value. Both questions get their due in Chapter 10. A theory of the normativity of aesthetic value does not stand upon an answer to either question, and we should not get sidetracked.

The network theory melds Sibley-style pluralism with socialized aesthetic agency by means of aesthetic profiles. Aesthetic profiles are distinct patterns of distribution between items' aesthetic values and the other properties, whatever they are, that make a difference to whether or not an item has a given aesthetic value.

Valence

Thinking of aesthetic values as determinates of aesthetic goodness is a simplification for the sake of convenience. Some aesthetic values are aesthetic demerits. To discharge the simplification, two questions need answers. What makes some aesthetic values merits and others demerits? And how do aesthetic merits and demerits figure, as such, in the practical reasons of aesthetic agents?

The tenets of three schools of thought speak to the valence of aesthetic values. Disciples of the heroic school maintain that some aesthetic values are invariably merits or invariably demerits. Beardsley (1962) champions exactly three invariably positive aesthetic values: unity, complexity, and intensity of regional quality. Unity is always an aesthetic merit and never a demerit, for Beardsley, whereas grace is a merit in many items but a demerit in some. The heroic school retreated under a barrage of counterexamples—items whose unity, complexity, or intensity are demerits (Sibley 2003a: 110–13). Sibley (2003a) speaks for a second school, professing that no determinate aesthetic values are invariably merits or invariably demerits, but some are inherently merits or inherently demerits. Grace is an aesthetic merit when taken in isolation from any item, though it is an aesthetic demerit in some cases. The third school teaches that no determinate aesthetic values are invariably or inherently merits and none are invariably or inherently demerits (e.g. Mothersill 1984; Goldman 1995: 139–42).

Setting aside the heroic school, we are left with a consensus that an aesthetic merit in one item might be an aesthetic demerit in another item. The disagreement concerns whether some aesthetic values are inherently merits or demerits. However, Sibley's claim that grace is an aesthetic merit when taken in isolation should be heard as epistemic rather than metaphysical. His idea cannot be the confused one that a property can have a valence when it is not instantiated that differs from the valence it has when it is instantiated. Rather, he argued that there are some general yet defeasible principles of the form "V is an aesthetic merit." To say that grace is an inherent merit is just to say that it is a generally true but defeasible principle that grace is an aesthetic merit. What matters for present purposes is the metaphysical consensus. What can be said about the valence of aesthetic values, given that what has positive valence in one case can have negative valence in another case?

As we saw in Chapter 5, Sosa highlights cases where all the goods in a domain of performance are organized by a fundamental good (2007: 78). The bull's eye is the fundamental good of archery: what is good in archery—good bows, good shots, good conditions—conduces to bull's eyes. Tasty coffee is the fundamental good of the barista, for other espresso goods, such as good burr grinders and good roasts, conduce to tasty coffee. Aesthetic hedonists will follow suit: finally good experiences are the fundamental goods of aesthetic practices. By contrast, the network theory does not posit a fundamental aesthetic good, because each specialized act-type has its own success conditions and none enjoys special privilege.

Why not reverse priority? In some domains of performance, goodness determines success; in others, the priority reverses and success determines goodness. In aesthetic domains, success determines goodness:

> MERIT: V is an aesthetic merit in x = the fact that x is V is reason for A to φ in C in K, and A's success in φing in C contributes to promoting V in K.

A value is promoted in a practice just when it tends to spread to a larger fraction of items in the practice, all else being equal (i.e. excluding external factors in the value's spread). Turning to negative valence,

> DEMERIT: V is an aesthetic demerit in x = the fact that x is V is reason for A to φ in C in K, and A's success in φing in C contributes to suppressing V in K.

A value is suppressed in a practice just when it is found in a shrinking fraction of items in the practice, all else being equal (i.e. excluding external factors in the value's retreat).

Recognizing the quirky surrealism of a shot, Abbott includes it in *The World of Atget*. Her editorial act is successful at bringing Atget's work into the canon. As a result of her success, quirkiness tends to spread in modernist photography. The quirkiness is a merit in the photograph. Recognizing the triteness of another shot, she excludes it from the book—a decision that protects her success in bringing Atget's work into the canon and that contributes to a tendency that suppresses triteness in photographic modernism. Being trite is a demerit in the shot.

A merit in one item might therefore be a demerit in another in the same practice. Quirkiness is a merit in Atget's photographs, but would be no merit in a photograph by Abbott, with its forthright realism. Abbott does not print a quirky shot on one of her contact sheets and her omission is an achievement—a success out of competence. The shot's quirkiness is a demerit because her success helps to suppress quirkiness in the practice. MERIT and DEMERIT accommodate the post-heroic consensus on aesthetic valence.

An aesthetic value's valence can also vary from item to item within a practice. Indeed, an item can have an aesthetic value whose valence varies by act type and circumstance. The provocative intimacy of an image in Robert Mapplethorpe's X Portfolio is an aesthetic reason for Danto to write an essay about it (1995). At the same time, it is an aesthetic reason for the tourist bureau to omit to display it on the billboard next to the amusement park. If the tourist bureau's success contributes to suppressing provocatively intimate images, then the image's provocative intimacy is a demerit in it. At the same time, its provocative intimacy is a merit in it if the philosopher's success contributes to promoting provocatively intimate images.

Positive and negative valence are to aesthetic value as positive and negative valence are to the adaptive value of genes. Aesthetic merit is to aesthetic success as adaptive merit is to reproductive fitness. There is no function that a gene performs such that its successfully performing the function consists in its getting some good. Rather, a gene has positive adaptive value just when it codes for a behaviour whose success in an environment tends to spread the gene in the population. In the same way, an item has aesthetic merit just when it calls for an act whose successful performance tends to spread the merit among the population of items in the practice.

Think of an item's merits and demerits as vectors pushing with more or less force towards their greater or lesser dispersion in the population of items in a practice. Aesthetic merit spreads aesthetic merit: aesthetic merits figure in reasons for agents to achieve, and when they achieve, they spread the very merits that figure in their reason to achieve.

Core Aesthetic Norms

What it takes to succeed varies from one type of aesthetic agent to the next in an aesthetic practice. Each has their own aims, with their own success conditions. Since competence befits success, what it takes to achieve also varies from one type of agent to the next. Nevertheless, all aesthetic agents rely, for their achievement, on core aesthetic competence—competence in aesthetic evaluation. Obviously, core aesthetic competence implies a competence in evaluating in accordance with the aesthetic profile of the relevant aesthetic practice. Every aesthetic practice is sustained by a pair of core aesthetic norms that bear upon and stabilize its aesthetic profile.

One core aesthetic norm is: get the object right. For participants in K: aesthetically evaluate an item using K's aesthetic profile only if it is an item in K (cf. Knight 1967: 155–7; Walton 1970; Olsen 1981; Eaton 1989: 178; Lopes 2014a: 154–6). A netsuke collector mistakes a piece of Appalachian whittling for a netsuke. Having made the mistake, she finds it beautifully rustic, though it is exquisite—not rustic—on the aesthetic profile of Appalachian whittling. In collecting the piece, she fails to achieve what netsuke collectors set out to achieve, and her failure springs from an episode of incompetence. Precisely what incompetence? When evaluated as a netsuke, the carving is rustic. She is not wrong there. Rather, her mistake lies in aesthetically evaluating an item on the aesthetic profile for netsuke when it is not a netsuke. As a rule, an agent's chance of aesthetic achievement in K hangs on her aesthetically evaluating only items in K on the aesthetic profile of K. She fails to do as an expert would. The demands of aesthetic achievement impose the norm: get the object right.

Another core aesthetic norm is: get the practice right. For participants in K: do not make aesthetic evaluations of items in K that are inconsistent with the pattern of correlations that really is K's aesthetic profile (cf. Lopes 2014a: 156–7). A Californian wine lover has mostly tasted heavily oaked Chardonnays loaded with diacetyl. Tasting a Chablis, she finds it screaming bright. However, the Chablis is not screaming bright in the aesthetic profile for Chardonnays. Exposed to a biassed sample, the wine lover has got the Chardonnay aesthetic profile wrong. Her chance of aesthetic achievement in the world of wine hangs on her getting right the Chardonnay aesthetic profile. The demands of aesthetic achievement impose the norm: get the practice right.

Sherri Irvin observes that fakes and forgeries present a special kind of aesthetic threat (2007: 305–6). Translated into the vocabulary of the network theory, they subvert core aesthetic competence so as to pollute the aesthetic profile of an aesthetic practice. Experts duped by Van Meegeren's Vermeers came to take features of the Van Meegerens as diagnostic of Vermeers, making it easier to admit more Van Meegerens into the Vermeer oeuvre. A vicious cycle develops that makes it harder and harder to comply with the core aesthetic norms. The norm to get the practice right is harder to follow when we frequently enough fail to get the item right, and the norm to get the item right is harder to follow when we frequently fail to get the practice right. The two core aesthetic norms go hand in hand.

The final pass at the network theory introduces the requirement that an agent's competence to φ be aligned upon the aesthetic profile of K. Its members do not make an aesthetic practice the one that it is; rather, their aligning on its aesthetic profile makes an aesthetic practice the one that it is. We now have resources to understand what it is for an agent to be aligned on an aesthetic profile. An agent's competence is aligned on K's aesthetic profile just when they are subject to, and closely enough comply with, K's core aesthetic norms.

To illustrate, let us have one last go at my wonky lanyard. My attempt to save face by claiming expertise in tying gnots is hopeless because there is no aesthetic practice of tying gnots. The gnot aesthetic profile exists, since it is merely a pattern that can be instantiated. (Compare: Walton's category of guernicas exists, and it has one instance, namely *Guernica*.) What does not exist are core aesthetic norms for a gnot aesthetic practice. A norm is a rule that explains a pattern of behaviour. That is,

> a rule of action, R, for circumstances, C, is a norm in population, P, = (1) enough agents in P know that R applies in C and (2) conform to R in C on condition that (3) they expect enough others in P to conform to R in C and (4) they expect enough others in P to expect them to conform to R in C.

There is no pattern of action in a population that is explained by anyone's acting on a norm to get the gnot aesthetic profile right, or a norm to aesthetically evaluate an item as a gnot only if it is a gnot.

The only aesthetic norms in the vicinity are those of knot tying. Like it or not, I am subject to those aesthetic norms, and I do have a core aesthetic competence that brings me into close enough compliance with them. Those are simply social facts. To get the item right, I must evaluate my lanyard on the aesthetic profile for knots. To get the practice right, I must not evaluate my lanyard in a way that is inconsistent with the pattern of correlations that is the aesthetic profile for knots.

Therefore, my lanyard is just wonky. My rationalization of its being a *wabi-sabi* gnot requires a claim to a type of expertise that does not exist, because experts are experts in practices. Attempting the impossible is bad enough. I also make an evaluation that I should not make.

Do not forget that cognitive schemas are often implicit. Participants in aesthetic practices need not have full awareness of the norms with which they comply. They might be unable to articulate their norm-constituting expectations, they might heap scorn upon the assertion that their actions are patterned upon any aesthetic profile, and they might not even possess the concept of a norm, let alone the concept of an aesthetic profile. As Mothersill explains, participants in a practice "can afford the economy of ellipsis. Not everything needs to be spelled out. Practical deliberation, where goals and interests are shared, can get along using only minor premises" (1984: 9).

Plain Vanilla Aesthetic Normativity

Parents teach their children: whatever you do, do it well. No rule of action is more generic than: do it well. All else being equal, agents do well to the extent that their acts succeed as a result of their bringing their competence to bear. Aesthetic agents are no exception. Part of what makes them agents at all is that they do well by achieving. They have reasons to act that are reasons to act well that are reasons to achieve. So the network theory appeals to plain vanilla normativity. Aesthetic values inherit their practical normativity from a basic condition of all agency—agents must use what they have to perform successfully.

President Obama's 2008 speech on "A More Perfect Union" is powerful—sombre, thoughtful, and yet rousing. According to VALUE, aesthetic values figure in reasons to act aesthetically. Being powerful is an aesthetic value only if the fact that the speech is powerful lends weight to the proposition that someone aesthetically should get moving and do something. Thomson's principle adds that what anyone should do in a practical arena is what the expert would do. Aesthetic experts have competence for aesthetic achievement (see EXPERT). So, here is why being powerful is reason-giving. The fact that the President's speech is powerful lends weight to its being an achievement for an agent of a certain kind to get moving and φ. Not any agent, however, but an agent who participates in an aesthetic practice—one centred on political speeches, for example. For such an agent, being powerful is reason-giving. It gives them aesthetic reason to act, to act well, and to achieve.

The fact that the speech is powerful is an aesthetic reason for an agent to φ, to φ well, and to achieve by φing. An aesthetic reason is a fact that answers a question such as, what reason did you have to include that speech in the Norton Anthology? The answer is: the speech is powerful. True, one might answer: by including it, I acted well. One might also answer: by including it, I achieved. While it is true that anyone who has reason to act thereby has reason to act well and has reason to achieve, these reasons are not aesthetic reasons. Aesthetic reasons are aesthetic value facts, such as the fact that Obama's speech is powerful.

Put another way, a fact is not an aesthetic reason just because it explains why another fact is an aesthetic reason. Assume that the fact that x is V is aesthetic reason for A to φ. According to the network theory, the fact that A achieves by φing explains why the fact that x is V is an aesthetic reason for A to φ. However, a fact that explains why the fact that x is V is an aesthetic reason to φ is not another aesthetic reason that A has to φ. The only fact that is an aesthetic reason to φ is the fact that x is V.

Aesthetic normativity is a special case of a plain vanilla normativity that localizes to practical arenas. Facts that are reasons for biologists, investment bankers, and golf fans to act and achieve are not facts that are reasons for anthropologists, dry cleaners, or hockey referees to act and achieve.

The practical significance of an item's aesthetic value for an agent is a function of their aesthetic identity. You are an image meme aficionado. Along comes a wicked take on Hipster Dog. In view of your location in a practical arena, whose coordinates are your competence in a social context, the wickedness of the image means you aesthetically should propagate a new twist on it. Since I am not into image memes, there is no question of my acting or achieving in the same arena, and the wickedness of the image gives me little or no reason to act. Aesthetic values do not have practical significance for just anyone. For any aesthetic value, the achievement of an agent in an aesthetic practice lies in doing what would be done by an expert in the practice.

Mothersill countered Hume's thought that some items are ones that every qualified observer finds beautiful with the "better idea" that every qualified observer finds something beautiful (1984: 261). The network theory runs with Mothersill's better idea: we position ourselves to get a bead on an item's aesthetic value and hence what it asks of us. Not everyone eats the same food when all eat the hundred mile diet. Montréalais on the hundred mile diet should not eat the Mombasa diet. Aesthetic normativity is the same for all, but what each aesthetically should do reflects who they are, and where they are.

Two Counterexamples

Intuitions about aesthetic value are bound to be so heavily infused by aesthetic hedonism that we must not take them at face value. Nevertheless, here are a pair of cases that instructively pump some intuitions against the network theory.

Riggle shares this anecdote:

REGGAETON. The other day my wife and I were trying a taco shop near our new house. A song came on in the middle of our meal and it immediately piqued our interest. The rhythm of the beat, the syntactical complexity of the lyrics, the vocal character and melody—it was so good! We found out it was "Me Rehúso" by Danny Ocean. Now, we know exactly nothing about Latin mega pop, let alone whatever specific genre this pop song falls into. But we loved it. We downloaded it and have been sharing it with friends when they come over or ride in our car. We dance to it, we sing it with smiles, we joke about not knowing some of the Spanish lyrics—the song became integrated into our social lives and will no doubt partly define our summer looking back. In doing so, we might have engaged with the exact song that a local aesthetic expert would recommend. But if I should strive to be like a local aesthetic expert, then our forging ahead with our enthusiasm looks rash and naïve. (personal correspondence)

A theory of aesthetic value that throws cold water on our newly acquired aesthetic enthusiasms should have its premises examined.

Happily, the network theory is not as forbidding as REGGAETON suggests. To begin with, Brett and Nick might simply get (heaps of) pleasure from the song: moving on from aesthetic hedonism liberates us to get our kicks where we may (more on pleasure in Chapter 8.) However, that cannot be the whole response, for we can be good at tuning in aesthetic value in new places. Are we really subject to the norms of an aesthetic practice on first encounter?

Suppose that Brett and Nick found the song laid back in its attitude to a painful breakup, and suppose that they are wrong about this. Perhaps a reggaeton expert would know that the song is laden with irony—a Latin "Hey, That's No Way to

Say Goodbye." The network theory gives our couple two options. If they recognize that they have reason to give the song another listen, then they accept that the expert is normative for them. Alternatively, if they shrug off the expert, then they decline the invitation to enter the reggaeton aesthetic practice. They are in it for pleasure, or for appreciation within some wider aesthetic practice, such as pop music. Either option is open. What the network theory rules out is a third option, of their accepting the invitation while ignoring their host.

Switching from a worry that the theory is too demanding to a worry that it is too permissive, Shelley poses this case:

> VANDALS. Suppose a practice arises (or exists) consisting of aesthetic vandalism—that is, of defacing or destroying items typically preserved in some other practice. The vandals must be attuned to the very same values that the preservationists are in order to act in their destructive ways. Yet the network theory implies that such acts of vandalism are aesthetic achievements: gracefulness is reason-giving = the fact that the Arch of Triumph at Palmyra was graceful lent weight to the proposition that it was an aesthetic achievement for vandals to destroy it in 2015, where it is an item in a practice of aesthetic vandalism, and the aesthetic vandal's competence is aligned upon the aesthetic profile of aesthetic vandalism. (personal correspondence)

Caveat: aesthetic vandals are not Daesh, which did not act upon any aesthetic reasons in destroying the antiquities at Palmyra. Moreover, whatever we say about the coherence of the practice of aesthetic vandalism, nobody denies that there are lots of overwhelming non-aesthetic reasons not to destroy monuments.

VANDALS brings out affronts to our intuitions that stem from two features of the network theory. First, the theory does not restrict the success conditions on aesthetic acts. In particular, it does not require aesthetic acts to promote some overall good. The theory assumes that aesthetic goods fill in for V in facts of the form "x is V." We cannot say what we want to say, namely that the whole practice of aesthetic vandalism is just no dang good. Second, according to MERIT, what gives a value a positive valence is that successful aesthetic acts spread its incidence among items in the practice. Hence, as aesthetic vandals succeed in destroying things, what is a merit in an item's "home" practice becomes a demerit in the practice of aesthetic vandalism. Although grace is a merit in the Roman architecture of which the Arch is an instance, the vandals' success means there is less grace in their aesthetic inventory. Yet, we want to say that grace cannot be a demerit.

On the second point, the thing to do is dig in the heels. Grace is not always a merit. It is a demerit in: punk songs, hip hop clothing, the decadent aesthetic of

Huysmans and his circle, the English bulldog, and de Kooning's paintings. Turning to the first point, it is a technical matter that aesthetic values are values in items. If we want to say that an aesthetic practice can be no dang good, even if it thrives in its own terms, then why not find a way to say that? After all, the aesthetic vandals' successes interfere with the aesthetic agency of many others. They perpetrate an aesthetic injustice. Chapter 12 supplements the network theory of aesthetic value with a theory of aesthetic justice.

Explaining Local Aesthetic Expertise

The main argument for the network theory is a limited contrastive inference to the best explanation. Chapter 4 argued that aesthetic hedonism does not explain six facts about aesthetic experts set out in Chapter 1. The network theory is true if it does a better job explaining these facts.

1. Aesthetic experts disperse into almost all demographic niches. Aesthetic activity and achievement cut across boundaries of gender and ethnicity, culture and socio-economic status. As Bourdieu wrote, "there are beautiful ways of ploughing or trimming a hedge, just as there are beautiful mathematical solutions or beautiful rugby manoeuvres. Thus, most of society can be excluded from the universe of legitimate culture without being excluded from the universe of aesthetics" (1990: 7–8). The network theory explains why.

Agents, being agents, do well to achieve. Whatever their walk of life, agents who act upon a rudimentary capacity to tune in the aesthetic value of some items automatically have reason to do better. Since specialized agents boost their chances of aesthetic achievement, their aesthetic reason to act is reason to plug into networks of specialists. Networked specialists must converge on an aesthetic profile, and the core of aesthetic expertise is the capacity to evaluate items in the relevant aesthetic profile. In other words, as long as a population contains agents who often enough act upon their aesthetic reasons, they will act in ways that channel them towards specialization.

Moreover, specialist networks are unlikely to arise independently of other social formations. Neighbourhood is a factor. Coast Salish carving evolved as it did partly because there was no contact with Makonde carving. Social class is another factor: guys who work on cars for a living are more likely to airbrush paintwork than the chaps with clean fingernails. Cosmetic practices for men and women in European culture reiterate and reinforce broader gender concepts. (Chapter 12 looks at what to do about aesthetic injustice that breeds and is bred of social injustice writ large.)

In sum, the ingredients needed to brew up aesthetic activity are some ability to detect aesthetic value, an orientation on doing better by developing competence, and such modest social wherewithal as is needed to join forces with others. No social setting lacks any of these, every social setting exploits them in its own way, and every social setting breeds its own experts. The network theory predicts the aesthetic saturation of social life.

2. Aesthetic experts jointly inhabit the whole aesthetic universe. The network theory predicts that, taken together, aesthetic experts sweep the great world of the aesthetic, from popular art to the fine arts, from mainstream to the fringe, from nature to design, from private life to the public sphere.

An agent boosts their chance of aesthetic achievement by networking with others in an aesthetic practice. The character of the practice that they join depends on their own suite of aesthetic competences and on the mix of aesthetic competences possessed by their neighbours. Since members of a group with a mix of competences must converge on an aesthetic profile, they have reason to migrate to a practice centred on that profile. In this way, practices' aesthetic profiles are attractors for competent agents. Aesthetic profiles that fail to attract competent practitioners centre unstable practices that are in peril of disappearing.

Hence, where there are aesthetic experts, there is an aesthetic practice, and where there is an aesthetic practice, there are aesthetic experts. Without experts to sustain them, aesthetic practices wither, and without practices that breed expertise, agents will look elsewhere to achieve. The network theory predicts that the aesthetic universe is saturated with aesthetic activity.

3. Aesthetic experts specialize by aesthetic domain. Nobody pretends expertise, or even competence, in any more than one or perhaps a few local aesthetic domains. Aesthetic agency channels into categories of art, design, and nature. The network theory predicts that aesthetic agents will not crowd into a single aesthetic mega-practice, but will instead participate in many hundred mile aesthetic practices.

Agents are subject to the contingencies of socialization. Inborn differences in aptitude do not track social arrangements, but processes of socialization shape agents' aptitudes by transmitting cognitive schemas and pools of resources, including aesthetic profiles and norms. Moreover, social structures are self-perpetuating. Agents whose acts have been scaffolded will perform scaffolded acts, which transmit the cognitive schemas and replenish the pools of resources that do the scaffolding. Differences in aptitude, amplified by social structures, proliferate aesthetic practices.

Externalities also play a role, as aesthetic practices exploit technologies and material resources that vary from one population to another. Contrast the aesthetic profile suited to the furs and knits of Nunavut with the aesthetic profile suited to the cargo shorts of southern California.

Scaffolding is constraint, but it also nourishes aesthetic diversity. Aesthetic values are determinates of generic aesthetic value—distinct ways of being aesthetically valuable. Savion Glover's emphatic stomp is not Misty Copeland's emphatic *pas coupé*. To lose tap is not to lose the emphatic but it is to lose tap emphatic, which is different from other ways of being emphatic. Just as a loss of biodiversity amounts to a loss of genetic materials, a loss of aesthetic diversity amounts to a loss of aesthetic values.

4. Aesthetic experts specialize by activity. Local experts make specialized contributions to their aesthetic domains by editing, curating, collecting, conserving, exhibiting, teaching, and connecting audiences. Here too the network theory passes with flying colours, predicting what we observe.

To specialize is to trade off all-around competence in order to get a boost in effectiveness. Trading off is a good idea when others better perform the tasks that come to lie beyond an agent's area of specialization, so that more can be achieved. Having achieved more, the prospects of further achievement come into view. Provided that specialists can count on each other to deliver, because all reliably cooperate around an aesthetic profile, the result is a cascade towards a deeper division of aesthetic labour. Finer and finer divisions of aesthetic competence fuel ever higher levels of aesthetic competence, which drive finer divisions of aesthetic labour.

The engine driving specialization is the normative force of agency itself, which makes a reason to act into a reason to act well and hence a reason to achieve. At the same time, divisions of aesthetic competence are a good idea only with enough convergence on an aesthetic profile and enough compliance with core aesthetic norms. The network theory explains why agents have reason to divide aesthetic labour given convergence on aesthetic profiles.

5. Specializations by activity and domain interact. Agents have reason to specialize by activity when they share an aesthetic domain, and they have reason to perform differently where they belong to different aesthetic domains. Poets only work with editors who are "on the same page," and different skill sets go into editing contemporary poetry, pop song lyrics, analytic philosophy texts, or Bollywood movie scripts. Figure 1.1 represents the interactive specialization space. A selling point of the network theory is its predicting the interaction.

Achievement-oriented agents have aesthetic reasons to act in ways that situate them within practices and to develop competences for specialized activities. In acting on the aesthetic reasons they have, they steer themselves toward some regions of the two-dimensional specialization space, and that space continuously subdivides. Dividing aesthetic labour divides aesthetic domains and dividing aesthetic domains divides aesthetic labour.

That expertise is acquired and sustained through social practices that determine ways of being good and that endow agents with a form of identity—this cluster of ideas arguably goes back to Hume and remains attractive among contemporary thinkers (Wiggins 1998; see also Blum 1998; Mason 1998: 192). In one famous definition, a practice is a

> coherent and complex form of socially established cooperative human activity through which goods internal to that form of activity are realized in the course of trying to achieve those standards of excellence which are appropriate to, and practically definitive of, the form of activity, with the result that human powers to achieve excellence, and human conceptions of the ends and goods involved, are extended.   (MacIntyre 1984: 175)

The network theory fills in the details by deploying aesthetic profiles and core aesthetic norms to explain the reasons agents have to act in ways that can make aesthetic practices real. That reality is a product of a virtuous spiral put in motion by a mechanism whereby dividing aesthetic labour divides aesthetic practices and dividing aesthetic practices divides aesthetic labour.

6. *Aesthetic expertise is stable.* Local aesthetic experts seem to have stable traits that enable them to act well reliably. Not all domains of human endeavour house genuine experts. Evidence suggests moral expertise is a myth, for example (Harman 1999; Doris 2002). Why think that there are genuine aesthetic experts?

The key to stable expertise is consistency in behaviour across relevantly similar situations, and the more the similarity the better the prospects for consistency. Daniel Kahneman, an expertise pessimist, and Gary Klein, an optimist, agree that expertise requires an environment regular enough to be predictable and to afford opportunities to learn regularities through prolonged practice (2009: 520). They contrast the low-validity environment of stock-pickers and political pundits with the disciplined environments where trauma surgeons, firefighters, and athletes are trained to perform.

Such reliability as we see in the performances of aesthetic agents is explained by the network theory. The theory depicts aesthetic agents as achieving when they succeed by exercising personal competence scaffolded by social reality. Very specific aesthetic practices come with specific aesthetic profiles and norms, which are entrenched in materials and technologies. Social structures regularize the environment and provide opportunities for methodical training. By acting on reasons that channel them into specializations, aesthetic agents help to secure the stability of their expertise.

At the same time social structures are dynamic and aesthetic practices change (see Chapter 9). Some change is due to externalities, such as political instability and technological invention. Some change is internal, induced by high achievers whose strivings subdivide the practice and spur specialized activity. The network theory predicts stability within a context of change that is for the most part relatively gradual, unfolding over years or decades. To adapt Blackburn's metaphor, the theory predicts a speed limit on aesthetic dynamism (1998: 67).

Whereas aesthetic hedonism attempts to fix protean pleasure to a standard of taste, the network theory predicts that aesthetic expertise as no less and no more stable than the social practices in which it flourishes.

Raz advises that we do value theory well when we "thicken the texture of goods, allowing them to develop greater subtlety and nuance" (1999a: 205). Here Raz gives voice to this book's deepest commitment. We cannot stale beauty's infinite variety.

So concludes the limited, contrastive abductive argument for the network theory of aesthetic value. Whereas aesthetic hedonism might be consistent with the explananda, it does not predict them all, as does the network theory. Therefore, the network theory offers the better explanation. We should infer its truth. Supplementing the main argument are five bonus arguments, three of them presented in Part IV. In the course of thinking things through, questions sometimes arise that it would be good to answer. What is the role of pleasure? What should we say about aesthetic disagreement? What about the metaphysics of aesthetic value? The network theory helps to articulate what is genuinely at stake in these questions, and then it provides the answers. A theory that is good at answering good questions is a good theory.

PART IV

8

By Happy Alchemy of Mind

What would be our situation were the network theory correct? It had better be the situation we are actually in! Start with our psychological situation. All hands agree that aesthetic encounters have something to do with pleasure. Aesthetic hedonism makes the connection constitutive; the network theory makes it contingent. Three questions arise. First, what explains how we come to act aesthetically, if not hedonic desires? Second, what explains aesthetic pleasure, if it is not built into experiences of items with aesthetic value? Third, what is aesthetic appreciation, and where does pleasure come into it? To answer these questions, the network theory performs two tasks. It first articulates our psychological situation and then makes sense of it.

Aesthetic Motives, Pure and Mixed

Aesthetic reasons are worldly facts, facts that lend weight to what agents aesthetically should do. The network theory answers the normative question by stating what it is about V that makes it the case that the fact that x is V lends weight to what an agent aesthetically should do. As we all know from our own experience, an agent who has decisive aesthetic reason to perform an act might yet fail to do the act. An aesthetic expert is an agent so configured that they routinely act on the aesthetic reasons that they have, but we are not all experts. Non-experts sometimes lack the expert's motives, where motives are psychological states that explain action. The question is precisely what motives must an aesthetic expert have?

On the standard (Humean) theory, introduced in Chapter 3, motives are belief–desire pairs. Beliefs do not suffice to motivate action; desires are also needed. Furthermore, ACT stipulates that someone acts aesthetically only when their making an aesthetic evaluation helps explain their acting. So an agent who acts aesthetically is partly motivated by an aesthetic evaluation—a representation of an item as having some aesthetic value. What about the desire that pairs with the evaluation?

For purists, aesthetic motives pair aesthetic evaluations with aesthetic desires. Just as an aesthetic evaluation represents an item as having an aesthetic value, an aesthetic desire also represents an aesthetic value. Aesthetic hedonism easily accommodates purism (see Chapter 3). A springboard fan watches a diver execute a triple pike because they judge the pike is crisp and they want to see the crispness. According to aesthetic hedonism, crisp dives please. Moreover, pleasure is by nature desirable. So, purists embrace a desire-based theory of aesthetic reasons along the lines of

DESIRE: necessarily, p is an aesthetic reason for A to φ in C only if A has a p-representing desire that would be satisfied by A's φing in C and the fact that p explains why the desire would be satisfied by A's φing in C.

The fact that the triple pike is crisp is an aesthetic reason for the fan to watch it only because the fact that it is crisp explains why their desire for pleasure would be satisfied by their watching it. In general, abstracting away from aesthetic hedonism, the purist's understanding of aesthetic motives (as combining aesthetic evaluations with aesthetic desires) takes aesthetic reasons to be facts of a kind that are represented in aesthetic desires (as well as evaluations) in order to explain aesthetic action. DESIRE articulates the purist understanding of aesthetic motives.

The trouble is that the network theory is inconsistent with DESIRE. Desconocido's *Besos* in Bogotá is biting. Being biting is reason-giving, and the network theory explains why. The fact that *Besos* is biting lends weight to its being an aesthetic achievement for Andrea Baldini to include it in a volume on political street art, for instance. Unlike pleasure, however, aesthetic achievement is not by nature desirable. In having an aesthetic reason to include *Besos* in his book, Baldini does not thereby have a desire such that the fact that *Besos* is biting explains why that very desire would be satisfied by his undertaking the venture. He need have no desire that represents the fact that *Besos* is biting: he need not want biting street art in his book, and he need not want to achieve. Yet he has aesthetic reason to include the work in his volume.

True, aesthetic reasons can and do generate additional, more complex, non-aesthetic reasons to have desires. When the fact that x is V is an aesthetic reason for an agent to φ, then the further fact that they have aesthetic reason to φ gives them reason to want to φ. The fact that *Besos* is biting gives Baldini reason to write it up, and that further fact, about the aesthetic reason he has, gives him reason to want to write it up. Perhaps we necessarily want to have the desires we have reason to have. Still, Baldini might not want to write it up, and he has reason to write it up even if he does not want to. Aesthetic reasons are facts of the form "x is V" (not facts of the form "x is V is an aesthetic reason to φ"), and they do not implicate desires, on the network theory.

Assume the network theory is true. Since the theory is inconsistent with DESIRE, DESIRE is false. As we saw in Chapter 2, DESIRE is implied by the standard theory of motivation conjoined with

AESTHETIC REASON INTERNALISM: necessarily, p is an aesthetic reason for A to φ in C only if A can be motivated by a p-representing state to φ in C.

By modus tollens, either the standard theory of motivation or AESTHETIC REASON INTERNALISM is false. Grant the standard theory of motivation (see Chapter 4). It follows that AESTHETIC REASON INTERNALISM is false.

To deny reason internalism is to hold that an agent has a reason to act even though the reason finds in them no motivational echo. According to

AESTHETIC REASON EXTERNALISM: possibly, p is an aesthetic reason for A to φ in C but A cannot be motivated by a p-representing state to φ in C.

Here "cannot" indicates rational impossibility. The agent's existing motivational makeup does not already include the required motive, and they have no path to the required motive just by correctly reasoning from their current motives. The claim is that an agent can have an aesthetic reason to act even if they lack, and cannot reason themselves into, having purely aesthetic motives that would explain their so acting. Their aesthetic reasons are not restricted by what is in their rationally extensible set of aesthetic motives.

Now we see the alternative to the purist line on what motivates aesthetic acts. According to ACT, every aesthetic act is motivated by an aesthetic evaluation. Agents who belong to an aesthetic practice can always make aesthetic evaluations more or less in line with the aesthetic profile of the practice. A member of the street art community who initially judges *Besos* on non-aesthetic grounds can always be brought round to judging it aesthetically. At the same time, AESTHETIC REASON EXTERNALISM says that they need not have or be capable of acquiring aesthetic desires—desires that attribute aesthetic values. They can act from impure motives that pair an aesthetic evaluation with a non-aesthetic desire.

Aesthetic Indifference

In the last couple of decades of his life, Ernst Gombrich reported that he was able to judge whether a painting was beautiful or graceful, but it left him completely cold (Nanay 2016: 15). Nothing could warm his heart to painting after a lifetime dedicated to its study. His was a case of locked-in aesthetic indifference: he could not be reasoned into caring. According to the network theory, Gombrich still had aesthetic reasons to perform many aesthetic acts. Suppose that he did sometimes advise important galleries on acquisitions. In proffering his advice, he must have been motivated by a mixture of an aesthetic evaluation and some non-aesthetic desire.

An advantage of the network theory is that it correctly predicts our psychological situation. It predicts the possibility of agents like Gombrich, who engage in aesthetic action despite locked-in aesthetic indifference, because it takes aesthetic action to require only aesthetic evaluation, not aesthetic desire. Even aesthetic experts can engage in aesthetic action despite their locked-in aesthetic indifference. (Nobody is an aesthetic expert, if not Gombrich.)

Wagner is all the rage. The arts councils pour gargantuan sums into productions, the best venues compete for those productions, and the opera schools ensure placement success by loading their curricula with Wagnerian materials taught by their most effective instructors. Students see the writing on the wall. One turns out to be especially gifted at Wagnerian set design, and she becomes the premier designer. She homes in on the aesthetic values of the operas and sees what kinds of sets those values give her reason to build. Even so, the enterprise leaves her cold. She loathes Wagner's philosophy, and she would have to give up too much of who she is in order to make his music hers. Her reasons are aesthetic; her motives are a mixture of accurate aesthetic evaluations and, on the conative side, what some (too snickeringly) call careerist ambitions.

Raffi is all the rage. The recording studios pour astonishing sums into recording and marketing, tickets sell out at Carnegie Hall, and producers learn the tricks that present the music at its best. One producer turns out to have a perfect knack in the recording studio. He homes in on the aesthetic values of the songs and sees exactly what kinds of arrangements those values give him reason to concoct. He wins kudos and prizes. Yet the business leaves him cold. Chopin is his true passion, and there is no sound deliberative route that leads from a passion for Chopin to a conative makeup that echoes the aesthetic reasons he has and acts upon when he produces Raffi. The only path open would infantilize him.

In both cases, aesthetic experts both have and routinely act upon aesthetic reasons. What actually motivates them is a mixture of accurate aesthetic evaluations with non-aesthetic desires. Moreover, their aesthetic indifference is locked in: the set designer cannot be reasoned round to wanting that a set perfectly echo some Wagnerian profundity, and the music producer cannot be reasoned round to wanting that an arrangement be so sweet. Aesthetic experts routinely act on the aesthetic reasons they have because they are motivated by correct aesthetic evaluations. Their motives must also include desires, but the desires need not represent aesthetic values.

The point is not to champion the prevalence of locked-in aesthetic indifference. Of course the condition is uncommon, but its possibility teaches four lessons.

To begin with, purism about aesthetic motives depends upon a kind of individualism, which regards aesthetic agents as having a kind of motivational integrity that is proof against social interference. In fact, agents can act on their aesthetic reasons, despite their indifference, because social structures, including sanctions and incentives, shape their conative motives. Agents interacting with one another must be able to count on each other to act on the aesthetic reasons they have, like it or not. Aesthetic practices nudge their members to act on the aesthetic reasons they have, even if that means harnessing non-aesthetic desires.

A second lesson is developmental. While it is rarely locked in, aesthetic indifference is more commonly recalcitrant. All else being equal, someone into street art, who often acts on the aesthetic reasons he has, will line his conative motives up with his aesthetic evaluations, acquiring aesthetic desires. As we have seen, the fact that an agent has aesthetic reason to φ gives them reason to want to φ. Moreover, desire is plastic. Only special circumstances inhibit the plasticity of the desires of the Raffi arranger, the Wagnerian set designer, and the distinguished art historian. In the normal course of events, agents who design sets that evoke Wagnerian profundity, arrange songs sweetly, and recommend paintings for their subtlety will come to want the sets to be profound, the songs to be sweetly arranged, and the gallery's acquisitions to be subtle.

Chapter 11 will return to the thought that our aesthetic labours are often labours of love that contribute to the goodness of our lives. Notice, for now, that it does not follow from this that aesthetic agency is constitutively a labour of love. The third lesson is an error theory. Having observed how being good at doing something often goes with loving to do it, we tend to reason that we must love what we are good at doing. But we reason fallaciously. We can sacrifice what we want on the altar of achievement. The fallacy explains intuitive resistance to externalism about the configuration of aesthetic agency.

The final lesson concerns the limits of indifference, which trace the boundaries of aesthetic practices. Wikipedia's lists of music genres taxonomize incredibly diverse aesthetic ecosystems, where most niches have few occupants. Chances are that you and I are indifferent to boom bap (a genre of hip hop), and the moment has long since passed for us to make our way to boom bap from our present aesthetic interests. As we are not participants in the boom bap practice, we are not specialists for whom boom bap experts are normative. We do not have any boom bap reasons. If we do not have any boom bap reasons, then there is no question of our having boom bap reasons without motivational echoes. Aesthetic externalism only imposes aesthetic reasons on those who participate in an aesthetic practice. To make sense of this is to appreciate how an aesthetic practice structures the desires of its members, as well as their aesthetic evaluations.

A designer who bumbles a dress cannot shrug off their failure by saying that they did not see the flaw. They have aesthetic reason to do the act that the expert would do. Peter Railton adds that they cannot shrug off their failure by saying, "Yes, but I don't care how it looks" (2003: 121). Their indifference cannot mean that they did not fail to do as they aesthetically should have done, and the network theory explains why.

The Blame Argument

An argument given by Russ Shafer-Landau against generic reasons internalism also fits the aesthetic case (2003: 187–8). According to a principle of fair criticism, A merits criticism for not φing, in the context of K, only if A has aesthetic reason to φ. AESTHETIC REASON INTERNALISM says that A has an aesthetic reason to φ only if A can be motivated to φ by that reason. From these two claims it follows that A merits criticism for not φing, in the context of K, only if A can be motivated to φ by that reason. Yet, observe that some agents do merit criticism for not φing in the context of K, though they cannot be motivated to φ by an aesthetic reason. The triad is inconsistent: if the observation is correct, then either the principle of fair criticism or AESTHETIC REASON INTERNALISM is false. The principle of fair criticism is solid, and it is arguably implied by norms of criticism and advice-giving in social practices, including aesthetic ones. Ergo, AESTHETIC REASON INTERNALISM is false and AESTHETIC REASON EXTERNALISM is true.

Is the argument sound? Do some agents merit criticism despite their aesthetic indifference?

Take inexpert counterparts of the Raffi producer and the Wagnerian set designer. One mixes a little too much electric guitar noise into "Bananaphone;" the other gets it just a bit wrong in setting *Die Meistersinger* in a Brooklyn hipster microbrewery. Each has failed to do as their expert counterpart would do. For this they merit criticism, because they belong to practices where the achievement of each depends on others' achievements. Why should an agent's indifference mean they merit no criticism on the part of other agents in a common enterprise, where achievements interdepend?

Williams's (1981) defence of reason internalism stresses the impropriety of blaming and browbeating indifferent agents. Shafer-Landau replies that it can be inappropriate to blame or browbeat agents who nevertheless merit criticism (2003: 176–8). Meriting criticism neither obliges nor licenses others to get down to some criticizing.

Moreover, it is a mistake to conflate criticism, on one hand, with blaming or browbeating, on the other. Criticism is discourse aimed at changing behaviour. Agents in aesthetic practices have reason to exchange words in order to improve each others' performance. As we shall see in Chapter 9, an important function of aesthetic discourse is the mutual calibration of competences of members of a practice to bring them into alignment with each other on the practice's aesthetic profile. Criticism can help an agent to see what aesthetic reasons they have, even when the aesthetic reasons they have find no echo in their conative aesthetic motives.

Snobs: An Objection

Really? Aesthetic experts with careerist motives! The network theory originates as a way of filling in Thomson's principle. What someone aesthetically should do is what the relevant aesthetic expert would do, where the relevant aesthetic expert is an agent who is as good as a kind of aesthetic agent as an aesthetic agent of that kind can be (see Chapter 5). Surely, an aesthetic expert is as good as an aesthetic agent as an aesthetic agent can be only if they are equipped to act from the best motives. A disposition to careerism is not a good trait of character. How could it serve as an expert's motive? In its commitment to AESTHETIC REASON EXTERNALISM, the network theory betrays its roots in Thomson's principle.

For some virtue theorists in ethics and epistemology, virtues are competences that include characteristic motivational profiles (e.g. Zagzebski 1996; Hursthouse 1999; Baehr 2011). An agent does not perform from virtue unless they act out of an appropriate conative motive. Writing a cheque for the tax break might be an act of charity, but it does not display a charitable character, because the truly charitable person helps the needy out of moral concern. In aesthetics, some virtue theorists follow suit: a virtuous aesthetic agent exercises their competence out of a characteristically aesthetic conative motive (e.g. Goldie 2007; Goldie 2008; Lopes 2008).

Kieran's (2009) exposé of snobs brings the challenge down to earth (see also Patridge 2016). Some people are snobs. Their being snobs is a blot on their characters. Though we might not lay into them for it, we often want to, and the reprimand would be deserved. Ultimately, Kieran thinks, the problem with snobs lies with their conative motives.

Who is a snob? Felix buys a season pass to the Met. His act is aesthetic because it counterfactually depends on an aesthetic evaluation of the season—Felix has it on good authority that Met seasons are the best, and he would not subscribe were he to suspect otherwise. At the same time, he is motivated to buy the pass out of a desire to impress his peers, attract boyfriends, and establish his standing in the Upper West Side cultured set. Snobs are those who are disposed to act—and often enough do act—as Felix does here. Snobs' aesthetic acts are often enough motivated by concerns for "social" status.

The scare quotes signal the need for delicacy around identifying the snob's non-aesthetic motives with a desire for social status. After all, the network theory understands agents as participating in aesthetic practices, and being a participant in an aesthetic practice is a social status. A landscape architect's motive, when they specify a grass for a green roof, is predicated upon an understanding of and concern for their professional standing. They want to act professionally, and rightly so. Hence, snobs' concerns cannot be characterized simply as "social." Rather, snobs act from a notorious subset of social motives—desires to impress peers, attract mates, and the like. Henceforth, assume we have no trouble recognizing the notorious "snobcial" motives characteristic of snobbery.

With the snob's portrait sketched, Kieran argues that, because snobs are motivated by snobcial concerns, no genuine aesthetic expert can be a snob. If true, this conclusion spells serious trouble for the network theory. An aesthetic agent is not as good an aesthetic agent as they can be if they often enough act from snobcial motives, so an aesthetic expert must routinely act out of desires that represent aesthetic reasons. The network theory must be jettisoned, or redrafted to say that for an aesthetic value to be reason-giving is for it to figure in an aesthetic reason that lends weight to the proposition that it would be an achievement for an agent to act out of pure aesthetic motives.

Why think that snobcial motives disqualify snobs for expert status? Kieran gives two answers.

First, snobs tend to be unreliable, prone to error. Their motives make them prey to "confabulation, over-generalization, and selective focusing of attention" that trip them up in circumstances where doing what gets snobcial esteem is not the aesthetic best (Kieran 2009: 254). In other words, an agent with the wrong desires will tend to make wrong evaluations: snobbery compromises the core aesthetic competence that makes for expertise.

The trouble with this answer is that it overlooks the social scaffolding of aesthetic reasons. To see this, notice how plausible the answer is, given aesthetic hedonism. If an aesthetic evaluation measures the power to please, then an agent makes an aesthetic evaluation either by gauging their own response or by deferring to experts. A snob who is an expert does not defer to experts, so they must gauge their own response. Not implausibly, snobbish motives interfere with an agent's own pleasure response, rendering it useless as a measure of hedonic value (Melchionne 2010).

By contrast, the network theory proposes that core aesthetic competence consists in being aligned on the aesthetic profile of the relevant aesthetic practice. A practice's aesthetic profile is the pattern of correlations that obtains between the aesthetic value properties of items in the practice and some other properties they have. Aesthetic experts competently track the pattern of correlations. To do this, they do not inspect their own responses. Instead, they look outward, to the actions of others in the practice, with whom they form an interactive network. Confabulation, overgeneralization, and selective focusing of attention can get in the way, as they do in any endeavour, but they pose no heightened, existential threat. Agency is scaffolded in aesthetic practices precisely in order to secure against such threats.

The question was, why should their characteristic motives disqualify snobs for expert status? Kieran's second answer grants that snobbery need not compromise reliability. Let Felix be a snob with core aesthetic expertise. Not wanting to be unmasked as a poser by betraying his ignorance at the Met, he has put in the hours and has nailed the aesthetic profile of opera. Yet he attends *Turandot* only out of desires for snobcial status. Kieran describes him as a kind of aesthetic psychopath: he is missing the wiring that should make the "connection between the possession of aesthetic knowledge and the point of it" (Kieran 2009: 260).

What is the point of exercising core aesthetic competence? Kieran answers, to get pleasure. However, according to the network theory, the point of exercising aesthetic agency is to succeed at some aesthetic task out of competence. Success takes many forms, for there are many different types of aesthetic tasks that agents have to perform. Aesthetic success is not always getting a hit of pleasure. Therefore, some aesthetic agents are experts, who reliably succeed out of competence, though what motivates them is a desire to win fame or fortune, make their children proud, glorify their nation, or squash their rivals.

Facilitating Pleasure

The network theory makes sense of the psychological situation of aesthetic agents. It explains how we come to act aesthetically, if not by acting on hedonic desires. A second question is, what explains aesthetic pleasure, if it is not built into experiences of items with aesthetic value?

Nobody denies the tremendous pleasures that we are minded to take in things of beauty, and nobody doubts pleasure's close alliance with aesthetic value. In folk metaphysics, what is most striking in a phenomenon is often taken to belong to it by nature, but it is a fallacy to infer aesthetic hedonism from the tremendous pleasure that comes from beauty. What is important about a phenomenon might not make the phenomenon what it is. According to the network theory, pleasure is contingent to, not constitutive of, aesthetic acts. The story of aesthetic pleasure is an empirical one, and indeed the brain and behavioural sciences are on the case (e.g. Shimamura and Palmer 2011). That said, in view of our deep attachment to aesthetic hedonism, it would be wise to give some thought to how we might explain aesthetic pleasure, given the network theory.

Consider the principle that John Rawls names for Aristotle: "other things equal, human beings enjoy the exercise of their realized capacities" (1971: 426). So stated, Aristotle's principle is incomplete. Performances can succeed, they can be competent, and they are achievements when they succeed out of competence. Competent performance typically brings pleasure, but so do success and achievement. We far less enjoy competent performances when bad luck scotches success—consider how frustrating it is to write clearly, only to be misread. We also enjoy success less when it springs from luck—consider the letdown of winning a prize when the competition is weak. So we most enjoy achievement—consider the pleasure of having convinced an opponent to change their mind through rigorous and imaginative argumentation. (We can dream.) When completed, Aristotle's principle says that, all else being equal, we human beings enjoy the successful exercise of our realized capacities.

Aristotle's principle is a psychological truth with a plausible biological explanation. Mohan Matthen (2015; 2017) distinguishes effortfully acquired skills from capacities that develop spontaneously. Elementary language, numeracy, and motor skills reach a level of proficiency nearly without effort. Writing spoofs, solving proofs, and shooting hoops require practice and learning. Practice and learning are difficult, but many effortfully acquired skills are beneficial. Matthen's hypothesis is that we have evolved a system that immediately rewards our efforts as an incentive to learning. In particular, we feel pleasure in doing activity that is fluent and matches our desires for skill development (2015: 186; cf. Cutter and Tye 2011). The feeling is a "facilitating pleasure," a felt positive evaluation that arises directly from an awareness of performing a difficult and costly activity and that activates a competence that facilitates and optimizes the activity. As Matthen writes, "pleasure taken in an activity...enables productive agency" (2017: 13).

By rewarding activities from which they arise, facilitating pleasures make it more likely that those activities will be pursued, and by rewarding success, they make it more likely that those activities will be successfully pursued. Since aesthetic achievement requires core aesthetic achievement, core aesthetic pleasure comes from an exercise of core aesthetic achievement. Moreover, aesthetic pleasure tends to track aesthetic merits because aesthetic merits are aesthetic values that spread in an aesthetic practice through successful aesthetic acts (see Chapter 7).

Pleasure plays a non-constitutive and non-essential but still important role in the configuration of aesthetic agency. Without it, many aesthetic agents would find themselves listless. That is our psychological situation. The network theory predicts that we enjoy aesthetic activity, it predicts that the pleasure will be explained by something like the reward mechanism Matthen describes, and it predicts a close but contingent tie between pleasure and merit.

Interesting factoid: Matthen is an aesthetic hedonist, which proves that we can detach the theory of pleasure invoked by an aesthetic hedonist from their theory of aesthetic value and then retrofit it to explain the contingent link between aesthetic value and pleasure. The proof of concept is enough: we need not do the rounds and pay call upon every theory of pleasure.

Pleasures and Motives

Have we returned, full circle, to the claim that aesthetic agents must be motivated by hedonic desires? No. From the fact that an activity is enjoyable, it does not follow that an agent who enjoys the activity must be—or ever is—motivated to do the activity by a hedonic desire (Elster 1983: 107; Foot 2003[1990]: 135–6).

Executing a triple axel is an achievement that Mao Asada enjoys, but she does not jump triple axels in order to get the pleasure. The pleasure facilitates her learning the jump and thereby enhances her chances of achievement, and it no doubt heightens her desire to jump a triple axel today. Nevertheless, she executes a triple axel today because she wants to meet and raise the standards of contemporary skating, win a medal, and push the limits of human performance.

Feeling into the tangled psychology of the characters in Alice Munro's "Fits" calls upon the exercise of effortfully acquired reading competence, which is pleasurable when successful. The pleasure facilitates learning how to read better, and it heightens your desire to read into the states of mind of Peg and Robert. However, you wrestle first with Peg's reaction to the events of the story, and then with Robert's reaction to Peg, because you want to understand them, discover something about the rest of us, or pass the time on a long flight. What motivates you is not a desire for the pleasure that comes from flexing your muscles as a reader.

Winfrey's achievement in bringing readers together came out of her exercising her effortfully acquired social skills. Her achievement might bring her pleasure, but she did not challenge her audience to read *Anna Karenina* out of a desire to feel her own biceps. She wanted to share a book whose merits matched, at just that point, her readers' own aesthetic aspirations.

Pleasure is nomologically necessary for learning, but not for acting. It can enter into a causal explanation of how an agent comes to achieve by acting, without showing up in intentional explanations of their act.

The Hedonic Function of Aesthetic Practices?

Similar points apply when we scale up to the level of aesthetic practices. Some aesthetic practices thrive—Bollywood cinema and gardening, for example—while others hold on precariously—for example, post-tonal music and smoking accessories (e.g. ashtrays and cigarette cases). Aesthetic practices sometimes thrive because they are efficient systems for delivering doses of pleasure. Some are tempted by the hypothesis that aesthetic practices arise in order to serve a hedonic function (e.g. Iseminger 2004). From this hypothesis one might infer, wrongly, that their hedonic function makes them what they are.

What is it for an aesthetic practice to serve a hedonic function? An item's etiological function is a service it renders that caused it to be selected in the past (Millikan 1984). Hearts render service in pumping blood, which caused them to be favoured by natural selection, so that pumping blood is their etiological function. Artifacts, including social practices, can also have etiological functions. Glenn Parsons and Allen Carlson propose that an artifact has an etiological function just when it is manufactured and distributed because its recent ancestors performed that function, thereby causing their success in the marketplace (2008: 75). Turning to practices, the service rendered by a practice is its etiological function just when it has a recent history of rendering that service, thereby causing it to attract and retain participants. The hypothesis is that aesthetic practices succeed in the marketplace, attracting and retaining participants, because they have a recent history of supplying their participants with doses of pleasure.

The hypothesis is empirical, and it is not obviously true. Chances are very high that a range of different factors explain why some aesthetic practices persist while others fade in their historical and cultural settings (Parsons and Carlson 2008: 219). Perhaps pop music thrives because it helps teenagers to cope with rapid emotional change. Perhaps post-tonal music survives on life support, in the form of public funding and cultural brownie points. Not implausibly, the tartan aesthetic soldiers on just because it celebrates Scottish national identity. Humanities scholars endlessly document how aesthetic practices thrive as instruments of privilege and oppression (see Chapter 12). The empirical evidence is not likely to bear out the hypothesis that all aesthetic practices serve a hedonic function.

Even were it true, the hypothesis would not imply that its hedonic function is constitutive of an aesthetic practice. In the marketplace of games, some games make it because they are fun to play. That fact does not speak against a non-hedonic theory of games (e.g. Suits 1978; see also Nguyen 2017).

Will is playing *The Sims*, trying to put in a swimming pool. Maybe *The Sims* persists because people enjoy playing it. Even so, what makes Will a game player is that he complies with the norms of the game practice, which coordinate activity around an aesthetic profile to boost achievement. Sam collects game code and is trying to reconstruct a bit of *SimAnt* source code. Possibly, there are game code collectors because people enjoy playing games. Again, what makes her a game code collector is her acting in accordance with the norms of the aesthetic practice of gaming, aligning her activities with the relevant aesthetic profile. A kind of the genetic fallacy consists in drawing inferences from a causal explanation of the persistence of a practice to the nature of the practice.

Suppose Elster is right and pleasure is an essential by-product of some aesthetic activities, which cannot bring pleasure when done in order to get the pleasure. In that case, a good way to get pleasure from these aesthetic activities is to structure aesthetic practices where agents derive enjoyment from acts done from non-hedonic motives. How so? Well, if aesthetic practices scaffold aesthetic achievement, then, by Aristotle's principle, they raise agents' chances of getting any pleasure that accrues as a by-product of achievement. Getting pleasure facilitates learning and amps up the desires that motivate aesthetic performance, redoubling agents' chances of aesthetic achievement. Riding the upward spiral, agents act in ways that promote the persistence of their aesthetic practices.

Pleasure configures aesthetic agency by rewarding learning, and it sometimes rewards participants in aesthetic practices by giving them a way to get pleasure from activities that yield no pleasure when done to get the pleasure. Again, pleasure can enter into a causal explanation of the social formation of aesthetic practices without figuring into an account of the nature of the practices.

The Practiced Eye: Aesthetic Appreciation

Most of us get pleasure from aesthetic appreciation. This book correctively spotlights non-appreciative aesthetic acts that are overlooked in thinking about aesthetic agency and value, but aesthetic appreciation obviously plays a key role in many aesthetic practices. As it turns out, spotlighting non-appreciative aesthetic acts will have paid off, for the network theory yields a rich picture of aesthetic appreciation (see also Lopes forthcoming).

Aesthetic appreciation is not aesthetic evaluation. Aesthetic evaluations are mental representations that attribute aesthetic values to items, and every aesthetic act implicates an aesthetic evaluation, but not every aesthetic act is an act of aesthetic appreciation. In other words, appreciating an item involves more than representing its aesthetic value. To return to the example from Chapter 2, Nick has consulted the good people at Lonely Planet and judges that there is a Poussin worth looking at in the National Gallery, but only once he arrives there can he begin to appreciate the painting. So far, not much has been said about what he begins to do when he begins to appreciate.

Thinly conceived, aesthetic appreciation is pleasure taken in, or consequent upon, aesthetic evaluation. It requires no competence except core aesthetic competence plus a capacity to take pleasure in things. On a thicker conception, aesthetic appreciation engages distinctive skills that vary from one aesthetic practice to another.

The "practiced eye" generalizes Michael Baxandall's metaphor of the period eye in his book on *Painting and Experience in Fifteenth-Century Italy*. The "eye" stands metonymically for any cognitive competence, and whereas the period eye changes over time, the practiced eye is shaped by social structures more generally.

First, Baxandall observes that agents differ in their cognitive styles, which are clusters of interpretation skills, category concepts, and habits of making inferences and drawing analogies (see also Nisbett 2003; Masuda et al. 2008). Then he supposes that differences in cognitive style impact attention, hence the contents of agents' experiences. A third point is that different picture-appreciators, exhibiting different cognitive styles, answer more or less well to the perceptual demands of any given image. For example, he writes that,

a virtuosity in classifying the ductus of flexing lines—a skill many Germans possessed in [the fifteenth century]—or a functional knowledge of the surface musculature of the human body would not find much scope on [Piero's] *Annunciation*. Much of what we call "taste" lies in this, the conformity between discriminations demanded by a painting and skills of discrimination possessed by the beholder. (1972: 34)

Finally, some visual skills are endogenous, acquired specifically for looking at pictures (e.g. skills in detecting traces of the efforts of the artist). Endogenous pictorial skills dominate our thinking because they are often taught formally, using rules and standards expressed in a specialized vocabulary. Yet, most of the visual skills that we bring to pictures are exogenous, originally acquired to serve tasks outside imaging practices. For Baxandall, each "must use on the painting such visual skills as he has, very few of which are normally special to painting, and he is likely to use those skills his society esteems highly. The painter responds to this: his public's visual capacities must be his medium" (1972: 40).

As a historian, Baxandall's immediate goal is to detail how quattrocento paintings address the visual capacities of their audiences, including exogenous capacities that were originally adapted to social life, religious practice, and business affairs. Perhaps most delightful is his account of the capacity of the quattrocento eye for commercial gauging. In a time before standardized measures, anyone involved in business learned geometrical methods for gauging quantities. Baxandall quotes a contemporary textbook:

There is a barrel, each of its ends being 2 bracci in diameter; the diameter at its bung is $2\frac{1}{4}$ bracci and halfway between bung and end it is $2\frac{2}{9}$ bracci. The barrel is 2 bracci long. What is its cubic measure?

This is like a pair of truncated cones. Square the diameter at the ends: $2 \times 2 = 4$. Then square the median diameter $2\frac{2}{9} \times 2\frac{2}{9} = 4\frac{76}{81}$. Add them together: $8\frac{76}{81}$. Multiply $2 \times 2\frac{2}{9} = 4\frac{4}{9}$. Add this to $8\frac{76}{81} = 13\frac{31}{81}$. Divide by 3 = $4\frac{112}{243}$.... Now square $2\frac{1}{4} = 2\frac{1}{4} \times 2\frac{1}{4} = 5\frac{1}{16}$. Add it to the square of the median diameter: $15\frac{5}{16} + 4\frac{76}{81} = 10\frac{1}{129}$. Divide by 3: $5\frac{1}{3888}$. Add it to the first result: $4\frac{112}{243} + 5\frac{1}{3888} = 9\frac{1792}{3888}$. Multiply this by 11 and then divide by 14: the final result is $7\frac{23600}{54432}$.

Baxandall dryly adds, "it is a special intellectual world" (1972: 86). What is special is not just the dizzying arithmetic but also what precedes it, the automatic and comprehensive analysis of complex forms into combinations of regular geometrical solids. Quattrocento Italians brought their geometer's skill to looking at pictures that were made to be looked at with the same trained eye.

In as much as its operations raise chances of success in aesthetic appreciation, the practiced eye is an aesthetic competence. The point of Baxandall's book is to document the aesthetic impact of the quattrocento eye, in particular. For example, the gauger's geometrical operations yield a rich and vivid "sense of concrete mass" (Baxandall 1972: 91). Competence for aesthetic appreciation varies from practice to practice.

Any competence raises the probability of success. According to Baxandall, an act of aesthetic appreciation succeeds when the appreciator meets the demands of a picture—when the "skills of discrimination possessed by the beholder" yield an experience that conforms to the "discriminations demanded by a painting" (1972: 34). Successful aesthetic appreciation is successful apprehension of features of an item as features that are responsible for its having the aesthetic values that it has.

Aesthetic appreciation is often, but contingently, a source of pleasure. Baxandall endorses Aristotle's principle, writing that "we enjoy our own exercise of skill.... If a painting gives us an opportunity for exercising a valued skill and rewards our virtuosity with a sense of worthwhile insights about that painting's organization, we tend to enjoy it" (1972: 34). Thus he details how quattrocento Italians enjoyed the geometrical joke in a depiction of a hat by Uccello (1972: 89–91). To appreciate an item aesthetically is to apprehend it, aiming to get right its features and aesthetic values, by bringing to bear a practiced eye. The exercise of the practiced eye, like the exercise of any aesthetic competence, typically evokes facilitating pleasures—pleasures that are taken in activities that subserve productive agency.

Quattrocento image appreciation is exceptionally rarified, and one might wonder how well it models aesthetic appreciation overall. Are we wrong to think of aesthetic appreciation as a purely receptive condition wherein we seem to give ourselves over to pleasure? The story is told of how Clement Greenberg would situate himself before a painting, in the dark, clear his mind, and then say "Hit me!" to have the lights on. Less pompously, we all know immersion in the world of a novel, putting on the headphones and letting the music flow through us, or the moment of intense focus on the first sip of a wine, and how its flavour unfolds in the mouth.

As alluring as it might be, the thin conception of aesthetic appreciation as purely receptive falsely identifies the practiced eye with a deliberative faculty. The second the lights are on, Greenberg's vast store of knowledge kicks in, along with his advanced picture-reading skills, and the operation of his practiced eye proceeds largely automatically. We underestimate how much goes into learning, from infancy onwards, how to listen to music and taste flavours. Each act of aesthetic appreciation is the tip of an iceberg, floating atop a vast psychological infrastructure.

Fried tells how a painting in eighteenth-century France "had to call to someone, bring him to a halt in front of itself, and hold him there as if spellbound and unable to move" (1980: 92). Yet rapture was not simply visited upon habitués of the Parisian salons. Eighteenth-century salon-goers had to position themselves to meet the demand to be held spellbound. Meeting the demand put them in an impossible situation: since the spell was broken the minute they recognized their self-positioning, they had to maintain the dizzying pretence that the experience was induced in them by the painting alone. They had to mask their own pretence from themselves. In aid of this, one early ploy was to depict figures as utterly absorbed in some activity, hence unaware of the spectator, as in Chardin's *Soap Bubbles*. Maintaining the pretence that the absorbed figures were not in fact put there precisely so as to be caught unaware demanded exquisite mental manoeuvring, and the routine soon became too hard to keep up. New ploys had to be devised, and Fried (2008) argues that the game of cat and mouse continues to this day. At any rate, Fried's account suggests how pleasure can accrue as a by-product of our engaging in acts of aesthetic appreciation of which we make ourselves unaware.

For Baxandall and Fried, pictures demand specific appreciative competences. Aesthetic appreciators act within aesthetic practices where they operate at an artificially high level of competence, buoyed by the high level of competence exercised by coordinate experts, so that, on a good day, each achieves more than they would by operating solo. In many aesthetic networks, aesthetic appreciators occupy a key node. If Diana Raffman (2003) is right, composers of post-tonal music fail to achieve because they write pieces that demand appreciative competences that nobody can acquire. Without aesthetic appreciators, the practice is at risk. By the same token, aesthetic appreciators could not achieve success through the exercise of their competence without artists, editors, collectors, and other aesthetic specialists. None can do (literally do) without the others.

Is aesthetic appreciation essential to aesthetic practices? Without aesthetic evaluation, there can be no aesthetic acts, hence no aesthetic achievements, and no aesthetic agency. However, aesthetic appreciation is more demanding than aesthetic evaluation. Imagine post-tonal music losing its audience entirely... and yet persisting. Composers continue to write it, performers continue to play it, and critics continue to write texts that would guide the appreciations of its (counterfactual) target audience. Admittedly, the scenario is speculative. Notice, instead, the existence of aesthetic practices where there is no aesthetic appreciation, though competence in aesthetic appreciation is well within reach. Muzak, for example. The minute you turn your appreciative skill on some elevator music, you cease to appreciate it as music meant to remain in a background from which it can spread subliminal calm.

To sum up, aesthetic appreciation is a distinctive aesthetic act-type that implicates the exercise of a competence suited to the relevant aesthetic practice. Exercising the competence typically brings pleasure, though aesthetic appreciation is not in essence a pleasure-seeking activity. Finally, aesthetic appreciation is key to many, but not all, aesthetic practices.

A theory of aesthetic value had better place us in a situation that is the situation we are in. Since our perception of our situation is theory-laden, we can easily get it wrong. By first revealing and then pointing to explanations of the psychological situation of aesthetic agents, the network theory holds some surprises.

9

Endless to Dispute

The network theory had better represent our situation accurately, and that includes our discursive situation. Some have looked into the nature and point of aesthetic or critical discourse from a general point of view (e.g. Carroll 2009; Grant 2013). However, our discursive situation is pressing for a special reason. In 1956, W. B. Gallie wrote that,

> if we should hear about or happen upon a society whose aesthetic valuations showed as high a degree of uniformity, in respect both of particular assessments and general point of view, as do, say, our valuations of scientific achievement, we should be inclined to say that...its artistic life...was of an unhappily stinted kind. The question might even arise whether...they had an adequate appreciation of works of art at all. At any rate this supposition helps us to recognise that uniformity of judgment and appraisal, although so necessary in many fields of activity, is by no means necessary or even desirable in all. In any field of activity in which achievements are prized because they renew or advance a highly complex tradition, the point of view from which our appraisals are made...would seem always to be of the kind I have called "essentially contested." (1956: 114)

The past sixty years have piled on the evidence that Gallie was on the mark. Aesthetic discourse is shot through with aesthetic disputes, which do seem to be an essential fixture of the aesthetic realm. Yet, according to the network theory, interactions between agents in an aesthetic practice require them to form a consensus around an aesthetic profile. Does the theory get our aesthetic situation right? Is there consensus or is dispute essential? As in Chapter 8, the task is to use the theory both to obtain an accurate read on our situation and then also to explain it.

Both Sides Now

Let us begin, aptly enough, with the meta-dispute about aesthetic disputes.

From an early age we are taught that there is no disputing taste (Nichols and Folds-Bennett 2003; Cova and Pain 2012). Old saws aside, there are scads of disputes concerning aesthetics. As Hickey remarks, exclamations of beauty are "more often than not... followed by talk—by comparisons, advocacy, analysis, and dissent" (2009: 70). Running through much of the chatter as you exit the cinema, or the car dealership, are frank, sincere, passionate, and persistent exchanges about aesthetic merits and flaws. No surprise here: *Homo sapiens* is *Homo disputans*. The philosophy gets interesting with the claim that aesthetic disputes are faultless disagreements. That is, parties to aesthetic disputes frequently disagree, when their disagreement is not due to inattention, ignorance, insincerity, pretence, or inadvertence (Goldman 1990: 34–5; Bender 1996: 371–2).

In many other domains, disagreement is welcome and yet to be overcome, and the task of overcoming it is treated with some urgency. Not so when it comes to aesthetic disputes. Isabel Hungerland observes that "in moral matters, we must achieve some large measure of agreement or be annihilated. In science, we must require agreement or abandon the project.... In art, we can be out of step with the rest of the world without endangering a single soul or abandoning the enterprise" (1968: 288; see also Goldman 1995: 144–7). Perhaps Hungerland understates how much the charm of our aesthetic activities seemingly hangs on in their freeing us to be quite safely and enjoyably out of step with one another. Nobody puts it better than Nehamas:

imagine, if you can, a world where everyone likes, or loves, the same things, where every disagreement about beauty can be resolved. That would be a desolate, desperate world.... What is truly frightful is not *what* everyone likes but simply the fact that *everyone* likes it. Even the idea that everyone might share *one* of my judgements sends shivers down my spine. (2007: 83–4)

In philosophy and science, disagreement can bring us closer to the truth, but those enterprises ultimately aim to extinguish disagreement. If Nehamas is right, aesthetic disagreement is not to be used to hasten its own demise.

That is one take on our situation, and the network theory suggests a very different take.

When it comes to what we like, there is very often little pressure for appreciators to converge. Standardized aesthetic hedonism turns up the pressure, in as much as it implies that we aesthetically ought to take the same amount of pleasure in the same things. That said, the most we lose when we do diverge is some opportunity for pleasure, so the pressure to converge remains relatively low.

By contrast, the network theory takes aesthetic reasons to be practical reasons for agents to conduct all kinds of aesthetic business within cooperative social networks. Their disputes about what to do are likely to obstruct immediate action and to inhibit future cooperation. Network theorists cannot sign off on Hungerland's alluring idea that aesthetic agents can carry on out of step without endangering the enterprise. Like other practical disputes, aesthetic disputes are to be overcome, not embraced.

Where there is cooperation, advice-giving is never far off, and aesthetic practices include practices of giving advice. As we tend to our own aesthetic capabilities, we also attend to others', and we have every reason to exchange appraisals of those we rely upon to perform well. Obviously, practices of giving advice wither unless advice is taken, and advice is taken only when there is a decent chance of agreement. The fact that aesthetic agents (have reason to) exchange advice seems to tug against observations about widespread faultless aesthetic disagreement.

Data: Beyond Faultless Disagreement

Disputes are verbal, expressed in words. Therefore, to get an accurate read on our discursive situation, we need to know what we are saying and why, so we need some apparatus to characterize first the semantics and then the point of aesthetic discourse. Some argue that faultless aesthetic disagreement is best explained on a relativist semantics (Kölbel 2003; Kölbel 2004; Lasersohn 2005; Kölbel 2008; MacFarlane 2005; Stephenson 2007; García-Carpintero and Kölbel 2008; Egan 2010; Brogaard 2017). The alternative semantics is indexicalist or perspectivist (Beardsley 1983; López de Sa 2007; Sundell 2011; Barker 2013; Mole 2016; Davies 2017; Lopes 2017b, Sundell 2017; see also Wright 2010). The network theory implies aesthetic perspectivism, which reconciles the existence of faultless aesthetic disagreement with pressure on aesthetic agents to reach consensus and get on with things.

The logic is this. The network theory implies a perspectivist semantics for aesthetic discourse, which yields a good read on our discursive situation. Aesthetic perspectivism and aesthetic relativism are contraries. The classic argument for aesthetic relativism is that it best explains faultless aesthetic disagreement. The argument for aesthetic perspectivism is that it better explains all the facts about aesthetic disputes. This section lays out the facts; the next, on "The Relativist Challenge," characterizes the two semantic options.

Five facts need explaining, and the first is that aesthetic disputes are verbal exchanges that deserve to be called disagreements. Parties to a disagreement must be at odds with each other; there must be some conflict. The conflict must be aesthetic in the sense that it withstands agreement on all the relevant non-aesthetic facts. Parties disagree aesthetically about an item only if joint acceptance of a complete, non-aesthetic description of the item would not bring them into full agreement. Beyond this, some care is needed to home in on what counts as disagreement.

An obvious proposal is that A and B disagree only if some utterance by A expresses a proposition, p, and an utterance by B expresses a proposition, q, where q entails not-p. However, the obvious proposal will not do. As Timothy Sundell points out, there are disagreements where parties assert consistent propositions (2017: 88). In his example,

A: Vegemite tastes good to me.
B: Well, it doesn't taste good to me. Try it again. Have you noticed how salty it is?

To capture the full gamut of cases, let disagreement be the relation between speakers that licenses linguistic denial (Sundell 2011: 274). Linguistic denials fit the general schema:

A: p.
B: Nope, q.

An aesthetic disagreement occurs whenever linguistic denial is felicitous.

Second, aesthetic disagreements are sometimes faultless. By itself, disagreement is unremarkable. What is remarkable is that it sometimes seems that, as Andy Egan puts it, "both parties to the dispute are getting it right" and neither is "warranted in making the assumption that one or the other of them must be getting it wrong" (2010: 263; see also Foot 2003[1979]: 22). Put another way, it would not be an improvement for either party to give up what they assert; there is nothing that either of them could learn that would make it better for them to end the dispute (Kölbel 2003: 53–4). Needless to say, parties to aesthetic disputes are sometimes at fault, impaired by ignorance, bias, wonky logic, or some other pertinent cognitive shortcoming. Only some cases of aesthetic disagreement are faultless.

Third, aesthetic disagreements appear to track, and mark, social boundaries. Some boundaries are cultural, as in Derek Matravers's example of "a Japanese critic who finds Wright of Derby clunky and unsubtle and a British critic who finds Utamaro's flower pictures overly pretty and sentimental" (2010: 1). More finely individuated social groups also tend to aesthetic disagreement—contrast adolescent inhabitants of the San Fernando Valley with BFA students at California Institute of the Arts (CalArts). Within any group, aesthetic agreement is regulated. Readers of this book who venture that *Paradise Lost* is frivolous or who deny the ardour of Foofwa d'Imobilité's dance performances jeopardize their standing in the academic elites to which they (aspire to) belong. They are likely to be accused of "extravagance," in Hume's diplomatic parlance (1777: 232).

Fourth, aesthetic disputes principally orient upon items of aesthetic interest, rather than traits of the disputing parties. In sharing our judgements with others, we sometimes do reveal ourselves and invite them to make reciprocal disclosures. Usually, though, we are less interested in ourselves and each other than in "A Love Supreme," Ferrante's Neapolitan novels, a champion Puli, or the Lulu Island tidal flats. When the aim is to reveal something personal, what we reveal is how we are attuned to items like these. Aesthetic disputes principally concern the aesthetic merits and flaws of objects of aesthetic evaluation and only secondarily concern the traits of aesthetic evaluators.

Finally, aesthetic disputes are persistent. I enjoy crème brûlée; you do not. Once we exchange the information, there is little more to say on the matter. Disputes about what we simply enjoy quickly fizzle. When it comes to aesthetic disputes, the norm is: put up a reason or shut up. Philippa Foot writes that,

> if we actually have something to say in criticism of the art of some other time or some other culture, as that it is sentimental, we expect to be able to show that this is so.... If there were genuinely nothing to say and nothing to show,... we would be most unlikely to insist that somehow, nevertheless, we must be right.   (2003[1972]: 15)

Through aesthetic disputes we characterize items of interest, like Ferrante's writing or the Lulu Island tidal flats, and we characterize ourselves to each other. To give characterizations of both kinds, we drill down into the details.

The Relativist Challenge

Looking over a Joseph Wright landscape painting, a Japanese and a British critic exchange words . . .

A: This painting is clunky.
B: No, it's not.

Here each asserts an aesthetic judgement, neither is at fault, but they disagree. The classic argument for aesthetic relativism is this: aesthetic relativism does a better job than aesthetic perspectivism at explaining faultless aesthetic disagreement. Since everyone who debates the matter assumes aesthetic hedonism, some fiddling is needed to retrofit the argument as a challenge to the network theory.

Aesthetic perspectivism exploits the thought that what proposition a sentence expresses is determined by facts about its context of use and context of assessment. A sentence that expresses one proposition in one context of use or assessment expresses a different proposition in another context of use or assessment. In my mouth, "I'm Scottish" expresses the proposition that Lopes is Scottish, but it expresses the proposition that Brigitte Bardot is Scottish when she speaks it. Hence, according to aesthetic perspectivism, both A and B speak truly because what proposition each expresses is determined by a parameter whose value is a contextually determined aesthetic practice. Belonging to the *ukiyo-e* aesthetic practice, A expresses the proposition that the landscape is clunky by the lights of that practice. Belonging to the aesthetic practice of English romantic painting, B expresses the proposition that the landscape is not clunky by the lights of that practice. Both propositions are true, and both A and B speak truly. They differ in their use of "clunky," or in their idea of clunkiness.

Now the objection to perspectivism. Perspectivism explains why neither A nor B is at fault: each judges by the lights of their aesthetic practice. However, perspectivism does not represent their exchange as a disagreement, for it does not make one party out to assert a proposition that the other denies. A asserts that the landscape is clunky according to one perspective. B asserts that it is not clunky according to a different perspective. Neither denies what the other asserts.

To remedy the fault, aesthetic relativism represents one speaker as asserting the very same proposition as the other denies. On a relativist semantics, facts about the context of use and the context of assessment determine not what proposition is expressed but rather the truth of the proposition expressed. Contexts of assessment are commonly thought to be set by world and time parameters; aesthetic relativists add an aesthetic standard parameter. Thus the truth of one and the same proposition varies as it is assessed against different aesthetic standards.

Aesthetic relativism explains how some aesthetic exchanges can be faultless disagreements. A asserts the proposition that the landscape is clunky whereas B denies that very proposition, so they disagree in the sense that one denies a proposition that the other asserts. Yet the truth of that proposition varies with their aesthetic standard. A speaks truly by expressing a proposition that is true relative to the standard of her aesthetic practice, while B speaks truly by expressing a proposition that is true relative to the standard of his aesthetic practice. If each speaks truly and correctly and each applies the standard for their aesthetic practice, then neither is at fault.

So goes the classic argument for aesthetic relativism, and the argument initiates a challenge to the network theory, as long as the theory implies aesthetic perspectivism. Does the theory imply aesthetic perspectivism? Is it not consistent with aesthetic relativism?

On a relativist interpretation, A and B agree on the Wright's non-aesthetic features, and they exercise the same concept of clunkiness, but they correctly apply the concept to different items. A speaks truly relative to the standard of her aesthetic practice, while B speaks truly relative to the standard of his aesthetic practice. The idea is that aesthetic standards vary even as aesthetic value concepts remain fixed, and it is this idea that the network theory blocks.

Although the theory does understand aesthetic practices as providing different aesthetic standards, the standard for each practice is its aesthetic profile, where an aesthetic profile is a pattern of correlations that obtains between the aesthetic value properties of items in a practice and some other properties of the items. Those who conform to the *ukiyo-e* standard have a concept of clunkiness that applies to items having one range of non-aesthetic features, while those who conform to the English romantic standard have a different concept of clunkiness that applies to items having a different range of non-aesthetic features. According to the network theory, a difference in aesthetic standards implies a difference in the application conditions of aesthetic value concepts. If A and B have different concepts of clunkiness, then they cannot express the same proposition by describing the painting as clunky. The network theory is incompatible with aesthetic relativism.

In fact, as this reasoning suggests, the network theory implies aesthetic perspectivism. Aesthetic profiles correlate distributions of aesthetic values with distributions of certain other properties. The aesthetic profile of *ukiyo-e* correlates clunkiness with certain surface marks, masses, and colours that are not the same as those associated with clunkiness in the aesthetic profile of English romantic painting. Hence, A and B share a determinable concept of clunkiness but apply different determinate concepts. When A asserts that the painting is clunky, she speaks truly, because she expresses a proposition that applies the *ukiyo-e* concept of clunkiness. When B denies that the painting is clunky, he speaks truly because he expresses a proposition that applies the English romantic concept of clunkiness. A and B express different propositions, applying different aesthetic value concepts.

The challenge to the network theory can be put as a dilemma. On one hand, if A and B deploy the very same concept of clunkiness, then one asserts a proposition and the other denies that very proposition. A speaks truly relative to the standard of her aesthetic practice, and B speaks truly relative to the standard of his aesthetic practice. In that case, aesthetic standards are not aesthetic profiles, and the network theory is false. On the other hand, what if A and B do not deploy the very same determinate concept of clunkiness (even if they share a determinable concept)? Now they do not disagree in the sense that one asserts a proposition that the other denies. The network theory does not explain the phenomenon of faultless aesthetic disagreement. The theory is in a pickle.

Aesthetic Profiles in Perspective

The reply grasps the second horn of the dilemma. The network theory does imply aesthetic perspectivism, but aesthetic perspectivism better explains the facts about aesthetic discourse.

First, aesthetic disputes are verbal exchanges that deserve to be called disagreements. Parties to a disagreement must be at odds with each other; there must be some conflict. The classic argument is that, according to aesthetic perspectivism, A and B express consistent propositions, so they do not disagree in the sense that one expresses a proposition that the other denies. By contrast, on a relativist interpretation, A does indeed assert the very proposition that B goes on to deny.

However, while it is true that aesthetic relativism explains how A and B disagree, the same goes for aesthetic perspectivism, provided that disagreement does not require logical contradiction. Disagreement occurs whenever linguistic denial is felicitous, as it is in the exchange between A and B. Many circumstances license linguistic denial. For present purposes, one is important: linguistic denial is felicitous whenever speakers exchange words for the purpose of metalinguistic calibration.

Suppose that A is seconded from a French bistro to B's sushi bar and is helping to sharpen a *sashimi bōchō*:

A: This one is sharp.
B: No, not yet.

In this non-aesthetic disagreement, A and B use an adjective metalinguistically, to make precise what it means in the context (Barker 2002). Perhaps they agree about the absolute sharpness of the blade, but a knife whose edge is sharp for one context can be dull in another context. Their disagreement is a mechanism for determining what counts as sharp in context—for calibrating on the concept of sharpness that the context requires them to apply.

Aesthetic value concepts, such as clunky and elegant, are notoriously vague when we try to use them out of context, but they are extremely precise when applied to specific items in specific practices. What is playful elegance? It is a mug's game to think about that in abstraction. Go visit Kathryn Gustafson's Princess Diana Memorial Fountain in Hyde Park: it is easy to see exactly how it is playfully elegant.

According to the network theory, aesthetic concepts need to be made precise if they are to serve agents who are trying to cooperate with one another. Aesthetic disagreement is a mechanism for calibrating aesthetic concepts in accordance with the aesthetic profile that is in play in a context (Sundell 2011: 278–9; Barker

2013; Sundell 2017). To serve this purpose, aesthetic disagreement need not consist in parties asserting propositions that others deny. Consider the exchange over the Wright landscape painting. A and B assert consistent propositions. What counts as clunky is not the same in different painting practices, and the disagreement is a disagreement on what the practice is—that is, about its aesthetic profile, which correlates non-aesthetic features with being clunky.

Aesthetic perspectivism therefore explains how aesthetic disputes are disagreements, on a conception of disagreement that matters.

Second, aesthetic disagreements are sometimes faultless. Neither A nor B is troubled by ignorance, bias, wonky logic, or some other pertinent cognitive shortcoming. This fact aesthetic perspectivism also explains. According to aesthetic relativism, A and B speak truly in accordance with the relevant aesthetic standard. According to aesthetic perspectivism, both A and B speak truly in accordance with the aesthetic profile of the aesthetic practice to which they belong.

So, with respect to the first two explananda, aesthetic perspectivism and relativism are running neck and neck. What about the facts that aesthetic disputes are socially patterned, item-oriented, and persistent? How well does each semantic theory explain these facts? Start with aesthetic relativism.

The third explanandum was that aesthetic disagreement tracks, and marks, social boundaries. Aesthetic relativism explains this fact when paired with what might be called the "Michigan approach" to the point of aesthetic discourse. On the Michigan approach, aesthetic discourse either signals or brings about a shared aesthetic sensibility that conforms to an aesthetic standard (Railton 2000; Egan 2010; cf. Kivy 2015). Thus Egan argues that aesthetic disputes serve to signal a shared sensibility when disputants presuppose, and have to reason to presuppose, that they will respond alike. In cases where there is no presupposition of a shared sensibility, aesthetic disputes bring about a shared sensibility (Egan 2010: 273–4). For example, a speaker can make an assertion that would be felicitous only given a presumption of similarity, intending that the audience will recognize this fact and accommodate the assertion by bringing the similarity into effect. A schoolyard aesthetic bully, knowing that the new kids go in for *Barney and Friends*, yanks them into conformity by declaring, "Barney is lame." The new kids understand that the bully is presuming that they will share her taste, and they accommodate her assertion by coming to agree that Barney is lame.

With the Michigan approach as backstory, Egan explains that discovering a shared sensibility is important in "building and maintaining interpersonal relationships, and in establishing and maintaining ties to communities and groups. Very many groups and subcultures are defined, at least in part, by the common aesthetic sensibilities of their members" (2010: 260; see also Goldman 2006: 339). He consequently predicts that "we will have many more sensible aesthetic disputes with our friends and neighbors" than with those very different in sensibility (2010: 264).

The trouble is that the aesthetic relativist's explanation of the sociality of aesthetic disputes is in tension with their persistence and orientation on items.

The fourth fact was that aesthetic disputes principally concern the aesthetic merits and flaws of objects of aesthetic evaluation, and only secondarily concern the traits of evaluators. According to the Michigan approach, the point of aesthetic disputes is for parties to self-attribute aesthetic sensibilities, so that we attribute values to items in order to attribute sensibilities to ourselves. Granted, an item can sometimes serve as a litmus test for aesthetic sensibility. A candidate for employment at the haberdasher is asked for their view on the design of a necktie as a test of their suitability for the job. That granted, the point of aesthetic disputes is, in typical cases, to get right the item's features. Take the following exchange over Franzen's *Freedom* (Myers 2010; Tanenhaus 2010):

M: The book radiates a profound moral intelligence.
T: No, it's a 576-page monument to insignificance.

A tiff like this is not a roundabout way for Tanenhaus to contrast his post-Seinfeld style with Myers's Leavisite sensibility.

Finally, aesthetic disputes are persistent. Michiganers suggest the following. Wishing to signal our shared sensibility, you and I might announce opinions on an item's beauty. However, an exchange of simple verdicts fails to establish a common sensibility. We might agree to absolutely nothing except that Franzen's novel is good, though we seek a similarity in response over a range of cases. Hence aesthetic disputes persist by digging down to details. Imagine a disagreement about *Downton Abbey*:

R: The writing is sophisticated.
S: No, it isn't.

If the point is to detect or bring about a shared sensibility across a range of cases, then R might next try, "*House of Cards* is sophisticated" on the supposition that continued disagreement might indicate that S's sensibility is too highbrow for the entertainment R has in mind. The target of judgement might roam freely across genres, and the conversation might to turn to music or fashion.

While there is nothing irrational in such a conversation, a significantly different pattern of reasoning will occur when the topic is to make good on the initial verdict about *Downton Abbey*. For example:

    ... R: There are many plot twists and the characters change radically.
         S: But there's no attempt at distance or irony, as in *Gosford Park*.
         R: *Gosford Park* is Altman; *Downton Abbey* is soap in period dress.

Here R and S attempt to get the target right by understanding it in relation to its genre. When another item is brought in for comparison, it is to align on the aesthetic profile of the genre. This fact is not predicted by the hypothesis that the point of aesthetic disputes is principally to self-attribute an aesthetic sensibility.

Meanwhile, aesthetic perspectivism directly explains the facts with which aesthetic relativism struggles. Why do aesthetic disputes principally focus on items? And why do they persist as they do? Both questions get one answer. The purpose of an aesthetic dispute is to get an item right, by getting the practice right, by getting its aesthetic profile right. In the case of the exchange between A and B, the task is to find out what practice the Wright landscape belongs to—namely, English romantic landscape painting—and thereby to trace the contours of the relevant aesthetic profile. In the case of the Franzen, Myers and Tanenhaus know that *Freedom* is a work of American postmodern fiction: their task is to get it right by tracing the contours of the aesthetic profile of the practice.

How does this claim explain the item-orientation and persistence of aesthetic disputes? The way to trace the contours of an aesthetic profile is to survey correlations between aesthetic values and some other properties. That means examining items. Moreover, it can rarely suffice to look at one aesthetic value in one item. Disputes will persist because parties dig down into greater detail on an item, examining many aesthetic values and many other properties with which the values correlate. Disputes will also persist because aesthetic values are multiply realized, so that it makes sense to examine a range of items in the practice, as when S contrasts *Downtown Abbey* with *Gosford Park*. Only having gone through the exercise of examining items to trace the contours of an aesthetic profile can agents attribute to themselves such traits as having a concept of clunkiness, aligning on an aesthetic profile, or having a relevant competence in aesthetic evaluation.

On this hypothesis, aesthetic disputes no longer serve their purpose, and will tend to fizzle, once an interlocutor signals that they do not participate in the relevant practice. Imagine a further continuation of the *Downtown Abbey* debate:

    ... R: *Gosford Park* is Altman. *Downton Abbey* is soap in period dress.
         S: Yeah, so what?

Now S stands by his opening assertion by refusing to judge the series for what it is, and there is no point in a reply from R.

Only the third explanandum remains. Aesthetic disputes track, and mark, social boundaries. Aesthetic perspectivism obviously predicts this fact. If aesthetic disputes metalinguistically bring aesthetic value concepts into line with an aesthetic profile, then they track social practices, because aesthetic practices are social practices. Aesthetic relativism also predicts that we will tend to engage in aesthetic disputes with friends and neighbours. So does aesthetic perspectivism. If aesthetic practices are social practices, then they will tend to involve friends and neighbours as participants (see Chapter 7). In the dispute about the Wright landscape, a difference between the practices of *ukiyo-e* and English romantic painting will tend to map onto a cultural difference.

A semantics for aesthetic discourse should explain why it is fit to serve the purpose of aesthetic disputes. Parties to a dispute about a painting's clunkiness might disagree in the sense that linguistic denial is felicitous, and neither is at fault as long as they take the perspectives of different practices. The point of their dispute is to converge on what the practice is. Aesthetic perspectivism treats the clunkiness of the Wright landscape as it treats the sharpness of a *sashimi bōchō*. Disagreeing about the landscape's clunkiness is a way to sort out what aesthetic profile is in play. The dispute has a social dimension, even as it is persistently oriented on the landscape.

Whereas aesthetic relativism offers an explanation of the sociality of aesthetic disputes that is in tension with their persistence and their orientation on items, aesthetic perspectivism explains all three facts in one go. Since it better explains the facts, it is true. The network theory implies it: chalk one up for the network theory.

Dynamic Consensus

Equipped with a richer picture of the point of aesthetic disputes, and a semantics to suit, the time has come to reconcile the existence of faultless aesthetic disagreement with pressure on aesthetic agents to reach consensus and get on with things. On one hand, the network theory requires consensus on the aesthetic profile of a practice; on the other hand, the realm of the aesthetic seems to be essentially disputatious. The key to reconciliation is to recognize the dynamism of aesthetic practices.

Like most social practices, aesthetic practices are living entities that change over their lifetimes. While some are conservative, hardly changing, others exhibit a freewheeling dynamism. (Incidentally, the spectrum from conservative to freewheeling is not the spectrum from the traditional to the contemporary. It is pure myth that traditional aesthetic culture is slow to change. Tradition is what lasts, often by adapting itself, and the latest hot fad might fail to adapt.) An explanation of the dynamism of aesthetic practices should also explain why footloose practices do not change unchecked. To adapt Blackburn's metaphor, there must a speed limit on aesthetic dynamism, for where too much changes too fast, nothing can count as an ongoing practice (1998: 67).

The network theory already explains why participants in a practice have reason to go along with modifications to the practice's aesthetic profile. They have reason to go along with a modification when they will do better as aesthetic agents, raising their chances of aesthetic achievement. Just by acting on the aesthetic reasons they have, members of a practice can come to align today on an aesthetic profile that is a modification of yesterday's aesthetic profile. The mechanism is obviously inefficient, though. To gain efficiency, we can use our words. When change leaders, who fall out of step with their peers, give voice to their new vision, they can bring others along. Aesthetic disputes lubricate aesthetic dynamism.

Aesthetic perspectivism explains how. Imagine a greeting card practice that shifts from an aesthetic profile organized around an earnest sentimentality to one of gentle irony. Earnest E and ironic J exchange words.

E: Send this card. It's sweet.
J: No, it's not sweet enough.

Each presupposes that they judge the card in a practice whose aesthetic profile befits their judgement. In as much as what counts as sweet is not the same in different aesthetic profiles, their disagreement is about what the profile is for the practice. In disagreeing about the card's sweetness they attempt to establish the aesthetic profile. As their dispute persists, they drill down into the card's other aesthetic merits and demerits, as a way to zero in on the profile. The profile changes as J's way of seeing things, represented by her use of "sweet" and other value terms, catches on and becomes the norm, either bringing E on board, or leaving him in the dust. Given aesthetic perspectivism and the network theory, we should predict that aesthetic disputes play a major role in changing the profiles internal to aesthetic practices.

Meanwhile, aesthetic perspectivism also predicts the speed limit on aesthetic dynamism. Mere talk cannot induce breakneck dynamism. Suppose J is Judith Butler, who wants not gentle irony but the oppositional kind. She and her earnest interlocutor might find, as they drill down, that they use none of their aesthetic value terms alike. Without sufficient common ground, what reason have we to think that they disagree about the profile of one and the same practice, rather than two different practices?

Jonathan Neufeld (2015) shows how art practices are put under pressure to reform through acts of aesthetic disobedience—and the same goes for non-art aesthetic practices. Acts of aesthetic disobedience are communicative acts that violate the norms of a practice, in order to draw attention to conflicting norms and thereby promote reform within the practice.

So understood, aesthetic disobedience is something exceptional. Aesthetic disputes need not involve aesthetic disobedience, for disputants can modify the aesthetic profile of a practice without violating core aesthetic norms (see Chapter 7). They get the object right, evaluating only items in K using the aesthetic profile of K. They also get the practice right, never making aesthetic evaluations of items in K that are inconsistent with the pattern of correlations that really is K's aesthetic profile. The dynamism of aesthetic practices is often managed through disputes between parties who exercise core aesthetic competence.

Rarely is consensus static; aesthetic agents interact against a background of changing consensus. Some of the dynamism of aesthetic practices is driven by technological as well as larger social factors, but credit also goes to the avant-garde radicals, bold aesthetic visionaries, and unshakeable small-time innovators, who were out of step with their peers. Their disagreements lubricate aesthetic dynamism. In consequence, aesthetic perspectivism explains why Gallie is right about the essentially contested nature of aesthetic concepts, and the network theory implies aesthetic perspectivism.

Vulgar Relativism and the Limits of Aesthetic Disputes

If you have taught aesthetics to first- or second-year undergraduates, then you will know about some knee-jerk opposition to a crucial assumption of this chapter. So far, the assumption has been that faultless aesthetic disagreement typically serves a useful purpose. According to the Michigan approach, the point of aesthetic disputes is to signal an aesthetic sensibility in a search for others with a similar sensibility. According to the network theory, aesthetic disputes facilitate the interactions of aesthetic agents by bringing them into alignment with dynamic aesthetic profiles. Against this, the opposition insists that there really is no disputing matters aesthetic. Moreover, the opposition is so tenacious that regular arguments will not cut it; we need an error theory.

The knee-jerk opposition is a case of what Williams (1972) calls "vulgar relativism." Vulgar aesthetic relativism joins two thoughts. The first thought interprets the claim that there is no disputing matters aesthetic. Since people do in fact dispute matters aesthetic, the claim is normative, an injunction to the effect that we should not engage in aesthetic disputes with members of other aesthetic communities. For example, A should not dispute with B about the Wright landscape because A and B belong to different aesthetic communities. The second thought is a theory of the injunction. We should not engage in aesthetic disputes with members of other aesthetic communities because their evaluations are true, though inconsistent with our evaluations, which are also true (Williams 1972: 20).

Vulgar aesthetic relativism obviously straddles shaky ground. For one thing, aesthetic relativism does not entail the injunction—it is consistent with the Michigan approach to the point of aesthetic disputes. In addition, we have very good reason to prefer aesthetic perspectivism to aesthetic relativism. Nevertheless, vulgar aesthetic relativism taps a deep instinct we have about how we stand with respect to aesthetic practices to which we do not belong, and that instinct gets expressed as a combination of aesthetic relativism with the injunction against aesthetic disputes with outsiders. The situation calls for an error theory.

Vulgar aesthetic relativists prohibit aesthetic disputes whenever there is a confrontation between members of different aesthetic practices. Williams distinguishes real from notional confrontations (1975: 221–4). In a real confrontation, participants in one practice have a real option of going over to the other practice. That is, they could abide by its norms within their actual social and historical circumstances—the "could" represents social and historical possibility. Given variability in how much of a group's social and historical circumstances remains in place as they go over to a new practice, real options are a matter of degree. Aesthetic confrontations run the gamut from real to notional—from confrontations between nearby practices and confrontations between practices that are distant from each other.

Williams diagnoses vulgar relativism as an attempt to treat all confrontations as notional (1975: 226). In notional aesthetic confrontations, aesthetic disputes are pointless. They cannot signal a shared or shareable aesthetic sensibility, and they cannot help disputants to calibrate to an aesthetic profile. With the focus on notional confrontations, aesthetic relativism has its attractions. An entomologist describes a specimen of *Periplaneta americana* as handsome, and you just cannot go there. If you deny the very proposition that she asserts, because your exchange involves a very vague concept of being handsome, then perhaps it is best to think that you both speak truly, without fault, and chances are the dispute will not persist. Since nobody should engage in pointless aesthetic disputes, the injunction is reasonable.

In point of fact, not all aesthetic confrontations are notional. We should be grateful: were all aesthetic confrontations notional, we could not outgrow our childish interests and we would be locked in aesthetic silos. Surely it would be silly to invoke the injunction against an aesthetic dispute between experts in Russian River and Okanagan Pinot Noirs, or between them and a Burgundy expert. Vulgar aesthetic relativism is insanely pessimistic about real aesthetic confrontation. To be fair, some are possibly too optimistic. Greg Currie thinks that everything aesthetic is available to everyone: "there are no sheer aesthetic cliffs that require heroic endeavour before we can glimpse the riches above us" (2011: 111). Is aesthetic activity the exception to the rule that we each have our limits?

The network theory explains the attraction of vulgar aesthetic relativism. First, it predicts a spectrum of real to notional aesthetic confrontations. Second, it upholds an injunction against engaging in aesthetic disputes when confrontations are notional, or close to notional. Third, it predicts that many aesthetic confrontations will appear to be more notional than they are.

An agent's path to an unfamiliar aesthetic practice is all the smoother as its aesthetic profile overlaps with that of a familiar practice. What it takes for a tune to swing in big band is similar to what it takes for a tune to swing in bebop. The rhythmic differences are noticeable but not huge. By engaging in persistent exchanges with bebop insiders about what swings, a big band expert can efficiently calibrate on the bebop aesthetic profile.

By the same token, the path from a familiar to an unfamiliar aesthetic practice is going to be rockier the more their aesthetic profiles differ. Sometimes aesthetic profiles differ so much that some relatively determinable value properties fail to cross over. Nothing swings in lieder. When relatively determinable aesthetic value properties do cross over, the difference between their determinates can be considerable. The motion vectors that make for emphatic movements in tap are very different from those that make for emphatic movement in ballet. In cases such as these, disagreements about what swings or what is emphatic less effectively shift profiles.

Aesthetic disputes more effectively recalibrate on an unfamiliar aesthetic profile to the extent that a confrontation is more real and less notional. When confrontations are very notional, aesthetic disputes cannot recalibrate on the confronted aesthetic profile. Since nobody should engage in pointless aesthetic disputes, it is reasonable to invoke the injunction in notional confrontations. That was the second point.

Third, the network theory predicts that many aesthetic confrontations will appear to be more notional than they are. Core aesthetic competence in aesthetic evaluation is a skill acquired through repeated effortful trying. Even low-level perceptual, motor, and affective skills can be implicated. Studies of the unconscious and subconsciously controlled ocular saccades and fixations of subjects looking at paintings find marked differences between expert and non-expert viewers (Vogt and Magnussen 2007). Likewise, Richard Nisbett (2003) and his collaborators have studied differences in cognitive style between North Americans and East Asians—for example, East Asians attend more to social and contextual information than do North Americans. The same difference in cognitive style impacts the compositions of drawings and digital photographs made by North American versus East Asian subjects (Masuda et al. 2008).

The point is not that retooling core aesthetic competence is easier said than done, though that is true. Rather, it is impossible to imagine what it is, and what it takes, to acquire a core aesthetic capacity in an aesthetic practice whose profile is very different from any familiar profile. What is impossible to imagine is frequently imagined as impossible.

At the heart of vulgar relativism lies an instinct, which is a good one. Some confrontations are notional, where it makes sense to proscribe aesthetic disputes. All the same, notional confrontations are more and more the exception in our global village. Mostly, aesthetic disputes serve our needs as aesthetic agents.

The network theory predicts that the more we understand each other while preserving our differences, the more we will engage in sensible aesthetic disputes. Aesthetic disputes are part and parcel of aesthetic culture. So, too, is a commitment to suspend judgement when mutual understanding reaches, for now, its limits.

10

Beauty, Naturally

One last time... the situation where the network theory places us had better be the situation we are in. Aesthetic values occupy our familiar world alongside agents and the items they act upon. The buoyant scent of Creed's Vetiver fills the room, and we hear the sassiness of a duet by Tony Bennett and Lady Gaga. Being buoyant and being sassy are values with which we are acquainted. Yet the concrete reality of aesthetic values sometimes puzzles us, as when we feel the pull of an ancient though murky meme that opposes value to reality. Our puzzlement draws us into metaphysics.

Aesthetics Meets Metaphysics

As always, the network theory explains our situation partly by bringing into focus what needs to be explained. To this end, the prime directive is to never lose sight of the puzzlement that caused us to roll in the machinery of metaphysics in the first place. Care is needed to neutralize the effects of two distractors in particular.

One is moral metaphysics. Suppose we impose the standard map of the logical space of metaethics onto the landscape of aesthetics. Aesthetic cognitivism is the view that some evaluations accurately or inaccurately attribute aesthetic values, or some aesthetic judgements are truth-apt, or we sometimes assert that x is V. Aesthetic non-cognitivism holds the contrary, while aesthetic nihilism conjoins aesthetic cognitivism with the claim that no aesthetic evaluations are true or accurate. According to aesthetic realism, some facts are aesthetic value facts—facts of the form "x is V." Aesthetic non-realism denies that there are aesthetic value facts.

The metaethics map is useful because it locates areas of hot dispute in ethics. Not so when the map is imposed on aesthetics. Aesthetic non-cognitivism, nihilism, and non-realism are not positions that philosophers have seriously sought to win and hold. Maybe (just maybe) Isenberg (1949) is an aesthetic non-cognitivist. Those who bestir themselves to take a stand lean heavily to aesthetic cognitivism (Diffey 1967; Kivy 1980; Hopkins 2001; McGonigal 2006;

Meskin 2006; Kivy 2015; Strandberg 2016). Meanwhile, specialists have zero appetite for aesthetic nihilism (Mackie 1977 is no specialist). Finally, aesthetic non-realism has few takers, and only a tiny number have undertaken to make the case against it (Todd 2004 vs. Sibley 1968; Hopkins 2001; Meskin 2006; Mole 2016).

Philosophers, being philosophers, are too often tempted to occupy unoccupied positions for no better reason than that they find them unoccupied. Giving into the temptation risks losing sight of the puzzlement that prompted us to metaphysics in the first place. We end up doing metaphysics for its own sake. To neutralize the danger, grant aesthetic cognitivism and aesthetic realism (and give aesthetic nihilism nary a moment's thought).

The second, more powerful, distractor is the weight of history. Insiders will have noticed that no space was allocated on our map for the debate that sets those who regard aesthetic values as objective or response-independent against those who regard them as subjective or response-dependent. This debate ramped up among early modern thinkers, especially Hume (1739) and Kant (2000[1790]), and it chugs nicely along to this day (e.g. Sibley 1968; McDowell 1983; Pettit 1983; Wiggins 1987a; Goldman 1993; Levinson 1994; Bender 1996; Young 1997; Miller 1998; Vaida 1998; Raz 1999b; Railton 2000; Bender 2001; Levinson 2001; Todd 2004; Prinz 2006; Schellekens 2006; Budd 2007; Dorsch 2007; Alcaraz León 2008; Bourget and Chalmers 2014; Ross 2014; Mole 2016; Schellekens 2017). One might surmise that the philosophy of aesthetic value has just been this debate (aesthetic hedonism having been viewed as obvious). Traditionalists will find much of this book to have been irrelevant until just now.

Unfortunately, though, anyone who attempts the literature quickly begins to lose their fix on what is at stake. If we are drawn into metaphysics because we wonder how aesthetic values come so concretely to occupy our familiar world, then the debate about the subjectivity of aesthetic values cannot represent our puzzlement. On one hand, subjective values are those that are constituted by us, or by our reactions, and we are parts of our familiar world. On the other, how is confidence that aesthetic values are objective compatible with worries about their place in the world? Therefore, put debate on hold until the final section of the chapter, "Anthropocentric Aesthetics," when we will have addressed the true source of our puzzlement.

Our world is the natural world, a world whose horizons lie within our best empirical—scientific—understanding. Aesthetic values appear to belong to this world, but how can they?

Metaphysical naturalism is the view that all facts are natural facts. Routes to metaphysical naturalism include aesthetic non-cognitivism, nihilism, and non-realism, but these routes to metaphysical naturalism are closed. There are aesthetic value facts. Only one route to metaphysical naturalism remains open. Aesthetic naturalism is the view that aesthetic value facts are natural facts; they "offend against nothing else in our world view" (Blackburn 1998: 49).

Impulses to metaphysical naturalism stem from many sources, including a taste for parsimony, a yen for ontological innocence, and a zeal for science. The impulse to aesthetic naturalism is strong, for a special reason. Currie observes that aesthetic engagement is predicated upon our taking it for granted that "objects have aesthetic properties because they have properties of other kinds... Two objects cannot differ *only* in their aesthetic properties; they differ aesthetically because they differ in other ways" (1990: 243; see also Sibley 1959: 442). As a result, we know that the way to act upon an item aesthetically is by acting on some of its other properties. Notice how Currie's observation echoes the naturalism of W. V. O. Quine. As Quine put it, "nothing happens in the world, not the flutter of an eyelid, not the flicker of a thought, without some redistribution of microphysical states" (1981: 98).

Cormier's Blue Stick Garden is playful, and its being playful has everything to do with the natural fact that it is made of planting stakes painted three sides blue and one side orange-red. After all, nothing happens, aesthetically, without some intervention in the realm of natural facts. Presumably, an aesthetic fact is a natural fact if it is sensitive to intervention in the realm of natural facts. Therefore, the fact that the garden is playful is a natural fact too. Its playfulness is on all fours with its being made of planting stakes painted blue and orange. Aesthetic value facts are part of the familiar world because they lie within our reach. The agenda is now to make good on these observations, using the network theory to make a case for aesthetic naturalism.

Aesthetic Normativity Naturalized

Aesthetic naturalism is the view that aesthetic value facts are natural facts. Which facts are natural facts? In the usual procedure, some facts are taken to be fundamentally natural, while non-fundamental facts count as natural facts by standing in a sponsorship relation to the fundamental natural facts (for other procedures see Shafer-Landau 2003: 58–62). Accordingly, one task is to settle on the fundamental facts, a second is to specify what relation sponsors membership among the natural facts, and the final task is to see whether aesthetic value facts are so sponsored.

Suppose, with Quine, that the fundamental facts are those facts about microphysical states that would be explained by a perfected science of physics. Fundamental facts involve items having properties that figure in explanations in physics. Non-fundamental facts are natural facts if they stand to the fundamental facts in the relation that sponsors membership among the natural facts. Whatever the relation is, assume that it sponsors all the facts explained by the physical and life sciences, the behavioural sciences, and the social sciences, including history, economics, linguistics, and political science. Any fact is a natural fact if it is explained by any of the sciences. In particular, psychological and social facts are natural facts. If they are not, then the prospects of aesthetic naturalism are too bleak to proceed. One might even worry that the prospects for aesthetics are too bleak to contemplate (Lopes 2018).

The idea is that the facts that fall within the horizon of scientific understanding make up the facts about the familiar world, where aesthetic naturalism seeks a home for aesthetic value facts. Currie observes that aesthetic values have a home in this familiar world. Items are playful or buoyant or sassy because they have other features—because they are planting sticks painted blue and orange, or their earthy vetiver base is cut with ginger, or they are sung by an unlikely duo.

What is the sponsorship relation? Classical naturalism is reductive, where reduction consists in identifying properties that register in the admitted natural facts with properties that register in the facts seeking admission. An aesthetic naturalism that identifies aesthetic values with natural properties comes in two flavours.

According to analytic aesthetic naturalism, aesthetic values are identical to admitted natural properties, and the identity is an analytic truth, so that a correct analysis reveals the concept of playfulness to be identical to a concept of some natural property or properties. Moore's (1903) famous open question argument attacked the project of giving any analysis of value concepts as identical to hedonic concepts. One might concede that the Bennett–Lady Gaga duet is disposed to please and yet go on to ask, perfectly sensibly, "But is it any good?" It is not analytic that aesthetic values are identical to hedonic properties.

Nor does aesthetic hedonism imply that they are. The naturalism that Moore attacked is one flavour of classical naturalism; drop the analyticity requirement and what remains is substantive naturalism. According to substantive aesthetic naturalism, aesthetic values are identical to other natural properties, even though aesthetic value concepts are not identical to concepts of other natural properties. (Consequently, there are informative statements about what an item's aesthetic value consists in.)

Given aesthetic hedonism, the route is clear to substantive aesthetic naturalism. An aesthetic value is something like a power in an item to induce a kind of response that is bread and butter to psychologists. Aesthetic normativity is a natural phenomenon and aesthetic values belong among values that inhabit "a natural world, including humans and their responses... not being a further element of reality but, rather, created by humans' reacting approvingly to an element of reality when they are aware of its relevant features" (Griffin 1996: 22).

Equally straightforward is the route to substantive aesthetic naturalism, given the network theory. The network theory is designed to answer the normative question, which asks what it is about V that makes it the case that the fact that x is V lends weight to what an agent aesthetically should do. The theory answers by identifying V's being reason-giving with a complex fact concerning what raises an agent's chances of successfully performing a task by using their competence in the context of a social practice. Facts about the success conditions of acts (landing an arrow on a target, widening the audience for a jazz standard) are natural facts. So too are facts about competences—they are explained by a perfected psychology. Facts about practices are natural facts because they will be explained by the perfected social sciences. The network theory supplies a naturalistic reduction of aesthetic normativity.

However, a declaration of victory would be premature. Here are two facts. The first fact is the fact that Bennett's duet with Lady Gaga is sassy. The second fact is the fact that the first fact is an aesthetic reason. That is,

1. the duet is sassy
2. (1) is an aesthetic reason.

The normative question asks what it is about sassiness that makes (2) the case. The network theory answers the question by saying something about the role of the property of being sassy in the achievement of a networked agent. So it supplies a naturalistic reduction of aesthetic normativity, but it does not supply a naturalistic reduction of (1). Having accepted the network theory, we might still ask whether the fact that the duet is sassy is a natural fact. An account that naturalizes aesthetic normativity need not naturalize aesthetic value facts.

A loose end in the network theory yields another way to put the worry. Each aesthetic practice is constituted by its aesthetic profile, which Chapter 7 characterized rather neutrally as a pattern of correlations between the aesthetic values of items in the practice and other properties the items have. Why not think the pattern correlates non-natural and natural properties? Or, why think that the correlation sponsors natural facts?

A Sibleyan Challenge

Aesthetic naturalism is the view that aesthetic value facts are natural facts, where natural facts are any facts that stand in the sponsorship relation to other natural facts. Classical naturalism is reductive, identifying properties that register in the admitted natural facts with properties that register in the facts seeking admission. The challenge is this. Such facts as the fact that Creed's Vetiver is buoyant, the duet is sassy, and Cormier's garden is playful do not yield to reduction.

A line of thought due to Sibley (1959; 1965; 1974) blocks the path to analytic naturalism for aesthetic pluralists. For pluralists, being playful is identical to some massive disjunction of non-aesthetic properties. Playfulness is being made up of planting sticks painted orange and blue and sited next to a garden designed using Gertrude Jekyll's colour theory, or it is the drawing of a moustache on a reproduction of the *Mona Lisa*, or it is.... No analysis of the concept of playfulness is about to reveal the disjuncts. Malcolm Budd encapsulates Sibley's point in three theses (1999: 301). For aesthetic value, V, and a set of non-aesthetic properties, Γ,

1. there is no V and no Γ such that it is analytic that Vx = Γx
2. there is no V and no Γ such that it is analytic that if Γx then Vx
3. for some V and some Γ, it is analytic that if Vx then Γx.

Theses (2) and (3) are controversial (e.g. Ribeiro 2010). Still, (1) is universally accepted, and it scotches analytic aesthetic naturalism.

To make matters worse, the Sibleyan point extends beyond analytic reductions. The playfulness of the Blue Stick Garden lies in its being made of planting stakes painted blue and orange. The (more wicked) playfulness of *L.H.O.O.Q.* lies in its being a moustache on a masterpiece. If playfulness is identical to anything, then it is identical to a massively disjunctive property. Our having no idea what the disjuncts are is not a problem, since the point of substantive naturalism is that they are to be discovered empirically. Rather, the problem is that the big disjunctive property does not play an explanatory role in any perfected science. As we saw above, aesthetic facts are natural facts only if they stand in a sponsorship relation to natural facts that involve properties that are explained in the perfected sciences. The perfected sciences will have no truck with the massively disjunctive property wherein playfulness lies. If the big disjunctive property is not a natural property, then neither is playfulness.

While the case is not hopeless (e.g. Yablo 1992; Jackson 1998), it is worth seeking an alternative to classical naturalism.

Grounding Naturalism

Many assume that the only naturalizing sponsorship relation is property identity. However, granting reduction the monopoly on naturalism jeopardizes too much of the natural world. Naturalism does not require reduction. Another, weaker, relation will fit the bill.

Recall that we follow Quine: the fundamental facts are those explained by a perfected physics. Yet Jerry Fodor (1974) famously showed that the special sciences do not reduce to the physical sciences. The reduction of biology to physics would mean that every biological natural kind is identical to a physical natural kind, but biological natural kinds often parse out as massive disjunctions of physical properties that are not physical kinds because they play no explanatory role in physics. Taking an example from economics, he pointed out that some true economic theories concern monetary exchanges. However, a true description of monetary exchanges in the language of physics will be wildly disjunctive. Some involve strings of wampum, some involve banknotes, some involve cheques, and some involve appending to encrypted strings. Fodor asks, "What are the chances that a disjunction of physical predicates which covers all these events expresses a physical natural kind?" (1974: 103).

In response to Fodor's argument, fundamentalists say that all the facts are fundamental facts. They place aesthetic value facts in the same non-naturalist boat as facts about monetary exchanges and protozoa. Liberals jettison the assumption that property identity is required to naturalize a domain of facts (e.g. Railton 2003). They place aesthetic value facts in the same naturalist boat as facts about monetary exchanges and protozoa.

Fundamentalism suits those with a taste for parsimony or a yen for ontological innocence. Liberalism takes seriously the enterprise of understanding how nothing happens in the aesthetic world without some redistribution of the properties of aesthetic agents or the items upon which they act (Fodor 1974: 107).

What relation fills in when identity is retired by non-reductive naturalists? Recent work in metaphysics volunteers grounding. A combination of facts, γ, grounds the fact that p. Or we say that p obtains in virtue of γ, that p is due to γ, that p because γ, or that p by dint of γ. Usain's pain grounds a reason to stop running, the ball is disposed to roll because it is spherical, the shirt's being cerulean makes it blue, "grass is green" means grass is green in English by dint of linguistic conventions and certain facts about speakers, and the vase is beautiful in virtue of its being... (Audi 2012b: 659–60). Constructions such as these are hardly new in philosophy (Correia and Schnieder 2012: 2–10). What is new, and more useful, is inquiry into the grounding relation's character and role in theorizing (esp. Schaffer 2009; Rosen 2010; Audi 2012a; Fine 2012; Bliss and Trogdon 2014).

Unlike identity, grounding is irreflexive and asymmetric. Like identity, it is transitive and non-monotonic (where γ grounds p, it does not follow that adding facts to γ yields a set of facts that grounds p). Most also accept that full grounding carries metaphysical necessity:

if γ grounds p then, necessarily, if γ then p.

This claim represents γ as those facts that fully ground p; any proper subset of γ partially grounds p. The scope of the necessity is left open to serve the context—it might be logical, metaphysical, nomological, or otherwise regional. Perhaps aesthetic grounding carries necessity relative only to nearby possibilities. The final observation is that grounding obtains between facts, not properties, and the facts are worldly, not facts as we conceive them.

Grounding is well suited to serve in non-causal, metaphysical explanations. In Kit Fine's slogan, "ground stands to philosophy as cause stands to science" (2012: 40). Causal explanations do not answer all why-questions; grounding claims answer why-questions by telling us something about the non-causal determinant of what we are asking about (Audi 2012a: 104–5; see also Griffin 1996: 49–51). Usain's pain did not cause him to stop running, but it is the reason he had to stop running; the ball's being spherical did not cause it to be disposed to roll, but it explains why it has that disposition; and the shirt's being cerulean is why it is blue but does not cause it to be blue. In philosophy, expressions constructed with "in virtue of," "makes it," "due to," and "because" typically invoke grounding relations and thereby propose non-causal explanations.

Grounding equips us to fashion a non-reductive alternative to classical aesthetic naturalism. In "recursive naturalism," grounding is deployed in a recursion routine, starting with fundamental natural facts, to add layer upon layer of natural facts. Here is Gideon Rosen's portrait of normative naturalism:

> every fact p … is associated with a tree that specifies the facts in virtue of which p obtains, the facts in virtue of which those facts obtain, and so on. A path in such a tree is naturalistic when there is a point beyond which every fact in the path is non-normative. A tree is naturalistic when every path in it is naturalistic. Metaphysical naturalism is then the thesis that every fact tops a naturalistic tree. (2010: 111–12)

Aesthetic naturalists need not be metaphysical naturalists; they say only that every aesthetic value fact tops a naturalistic path. In a formula,

AESTHETIC VALUE NATURALISM: for any aesthetic value fact, p, there is a subset, γ, of the non-aesthetic natural facts such that γ grounds p.

Now we may sensibly ask whether the network theory fits the bill.

Recent interest in grounding expresses a shift in metaphysics from a taste for minimizing what there is to a curiosity about the layered structure of being

(Schaffer 2009). Grounding is what aesthetic naturalists are after, if they share the same curiosity.

Aesthetic Values Naturalized

The network theory supplies a naturalistic reduction of aesthetic normativity, but it does not provide a naturalistic reduction of aesthetic value facts, such as the fact that a duet is sassy. For that, we need grounding. Aesthetic value facts are natural facts because they are grounded by natural facts. The argument for AESTHETIC VALUE NATURALISM appeals to a supervenience thesis.

Some regard grounding claims as new to aesthetics (Audi 2012b; Benovsky 2012). What does come up is supervenience, and grounding is not supervenience. However, matters are not quite so simple, because the discussions of aesthetic supervenience are not as they might appear.

First, what flies under the banner of "supervenience" in philosophical aesthetics is not always supervenience in the strict and technical sense (an exception is Currie 1990). Frequently, the relation that seems to be in play is a grounding relation. For example, Sibley's claims couched in terms of "determination" and "dependence" are closer to grounding claims than supervenience claims, and he routinely deploys the "in virtue of," "responsible for," and "owes to" constructions (e.g. 1959; 1965; 1974; see also MacKinnon 2001b). Nick Zangwill also cashes out his use of "dependence" with a non-causal "because" (1995: 324–5). Levinson (1984) explicitly acknowledges that he is not advocating supervenience proper, and reaches in the direction of grounding. Recent work on grounding is best viewed as building on this tradition in aesthetics.

Second, the heated exchanges about aesthetic supervenience do not concern the technical details of the relation itself; they concern its relata. In particular, they concern which properties are supervenience base properties of non-value aesthetic properties (Sibley 1959; Pettit 1983; Levinson 1984; Bender 1987; Currie 1990; Zangwill 1999; Zangwill 2000; Fudge 2005; Hick 2012). Some say the base comprises only formal, expressive, and semantic properties; others admit genetic and contextual properties too. Obviously, any case for naturalizing aesthetic value facts bypasses the heat over the supervenience base of non-value aesthetic properties. What about aesthetic values? Under the hegemony of aesthetic hedonism, all writers take them to supervene, at least in part, on spectator responses (Goldman 1993; Levinson 1994; Goldman 1995: 39–45; Bender 2001).

Set aside the quarrel over base properties. All we need for AESTHETIC VALUE NATURALISM is the claim that aesthetic value facts are grounded in some admitted natural facts. The base properties on which aesthetic values supervene can be any properties that figure in natural facts. The real trouble with existing discussions of supervenience is that, by collapsing the distinction between supervenience and grounding, they miss the possibility arguing for AESTHETIC VALUE NATURALISM by appeal to the supervenience of aesthetic properties on natural properties. The first step is to get clear on supervenience proper.

Supervenience is a family of relations of covariation between supervening and base properties (McLaughlin and Bennett 2011 is a good summary). Aesthetic values supervene on base properties just when no two items can differ in aesthetic value unless they also differ with respect to their base properties. Equally, aesthetic values supervene on base properties just when any two items with the same base properties are guaranteed to have the same aesthetic value.

Now to details. As with grounding, the scope of the modality varies—it is logical, nomological, or regional. Members of the supervenience family also differ independently of modal scope. Contrast weak and strong versions of local aesthetic supervenience:

> aesthetic values weakly supervene on base properties if and only if, for any possible world, w, and any items, x and y in w, if x and y are indiscernible with respect to their base properties in w, then x and y are indiscernible with respect to their aesthetic value in w.

Here there is a covariation of aesthetic values and base properties among items in a world. In strong supervenience, the covariation holds across possibilities:

> aesthetic values strongly supervene on base properties if and only if, for any possible worlds, w_1 and w_2, and any items, x in w_1 and y in w_2, if x in w_1 and y in w_2 are indiscernible with respect to their base properties, then x in w_1 is indiscernible in aesthetic value from y in w_2.

For example, were there a structure indiscernible in its base properties from the Mirage Volcano, though it differed in its rebar reinforcement, it would have the same impressive cheesiness as that Las Vegas landmark. In a slogan, there can be no aesthetic value difference without a base difference.

Grounding is not supervenience. Supervenience is reflexive and not asymmetric, so it cannot carry priority and cannot represent how the less stands to the more fundamental. Moreover, some irrelevant properties supervene on aesthetic base properties. The property of not being a square circle supervenes on the very same properties as does being playful. The garden's playfulness is not explained by its supervenience on the properties upon which the property of not being a square circle also supervenes! Either way, the lesson is that supervenience does not serve in explanations. For that, we need grounding.

With the distinction between grounding and supervenience in place, here is the argument for AESTHETIC VALUE NATURALISM (cf. Epstein 2015: 72, 100–11). First, aesthetic values strongly supervene on natural properties—they change in sync with other natural properties across possibilities. Second, the best explanation of why aesthetic values strongly supervene on natural properties is that aesthetic value facts are grounded in other natural facts. Third, by abduction, aesthetic value facts are grounded in other natural facts. Fourth, facts grounded in natural facts are also natural facts. Ergo aesthetic value facts are natural facts.

The previous section, "Aesthetics Meets Metaphysics," made the case for recursive aesthetic naturalism, the premise that facts grounded in natural facts are also natural facts. That leaves the first two premises of the argument.

Start with the second. Why think that aesthetic values strongly supervene on natural properties because aesthetic value facts are grounded in natural facts? Are there no alternative explanations? Take the supervenience of the impressive cheesiness of the Mirage Volcano on its being more than 20 metres tall. One option is that the alleged grounders cause the aesthetic value facts. However, the fact that the Mirage Volcano is more than 20 metres high does not cause it to be impressive. Another option is that the supervenience is accidental. But if it is a fluke that aesthetic values sync with base properties, then aesthetic agents do not modify items' aesthetic values by tinkering with their base properties. Put another way, if the natural world does not control the aesthetic world, then the aesthetic world is out of control, but the aesthetic world is not out of control, so the natural world does control the aesthetic world and the aesthetic world is not one big accident. Is there a third option? Hearing none... aesthetic grounding best explains aesthetic supervenience. The fact that the Volcano is more than 20 metres high serves in a non-causal explanation of its being so impressively cheesy.

That leaves the first premise, the observation that aesthetic values strongly supervene on base properties. Ludwig Wittgenstein posed this teaser: "imagine this butterfly exactly as it is, only ugly instead of beautiful!" (1967: §199). One might reason: if we cannot conceive this, it is impossible, and if it is impossible, the beauty supervenes on the exact features we imagine the butterfly to have. Alas, inferences from inconceivability to impossibility are controversial.

As a fallback, consider how seriously we should take the ugly proposition, namely that a butterfly might be ugly while indiscernible in its base properties from this beauty here. We are only interested in nearby possibilities. Keep fixed the facts of human nature, roughly the path that human history has taken, our relationship with butterflies, and their natural history. For example, fix it that butterflies are not poisonous and that they are not the logo of a genocidal fascist state. Even the space of nearby possibilities is very large, of course. Maybe we can follow Wittgenstein's command because a butterfly's beauty depends on an act of imagination, where what is imagined is up to the imaginer, only softly guided by the item itself (MacKinnon 2001a). People much like us imagine differently, and each one of us imagines differently from occasion to occasion.

However, the task is to make a case for AESTHETIC VALUE NATURALISM given the network theory, and the suggestion is incompatible with the network theory. Aesthetic values cannot be hostage to the whims of individual imagination if agents are to coordinate around them in the context of aesthetic practices.

In sum, the supervenience of aesthetic values on natural properties is evidence for AESTHETIC VALUE NATURALISM. For any aesthetic value fact, p, there is a subset, γ, of the natural facts such that γ grounds p. Grounding carries metaphysical necessity: if γ grounds the fact that the Mirage Volcano is impressively cheesy then, necessarily, if γ then the Mirage Volcano is impressively cheesy. Grounding does not carry metaphysical dependence, and indeed it is not the case that if γ grounds the fact that the Mirage Volcano is impressively cheesy then, necessarily, if the Mirage Volcano is impressively cheesy then γ. To our everlasting delight, there are many ways to be cheesy.

Sibley might have grasped at another argument. Chapter 7 followed him in taking the relation between less specific and more specific aesthetic values to be the relation between determinables and determinates. For any V, to be V is always to be V in some particular way (Sibley 1974: 11–13). Rosen nicely proposes a link between the determinate–determinable relation and grounding (2010: 126). According to the

D–D LINK: if Γ is a determinate of V and x is Γ, then the fact that x is Γ grounds the fact that x is V.

If Γ is a determinate of impressive cheesiness and the Mirage Volcano is Γ, then the fact that the Mirage Volcano is Γ grounds the fact that it is impressively cheesy.

If Sibley is correct, every aesthetic value is a determinable of some super-determinate that is a combination of non-aesthetic properties. Every aesthetic value bottoms out in a set of non-aesthetic-value properties. Given the D–D LINK, all aesthetic value facts are grounded by natural facts. The network theory is Sibleyan in its naturalism.

Anchoring Aesthetic Practices

Metaphysical explanations answer why-questions by revealing the world as layered, and we badly need a model that explains the aesthetic layer of reality. Correction: the aesthetic layers of reality. Aesthetic reality is doubly layered.

Why is Bennett's duet with Lady Gaga sassy? The answer points to the facts that ground its being sassy—facts about its arrangement, who is singing it, the wink-wink of the song's title, and the switch-ups in the lyrics (as when Lady Gaga sings "This chick is a tramp"). What about the aesthetic practice? Do facts about the aesthetic practice of popular jazz vocals also ground the fact that the duet is sassy?

One might think the answer must be "yes:" facts about an item's aesthetic values are grounded in facts about the practice to which it belongs. Philosophers learn in their youth that an item's aesthetic value supervenes on its social-contextual properties (esp. Danto 1964; Walton 1970; Levinson 1980). On the standard story, indiscernible items can differ in aesthetic value. Warhol's *Brillo Boxes* is ironic, though it exactly (enough) mimics James Harvey's design for Brillo boxes, which is not ironic. If aesthetic values supervene on base properties, then no two items can differ in aesthetic value unless they also differ with respect to their base properties. Since *Brillo Boxes* differs in aesthetic value from the design for Brillo boxes, and since they are indiscernible, the relevant base properties must include contextual features. Hence, on the standard story, the irony of *Brillo Boxes* supervenes on its being a work in the aesthetic practice of pop painting, while the straightness of the Brillo box design supervenes on its belonging to the aesthetic practice of commercial packaging.

Surely the network theory is committed to the standard story! After all, *Brillo Boxes* is ironic given the aesthetic profile of pop painting, which grounds facts about irony in some other facts. The design for Brillo boxes is not ironic because the aesthetic practice of commercial packaging is constituted by a different aesthetic profile.

We miss a golden opportunity, however, if we fall too swiftly into line with the standard story. Philosophers are so accustomed to the standard story that its oddness has worn off. When we wonder what makes the duet sassy, we expect to hear about the arrangement, the lyrics, and the singers. What is odd is to hear that the duet belongs to the aesthetic practice of jazz vocals, as if this fact is a fact on all fours with facts about its arrangement, lyrics, and performers. We expect the practice to be named only when something special has gone wrong. To use a metaphor, the aesthetic practice is a framing device; it is not another bit of the scene in the frame. Appeal to the supervenience relation obscures this because supervenience is just covariation.

Unlike supervenience, grounding layers reality. Brian Epstein (2015) represents it as a general feature of social practices that they are doubly layered in a way that can make sense of the difference between explaining why the duet is sassy by pointing to the lyrics and what we are up to when we mention the aesthetic practice.

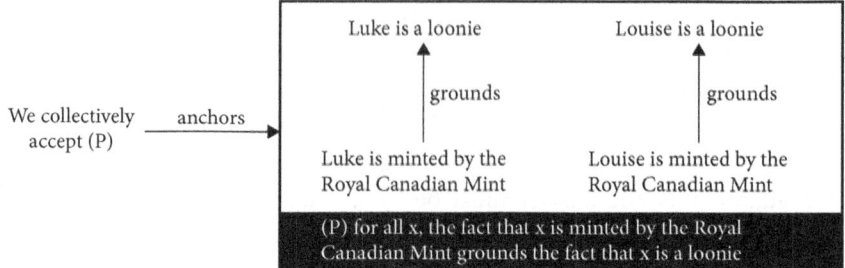

Figure 10.1 Anchoring a currency practice, grounding currency facts

The double layering of social reality pops out in what deserve to be called "Epstein diagrams." In Figure 10.1, facts about coins ground facts about Canadian dollars, nicknamed "loonies" (for the image of *Gavia immer* on the reverse). The fact that Luke is minted by the Royal Canadian Mint grounds the fact that Luke is a loonie, and the fact that Louise is minted by the Royal Canadian Mint grounds the fact that Louise is a loonie. In principle, the fact that a coin is minted by the Royal Canadian Mint grounds the fact that the coin is a loonie (and (P) can be restated modally). Obviously, (P) makes the practice what it is because it generalizes over the grounding facts. Meanwhile, the whole practice, in which some facts ground others, is set in place by facts about coin-users. Perhaps Canadians collectively accept (P) (Searle 1995). Their collective acceptance of (P) is what anchors the practice.

The Epstein diagram pictures two relations, grounding and anchoring. Anchoring might have the same logical character as grounding, but the relations have different relata. What is special about the pattern of grounding relations is that they constitute a practice. What is special about anchoring is that it stands a practice to facts about members of a population so as to explain what brings the practice into being.

Both grounding and anchoring serve in explanations, and distinguishing them makes it clear how two different explanations answer two different why-questions. Why is Louise a loonie? We seek an answer in facts about the history of the metal token that is Louise, not facts about the attitudes of Canadians. Why do the activities of the Mint create loonies? Now the answer points to the attitudes of Canadians.

Think of the distinction as protecting against what might be called "Skow's fallacy." Suppose that p is a reason why q and also suppose that r is a reason why (p is a reason why q). Bradford Skow points out that it does not follow that r is a reason why q (2016: 74–6). In his example,

Suzy throws a rock at a window but Billy sticks his mitt out, thereby catching the rock before it hits. The fact that Billy stuck his mitt out is a reason why the window didn't break. And the fact that Suzy threw the rock is a reason why (the fact that Billy stuck his mitt out is a reason why the window didn't break). But the fact that Suzy threw the rock is not a reason why the window didn't break. (2016: 76)

Likewise, the fact that Louise is minted by the Royal Canadian Mint is the reason why Louise is a loonie: the former fact grounds the latter. The fact that Canadians collectively accept (P) is the reason why the former fact grounds the latter: their collective acceptance anchors the practice. It does not follow that the fact that Canadians collectively accept (P) is a reason why that coin, Louise, is a loonie.

Now for an Epstein diagram of the aesthetic case. The box in Figure 10.2 represents the aesthetic profile that constitutes the practice, wherein aesthetic value facts are grounded in facts about non-aesthetic features. Unlike other social practices, no general principle adequately describes the set of aesthetic grounding relations in aesthetic practices (Isenberg 1949; Sibley 1959; Sibley 1974; Dancy 1983; Mothersill 1984; Bender 1995; Shelley 2002; Sibley 2003a; Shelley 2006; Audi 2014; cf. Beardsley 1981[1958]; 1962). Instead, we simply have the grounding pattern, the practice's aesthetic profile. What anchors the practice? According to the network theory, the practice is anchored by the fact that (enough) of its members act in ways that comply with its core norms, which centre on its aesthetic profile.

Why is Creed's Vetiver buoyant? The answer we expect points to the facts that ground the fact that it is buoyant—for example, the fact that it is cut with a ginger middle note. Why does the fact that it has a ginger middle note ground the fact that it is buoyant? In other words, why this aesthetic profile? Now the reason why points to facts that anchor the practice: members of the world of parfumerie comply with scaffolded core aesthetic norms centred on this very aesthetic profile. Recall Skow's fallacy, however. We err in jumping to the conclusion that compliance with the core aesthetic norms of parfumerie is a reason why Creed's Vetiver is buoyant.

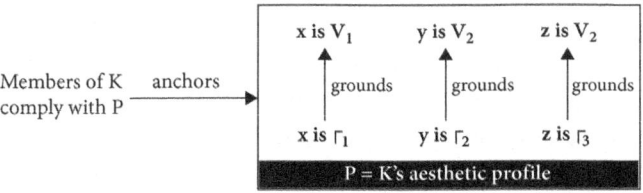

Figure 10.2 Anchoring an aesthetic practice, grounding aesthetic value facts

Aesthetic reality is doubly layered. Aesthetic value facts are grounded in certain other facts in an aesthetic practice, and the pattern of grounding makes the practice what it is. At the same time, the practice exists because it is anchored in facts about the doings of agents in a population.

Anthropocentric Aesthetics

We promised never to lose sight of what is at stake when we roll in the machinery of metaphysics. Much of what is at stake is earning our commitment to aesthetic cognitivism and realism (and our disregard for aesthetic nihilism) by housing aesthetic normativity and aesthetic value facts in the natural world. Having taken care of our real estate problem, what remains is the hoary debate about the subjectivity or objectivity of aesthetic value. The network theory takes the sting out of that debate.

Before proceeding with the operation of sting removal, it is important to acknowledge how the hoary debate expresses a pair of deep, and opposed, anxieties (cf. Rosen 1994).

On one hand, we experience ourselves as confronting or detecting aesthetic values, not as conferring or projecting them (cf. Nichols and Folds-Bennett 2003; Wolf 2011: 55; Cova and Pain 2012). As David Wiggins puts it, an agent "descries certain external properties in things and states of affairs. And the presence there of these properties is what invests them with importance in his eyes. The one thing that properties cannot be, at least for him, is mere projections" (1987b: 105). Check out the Solitaire MVB typeface and you will be struck by its perfect poise. Even if you cannot put your finger on what makes it poised, you do not experience yourself as painting poise onto it. Therefore, we hope that it is not "we who, with our desires or choices, make things good" but that, in Parfit's metaphor, "goodness gives us reasons in the way the sun gives us light, because it's out there, shining down" (2011: 1.46).

On the other hand, as Robbie Kubala pointed out when he read this, we are sometimes just as anxious that the objectivity of aesthetic values pose no threat to our access to them. Could we all be wrong in all our aesthetic evaluations, and have no method for discerning the aesthetic truth? We hope not! We hope, in other words, that the accuracy of our aesthetic evaluations is not wholly independent of how we are and the interests we have.

Assume that values are not subjective unless they are response-dependent. (Wiggins 1987a; Pettit 1991; Wright 1992; Johnston 1998; Schellekens 2006; Watkins and Shelley 2012; Kölbel 2016). On response-dependent accounts,

(1) necessarily, x is V if and only if x brings about response, R, in A in C, and
(2) x is V because x brings about R in A in C.

For example, according to standardized aesthetic hedonism, R is having a finally valuable experience, A is a true judge, and C are standard conditions for experiencing x. According to (2), the fact about the true judge's response metaphysically explains the aesthetic value fact.

One might surmise that the network theory is a response-dependent account. After all, the theory implies a social dependence thesis: there are aesthetic value facts only because there are aesthetic practices that sustain them (Raz 2003: 19). Moreover, there are aesthetic practices only because agents closely enough comply with core aesthetic norms—they often enough act by aligning with each other on aesthetic profiles. So, we do not track items for the values they have except by tracking each other's actions.

The path to this conclusion tramples the distinction between anchoring and grounding. What grounds values in a social practice is not what anchors the practice. What grounds the value of a chess move are facts about the state of play and the rules of the game, not facts about us that get us playing the game (Raz 1999b: 153). Or take agriculture. Organic and industrial agriculture are different practices and a foodstuff that is good in one might not have the same value in another—organic agriculture values variety where industrial agriculture values uniformity. The reason why a bushel of organic apples is good does not appeal to the collective acceptance of participants in the world of organics; it appeals to facts about the apples.

Likewise, the reasons why Solitaire MVB is poised have to do with facts about the shapes of the glyphs. These facts ground its being poised. The reason why those facts ground its being poised is that members of the aesthetic practice of type design track each other in complying with its core aesthetic norms. These facts about social behaviour are anchoring facts.

Trampling the distinction between grounding and anchoring lures us into a deep mistake: we mistakenly think that aesthetic value facts cannot be explained except with reference to us and our interests. In truth, a complete explanation of why Solitaire MVB is poised cites the grounding facts. None of the grounding facts are facts about our responses or interests. They are not response-dependent; they are as objective as you like.

At the same time, our collective responses and interests do play an ineliminable explanatory role. Why do those facts ground the fact that Solitaire MVB is poised? A complete explanation cites facts about the performances of members of the relevant aesthetic practice.

Notice how easy it is to go wrong. From the correct observation that we could very easily have different interests, we jump to the conclusion that the practice of type design could very easily have been different. Wrong! Were our interests different, we could very easily have gone in for a different practice. Compare: were we more interested in consistent spelling, we might have spoken Italian, but we could not have made English the same as Italian. Or, were our interests different, we might easily have anchored guernicas instead of paintings. No fact about us shows up in what it is for an aesthetic practice to be the practice of guernicas. The practice of guernicas is constituted by its aesthetic profile.

Echoing Wiggins (1987a) and John McDowell (1985), Michael Watkins and James Shelley say that a domain of facts is anthropocentric when it is of interest only because there are creatures like us (2012: 346–7). Aesthetic value facts are anthropocentric in the sense that aesthetic practices are anchored by the fact that aesthetic agents perform in line with their specialized competences. Were their interests and expectations different, they would converge on a different aesthetic profile, anchoring a different practice. Creatures with interests very different from ours might well anchor themselves to areas of aesthetic space beyond our reach, though we would try to reach them if we knew about them (Railton 2000: 66).

Approaching the idea from a different direction, Raz observes that the social dependence thesis explains why there is no point to value facts without valuers (Raz 2003: 27–8). Aesthetic value facts have a point for creatures like us only because creatures like us can act upon them, thereby anchoring them.

Parfit hoped that aesthetic values give us reasons in the way the sun gives us light—"because it's out there, shining down." He was right. At the same time, the sun radiates many wavelengths, though we see only some, a narrow band, and we must position ourselves to catch its rays. Aesthetic anthropocentrism is no surprise. Our values are the ones we ready ourselves to act upon.

PART V

11

Getting Personal

The main argument for the network theory is the limited, contrastive argument to the best explanation. As a bonus, the theory clarifies and explains our psychological, discursive, and metaphysical situations. Here is another bonus: it answers the primitive question of aesthetics. Socrates asked what ingredients go into a life lived well. The primitive question of aesthetics is: what is the place of aesthetic value in the good life? Or, what do aesthetic goods bring to my life, to make it a life that goes well? Or, how does beauty deserve the place we have evidently made for it in our lives? The time has come to address the primitive question, given an answer to the normative question.

Three Skeptics

Sam has been hard at work on a chunk of *Space Invaders* source code. So what? Why should anyone do like Sam? Here what looks like one question is really three questions that must be teased apart (cf. Foot 2001: 64–5). Each gives voice to a different brand of aesthetic skepticism.

Lite skeptics concede much. They concede that they should emulate expert performances and also that there are experts, who include Sam, in conserving and curating source code. Moreover, they are into video games. Nevertheless, they doubt that anyone has aesthetic reason to work on *Space Invaders*. In asking why they aesthetically should do like Sam, they are asking why a competent source code sleuth has aesthetic reason to work on *Space Invaders*. They want to know what facts about the game's value give anyone reason to devote their competence to it. Accordingly, a reply to lite skeptics refers them to Part III of this book. *Space Invaders* is intensely absorbing, hence disturbing in a way that fits its thematic content. A reply to the lite skeptic comes in the form of an assessment of the value of the video game.

Normative skeptics do not go along with the concessions of their lite peers. They are into video games, but they press the question of why they have aesthetic reason to do what Sam has aesthetic reason to do, because they doubt that expert performances are normative for them. They doubt that they should do what the video game expert does, whatever that turns out to be. What is so great about experts? they ask. In pressing the question, they need not embrace aesthetic value nihilism. They might well see what Sam sees in *Space Invaders*—its being disturbing. They simply doubt that this fact's practical significance for experts has much to do with its practical significance for them.

The reply to normative skeptics is just the network theory's answer to the normative question. Aesthetic experts are aesthetic high achievers who act well by using their competence to succeed in their aims. When agents have reasons to act at all, they have reasons to act well, hence to achieve. An agent with the same aims as Sam, and something approaching her competence, has aesthetic reason to do as she does just because he has reason to act well. Skeptics court incoherence if they think that they do not have reason to act well when they have reason to act at all.

Which queues up outsider skeptics. Just about any aesthetic practice has some curb appeal. Only a real sourpuss can see absolutely none of the appeal of video games. At the same time, no aesthetic practice draws in more than a fraction of those with aesthetic interests. All are niches. So, one side of the coin is the weak appeal for non-participants of any given aesthetic practice, and its flip side is that the weak appeal of aesthetic practices fuels the diversity of our aesthetic interests. An outsider skeptic asks why they aesthetically should do as Sam does because they want a case to be made for being into video games. They see the value of *Space Invaders* for Sam—its being disturbing. They also concede that, in general, they have reason to do as experts do. In particular, they concede that people into video games have reason to do as Sam does. Conceding all this leaves open the question of whether they have reason to regard as normative for them what experts do in aesthetic practices with mere curb appeal.

Outsider skepticism resonates because outsider skeptics are not mere theoretical posits. We are all outsider skeptics. Nobody goes in for, and has competence in, everything aesthetic. For each of us, there are zillions of aesthetic practices whose appeal is weak enough that we are outsider skeptics. If not video games, then something else.

By corollary, outsider skeptics are not anaesthetes, who have no aesthetic interests whatsoever. Mothersill remarked on the rarity of anaesthetes: "it takes more than bad taste and a sour humor to make a genuine anaesthete: the place to look would be the back wards of a state institution" (1984: 276). Normal human development includes induction into aesthetic life, with a base level acquisition of some aesthetic competence, and only serious trauma disrupts the normal developmental sequence.

The network theory is designed to address lite and normative skeptics. What about outsider skeptics? They press a line of questioning that articulates what is left of the primitive question once we have answered the normative question.

The View from Aesthetic Nowhere?

Outsider skeptics participate in some aesthetic practices, but they are cool to those to which they are not already committed. In extreme cases, they have trouble stretching to anything new, but we are all outsider skeptics because, for each of us, there is a limit to how far we stretch, and some aesthetic practices are beyond reach. Confronted with any aesthetic practice not already in their repertoire, the outsider skeptic asks a simple and excellent question: why is this for me? (Why not that?)

The assumption is that agents have aesthetic reasons to stretch (cf. Riggle 2015). Needless to say, people have loads of non-aesthetic reasons to sign on to a new aesthetic practice. The fact that friends and neighbours belong to an aesthetic practice is a reason to follow them and thereby share their interests (Egan 2010). The fact that an aesthetic practice forges a social identity that a person embraces is also reason for them to participate in the practice (Cohen 2001; cf. Riggle 2017). So is the fact that membership in an aesthetic practice brings wealth or prestige (Bourdieu 1984). Outsider skeptics will grant observations such as these while continuing to press their skepticism.

Aesthetic hedonism was purpose-built to answer outsider skeptics. According to the standard history, as leisure time became an issue for the new middle classes in the seventeenth and eighteenth centuries, writers answered the need for advice about worthy pursuits for persons of newfound means (Kristeller 1951–2; Shiner 2001). Standardized aesthetic hedonism supplies a principle to back the advice: the aesthetic value of an item is a property of it that stands it in constitutive relation to finally good experiences of true judges in joint verdict. Along with the principle comes the job description of true judges, who are "able to make comparative judgments across genres and art forms" (Levinson 2010: 228).

Viewed from the perspective of the outsider skeptic, the flexibility of the true judge is appealing indeed. That flexibility consists in a capacity to make comparative judgements across any aesthetic boundary. In technical parlance, standardized aesthetic hedonism models items as comparable in respect of aesthetic value (Chang 2013). That is, they can be ordinally ranked on a scale of goodness: for any two items, x and y, the ranking says that x is better than y in respect of V, y is better than x in respect of V, or they are equal in respect of V. Since the ordinal ranking obtains without regard to the boundaries of aesthetic practices, it answers outsider skeptics. If x is better than y in respect of aesthetic value, then choose x, even if it belongs to an unfamiliar K. An agent has superb aesthetic reason to stretch to an unfamiliar K: items in K will bring her more pleasure than she can get elsewhere.

The network theory is not ready, out of the box, with the same kind of answer to outsider skeptics, because it provides no tool for ranking the aesthetic values of items in a perfectly general way. Take two photographs, x and y, where x is V and y is V′, and take two agents, a photography collector and an appreciator. Maybe x is better than y in respect of aesthetic value and, at the same time, y is better than x in respect of aesthetic value. After all, it is possible that x is better to collect because it is V whereas y is better to look at because it is V′. There need be no ordinal ranking of x and y for any A, for any φ, in any C. The same goes if we hold act-type and agent competence fixed and vary the circumstances: maybe x is better to collect for the MoMA because it is V whereas y is better to collect for the FotoMuseum because it is V′.

The network theory contemplates ordinal rankings of items only where types of agent, their circumstances, and the aesthetic practice are held constant. You are at the MoMA, which is about to close, and you can look at x or y, both in the same genre. Either x is aesthetically better to look at than y, y is aesthetically better to look at than x, or one is as aesthetically good to look at as the other. Items can be ranked from the perspective of an agent faced with a task in a situation, but not by taking a "view from aesthetic nowhere."

Representing compared items as being V and V′ also papers over the network theory's pluralism (Chapters 7 and 10; see also Raz 1991; Anderson 1993: 49–58). Nothing is beautiful without being beautiful in some determinate way; there are countless determinate aesthetic values. Being sly and being quirky are ways of being aesthetically good, much as being teal and being turquoise are ways of being blue. Set a knowing and sly conceptual photograph by Jeff Wall next to a forthright modernist photograph by Dorothea Lange. Attempting to rank them from a neutral point of view is like attempting to rank the athletic value of a Sidney Crosby wrist shot against the athletic value of a Serena Williams serve.

Incidentally, these results do not mean that we cannot act, for good aesthetic reason, across the boundaries of aesthetic practices. Such would be the conclusion to draw only if it is not possible to make a choice involving incomparable values. On some views, we can make a rational choice between the *Best of Crosby* and the *Best of Williams,* although their values are incomparable (Chang 1997). Shelley recalls that, "faced with a choice between watching a movie or a TV show when I was kid, the good money was on the movie" (personal correspondence). He chose the movie, and for good aesthetic reason, but it does not follow that the movie came ahead of the TV show in an impersonal ranking of aesthetic value. This is hard to see for those weaned on aesthetic hedonism, which does nothing to discourage the dogma that there can be no rational choice without comparable values.

The Aesthetic View from Here

How bad is the news that there is no ordinal ranking of items, with respect to their aesthetic value, from the perspective of aesthetic nowhere? The answer hangs on whether we need such a ranking in order to satisfy outsider skeptics—those who wonder what aesthetic reason they have to stretch to aesthetic practices in which they are not already entangled.

Note that the task is to address outsider skeptics, not anaesthetes. Although standardized aesthetic hedonism supplies an ordinal ranking of items from an impersonal point of view, no hedonic ranking can draw anaesthetes into aesthetic life. Lacking any aesthetic interest whatsoever, they will shrug off any suggestion that items in K are the best source of aesthetic pleasure, asking why they should care about aesthetic pleasure at all. Standardized aesthetic hedonism only addresses outsider skeptics, who ask why they should stretch from where they are into unfamiliar regions of aesthetic space. Yet outsider skeptics already have aesthetic commitments; they have personal aesthetic perspectives. So standardized aesthetic hedonism affords a view from aesthetic nowhere that we do not need in order to address outsider skepticism. Outsider skeptics can be addressed from where they are. Therefore, so what if the network theory provides no ordinal ranking from an impersonal point of view? To answer the skeptics we yearn to answer, all we need are ordinal rankings from personal points of view.

One line of thought is that, since we all have reason to achieve, anyone has reason to join in aesthetic activities that offer them opportunities for achievement.

The underlying idea is correct, but it is not correctly stated. An aesthetic reason has the form "x is V;" it is a fact about an item. The problem is that, according to the network theory, aesthetic reasons are strong only for those already inside a practice. As a result, there is an asymmetry between the reasons insiders and outsiders have to achieve. If A, who is an insider to the relevant aesthetic practice, has aesthetic reason to φ, then A thereby has reason to achieve by φing. But an outsider to a practice will have no (or very weak) aesthetic reason to φ, so they have no (or very weak) reason to achieve by φing. Outsider skeptics grant that Sam has aesthetic reason to conserve *Space Invaders* and hence to achieve by conserving the game. Nevertheless, they point out, they have no reason to achieve by conserving *Space Invaders* unless they have aesthetic reason to conserve *Space*

Invaders. By definition, as outsiders, they have only the weakest aesthetic reason to conserve *Space Invaders*.

The point generalizes. As a philosopher working on value, I have strong reason to achieve philosophically by reading David Lewis (1989) on dispositional theories of value. University of British Columbia (UBC) students in kinesiology would achieve philosophically were they to read Lewis too. However, they have barely any reason to achieve by reading Lewis because they have barely any reason to read Lewis.

Take, by contrast, a literature student who is very good at thinking about literary value in an abstract way, using the methods of what the English department calls "theory." Surely she has pretty decent reason to get into aesthetics. Once she does, she will have reason to achieve philosophically by reading Lewis on value.

What we need is a conception of a reason to achieve by joining an aesthetic practice that is not a fact of the form "x is V." Instead, it is a fact about an unfamiliar K—a fact of the form "K is F"—that gives some agent reason to develop competence in K. Call such a fact a derived aesthetic reason. That is,

> the fact that K is F is derived aesthetic reason for A to acquire core aesthetic competence in K = the fact that K is F lends weight to the proposition that A would achieve were A to acquire core aesthetic competence in K.

The fact that K is F is obviously a fact that stands K in relation to A. Aaron, who is good at making North Indian curries, has strong derived aesthetic reason to learn to make Goan curries. Not so Rosalina, who does not cook.

Agents' existing capacities situate them to have derived aesthetic reasons to branch out into some unfamiliar domains of aesthetic activity, not others. No adequate presentation of the achievements of local aesthetic experts leaves out their biographies. Her prior understanding of the north, gained as a hunter, fisher, and trekker, set up for Elsie Reford's achievement in boreal horticulture. The success of Winfrey's book club came partly out of her understanding of her audience and an appreciation of how to communicate by telling stories on TV. Reford would have achieved less with bonsai and Oprah's Opera Club would have bombed. Facts about their competences and their social circumstances mean that agents are more likely to achieve aesthetically by signing up to some aesthetic practices rather than others.

Hence the network theory suggests an ordinal ranking of Ks from a personal perspective determined by an agent's circumstances and existing competences. K is better for A, in C, with respect to derived aesthetic value than is K′ just when A, in C, has better prospects for aesthetic achievement by acquiring aesthetic competence in K than K′. K and K′ are equal in derived aesthetic value for A in C when they offer the same prospects, in C, of upping the probability of A's aesthetic achievement.

Many factors go into agent-centred rankings of genres. One is overlap in competence for aesthetic act-type. Skill in food writing overlaps more with skilful movie reviewing than competence in playing the violin. All else being equal, an agent is likely to achieve more aesthetically by branching out from food writing to movie reviewing than by playing the violin. Another is overlap in core aesthetic competence, competence in aesthetic evaluation, which is a function of similarity of aesthetic profile. The aesthetic profiles of jump blues and rockabilly are more similar to each other than either is to the aesthetic profile of gamelan. Someone skilled at evaluating jump blues has more work to do in learning to evaluate gamelan than rockabilly, so they are more likely to achieve aesthetically by going in for rockabilly than gamelan.

The path dependence of the derived aesthetic value of an aesthetic domain for an agent has a welcome consequence. In so far as an agent's aesthetic biography expresses who they are, the path they have followed into new commitments can also express their aesthetic personality (see Chapter 4). Standardized aesthetic hedonism says we should all follow converging paths into the same top-ranked aesthetic domains. As Kant insists, "one cannot say that everyone has his special taste" (2000[1790]: 212–13). If the dream is that "we would all find beauty in the very same places," then, as Nehamas rightly complains, the "dream is a nightmare" (2007: 83). In this nightmare, we impose upon ourselves the goal of erasing our aesthetic personalities. By ranking genres from agent-centred points of view, the network theory secures a place for aesthetic personality at the heart of aesthetic life.

Aesthetic Personality

Reflecting on his upbringing during a period of "astonishing and unprecedented cultural abundance," A. O. Scott concludes that "the world had been organized to deliver an overwhelming variety of stimuli directly to my brain, which was quickly filled with pop-song hooks, sitcom catchphrases, movie montages, and stream-of-consciousness monologues from late-night talk shows and experimental novels." All this he calls "the architecture and furniture of my emerging self" (2016: 85–6). Let an agent's aesthetic personality be the sum of their aesthetic commitments—the Ks they participate in, whether they know it or not. In respect of aesthetic personality, everyone is in some ways like everyone else, in some ways like some others, and in some ways like very few others.

To acknowledge the sources and nature of aesthetic personality is not yet to account for why it matters to have one, but an idea lies not far off (for another, see Riggle 2015). Nehamas writes that "aesthetic character and style are an essential part of what distinguishes a person from the rest of the world" (2007: 86). Anyone's personality includes their aesthetic personality. Under the right conditions, simply being who we are matters to each of us.

Perhaps especially for humans of our era, being who we are matters under conditions of integrity and dignity, where integrity and dignity are properties of lives (Williams 1973; Taylor 1982). One's life has integrity just when it expresses a correct conception of the good. One's life has dignity just when basic commitments are undertaken freely, not as a result of the domination of others, or of forces that one cannot control. Does satisfying these conditions explain why it matters who we are, aesthetically speaking? A concern can be raised on each score, about dignity and integrity.

The concern about dignity grows out of the path dependence of aesthetic biography. In the normal course of things, aesthetic agents begin to acquire specialized competences in early childhood, under parental supervision. From then on, their options are at every turn subject to social regulations limiting access to aesthetic practices. Except for those rare high achievers who are able to drive change within an aesthetic practice, our aesthetic achievements are constrained by social forces we neither understand nor control. What else could explain the relatively high levels of aesthetic homogeneity within social groups? (When the kids revolt, they all revolt in the same way.)

An important feature of the network theory is its conception of aesthetic practices as scaffolding agency (Chapter 6). Agents constitutively use their competence to succeed, and social structures scaffold all but the most rudimentary aesthetic competences. Without social scaffolding, we have few, mostly poor, options for aesthetic commitment. The downside—and it is a serious downside, as we shall see in Chapter 12—is that social factors limit access to parts of the aesthetic universe.

The question is whether scaffolding offends against human dignity. Access to some goods is always cut off by scaffolding that enables access to other arenas for human activity, including athletics, the sciences, commerce, governance, even friendship and romantic love. What affronts human dignity must be more than path dependence in conditions of social scaffolding.

The second concern is about integrity. A life has integrity just when it expresses a correct conception of the good. Surely, though, to commit to what is good for the sake of being oneself is to sacrifice the good on the altar of narcissism. The concern echoes as a general concern about the primitive question. When we ask why aesthetic participation is part of a life lived well, we assume that we gauge the goodness of aesthetic participation by its place in a good life.

The time has come for a reminder that a reason is a fact that lends weight to the proposition that an agent should perform an act: it need not figure in their deliberations on what to do. Someone might work out a ranking of aesthetic practices as prospects for further aesthetic achievement, but agents can and do act as they have reason to act without representing to themselves the reasons they have.

Suppose a food writer simultaneously receives an invitation to review the new Mani Ratnam film for the Friday paper together with a violin lesson voucher that expires on Friday. She does not have time for both, and she realizes that she has stronger aesthetic reason to write the movie review than to take the violin lessons, because she calculates that she is very likely to write a decent review of the movie and she is very likely to sound terrible playing her first scales on the violin. As it happens, writing the review sends her down a path where she writes more reviews, builds the relevant competences, and becomes an expert movie critic. Acting solely through deliberation on her aesthetic reasons, she ends up doing what she has more derived aesthetic reason to do. In this way, we feel our way into new aesthetic practices without deliberating upon their derived aesthetic values.

Self-absorption is a fault, but being who one is under conditions of integrity does not require deliberation upon oneself; it only requires deliberation on what is good.

Another error also underlies the concern about integrity. The concern wrongly takes the proposal to imply that the reason an agent has to get into K rather than K' is that getting into K will better express their aesthetic individuality. An outsider skeptic asks why they aesthetically should do as Sam does. If the answer is that it will fit their aesthetic personality, then the skeptic might press on and ask why facts about their aesthetic personality are practical reasons.

Answering the skeptic in this way twists a good answer to the normative question into a bad answer to the primitive question. Nobody said that we have reason to act at all only because we have reason to be our best selves. Rather, we all have reason to do what our best selves would do (Foot 2001: 53). A food writer seeking a new gig has more reason to try her hand at movie reviewing than violin playing. In taking up movie reviewing, she does as she aesthetically should, and thereby lives a life that expresses her correct conception of the good. That her life will have integrity need not motivate her to take up movie reviewing.

Thomas Scanlon (1998a) regards inclusive goods as transparent to deliberation. An inclusive good is a good that is made up of other goods that are not made good by contributing to it. For example, having music in your life makes your life good, but the fact that having music in your life makes your life good is not what makes music good (Scanlon 1998a: 120). A good life is an inclusive good. For this reason, "it would be odd to make our everyday choices as 'artists of life' choosing each action with an eye to producing the best life, as an artist might select dots of paint with the aim of improving the value of the whole canvas" (1998a: 124). The concept of a good life is transparent to deliberation. To deliberate on the good life is just to deliberate on the things that make a life good—music, for example (see also Wolf 2010: 117–18).

The network theory backs Scanlon's idea that living well is an inclusive good that is transparent to deliberation. Someone who deliberates on the quality of their life, with an eye to possible aesthetic pursuits just deliberates on the quality of the pursuits. Having done that, assuming all goes as planned, they follow an aesthetic path that amounts to their being who they are, engaging in the various activities, including aesthetic ones, that make their life go well.

Meaning

One aspect of living well is being who you are as an aesthetic agent, under conditions of integrity and dignity. Though it might hold special importance to us nowadays, individual self-expression is not the sole aspect of living well. A meaningful life also tends to be a good life. No doubt there are many ways a life can have meaning. Ultimately, the task is to glean whether aesthetic activity can contribute to any kind of meaningful life, or whether it can contribute to only some kinds. If only some kinds, then why only those? For now, in proof of concept, just consider the meaningful life as it is portrayed by Susan Wolf (2010; see also Wiggins 1987b).

For Wolf, an agent's life is meaningful when they are actively and positively engaged in an activity where "subjective attraction meets objective attractiveness" (2010: 9). To unpack the slogan, think about what might be added to a meaningless life to give it meaning. Sisyphus is condemned to eternally roll a boulder to the top of a hill, from which it rolls back down. Richard Taylor imagines that the gods take pity on their victim and inject him with a potion that excites in him a powerful impulse to roll boulders (1970: ch. 18; see also Wiggins 1987b: 92–5). As long as his life lacks meaning just because he is bored and alienated, the potion fills him with meaning. Yet you might balk at Taylor's conclusion that subjective attraction suffices for meaning. Sisyphus' life lacks meaning not only because he is bored and alienated, but also because his task is pointless, utterly without value. To live meaningfully, he must engage in activities that he correctly sees to be worthwhile, quite apart from their satisfying his impulse. Wolf defines attractiveness as "objective" when it is independent of subjective attraction. Subjective attraction is affective, a feeling of fulfillment taken in engaging in an objectively attractive activity. Without an element of subjective attraction, a life dedicated to worthy activities lacks meaning—imagine a bureaucrat who just cannot get excited about the good they do.

In sum, an agent's life has meaning to the extent that they feel fulfilled by actively and positively engaging in projects that they correctly take to have objective worth.

Aesthetic engagements, from listening to music to pie baking, feature prominently among Wolf's many examples of activities that contribute to meaning. Genuinely feeling fulfilled comes from an agent's recognizing that they are making positive contributions to an endeavour that is bigger than them. Aesthetic projects fit the bill perfectly. To engage aesthetically is to participate in an aesthetic practice where there are standards of goodness independent of individual attitudes, where personal achievement supports the achievement of other participants in the practice, and where there is an opportunity to contribute to a group with a continuing history and traditions. Contributing to an aesthetic practice by acting in light of what is good within the practice warrants feelings of fulfillment.

According to the network theory, domains of aesthetic reasons are anthropocentric in the sense that they have interest only because there are creatures like us (Chapter 10). "Objectively" worthy activities, which warrant feelings of fulfillment, need not have value seen from outside the human perspective. They can be anthropocentric (anthropocentrism does not imply response-dependence). As we cooperate with each other in an aesthetic practice, we shine a light on items' aesthetic values in line with an aesthetic profile. The values are, in Wiggins's words, "*lit up* by the focus that the one who lives the life brings to the world" (1987b: 137).

Happiness

Recent interest in the meaningful life corrects for an overemphasis in ethics on happiness. Granting that happiness is one among many of the spices of life, one might still wonder whether aesthetic activity is a source of happiness, given the network theory. Much depends, of course, on what happiness is. If happiness is a net balance of pleasure, and if Chapter 8 is correct, then aesthetic activity is one source of happiness (see also Crisp 2006; Melchionne 2017). But is there a non-hedonic state deserving the name of happiness? Or, going for the prize, could happiness derive in part from being yourself and from living a meaningful life?

Among ethicists who write about happiness, Foot stands out for vigorously challenging the tendency to think of happiness as an occurrent state of mind like excitement or elation (2001: 86–9). Following Aristotle, she observes that we would not exchange adult happiness for a child's pleasures, even intense and enduring ones. If she is right, then there is a form of happiness that is, by its nature, beyond a child's reach. What is this deep happiness? Our instinct is to treat it, like regular happiness, as a state of mind that consists in its having a phenomenal character that can be fully captured independent of its objects. That is how it is with excitement and elation. However, deep happiness is not explicable in a way that detaches from its objects. Children can be happy, but not deeply happy, because they have not had the chance to encounter the sources of deep happiness.

Foot's reasoning finds an echo in James Griffin's conception of the good life as comprised of goods with a "long-term, life-structuring character" (1996: 85). Included among goods with a life-structuring character are basic agentive capacities such as autonomy and integrity, as well as self-understanding, close personal relationships, accomplishments, and the perception of beauty (Griffin 1996: 29–30). To secure goods such as these, an agent must be well launched in life.

As Michael Bishop (2015) interprets the data, psychology confirms the reality of deep happiness (cf. Sumner 1996; Haidt 2006). People who are happy tend to have positive affects, positive attitudes, and positive traits, all in combination with high levels of accomplishment. These elements of deep happiness are non-accidentally connected with each other in a self-maintaining or homeostatic network.

Bishop argues that deep happiness (or well-being) is the state of being in a positive causal network (2015: 10). Positive causal networks exhibit three features (Bishop 2015: 40–1). First, a positive causal network is made up of an agent's affects, attitudes, traits, actions, and accomplishments. Second, the components of the network form homeostatic clusters. That is, they tend to co-occur because the presence of some promotes the presence of others (Boyd 1999). For example, feeling good favours having an optimistic attitude, which inclines to success. Third, a positive causal network is positive in the sense that it includes enough of any of the following types of states: states that have positive hedonic tone, states that cause states with positive hedonic tone, states that the agent values, and states that the agent's community values.

A set of states might form a fragment of a positive causal network for an agent (Bishop 2015: 53–5). A fragment of a positive causal network for an agent is a set of states that either is or could be a causal driver for a full positive causal network for that agent, holding constant what kind of person they are. Suppose someone plays guitar in a successful band out of a sense of obligation to the other band members, getting no pleasure from playing (or from acting on obligation!) The guitarist instantiates a fragment of a positive causal network because her state is not self-maintaining. Still, it is a plus on the ledger: instantiating a fragment of a positive causal network contributes to her deep happiness.

Also note that being in a fragment of a positive causal network is relative to facts about the agent. In Bishop's example, a misanthrope is not in a fragment of a positive causal network just because she somehow ends up with a friend. Her having friends would promote and would be promoted by her feelings, attitudes, actions, and capacities only were she to undergo a radical metamorphosis in which she sheds her misanthropy.

Plainly, deep happiness is not being in state with a phenomenal character, on the model of excitement or elation. No state is identical to states with positive hedonic tone if it can include them.

Aesthetic practices are effective vehicles of deep happiness. In joining an aesthetic practice, an agent must acquire competences, which can lead to achievement, which can promote having positive affects and attitudes. Each of these—achievement and positive mental states—in turns promotes the competence. Competence so promoted pays off in boosted chances of achievement, which further inclines agents to optimism and feeling good. The virtuous spiral towards a self-maintaining positive causal network is one route to deep happiness.

True, the network theory of aesthetic value does not make achievement or positive affects and attitudes constitutive of aesthetic agency. Achievement is never guaranteed. Aesthetic agents can be alienated from their aesthetic labours: an accomplished and acclaimed performer or set designer might get no positive affect for their aesthetic efforts (Chapter 8). An alienated agent might not even have a fragment of a positive causal network.

Deeply happy members of practices will naturally tend to stick with the practice. That they tend to stick with the practice no doubt explains the persistence of some aesthetic practices. Yet, as we saw in Chapter 8, a fact that explains the persistence of an aesthetic practice need not be a fact that gives members of the practice aesthetic reasons to persist with it. Moreover, if deep happiness is an inclusive good, agents only deliberate on the goods that make it up. Someone who joins a practice undertakes to perform various acts. They do not intend to acquire a homeostatic cluster of traits, affects, attitudes, and accomplishments. Deep happiness is an essential byproduct of active aesthetic engagement.

Being for Beauty

Is the network theory an example of virtue aesthetics (Eaton 1989: 160–3; Brooks 1993; Woodruff 2001; Swanton 2005: 22–4; Goldie 2007; Goldie 2008; Lopes 2008; Kieran 2009; McGonigal 2010; Ransom 2017; Roberts 2018)? Virtue theories put the traits of idealized agents to work in explanations, and many link virtue to living a good life. Likewise, the network theory puts the traits of aesthetic experts to work in an explanation of aesthetic normativity, and it finds a place for aesthetic engagement in living well. The theory is a virtue theory, in the most general sense. However, some virtue theorists are rather particular either about which traits are virtues, or about the exact link between virtue and living well.

Some philosophers regard as virtues only traits with a special importance. They say, for example, that skill at knot tying is not a virtue. As very useful as it might be, it does not have the special importance of generosity, curiosity, creativity, and the other virtues. But what is this special importance?

One claim is that virtues, but not skills, have final value. In as much as a competence is a means to success, its value is instrumental, derived entirely from the value of the success. Skill in tying a bowline is good as a means to getting a strong knot that is also easy to untie. As long as its value is purely instrumental, skill in knot tying is not a virtue. The trouble is that when a competence makes for an achievement, the competence is also a constituent and not merely a cause of the goodness of the achievement (Sosa 2007: 74–80). Competence in tying a bowline is finally good if it contributes to an achievement's value (see also Lewis 1946: 486, 496–9). Anyone tempted to dismiss the achievement of tying knots need only spend a few minutes with Ashley's classic *Book of Knots* (1944).

Another claim takes virtues to be "deep qualities of a person, closely identified with her selfhood" (Zagzebski 1996: 104). Equally, virtues are the competences that we care about and that consequently reveal what we care about (Battaly 2015: 60–1). By this standard, most any competence can be a virtue. Ashley dedicated his life to skill in tying knots, and made a foundational contribution to it.

Aesthetic competences pass both the personality test and the final value test, so why not recognize aesthetic expertise as a virtue? No harm done, provided that the virtues are not thought to have some further, special importance as is possessed by generosity, curiosity, creativity, and their ilk. The price will be too high for philosophers who believe that aesthetic virtues keep company with moral and epistemic virtues, to the exclusion of skills like tying knots (Goldie 2007; 2008).

Exclusivists need a weightier conception of virtue. According to personal worth conceptions, virtues are competences that make their possessors excellent persons. Many competences make their possessors excellent kinds of persons—excellent knot tiers, dog walkers, or chess players—but virtuous agents are excellent simply qua persons (Baehr 2011: 91–6; Battaly 2015: 5–7). The task is then to make sense of being excellent simply as a person, and not any kind of person (cf. Thomson 2008).

Analytic personal worth conceptions of virtue make it a conceptual truth that having a given competence is part of being excellent qua person. Fill in the blank in "A is a —— but a good person" with an incompetence. If the result calls either for an explanation or an appended "otherwise," then the incompetence is a vice and the associated competence a virtue (Haack 1998: 15). Since "Allie is a liar but a good person" seems to call for an "otherwise" or some further explanation, honesty is a virtue. By contrast, "Abe is a disaster at chess but a good person" calls for no further explanation and appending an "otherwise" seems positively infelicitous. The same goes for "Axel is uncreative but a good person" and "Aida is a terrible editor but a good person." Aesthetic competences are not virtues on the analytic personal worth conception. Be that as it may, the trouble with analytic personal worth conception is that it is hostage to the virtue concepts we happen to have, which are overly moralized (Chappell 2013: 151–2).

Substantive personal worth conceptions jettison the conceptual link between having virtue and being an excellent person. A tradition with roots in Moore identifies being good qua person with having a positive orientation on what is good, for its own sake (Moore 1903; Nozick 1981: 429–33; Hurka 2001; Adams 2006; Lopes 2008). Writers disagree on what it is to have a positive orientation on what is good. Most identify the positive orientation with a pro attitude. In that case, the network theory implies that aesthetic competences are not virtues, for aesthetic competences are not constitutively attitudinal (see Chapter 8).

At the same time, the network theory can be read as articulating an alternative picture of a positive orientation on what is good. An agent has a positive orientation on what is good just when they are configured so as to act in ways that promote the good. In Nozick's list, they protect, guard, seek, and foster the good (1981: 429). Why not be more specific? Agents have a positive orientation on the good when they are configured to teach dance, reverse engineer source code, spread the habit of reading, edit photographs, or organize festivals. If aesthetic experts act from a state of being for beauty, then they act from virtues that make up part of their personal worth.

After all, the theme of this book, made explicit in the network theory, is that being for beauty does not consist in taking an attitude; it consists in a configuration of agency that kits us out to get in gear and act in accordance with our aesthetic reasons.

In sum, aesthetic expertise is a virtue on some but not all conceptions of virtue. How interesting is this result? The answer depends on what, if anything, is at stake in sorting virtue from mere competence.

Eudaimonist virtue theory is clear about what is at stake. Beginning with a prior, independent conception of the good life, eudaimonism identifies the virtues with competences whose exercise constitutes living well (e.g. MacIntyre 1984; Foot 2001; Annas 2011; cf. Hursthouse 1999; Swanton 2005). The challenge is to sort virtues, which are constitutive of well-being, from competences that are not (though they might benefit their possessors). Foot is optimistic that "for all the diversities of human life, it is possible to give some quite general account of human necessities... of what is quite generally needed for human good" (2001: 43). An account of what is quite generally needed for human good will reveal the virtues.

Here are two strategies for eudaimonist aesthetic virtue theorists. A direct strategy locates aesthetic activity among the Aristotelian necessities. A roundabout strategy argues that aesthetic competence serves non-aesthetic human necessities. Peter Goldie adopts the roundabout strategy when he argues that aesthetic virtues, exercised in engaging with art, boost moral response—they "can bind us together as fellow humans—can appeal to, and reveal, our shared experiences and our shared emotional responses to those experiences" (2007: 386).

Neither strategy is promising. No human life goes well without some aesthetic activity. Granting this addresses anaesthetes, not you and me, and it establishes only a minimum threshold. Your life and mine go well far above threshold levels, because we each have our specific enthusiasms. I am into K; you are into K'. My being into K spices up my life, but K need not do anything for you, so being into K is no human necessity. As to the thought that aesthetic activities always serve extra-aesthetic human needs, the trouble is not that they sometimes do not, but that their contributions to living well is not one bit diminished when they do not.

Nobody needs to be told their aesthetic pursuits express who they are, endow their life with meaning, bring them deep happiness, or fulfill their personal ideals. The puzzle is how our aesthetic pursuits can be so important in these ways. The deep anxiety is that they are pastimes, diversions from the serious business of life, mere trivialities. The overreaction is to insist on the great cultural significance of the fine arts. That throws the rest of our aesthetic lives under the bus. A better reaction embraces all aesthetic activity. Foot once imagined someone who reflects back on their life and says that they have wasted their time on "things that don't matter." Her response: "What are the things that 'matter' if they are not the trivial things on which we spend so much time?" (2003[1979]: 35).

12

Building Better Aesthetic Agents

Aesthetic agents populate aesthetic practices, which contribute to and derive support from a larger social fabric. Thriving societies typically lavish astonishing resources on aesthetic culture—G7 spending on the easily measurable aesthetic goods tops a trillion US dollars a year. Highly deliberative societies do not take the spending for granted. In some of the debates, especially in the United States, aesthetic differences trace rifts in the wider culture (Brooks 2001). Hence, the primitive question of aesthetics echoes at the collective level, when we ask what reason we have to adopt policies, at every scale from the household to the nation, that direct resources to what can appear to be rather frivolous aesthetic extras.

Aesthetic Policy and the Primitive Question

Let an aesthetic policy be a rule of action that is used and designed to make a difference to what aesthetic agents do. Aesthetic policies are either endogenous or exogenous, and exogenous aesthetic policies are either laissez-faire or interventionist.

Some aesthetic policies are endogenous because aesthetic practices include norms, and norms are policies. A sommelier and a chef are designing a tasting menu: their transaction is governed by a norm that they should each act in a way that is consistent with the aesthetic profile of the practice. As participants in the practice, it is their policy so to act.

While the norms of French cooking are endogenous aesthetic policies, we tend to speak of "aesthetic policies" with exogenous policies in mind. Families, companies, clubs, neighbourhoods, and subcultures routinely adopt aesthetic policies. And so do nation states. A policy of publicly funded aesthetic education might be used and designed to increase the general incidence of aesthetic appreciation, and a tax policy might be used and designed to incentivize preservation. Aesthetic policies such as these are designed and used to make a difference to what agents do, but they are exogenous to the aesthetic practices wherein those agents act.

(The distinction between endogenous and exogenous aesthetic policies is complicated because patrons are members of an aesthetic practice when their patronage is conditional on the nature of the practice—see Alexander 2014. Exogenous aesthetic policies are more content-neutral, either as a matter or fact or ideal.)

Why not define aesthetic policies as exogenous? The reason is that a group might adopt a policy, with respect to an aesthetic practice, that is laissez-faire, deferring to policies endogenous to the practice. A distinction between laissez-faire and interventionist policies presupposes a distinction between endogenous and exogenous policies.

Without the distinction between laissez-faire and interventionist policies, the primitive question collapses into the normative question. After all, the rationale for an endogenous aesthetic policy lies in the aesthetic reasons that agents have to act in compliance with it. Why should French cooking have the norms that it has? The network theory supplies an answer: the chef and the sommelier achieve most by following those norms. End of story. Yet, we sometimes take a standpoint outside the practice and ask whether it is better to leave the practice to its own druthers or to intervene in some way. Should the state fund French cooking classes, for example? As long as intervention is an option, the network theory supplies no answer; something of the primitive question remains.

We do have policies to devote public resources to support aesthetic activities. Are the policies reasonable? What reason do we have, if any, to adopt them? The question is part of what remains of the primitive question once we have an answer to the normative question.

Aesthetic Goods as Public Goods

Many take for granted that we have reason to adopt exogenous aesthetic policies, including interventionist policies, because aesthetic goods are public goods (cf. Black 1992; Brighouse 1995). The thought is that support for select aesthetic activities brings widespread benefits—benefits for all or most. What benefits? Scholars not directly engaged in making policy have answered by appeal to aesthetic hedonism. Scholars who attend more closely to the thick of politics focus on the instrumental benefits of aesthetic activity. Meanwhile, in its embrace of a hundred mile aesthetics, the network theory does not take for granted that any aesthetic good benefits all or most. (Why should the larger society do anything for my wee corner of the aesthetic universe, or yours?)

Assume that a community should have whatever benefits of aesthetic activity it wishes to obtain, at the cost necessary to secure them (Dworkin 1985: 221).

We are thought to have reason to adopt interventionist aesthetic policies when free markets fail to deliver the desired benefits. Markets often fail in this way due to externalities (Cwi 1980; Baumol 1985; Dworkin 1985; Heilbrun and Gray 2001: 222–38). An externality is a cost or benefit of a transaction that does not accrue to a party to the transaction. A physician is paid for vaccinating a child, who gains an immunity from disease, but the general public also benefits, as each inoculation is a step towards eradicating the disease. Disease eradication is a benefit external to those that accrue to the physician and her patient. The vaccination market fails when transactions between physicians and patients are not enough to yield an external benefit that is in the general interest. When the market fails, the state has reason to internalize the externality through incentives and sanctions. So, we have reason to adopt interventionist aesthetic policies when the desired benefits of aesthetic activity are not generated by aesthetic practices left to their own devices.

Any rationale for an interventionist aesthetic policy developed along these lines rests on a conception of the benefits that the policy is meant to secure. That is not all: the policy must be shown to be effective in securing the intended benefits without producing intolerable side-effects or violating principles of fairness (Kerr 1978: 8–9). For present purposes, though, what matters are the two approaches mentioned above: aesthetic hedonism and instrumentalism.

In his unjustly overlooked "Aesthetic Welfare," Beardsley lays out the aesthetic hedonist rationale for interventionist aesthetic policy (1970a). An item's aesthetic value is a property that stands in constitutive relation to finally valuable experiences of those who correctly understand the item. Aesthetic value is a potential to please. Accordingly, each time the item is experienced, some of that potential is made actual. Call the sum of all actualizations of an item's aesthetic value in a society its "total aesthetic worth." Whereas aesthetic value is a potential, total aesthetic worth is the actual benefit that an item brings to a society. It contributes to the society's "aesthetic welfare." For Beardsley, the aesthetic welfare of a society is the sum of all the aesthetic worths of all the items experienced by members of the society. Aesthetic welfare contrasts with aesthetic wealth, which is the set of all the aesthetically valuable items available to members of a society. In other words, aesthetic welfare is actualized aesthetic wealth.

Beardsley proposes that the rationale for any aesthetic policy is that it converts aesthetic wealth into aesthetic welfare. A laissez-faire policy is reasonable if aesthetic agents maximize aesthetic welfare when they all act on their own druthers. Interventionist policies are reasonable when exchanges between aesthetic agents produce aesthetic benefits for third parties at significantly suboptimal levels, and the policies optimize the externalities. For example, converting aesthetic wealth into welfare requires that people understand items of value and align their hedonic responses upon them, so it might be reasonable to adopt policies that expand the audience for items whose current total worth falls short of their great aesthetic value. Beardsley has in mind complex and sophisticated works of art.

Some of those writing on arts or aesthetic policy follow Beardsley's lead (e.g. Smith 1975; Pankratz 1983). However, the hedonist's rationale for aesthetic policy is not frequently voiced when policy is actually set. Rarely does it appear in the mission statements of arts institutions and funding bodies, for example. There are empirical challenges, of course. Externalities are ubiquitous and do not warrant intervention unless there is a significant shortfall in general benefit. In Nozick's lovely example, "a person who dresses well and pleasingly and walks in public provides benefits for other people in the pleasure of seeing someone looking nice," but that is no reason for state-subsidized tailoring, or incentives for walking in public (1985: 163). To have reason to intervene, we must measure a significant shortfall in general benefit. At the same time, one of the strengths of aesthetic hedonism is that it allows for ordinal rankings that can be used to address the empirical challenges. One can only speculate about why Beardsley's approach has not caught on among aesthetic policy makers.

For Beardsley, the benefits of aesthetic activity are final aesthetic goods, but aesthetic benefits can also be instrumental, and political and public discourse has centred on these. In fact, since most state-level aesthetic policy is arts policy, the discussion centres on the instrumental benefits of the arts (Cwi 1980; Baumol 1985; Heilbrun and Gray 2001: 226–30; Kidd 2012). Economic spillovers get top billing: the arts are said to bring in tourists, boost exports, create jobs, raise tax revenues, and attract skilled workers. Non-economic spillovers are also acknowledged: the arts are said to incubate innovation, lend prestige, cement national identity, facilitate the acceptance of diversity, inculcate moral character, and promote democratic citizenship. Turning to the philosophers, Ronald Dworkin (1985) argues that the arts equip us with a rich, complex, and deep "cultural structure" to pass on to future generations, Scanlon (1985) proposes that the arts help us to reflect on what we want and value in our lives, and Wollheim (1985) offers that they benefit us by showing us how pleasure can be obtained in ways we would not have imagined, encouraging us to form new conceptions of personal happiness.

Without a doubt, the arts do sometimes generate each benefit on the list, but critics point out several unhappy features of the instrumental approach (e.g. Cwi 1980; Nozick 1985; Carroll 1987; Feinberg 1994; Schwartz 1995; Heilbrun and Gray 2001: 244–9; Cohen, Schaffer, and Davidson 2003; Rushton 2003; O'Hagan

2016). On one hand, the approach is too restrictive, since it is unlikely that all the arts yield the benefits, all with high efficacy. On the other hand, the approach is not restrictive enough, as it is likely that many non-art and non-aesthetic activities bring the same benefits, often more effectively. A great deal rests on the empirical evidence that the arts are the most effective vehicles for the anticipated benefits, and the evidence is not there.

Interestingly, calls for a non-hedonic theory of aesthetic value are more often heard in writing on aesthetic policy than in work squarely on the topic of aesthetic value (e.g. Baumol 1985: 224; Nagel 1985; Feinberg 1994; cf. Wolf 2011). These writers question the assumption that exogenous aesthetic policies are reasonable just when they secure widespread benefits, hedonic or instrumental. As Thomas Nagel urges, "some things are wonderful and important in a measure quite beyond the value of the experiences or other benefits of those who encounter them" (1985: 237). Unfortunately, none of these writers provides a theory of aesthetic value that gives wind to their claims on its behalf.

The good news is that the network theory does not represent aesthetic goods as benefits—as good for people. What makes the flinty smokiness of a Pouilly-Fumé an aesthetic value is this: the fact that the wine has that quality is a reason for this sommelier to pair it with that chef's tasting menu. The wine's flinty smokiness is also a reason for a connoisseur to appreciate it, and she might derive pleasure from the act, but its aesthetic value does not lie in its affording pleasure in appreciation.

The bad news is that, according to the network theory, agents have aesthetic reasons to act only in the context of aesthetic practices, where they engage cooperatively with other members of the practice. No aesthetic value figures in a reason to act outside the practice, so no aesthetic values figure in reasons to adopt exogenous aesthetic policies, whether they be laissez-faire or interventionist. The network theory seems only to license endogenous aesthetic policies.

Aesthetic Opportunity

Having led us into philosophy, primitive questions are retooled as philosophical questions, but care must be taken in the retooling. We ask what reason we have to adopt exogenous aesthetic policies. In tackling the primitive question, it was taken for granted that some aesthetic goods are public goods, so that the primitive question became: what benefits do we get from aesthetic activities? The network theory suggests another question. What reason have we to maintain the social infrastructure of aesthetic practices, beyond participating in them?

In a hundred mile aesthetics, few or no aesthetic practices are for everyone, but almost all of us live within the ambit of some aesthetic practice. Outsiders are very common, for only a tiny fraction of us belongs to any given aesthetic practice, but anaesthetes are exceedingly rare, as just about everyone engages in some aesthetic practice. Hence, almost every person accesses some goods that are specific to some region of aesthetic space.

Chapter 11 distinguished aesthetic reasons, which are reasons to perform aesthetic acts within aesthetic practices, from derived aesthetic reasons, which are reasons for an agent to become a member of an aesthetic practice. Aesthetic hedonism provides for an impersonal conception of derived aesthetic reasons. Put bluntly, some aesthetic domains offer such high-calibre experiences that anyone, no matter who, has reason to refashion themselves so as to enjoy them. The claim is the linchpin of Beardsley's approach to aesthetic policy. By contrast, the network theory represents derived aesthetic reasons personally. Aesthetic kinds rank ordinally only when viewed from the perspective of an agent's circumstances and existing competences. K is better for A, in C, with respect to derived aesthetic value than is K' just when A, in C, has better prospects for aesthetic achievement by acquiring aesthetic competence in K than K'.

Agent-centred rankings of aesthetic kinds reflect the path dependence of our individual aesthetic lives. Existing competences, especially core competences, put some new aesthetic kinds within closer reach than others. An agent skilled at evaluating French wines has more work to do in learning to evaluate sour ales than Italian wines. Social factors also determine an agent's aesthetic opportunities. Wine is not widely available in Japan. Jazz was born of certain otherwise lamentable events blending church music with African musical traditions. Most humans designated male are not permitted to wear dresses. The contemporary visual arts require a schooling that puts them well out of reach of all but those with high cultural capital.

Imagine a monoculture where, through accidents of history or authoritarian dictates, all aesthetic activity is consigned to a tiny number of aesthetic domains. Perhaps everyone is alike enough in their basic psychological capacities that they come to have stronger derived aesthetic reason to participate in the available practices than in those that would have been available otherwise. Yet, as long as people do vary considerably in their aesthetic capabilities, they are very unlikely to have strong derived aesthetic reasons to fall into line with the monoculture. As a result, most will have poorer chances of aesthetic achievement than they would have had otherwise: they will find themselves hapless and clumsy as they try to act aesthetically within the confines of the monoculture. Their practical reality will alienate them from their aesthetic ideals. Therefore, to the extent that we are all cut of different cloth, a diversity of aesthetic opportunity is better than aesthetic monoculture.

What is aesthetic opportunity? Beardsley toys with the idea that aesthetic policy should do more than turn aesthetic wealth into aesthetic welfare; it should distribute to each their fair share of aesthetic welfare (1973: 53–5). The network theory obviously does not model aesthetic opportunity as a fair distribution of pleasure. Rather, a society provides for aesthetic opportunity to the extent that members of the population can join those aesthetic practices that they have strongest derived aesthetic reason to join. An aesthetic opportunity index would measure the diversity of practices, the share of the population that can join the practices they have most reason to join, and how easily they can do so. (Existing measures of cultural richness might be good indirect measures of aesthetic opportunity—e.g. Toffler 1967; Kushner and Cohen 2010.)

Why should aesthetic policy ensure any level of aesthetic opportunity? Agents committed to their own basket of aesthetic practices, seeing what practices they might soon join, given the path they are on, have reason to applaud any support that flows to their personal aesthetic priorities. None would be worse off, aesthetically, were their game to become the only game in town. From this there is no argument to aesthetic opportunity for all.

Each of us has reason to endorse what anybody would have reason to endorse, no matter who they are, and a well-known technique can be adapted to suss out what anybody would endorse no matter who they are (Rawls 1971). Anybody has reason to endorse what they would endorse were they placed behind a veil of aesthetic ignorance. From behind this veil, they know some things. They know that they are not anaesthetes. In knowing this, they know that they will have reasons to perform some aesthetic acts, hence to act well, hence to achieve aesthetically. They also know that their prospects of achievement will be determined by their psychological and social endowment. For all this, however, they have no idea of their actual social or psychological lot, and they have no idea what aesthetic acts they will attempt. As far as they know, they might or might not have what it takes to act well in a practice, that practice might or might not exist in their society, and it might or might not be within their reach, if it does exist.

Now, the question they face is this. They have a choice between a society with an aesthetic policy that diversifies aesthetic kinds and ensures efficient access to them for the greatest number, versus a society whose policy will not have these effects. They have reason, rooted in their derived aesthetic reasons, to select the society whose policy secures wide aesthetic opportunity.

The argument can be extended to gel with the picture presented in Chapter 11 of the contribution of aesthetic involvement with living well. One aspect of a life lived well is deep happiness. If each agent initiates a positive causal network by participating in some (but not any) aesthetic practice, then policies promoting aesthetic opportunity also promote deep happiness. Another aspect of a life lived well is living a meaningful life, where subjective attraction meets objective attractiveness. Aesthetic policies promote meaning when they give access to those practices where objective values are subjectively attractive. A third aspect of the good life is obtained by being oneself under conditions of dignity and integrity. One of the more interesting chapters in the story of Abbott's life is her decision to divide her time between making her own photographs and campaigning for Atget's. Presumably, she saw she had reason to campaign for Atget. In acting, with dignity and integrity, on the reason she had, she bound together her own work with her work for Atget as elements of her aesthetic personality.

Rationales for exogenous aesthetic policies can take as their major premise an "aesthetic opportunity principle:" larger social groups have reason to foster the aesthetic opportunities available to their members. Sometimes a laissez-faire policy is warranted: we get as much aesthetic opportunity as we could hope for simply by participating in aesthetic practices. Sometimes, interventionist aesthetic policies are in the cards. Minor premises are needed to bring in the relevant, circumstantial facts that point to specific policies, given the aesthetic opportunity principle.

Arts Education for Aesthetic Opportunity

A larger social group has reason to adopt policies that favour aesthetic opportunity, which is a function of how efficiently members of the group can join the aesthetic practices that they have strongest derived aesthetic reason to join. Put this way, it is easy to think of aesthetic policy as building capacity by means of direct subventions to aesthetic practices and by removing barriers impeding access to aesthetic practices. We build opera houses and sponsor literary prizes; we subsidize theatre companies to keep ticket prices within reach for a large audience and we provide grants to local museums to bring in travelling exhibitions. All these initiatives open doors to regions of aesthetic space. At the same time, however, aesthetic policy builds aesthetic opportunity by building up agents' aesthetic competences.

Aesthetic education is ubiquitous. Every healthy aesthetic practice includes mechanisms for transmitting competences from generation to generation. Often, pedagogical expertise is distributed: nobody is dedicated to teaching how to hack video game source code; each expert transmits their expertise forward. Sometimes pedagogical expertise is a specialization in its own right, as when some dancers become professional dance teachers. In addition, at least since the founding of the French academies, societies have adopted interventionist policies on aesthetic education, which now shows up in school curricula around the world. So, one good question is, why should we have interventionist policies on the side of aesthetic education?

Answers to this question are rarely content-neutral. To take the obvious case, aesthetic practices number in the zillions, but the state mostly intervenes in arts education. As to the rest, the policy is laissez-faire. Refining the initial question, we ask, why intervene in aesthetic education only when it comes to some aesthetic practices, namely the arts?

Arts educators have given a great deal of thought to the more refined version of the question: some take an external approach; some take an internal approach. A pair of challenges motivate both approaches. One challenge stems from the prevalent perception that the arts (and other aesthetic practices) are for leisure, ornaments to the serious business of life, hence destined to play second fiddle to the academic core. An early educational theorist wrote that, "as they occupy the leisure part of life, so should they occupy the leisure part of education" (Spencer 1861: 68). The second challenge targets the feasibility of arts education (cf. Elgin 2009: 319–22). On one hand, aesthetic activities are ubiquitous, they arise in the normal course of social life, and the competences they require are absorbed from the cultural environment. On the other hand, true attainment in the arts requires talent, which is not teachable. Either way, school is simply the wrong tool for cultivating artistic capacity.

External approaches tackle the second challenge by claiming that arts education calls upon and fosters motivations and competences that are not art-specific (e.g. Reid 1948; Meske 1987; Levi and Smith 1991; Efland 2002; Eisner 2002; Gee 2004; Elgin 2009; Choo 2014). From here it is a short step to an answer to the first challenge. By cultivating general traits, arts education contributes to performance in other subjects. Benefits accrue to education beyond the arts classrooms. Incidentally, cognitive transfer is a two-way street, for if music benefits math because they require common competences, then more math should mean better music, but who touts this as a benefit of the math curriculum? Arts education plays second fiddle to core academic subjects, but it is a useful second fiddle.

Some of the external benefits claimed on behalf of arts education are direct and easy to measure: improved creativity and better performance in reading and math, either as a result of cognitive transfer or of better self-awareness and self-esteem, which motivate scholastic engagement. Other alleged benefits are harder to measure: boosts to moral formation, including tolerance of difference, and a deeper understanding of human meaning-making and the human condition. Sadly, the measurables have been measured, and the news is not good. Lois Hetland and Ellen Winner (2000) orchestrated a massive suite of meta-studies, accumulating millions of data points (see Hetland and Winner 2004 for an overview). The results are that experience in theatre modestly improves reading, and music boosts spatial reasoning for a few minutes, but otherwise the predicted spillovers of arts education are just not real. With such disappointing news about the easy measures, optimism about the less easy ones is imprudent.

The scientists conducting the meta-studies conclude that "the arts deserve a justification on their own grounds, and advocates should refrain from making utilitarian arguments in favor of the arts. Such arguments betray a misunderstanding of the inherent value of the arts" (Winner and Cooper 2000: 66). Catherine Elgin grants the soundness of the argument that "education that improves the ability to make and appreciate art is valuable because it enables students to achieve an intrinsically valuable end" (2009: 328). An argument along these lines is internal in the sense that it justifies arts education for its impact on students' capacities to engage with the arts.

Internal approaches mostly take aesthetic hedonism for granted (e.g. Broudy 1972: 50–7; Smith 1984; Koopman 2005: 91–3). In a slogan, "society can have no more legitimate aim for its policies then improving the quality of experience of its members" (Smith and Smith 1977: 119). In order to achieve this aim, arts educators mould students' capacities to correctly understand items that are high in aesthetic value, so as to be able to have finally valuable experiences of the items. Arts education inculcates skills in sensory discrimination, recognizing formal patterns and expressive properties, and interpretation, while providing the knowledge of materials and backstory needed to apply these skills appropriately. Having learned what it takes to experience items with understanding, one then exposes oneself to them, attending to their aesthetic merits. Since this is not sufficient to induce positive experiences, arts education must also shape hedonic responses, perhaps on the principle of fake it till you make it (Melchionne 2010; Goldie 2011).

The whole scheme requires what aesthetic hedonism supplies, an ordinal ranking of items with respect to aesthetic value, atop which we presumably find outstanding works of art. Aesthetic education is fine arts education because the arts offer the greatest aesthetic rewards, but they are complex and esoteric, so getting those rewards requires a level of learning that is not required for popular art and other aesthetic practices. Some add that arts education also removes a barrier to maximal enjoyment when it equips students with a criticality that enables them to resist the allures of popular aesthetic practices (Di Blasio 1992: 28–30). Whatever the attractions of this line of thought, at least for some, it can hardly be said even to aim at fostering aesthetic opportunity by building up aesthetic competences in a diverse range of aesthetic practices.

(Internal approaches to arts education need not stop at aesthetic value. Some distinguish aesthetic value either from artistic value or from musical value, literary value, pictorial value, and the like—e.g. Nussbaum 1990; Carroll 1996; Kieran 2001; Stecker 2005; Kieran 2006; Gaut 2007; Eaton 2012; Huddleston 2012; Stecker 2012; Hanson 2013; Lopes 2014a: ch. 5. Values such as these include aesthetic values alongside other values, especially cognitive ones. An argument could be made that arts education is justified in so far as it secures access to these values.)

At first glance, chances seem slim for extracting a rationale for arts education from the network theory. Suppose that we have reason to build aesthetic opportunity by building up agents' aesthetic competences. Then recall the challenges to any rationale for arts education. Aesthetic education is ubiquitous, for it is integrated into any healthy aesthetic practice, and there are zillions of those. Why single out some practices as beneficiaries of interventionist policies? Why intervene especially when it comes to the fine arts? From an impersonal point of view, aesthetic practices are on a par with respect to their derived aesthetic value. From a personal point of view, each of us has strong reason to follow their own aesthetic path. Arts education compels most of us to pack bags for trips we will never take.

Appearances notwithstanding, the network theory does suggest a rationale for arts education. Unlike external approaches, it is not quite so hostage to empirical fortune. Unlike aesthetic hedonism, it aims at genuine aesthetic opportunity. We need two ideas.

First, participation in any aesthetic practice calls upon two kinds of competence. One is core competence, competence in making aesthetic evaluations in conformity with the practice's aesthetic profile. Members of K with core competence are skilled at relating the non-aesthetic features of items in K with their aesthetic merits and demerits. In addition, members of K specialize in the types of acts they perform. Some create, some appreciate, some conserve, and some edit. Competence in these acts combines core competence with some further competence.

Second, within a larger social group where a number of aesthetic practices are endemic, it is possible that some will foster competences that more easily transfer to many others. Imagine a space where lines between practices represent a more or less straightforward transfer of competence. Some aesthetic practices might be hubs, with spokes connecting outward to many practices that are not themselves hubs. An agent with a hub competence is more likely to have derived aesthetic reason to travel many places. An agent with derived aesthetic reason to travel to a practice has derived aesthetic reason to transit the hubs along the way. Moreover, the hub-and-spoke arrangement is not only possible but also likely, because it is efficient. A society where agents routinely act on the aesthetic reasons and the derived aesthetic reasons they have is likely to end up in a region of aesthetic space with hubs and spokes.

Factoring in their existing aesthetic competences, agents have derived aesthetic reasons to learn what it takes to do well in different aesthetic practices. In a hub-and-spoke universe, many of them have derived aesthetic reason to converge on some hubs on their way to their niches. Some hubs will be ones where core competence transfers; other hubs will be ones where specialist competence transfers. The claim is that a group has reason to adopt an interventionist policy of aesthetic education when the policy indirectly promotes access to activity across the whole space by directly supporting activity at the hubs.

Viewed impersonally, an agent has no more derived aesthetic reason to join one practice than any other. Viewed personally and in social context, their having derived aesthetic reason to set off for a destination gives them derived aesthetic reason to transit intermediate hubs. The claim is not that a hub must be our final destination. As long as we have derived aesthetic reason to travel anywhere, we have reason to transit a hub. Therefore, supporting the hubs engineers aesthetic opportunity.

What about arts education in particular? The question comes down to whether it is likely that the arts are aesthetic hubs in societies like ours, history being what it is. Historically, the arts enjoyed special stature and were showered with resources of all kinds. As a result, learning to be a good appreciator of one of the arts, where there is a tradition of written criticism and open discussion of how criticism works, is good background for acquiring core competence in neighbouring aesthetic practices.

No rationale for arts education is purely a priori. External approaches rely on empirical claims about the benefits of arts education for performance in non-arts subjects. Aesthetic hedonists rely on empirical claims about the ranking of art works over other items. The rationale just sketched relies on an empirical picture about the central role that the arts have come to play in building competences that transfer to other aesthetic practices.

Since the details will vary from one context to another, aesthetic education should not be applied on the cookie cutter model. The modern system of the arts has dominated European aesthetic culture since the eighteenth century; it does not fit all non-European cultures, where aesthetic kinds that we do not count as fine arts might functions as hubs. Perhaps some of the fine arts are now beginning to lose their roles as hubs. That the rationale is in this way hostage to empirical fortune is no knock against it. Arts education should adapt itself to its context, and change with the times.

Communication Gateways

One reason to adopt interventionist policies in arts education is that they prepare us for aesthetic agency beyond the arts, so long as the arts are effective gateways to swaths of aesthetic space to which we have derived aesthetic reason to travel (see also Kaelin 1989: 61–2). A similar line of thought suggests why we have reason to adopt policies that smooth communication among aesthetic agents. Indeed, the specific policies we should adopt depend on the nature of existing infrastructures of aesthetic communication.

Infrastructures of aesthetic communication fall into three broad modes, and the third is new. First are the intimate modes of communication that take place conversationally, among two or a few parties. In its intimate mode, communication rarely builds in a power disparity, but its reach is short, and it can only support local micro-practices. As local micro-practices tend to remain isolated from each other, intimate communication leads to an aesthetic landscape of great diversity.

The second mode of communication is broadcasting, where the same message is delivered to huge numbers of receivers at the same time. Technologies, from the printing press to television, vastly expanded the scope of broadcast communication, facilitating information transfer on a global scale. However, broadcast technologies are so costly that only a tiny number of super-experts have access to transmission facilities, while the receiver base is populated by a large number of people who are required to have only a minimal competence (Carroll 1998). Broadcasting culture sweeps local practices into a global aesthetic, killing off aesthetic diversity. An increase in overall aesthetic participation comes at the cost of aesthetic opportunity.

A third mode of communication exploits social media, which support globally distributed micro-practices (Lopes 2016a: 101–3). Take Flickr, which is made up of groups organized around some common purpose, sometimes a shared interest in subject matter—cats or cakes, for example—but sometimes a shared aesthetic interest. Soon after cameras became widely available, amateur photographers set up neighbourhood clubs to share know-how and equipment, but also to converge on norms, thereby establishing local aesthetic micro-practices. Flickr also provides a venue where aesthetic practices can develop around photography, beyond the control of the galleries and the art press. Unlike the photo club, though, its members can be anywhere. As a result, micro-practices now proliferate: chances are slim of finding fifty other photographers in your neighbourhood who share as much with you aesthetically as fifty people anywhere in the world, brought together by Flickr.

A delightful example is provided by a prankster who posted to a Flickr group a classic photograph by Cartier-Bresson, as if it was their own work, inviting comment (Heffernan 2008). Group members laid into it as "gray, blurry, small, odd crop." When the prank was revealed, the group came in for considerable mockery. How could anyone serious about photography fail to recognize a Cartier-Bresson? How could they get it so wrong? The mockery is mistaken, because it assumes a monolithic practice of photography. What is wonderful about this group is that it had developed an aesthetic practice with norms and traditions free of official art photography. Social media permit small-scale practices to arise by bringing together a super-specialized membership from almost anywhere on the planet.

The book has yet to be written on the role of technologies such as the YouTube video and the Etsy shop in fostering the new antiquarian aesthetics of hipsters and millennials. Much work remains to be done if we are to understand the workings of global micro-practices—how, for example, can we measure participation in mode three networks (Johanson, Glow, and Kershaw 2014)?

Laissez-faire aesthetic policies that make sense in societies where aesthetic communication is mostly intimate, might fail a society where broadcast communication dominates. Third-mode aesthetic communication calls for a new approach again. A report for the MacArthur Foundation argues that social media afford participatory culture, characterized by "relatively low barriers to artistic expression and civic engagement, strong support for creating and sharing one's creations, and some type of informal mentorship whereby what is known by the most experienced is passed along to novices" (Jenkins et al. 2006: 3). In as much as navigating globally distributed micro-practices requires special skills and knowledge, then perhaps a case can be made for curricula that build some of the needed skills (Jenkins et al. 2006: 7–8).

Aesthetic agents venture down paths from practice to practice. One rounds a treacherous cape, having made meticulous preparations to ready their vessel and lay in a course. Another wings it, selecting a destination based on a brochure, or some hearsay, showing up ready to take in whatever they find. The network theory allows for both. Sometimes we act having carefully sized up our derived aesthetic reasons. Sometimes, knowing that all aesthetic practices are on a par from an impersonal point of view, and that many are on a par from a personal point of view too, we sample, relying on some communication. Communication is a fundamental driver of aesthetic opportunity, to be given a special place in aesthetic policy.

Social Intersections

So far, these twelve chapters have treated aesthetic values in their own terms, as deserving a kind of full and undivided attention that they have rarely received. Attention is tactical and not substantive: it does not follow that aesthetic reasons are autonomous. On the contrary, they intersect with other practical reasons and with all kinds of non-aesthetic facts. Still, the danger in bracketing the intersections is that we end up with an "ideal theory" in Charles Mills's (2005) pejorative sense. A too rosy picture of aesthetic practices overlooks what has led arts scholars to view aesthetic value with suspicion, even derision (see the Introduction). Aesthetic values have been instruments of oppression, and aesthetic practices are not isolated from larger social mechanisms of oppression (see James 2013 for an overview). In abstracting away from all this, does the network theory turn out to be an ideal theory? Is what appears to be a straightforward truth claim really a move in an oppressive system that obscures the truth? The reply in defence of the network theory is to grant that aesthetic practices can be instruments of oppression, but to add that aesthetic policies can serve as anti-oppressive social policies (see also Eaton 2016; Yancy 2016).

Take as cases what Paul Taylor calls the beauty–gender nexus and the beauty–race nexus (2016: 20–3; see also Roelofs 2005; Irvin 2016). Running in one direction, the social formation of gender and race yields conceptions of beauty or aesthetic value. To be a woman is partly to conform to a standard of beauty; in some places, to be black is partly to fail to meet another standard, one associated with whiteness. Running in the other direction, the aesthetic practices that dominate in a society are precisely those that echo its conceptions of gender and race. Not only is access to aesthetic practices managed along lines of race and gender but, in addition, aesthetic practices are constituted by racialized and gendered ideals of beauty. Structuring aesthetic practices around race and gender perpetuates and is perpetuated by the social formation of race and gender. Since each nexus privileges some and oppresses others, aesthetic practices are "technologies" and "pedagogies" of privilege and oppression (James 2013: 106–8; Irvin 2017). As a result, we have ample non-aesthetic reason, including moral reason, to defang the offending aesthetic standards.

Sara Protasi's (2017) paper on the "perfect bikini body" represents skepticism about the availability, within the domain of aesthetic value, of resources for fashioning an anti-oppressive beauty ideal. She argues, by process of elimination, that an anti-oppressive beauty ideal must incorporate some ethical elements; it cannot be generated solely from aesthetic reasons.

The first view to be eliminated is the no-standards view, according to which everyone is maximally or equally beautiful (cf. Irvin 2017). Protasi objects that the view is insufficiently aspirational: without meaningful aesthetic comparisons between human bodies, we can have no target that we should strive to attain (2017: 96). In addition, she claims, an item's beauty is a positional good, one whose absolute value depends on the item's place in the distribution of the good. So, "if we were all beautiful, beauty would not be as valuable" (Protasi 2017: 96).

An alternative is a multiple standards view. If the goal is that "women stop trying to conform to standards that are excessively narrow and often impossible to obtain, and shaped by oppressive, demeaning norms," then multiple, inclusive standards fit the bill (Protasi 2017: 97). Whence the standards? Protasi considers grounding beauty in health, so that a healthy body is a beautiful one and bodies are ugly when they are unhealthy or abnormal. However, she objects, the proposal is ableist: it renders incoherent the proposition that physically disabled bodies can be beautiful. Since physically disabled bodies can be beautiful, the view is false (Siebers 2011).

By process of elimination, we arrive at the moralized view. For a person to be beautiful is for them to be an appropriate object of a loving gaze, and what makes someone an appropriate object of a loving gaze is their moral character, independent of their outward appearance (Protasi 2017: 99). The view retains beauty's positionality: some are more beautiful than others. At the same time, the ranking is determined by morally relevant features. "Those who are most beautiful on the inside are," Protasi writes, "the most beautiful on the outside" (2017: 99).

The misstep in this argument from elimination should be obvious, if the network theory has made any impression at all. The view that grounds personal beauty in healthy appearances is not the best version of a multiple standards view.

According to the network theory, nothing is beautiful without being beautiful in some more determinate way. Instead of speaking of multiple "standards" of beauty, we should say that there are many beauties, or many ways of being aesthetically good. For each aesthetic practice, there is an aesthetic profile—a scheme correlating non-aesthetic features with aesthetic values—that represents a distinct set of ways of being aesthetically good. Members of the practice follow the norm of acting on the basis of the relevant aesthetic profile. In principle, there are many aesthetic practices around the human body, and some ground aesthetic value facts in facts about health, or moral character.

Ideally, all it takes to displace a pernicious beauty ideal is to start to act around a new aesthetic profile. A theory of aesthetic value that says this and can say nothing more is fit to be impeached as an "ideal theory" in Mills's sense. In non-ideal reality, those who need to vote with their feet find themselves in a systematically gerrymandered space. They have reason—aesthetic and non-aesthetic—to travel to certain aesthetic practices, yet their paths are blocked by a nexus of aesthetic and non-aesthetic forces, some of which obscure for them the reasons they have.

Political theorists disagree about what strategies effectively resist oppression. Assume that resisting oppression, when oppression enlists our aesthetic practices, consists in aesthetic self-determination. Aesthetic policies promote self-determination when they are licensed by the aesthetic opportunity principle, namely that larger social groups have reason to foster the aesthetic opportunities available to their members. It is baked into the network theory that aesthetic agency is social agency, and that it is compromised by incompetence. The aesthetic opportunity principle charges us with doing what we can in the circumstances.

Any theory that promises an anti-oppressive silver bullet is an "ideal theory." No algorithm destabilizes the homeostatic system that is a beauty–gender or beauty–race nexus—or a beauty–ability, beauty–caste, or beauty–hetero nexus. "Doing what we can" is the most to hope for. Taylor eloquently articulates the challenge: we are in "an ongoing struggle to deal responsibly and experimentally with the forces that condition our choices" (2016: 115). He also hints at a parity argument (2016: 125). If aesthetic practices can be enlisted to serve oppressive social programs, then they have some oomph in the social world, and that oomph can be harnessed towards self-determination. In the case of race, he salutes how much progress has been made by "insisting on black dignity, humanity, and beauty, and cultivating these virtues and capacities in distinctively black public and private spaces" (2016: 122).

The network theory accommodates the importance of non-aesthetic spaces to incubate anti-oppressive aesthetic practices.

Nothing resonates more for us, nowadays, than Beardsley's agonies, in 1968, about the seeming absurdity of aesthetics in times troubled by violence, hate, environmental breakdown, and calamitous assaults on liberal democracy. In truth, however, our aesthetic commitments are not optional. We cannot down tools and make for the barricades. We will take our tools with us.

List of Theses

Common Ground

EVALUATION: a state is an aesthetic evaluation = the state is a mental representation of some item as having some aesthetic value.

ACT: A's φing is an aesthetic act = A's φing counterfactually depends on the content of A's aesthetic evaluation of x, where A's φing operates on x.

REASON: the fact that x is V is an aesthetic reason for A to φ in C = the fact that x is V lends weight to the proposition that A aesthetically should φ in C.

VALUE: necessarily, V is an aesthetic value only if the fact that x is V lends weight to the proposition that A aesthetically should φ in C.

Aesthetic Hedonism

AESTHETIC HEDONISM: an aesthetic value is a property of an item that stands in constitutive relation to finally valuable experiences of subjects who correctly understand the item.

SAH: an aesthetic value, V, is reason-giving = the fact that x is V lends weight to the proposition that it would maximize A's pleasure were A to φ in C, were A's hedonic responses calibrated to those of true judges in joint verdict.

AESTHETIC REASON INTERNALISM: necessarily, p is an aesthetic reason for A to φ in C only if A can be motivated by a p-representing state to φ in C.

DESIRE: necessarily, the fact p is an aesthetic reason for A to φ in C only if A has a p-representing desire that would be satisfied by A's φing in C and the fact that p explains why the desire would be satisfied by A's φing in C.

The Network Theory

EXPERT: A has aesthetic expertise = A has competence for achievement in φing, where φing is an aesthetic act.

NETWORK THEORY: an aesthetic value, V, is reason-giving = the fact that x is V lends weight to the proposition that it would be an aesthetic achievement for some A to φ in C, where x is an item in an aesthetic practice, K, and A's competence to φ is aligned upon an aesthetic profile that is constitutive of K.

MERIT: V is an aesthetic merit in x = the fact that x is V is reason for A to φ in C in K, and A's success in φing in C contributes to promoting V in K.

DEMERIT: V is an aesthetic demerit in x = the fact that x is V is reason for A to φ in C in K, and A's success in φing in C contributes to suppressing V in K.

AESTHETIC REASON EXTERNALISM: possibly, p is an aesthetic reason for A to φ in C yet A cannot be motivated by a p-representing state to φ in C.

AESTHETIC VALUE NATURALISM: for any aesthetic value fact, p, there is a subset, γ, of the non-aesthetic natural facts such that γ grounds p.

References

Abbott, Berenice. 1930. *Atget, photographe de Paris*. Paris: Henri Jonquières.
Abbott, Berenice. 1939. *Changing New York*. New York: Dutton.
Abbott, Berenice. 1941. *A Guide to Better Photography*. New York: Crown.
Abbott, Berenice. 1951. What the Camera and I See, *Art News* (September): 36.
Abbott, Berenice. 1964. *The World of Atget*. New York: Horizon.
Abbott, Berenice. 1969. *The Attractive Universe: Gravity and the Shape of Space*. Cleveland, OH: World.
Abell, Catharine. 2012. Art: What It Is and Why It Matters, *Philosophy and Phenomenological Research* 85/3: 671–91.
Acord, Sophia Krzys, and Tia DeNora. 2008. Culture and the Arts: From Art Worlds to Arts-in-Action, *Annals of the American Academy of Political and Social Science* 619/1: 223–37.
Adams, Robert Merrihew. 2006. *A Theory of Virtue: Excellence in Being for the Good*. Oxford: Oxford University Press.
Addison, Joseph. 1712. *The Spectator* 369.
Alcaraz León, María José. 2008. The Rational Justification of Aesthetic Judgements, *Journal of Aesthetics and Art Criticism* 66/3: 291–300.
Alexander, Victoria D. 2014. Art and the Twenty-First Century Gift: Corporate Philanthropy and Government Funding in the Cultural Sector, *Anthropological Forum* 24/4: 364–80.
Alvarez, Maria, and Aaron Ridley. 2017. Acting for Aesthetic Reasons, *Estetika* 54 10/1: 65–84.
Anderson, Elizabeth. 1993. *Value in Ethics and Economics*. Cambridge, MA: Harvard University Press.
Annas, Julia. 2011. *Intelligent Virtue*. Oxford: Oxford University Press.
Anonymous. 2013. *Fixing E. T. The Extra-Terrestrial for the Atari 2600* (February) <http://www.neocomputer.org/projects/et>.
Anscombe, G. E. M. 1963. *Intention*, 2nd edn. Oxford: Blackwell.
Archer, Alfred. 2013. Aesthetic Judgements and Motivation, *Proceedings of the European Society for Aesthetics* 5: 67–85.
Archer, Alfred, and Lauren Ware. 2017. Aesthetic Supererogation, *Estetika* 54 10/1: 102–16.
Ashley, Clifford W. 1944. *The Ashley Book of Knots*. New York: Doubleday.
Audi, Paul. 2012a. A Clarification and Defense of the Notion of Grounding, *Metaphysical Grounding: Understanding the Structure of Reality*. Cambridge: Cambridge University Press, pp. 101–21.

Audi, Paul. 2012b. Grounding: Toward a Theory of the *In-Virtue-of* Relation, *Journal of Philosophy* 109/12: 685–711.
Audi, Robert. 2014. Normativity and Generality in Ethics and Aesthetics, *Journal of Ethics* 18/4: 373–90.
Augustin, Dorothee M., and Helmut Leder. 2006. Art Expertise: A Study of Concepts and Conceptual Spaces, *Psychology Science* 48/2: 135–56.
Baehr, Jason. 2011. *The Inquiring Mind: On Intellectual Virtues and Virtue Epistemology*. Oxford: Oxford University Press.
Baldwin, Gordon. 2000. *Eugène Atget: Photographs from the J. Paul Getty Museum*. Los Angeles: J. Paul Getty Museum.
Barker, Chris. 2002. The Dynamics of Vagueness, *Linguistics and Philosophy* 25/1: 1–36.
Barker, Chris. 2013. Negotiating Taste, *Inquiry* 56/2–3: 240–57.
Battaly, Heather. 2015. *Virtue*. Cambridge: Polity.
Baumol, William J. 1985. Public Support for the Arts, *Columbia Journal of Art and the Law* 9/208: 214–28.
Baxandall, Michael. 1972. *Painting and Experience in Fifteenth-Century Italy: A Primer in the Social History of Pictorial Style*. Oxford: Oxford University Press.
Baxandall, Michael. 1985. *Patterns of Intention: On the Historical Explanation of Pictures*. New Haven, CT: Yale University Press.
Beardsley, Monroe C. 1962. On the Generality of Critical Reasons, *Journal of Philosophy* 59/18: 477–86.
Beardsley, Monroe C. 1969. Aesthetic Experience Regained, *Journal of Aesthetics and Art Criticism* 28/1: 3–11.
Beardsley, Monroe C. 1970a. Aesthetic Welfare, *Journal of Aesthetic Education* 4/4: 9–20.
Beardsley, Monroe C. 1970b. The Aesthetic Point of View, *Metaphilosophy* 1/1: 39–58.
Beardsley, Monroe C. 1973. Aesthetic Welfare, Aesthetic Justice, and Educational Policy, *Journal of Aesthetic Education* 7/4: 49–61.
Beardsley, Monroe C. 1979. In Defense of Aesthetic Value, *Proceedings and Addresses of the American Philosophical Association* 52/6: 723–49.
Beardsley, Monroe C. 1981[1958]. *Aesthetics: Problems in the Philosophy of Criticism*, 2nd edn. Indianapolis, IN: Hackett.
Beardsley, Monroe C. 1982. Aesthetic Experience, *The Aesthetic Point of View*. Ithaca, NY: Cornell University Press, pp. 285–97.
Beardsley, Monroe C. 1983. The Refutation of Relativism, *Journal of Aesthetics and Art Criticism* 41/3: 265–70.
Becker, Howard S. 2008. *Art Worlds*, 2nd edn. Berkeley and Los Angeles, CA: University of California Press.
Bell, Clive. 1914. *Art*. London: Chatto and Windus.
Bender, John. 1987. Supervenience and the Justification of Aesthetic Judgments, *Journal of Aesthetics and Art Criticism* 46/1: 31–40.
Bender, John. 1995. General but Defeasible Reasons in Aesthetic Evaluation: The Particularist/Generalist Dispute, *Journal of Aesthetics and Art Criticism* 53/4: 379–92.
Bender, John. 1996. Realism, Supervenience, and Irresolvable Aesthetic Disputes, *Journal of Aesthetics and Art Criticism* 54/4: 371–81.

Bender, John. 2001. Sensitivity, Sensibility, and Aesthetic Realism, *Journal of Aesthetics and Art Criticism* 59/1: 73–83.
Benovsky, Jiri. 2012. Aesthetic Supervenience vs Aesthetic Grounding, *Estetika* 49 5/2: 166–78.
Bernstein, Joe. 2014. Meet the Men Trying to Immortalize Video Games, *Buzzfeed* (October 27) <http://www.buzzfeed.com/josephbernstein/meet-the-men-trying-to-immortalize-video-games>.
Bicchieri, Cristina. 2006. *The Grammar of Society: The Nature and Dynamics of Social Norms*. Cambridge: Cambridge University Press.
Bishop, Michael. 2015. *The Good Life: Unifying the Philosophy and Psychology of Well-Being*. Oxford: Oxford University Press.
Black, Samuel. 1992. Revisionist Liberalism and the Decline of Culture, *Ethics* 102/2: 244–67.
Blackburn, Simon. 1998. *Ruling Passions: A Theory of Practical Reasoning*. Oxford: Oxford University Press.
Bliss, Ricki, and Kelly Trogdon. 2014. Metaphysical Grounding, *Stanford Encyclopedia of Philosophy* <http://plato.stanford.edu>.
Bloom, Paul. 2010. *How Pleasure Works: The New Science of Why We Like What We Like*. New York: W. W. Norton.
Blum, Lawrence. 1998. Community and Virtues, *How Should One Live? Essays on the Virtues*, ed. Roger Crisp. Oxford: Oxford University Press, pp. 231–50.
Bonzon, Roman. 1999. Aesthetic Objectivity and the Ideal Observer Theory, *British Journal of Aesthetics* 39/3: 230–40.
Bonzon, Roman. 2009. Thick Aesthetic Concepts, *Journal of Aesthetics and Art Criticism* 67/2: 191–9.
Bourdieu, Pierre. 1977. *Outline of a Theory of Practice*, trans. Richard Nice. Cambridge: Cambridge University Press.
Bourdieu, Pierre. 1983. The Field of Cultural Production, Or the Economic World Reversed, *Poetics* 12/4–5: 311–56.
Bourdieu, Pierre. 1984. *Distinction: A Social Critique of the Judgement of Taste*, trans. Richard Nice. Cambridge, MA: Harvard University Press.
Bourdieu, Pierre. 1990. *Photography: A Middle-Brow Art*, trans. Shaun Whiteside. Stanford, CA: Stanford University Press.
Bourget, David, and David Chalmers. 2014. What Do Philosophers Believe? *Philosophical Studies* 170/3: 465–500.
Boyd, Richard. 1999. Homeostasis, Species, and Higher Taxa, *Species: New Interdisciplinary Essays*, ed. Robert Wilson. Cambridge, MA: MIT Press, pp. 141–85.
Bradford, Gwen. 2015. *Achievement*. Oxford: Oxford University Press.
Brady, Emily. 2003. *Aesthetics of the Natural Environment*. Edinburgh: Edinburgh University Press.
Brady, Emily. 2006. The Aesthetic Practice of Agricultural Landscapes, *Ethics, Place, and Environment* 9/1: 1–19.
Braudel, Fernand. 1979. *The Structures of Everyday Life: The Limits of the Possible*. New York: Harper and Row.
Brighouse, Harry. 1995. Neutrality, Publicity, and State Funding of the Arts, *Philosophy and Public Affairs* 24/1: 35–63.

Brogaard, Berit. 2017. A Semantic Framework for Aesthetic Expressions, *Semantics of Aesthetic Judgement*, ed. James O. Young. Oxford: Oxford University Press, pp. 121–39.

Brooks, Arthur C. 2001. Who Opposes Government Arts Funding? *Public Choice* 108/3–4: 355–67.

Brooks, David. 1993. Taste, Virtue, and Class, *Virtue and Taste: Essays on Politics, Ethics, and Aesthetics in Memory of Flint Schier*, ed. Dudley Knowles and John Skorupski. Oxford: Blackwell, pp. 65–82.

Broudy, Harry S. 1972. *Enlightened Cherishing: An Essay on Aesthetic Education*. Urbana, IL: University of Illinois Press.

Budd, Malcolm. 1995. *Values of Art: Painting, Poetry, and Music*. London: Penguin.

Budd, Malcolm. 1999. Aesthetic Judgements, Aesthetic Principles, and Aesthetic Properties, *European Journal of Philosophy* 7/3: 295–311.

Budd, Malcolm. 2002. *The Aesthetic Appreciation of Nature: Essays on the Aesthetics of Nature*. Oxford: Oxford University Press.

Budd, Malcolm. 2003. The Acquaintance Principle, *British Journal of Aesthetics* 43/4: 386–92.

Budd, Malcolm. 2007. The Intersubjective Validity of Aesthetic Judgements, *British Journal of Aesthetics* 47/4: 333–71.

Budd, Malcolm. 2008. Aesthetic Essence, *Aesthetic Experience*, ed. Richard Shusterman and Adele Tomlin. London: Routledge, pp. 1–14.

Burge, Tyler. 2010. *Origins of Objectivity*. Oxford: Oxford University Press.

Burnham, Douglas, and Ole Martin Skilleås. 2012. *The Aesthetics of Wine*. Oxford: Wiley-Blackwell.

Cage, John. 2010[1952]. Juilliard Lecture, *A Year from Monday: New Lectures and Writings*. Middletown, CT: Wesleyan University Press.

Cahn, Walter. 1979. *Masterpieces: Chapters on the History of an Idea*. Princeton, NJ: Princeton University Press.

Carlson, Allen. 2000. *Aesthetics and the Environment: The Appreciation of Nature, Art, and Architecture*. London: Routledge.

Carroll, Noël. 1987. Can Government Funding of the Arts Be Justified Theoretically? *Journal of Aesthetic Education* 21/1: 21–35.

Carroll, Noël. 1996. Moderate Moralism, *British Journal of Aesthetics* 36/3: 223–38.

Carroll, Noël. 1998. *A Philosophy of Mass Art*. Oxford: Oxford University Press.

Carroll, Noël. 1999. *Philosophy of Art: A Contemporary Introduction*. London: Routledge.

Carroll, Noël. 2002. Aesthetic Experience Revisited, *British Journal of Aesthetics* 42/2: 145–68.

Carroll, Noël. 2007. Aesthetic Experience, Art, Artists, *Aesthetic Experience*, ed. Richard Shusterman and Adele Tomlin. London: Routledge, pp. 45–65.

Carroll, Noël. 2009. *On Criticism*. London: Routledge.

Cavedon-Taylor, Dan. 2017. Reasoned and Unreasoned: On Inference, Acquaintance, and Aesthetic Normativity, *British Journal of Aesthetics* 57/1: 1–17.

Chang, Ruth, ed. 1997. *Incommensurability, Incomparability, and Practical Reason*. Cambridge, MA: Harvard University Press.

Chang, Ruth, 2013. Incommensurability (and Incompatibility), *International Encyclopedia of Ethics*, ed. Hugh LaFollette. Oxford: Blackwell, pp. 2591–604.

Chappell, Timothy (Sophie Grace). 2013. Virtue and Virtue Ethics in the Twentieth Century, *Cambridge Companion to Virtue Ethics*, ed. Dan Russell. Cambridge: Cambridge University Press, pp. 149–71.
Choo, Suzanne S. 2014. Cultivating a Cosmopolitan Consciousness: Returning to the Moral Grounds of Aesthetic Education, *Journal of Aesthetic Education* 48/4: 94–110.
Cohen, Randy, William Schaffer, and Benjamin Davidson. 2003. Arts and Economic Prosperity: The Economic Impact of Nonprofit Arts Organizations and their Audiences, *Journal of Arts Management, Law, and Society* 33/1: 17–31.
Cohen, Ted. 1993. High and Low Thinking about High and Low Art, *Journal of Aesthetics and Art Criticism* 51/2: 151–6.
Cohen, Ted. 1998. On Consistency in One's Personal Aesthetics, *aesthetics and Ethics: Essays at the Intersection*, ed. Jerrold Levinson. Ithaca, NY: Cornell University Press, pp. 106–25.
Cohen, Ted. 1999. High and Low Art, and High and Low Audiences, *Journal of Aesthetics and Art Criticism* 57/2: 137–43.
Cohen, Ted. 2001. Sibley and the Wonder of Aesthetic Language, *Aesthetic Concepts: Essays after Sibley*, ed. Emily Brady and Jerrold Levinson. Oxford: Oxford University Press, pp. 23–34.
Coleman, James S. 1990. *Foundations of Social Theory*. Cambridge, MA: Harvard University Press.
Collingwood, R. G. 1938. *The Principles of Art*. Oxford: Oxford University Press.
Connor, Steven. 2011. Doing Without Art, *New Literary History* 42/1: 53–69.
Correia, Fabrice, and Benjamin Schnieder. 2012. Grounding: An Opinionated Introduction, *Metaphysical Grounding: Understanding the Structure of Reality*. Cambridge: Cambridge University Press, pp. 1–36.
Cova, Florian, and Nicolas Pain. 2012. Can Folk Aesthetics Ground Aesthetic Realism? *Monist* 95/2: 241–63.
Crisp, Roger. 2006. Hedonism Reconsidered, *Philosophy and Phenomenological Research* 73/3: 619–45.
Cross, Anthony. 2017a. Obligations to Artworks as Duties of Love, *Estetika* 54 10/1: 85–101.
Cross, Anthony. 2017b. Art Criticism as Practical Reasoning, *British Journal of Aesthetics* 57/3: 299–317.
Crowd. 2015. List of Commercial Video Games with Available Source Code, *Wikipedia: The Free Encyclopedia* (Update of August 19) <http://en.wikipedia.org/w/index.php?title=List_of_commercial_video_games_with_available_source_code&oldid=676890394>.
CSLA. 2001. 2001 National Honour: Blue Stick Garden. <http://www.csla-aapc.ca/awards-atlas/blue-stick-garden>.
Currie, Gregory. 1990. Supervenience, Essentialism, and Aesthetic Properties, *Philosophical Studies* 58/3: 243–57.
Currie, Gregory. 2011. Art and the Anthropologists, *Aesthetic Science: Connecting Minds, Brains, and Experience*, ed. Arthur Shimamura and Steven Palmer. Oxford: Oxford University Press, pp. 107–28.
Cutter, Brian and Michael Tye. 2011. Tracking Representationalism and the Painfulness of Pain, *Philosophical Issues* 21/1: 90–109.
Cutting, James E. 2003. Gustave Caillebotte, French Impressionism, and Mere Exposure, *Psychonomic Bulletin and Review* 10/2: 319–43.

Cwi, David. 1980. Public Support of the Arts: Three Arguments Examined, *Journal of Cultural Economics* 4/2: 39–62.
Dammann, Guy, and Elisabeth Schellekens. 2017. On the Moral Psychology and Aesthetic Force of Aesthetic Reasons, *Estetika* 54 10/1: 30–9.
Dancy, Jonathan. 1983. Ethical Particularism and Morally Relevant Properties, *Mind* 92/368: 530–47.
Dancy, Jonathan. 2004. *Ethics Without Principles*. Oxford: Oxford University Press.
Danto, Arthur C. 1964. The Artworld, *Journal of Philosophy* 61/19: 571–84.
Danto, Arthur C. 1981. *Transfiguration of the Commonplace*. Cambridge, MA: Harvard University Press.
Danto, Arthur C. 1995. *Playing with the Edge: The Photographic Achievement of Robert Mapplethorpe*. Berkeley and Los Angeles: University of California Press.
Danto, Arthur C. 2003. *The Abuse of Beauty: Aesthetics and the Concept of Art*. Chicago, IL: Open Court.
Davidson, Donald. 1963. Actions, Reasons, and Causes, *Journal of Philosophy* 60/23: 685–700.
Davies, David. 2006. Against Enlightened Empiricism, *Contemporary Debates in Aesthetics and the Philosophy of Art*, ed. Matthew Kieran. Oxford: Blackwell, pp. 22–34.
Davies, David. 2017. The Semantics of Sibleyan Aesthetic Judgements, *Semantics of Aesthetic Judgement*, ed. James O. Young. Oxford: Oxford University Press, pp. 106–20.
Davies, David. forthcoming. Analytic Philosophy of Music, *Oxford Handbook of Western Music and Philosophy*, ed. Tomas Macauley, Jerrold Levinson, and Nanette Nielsen. Oxford: Oxford University Press.
De Clercq, Rafaël. 2002. The Concept of an Aesthetic Property, *Journal of Aesthetics and Art Criticism* 60/2: 167–76.
De Clercq, Rafaël. 2008. The Structure of Aesthetic Properties, *Philosophy Compass* 3/5: 894–909.
DeNora, Tia. 2003. Music Sociology: Getting the Music into the Action, *British Journal of Music Education* 20/2: 165–77.
Devereaux, Mary. 1998. Beauty and Evil: The Case of Leni Riefenstahl's *Triumph of the Will*, *Aesthetics and Ethics: Essays at the Intersection*, ed. Jerrold Levinson. Cambridge: Cambridge University Press, pp. 227–56.
Devereaux, Mary. 2004. Moral Judgements and Works of Art: The Case of Narrative Literature, *Journal of Aesthetics and Art Criticism* 62/1: 3–11.
Dewey, John. 1934. *Art as Experience*. New York: Putnam.
DiBlasio, Margaret Klempay. 1992. The Road from Nice to Necessary: Broudy's Rationale for Art Education, *Journal of Aesthetic Education* 26/4: 21–35.
Dickie, George. 1974. *Art and the Aesthetic: An Institutional Analysis*. Ithaca, NY: Cornell University Press.
Dickie, George. 1984. *The Art Circle*. New York: Haven.
Dickie, George. 1988. *Evaluating Art*. Philadelphia, Penn: Temple University Press.
Diffey, Terry J. 1967. Evaluation and Aesthetic Appraisals, *British Journal of Aesthetics* 7/4: 358–73.
Doris, John. 2002. *Lack of Character: Personality and Moral Behavior*. Cambridge: Cambridge University Press.

Dornenburg, Andrew, and Karen Page. 1996. *Culinary Artistry*. New York: Wiley.
Dorsch, Fabian. 2007. Sentimentalism and the Intersubjectivity of Aesthetic Evaluations, *Dialectica* 61/3: 417–46.
Dorsch, Fabian. 2013. Non-Inferentialism about Justification: The Case of Aesthetic Judgements, *Philosophical Quarterly* 63/253: 660–82.
Ducasse, Curt John. 1966[1929]. *The Philosophy of Art*, 2nd edn. New York: Dover.
Dworkin, Ronald. 1985. Can a Liberal State Support Art? *A Matter of Principle*. Oxford: Oxford University Press, pp. 221–33.
Eaton, A. W. 2012. Robust Immoralism, *Journal of Aesthetics and Art Criticism* 70/3: 281–92.
Eaton, A. W. 2016. Taste in Bodies and Fat Oppression, *Body Aesthetics*, ed. Sherri Irvin. Oxford: Oxford University Press, pp. 38–59.
Eaton, Marcia Muelder. 1989. *Aesthetics and the Good Life*. Rutherford, NJ: Fairleigh Dickinson University Press.
Eaton, Marcia Muelder. 2008. Aesthetic Obligations, *Journal of Aesthetics and Art Criticism* 66/1: 1–9.
Efland, Arthur D. 2002. *Art and Cognition: Integrating the Visual Arts in the Curriculum*. New York: Teachers College Press.
Egan, Andy. 2010. Disputing about Taste, *Disagreement*, ed. Richard Feldman and Ted A. Warfield. Oxford: Oxford University Press, pp. 247–92.
Eisner, Elliot W. 2002. *Arts and the Creation of Mind*. New Haven, CT: Yale University Press.
Elgin, Catherine Z. 2009. Art and Education, *Oxford Handbook of Philosophy of Education*, ed. Harvey Siegel. Oxford: Oxford University Press, pp. 319–31.
Elster, Jon. 1983. *Sour Grapes: Studies in the Subversion of Rationality*. Cambridge: Cambridge University Press.
Epstein, Brian. 2015. *The Ant Trap: Rebuilding the Foundations of the Social Sciences*. Oxford: Oxford University Press.
Ericsson, Karl Anders, and Jacqui Smith. 1991. Prospects and Limits of the Empirical Study of Expertise, *Toward a General Theory of Expertise: Prospects and Limits*, ed. Karl Anders Ericsson and Jacqui Smith. Cambridge: Cambridge University Press, pp. 1–38.
Feinberg, Joel. 1994. Not with My Tax Money: The Problem of Justifying Government Subsidies for the Arts, *Public Affairs Quarterly* 8/2: 101–23.
Fine, Gary Alan, and Corey D. Fields. 2008. Culture and Microsociology: The Anthill and the Veldt, *Annals of the American Academy of Political and Social Science* 619: 130–48.
Fine, Kit. 2012. Guide to Ground, *Metaphysical Grounding: Understanding the Structure of Reality*. Cambridge: Cambridge University Press, pp. 37–80.
Fisher, John A. 2013. High Art Versus Low Art, *The Routledge Companion to Aesthetics*, 3rd edn., ed. Berys Gaut and Dominic McIver Lopes. London: Routledge, pp. 473–84.
Fodor, Jerry. 1974. Special Sciences (Or: the Disunity of Science as a Working Hypothesis), *Synthese* 28/2: 97–115.
Foot, Philippa. 2001. *Natural Goodness*. Oxford: Oxford University Press.
Foot, Philippa. 2003[1972]. Morality and Art, *Moral Dilemmas*. Oxford: Oxford University Press, pp. 5–19.
Foot, Philippa. 2003[1979]. Moral Relativism, *Moral Dilemmas*. Oxford: Oxford University Press, pp. 20–36.

Foot, Philippa. 2003[1990]. Locke, Hume, and Modern Moral Theory, *Moral Dilemmas*. Oxford: Oxford University Press, 117–44.
Forsey, Jane. 2013. *The Aesthetics of Design*. Oxford: Oxford University Press.
Fried, Michael. 1980. *Absorption and Theatricality: Painting and Beholder in the Age of Diderot*. Berkeley and Los Angeles, CA: University of California Press.
Fried, Michael. 2008. *Why Photography Matters as Art as Never Before*. New Haven, CT: Yale University Press.
Fudge, Robert. 2005. A Vindication of Strong Aesthetic Supervenience, *Philosophical Papers* 34/2: 149–71.
Gallagher, James. 2014. Mathematics: Why the Brain Sees Maths as Beauty, *BBC News Online* (February 13) <http://www.bbc.com/news/science-environment-26151062>.
Gallie, W. B. 1956. Art as an Essentially Contested Concept, *Philosophical Quarterly* 6/23: 97–114.
García-Carpintero, Manuel, and Max Kölbel, eds. 2008. *Relative Truth*. Oxford: Oxford University Press.
Gardner, Howard. 2011. *Truth, Beauty, and Goodness Reframed: Educating for the Virtues in the Twenty-First Century*. New York: Basic Books.
Garthwaite, Craig L. 2014. Demand Spillovers, Combative Advertising, and Celebrity Endorsements, *American Economic Journal: Applied Economics* 6/2: 76–104.
Gaut, Berys. 2007. *Art, Emotion, and Ethics*. Oxford: Oxford University Press.
Gaut, Berys. 2010. *A Philosophy of Cinematic Art*. Cambridge: Cambridge University Press.
Gaut, Berys, and Dominic McIver Lopes. 2013. *Routledge Companion to Aesthetics*, 3rd edn. London: Routledge.
Gee, Constance Baumgarner. 2004. Spirit, Mind, and Body: Arts Education the Redeemer, *Handbook of Research and Policy in Art Education*, ed. Elliott W. Eisner and Michael D. Day. New York: Lawrence Erlbaum, pp. 115–34.
Giddens, Anthony. 1984. *The Constitution of Society: Outline of the Theory of Structuration*. Berkeley and Los Angeles, CA: University of California Press.
Godlovitch, Stanley. 1990. Boors and Bumpkins, Snobs and Snoots, *Journal of Aesthetic Education* 24/2: 65–73.
Goldblatt, David A. 1976. Do Works of Art Have Rights? *Journal of Aesthetics and Art Criticism* 35/1: 69–77.
Goldie, Peter. 2007. Towards a Virtue Theory of Art, *British Journal of Aesthetics* 47/4: 372–87.
Goldie, Peter. 2008. Virtues of Art and Human Well-Being, *Aristotelian Society Supplementary Volume* 82/1: 179–95.
Goldie, Peter. 2011. The Ethics of Aesthetic Bootstrapping, *The Aesthetic Mind: Philosophy and Psychology*, ed. Elisabeth Schellekens and Peter Goldie. Oxford: Oxford University Press, pp. 106–15.
Goldman, Alan H. 1990. Aesthetic Qualities and Aesthetic Value, *Journal of Philosophy* 87/1: 23–37.
Goldman, Alan H. 1993. Realism about Aesthetic Properties, *Journal of Aesthetics and Art Criticism* 51/1: 31–7.

Goldman, Alan H. 1995. *Aesthetic Value*. Boulder, CO: Westview.
Goldman, Alan H. 2006. The Experiential Account of Aesthetic Value, *Journal of Aesthetics and Art Criticism* 64/3: 333–42.
Gombrich, E. H. 1960. *Art and Illusion*. London: Phaidon.
Good, Owen S. 2014. Museum Acquires "Virtually Complete" Source Code from Atari's Arcade Heyday, *Polygon* (April 22) <http://www.polygon.com/2014/4/22/5640114/maze-invaders-atari-arcade-source-code-strong-museum-icheg>.
Goodman, Nelson. 1976. *Languages of Art: An Approach to a Theory of Symbols*, 2nd edn. Indianapolis: Hackett.
Gracyk, Theodore. 1990. Having Bad Taste, *British Journal of Aesthetics* 30/2: 117–31.
Grant, James. 2013. *The Critical Imagination*. Oxford: Oxford University Press.
Greco, John. 2010. *Achieving Knowledge: A Virtue-Theoretic Account of Epistemic Normativity*. Cambridge: Cambridge University Press.
Griffin, James. 1996. *Value Judgement: Improving Our Ethical Beliefs*. Oxford: Oxford University Press.
Griffiths Ronald R., William A. Richards, Matthew W. Johnson, Una D. McCann, and Robert Jesse. 2008. Mystical-Type Experiences Occasioned by Psilocybin Mediate the Attribution of Personal Meaning and Spiritual Significance 14 Months Later, *Journal of Psychopharmacology* 22/6: 621–32.
Guyer, Paul. 2005. The Standard of Taste and the "Most Ardent Desire of Society," *Values of Beauty: Historical Essays in Aesthetics*. Cambridge: Cambridge University Press, pp. 37–74.
Haack, Susan. 1998. *Manifesto of a Passionate Moderate: Unfashionable Essays*. Chicago, IL: University of Chicago Press.
Haidt, Jonathan. 2006. *The Happiness Hypothesis: Finding Modern Truth in Ancient Wisdom*. New York: Basic Books.
Hall, Lars, Petter Johansson, Betty Tärning, Sverker Sikström, and Thérèse Deutgen. 2010. Magic at the Marketplace: Choice Blindness for the Taste of Jam and the Smell of Tea, *Cognition* 117/1: 54–61.
Hampshire, Stuart. 1954. Logic and Appreciation, *Aesthetics and Language*, ed. William Elton. Oxford: Blackwell, pp. 161–9.
Hampton, Jean. 1998. *The Authority of Reason*. Cambridge: Cambridge University Press.
Hanson, Karen. 1990. Dressing Down Dressing Up: The Philosophic Fear of Fashion, *Hypatia* 5/2: 107–21.
Hanson, Louise. 2013. The Reality of (Non-aesthetic) Artistic Value, *Philosophical Quarterly* 63/252: 492–508.
Harman, Gilbert. 1999. Moral Philosophy Meets Social Psychology: Virtue Ethics and the Fundamental Attribution Error, *Proceedings of the Aristotelian Society* 99: 315–31.
Haslanger, Sally Anne. 2012. *Resisting Reality: Social Construction and Social Critique*. Oxford: Oxford University Press.
Haslanger, Sally Anne. 2014. Social Meaning and Philosophical Method, *Proceedings and Addresses of the American Philosophical Association* 88/1: 16–37.
Hébert, Karine. 2009. Elsie Reford, Une Bourgeoise montréalaise et métissienne: Un Exemple de spatialisation des sphères privée et publique, *Revue d'histoire de l'Amérique française* 63/2–3: 275–303.

Heffernan, Virgina. 2008. Sepia No More, *New York Times Magazine* (April 27): 18–19.

Hegel, G. F. W. 1975[1832]. *Aesthetics: Lectures on Fine Art*, trans. T. M. Knox. New York: Oxford University Press.

Heilbrun, James, and Charles M. Gray. 2001. *Economics of Art and Culture*, 2nd edn. Cambridge: Cambridge University Press.

Hein, Hilde. 1978. Aesthetic Rights: Vindication and Vilification, *Journal of Aesthetics and Art Criticism* 37/2: 169–76.

Herrington, Susan. 2004. Taste Buds: Cultivating a Canadian Cuisine, *Eating Architecture*, ed. Jamie Horwitz and Paulette Singley. Cambridge, MA: MIT Press, pp. 33–50.

Hetland, Lois, and Ellen Winner, eds. 2000. Special Issue on the Arts and Academic Achievement: What the Evidence Shows, *Journal of Aesthetic Education* 34/3–4.

Hetland, Lois, and Ellen Winner. 2004. Cognitive Transfer from Arts Education to Non-Arts Outcomes: Research Evidence and Policy Implications, *Handbook of Research and Policy in Art Education*, ed. Elliott W. Eisner and Michael D. Day. New York: Lawrence Erlbaum, pp. 135–62.

Hick, Darren Hudson. 2012. Aesthetic Supervenience Revisited, *British Journal of Aesthetics* 52/3: 301–16.

Hickey, Dave. 2009. *The Invisible Dragon: Essays on Beauty*, 2nd edn. Chicago, IL: University of Chicago Press.

Hieronymi, Pamela. 2005. The Wrong Kind of Reason, *Journal of Philosophy* 102/9: 437–57.

Hopkins, Robert. 2000a. Beauty and Testimony, *Philosophy, the Good, the True, and the Beautiful*, ed. Anthony O'Hear. Cambridge: Cambridge University Press, pp. 209–36.

Hopkins, Robert. 2000b. Touching Pictures, *British Journal of Aesthetics* 40/1: 149–67.

Hopkins, Robert. 2001. Kant, Quasi-Realism, and the Autonomy of Aesthetic Judgement, *European Journal of Philosophy* 9/2: 166–89.

Hopkins, Robert. 2005. Aesthetics, Experience, and Discrimination, *Journal of Aesthetics and Art Criticism* 63/2: 119–33.

Hopkins, Robert. 2006a. Critical Reasoning and Critical Perception, *Knowing Art: Essays in Aesthetics and Epistemology*, ed. Matthew Kieran and Dominic McIver Lopes. Dordrecht: Springer, pp. 137–53.

Hopkins, Robert. 2006b. Painting, History, and Experience, *Philosophical Studies* 127/1: 19–35.

Hopkins, Robert. 2011. How to Be a Pessimist about Aesthetic Testimony, *Journal of Philosophy* 108/3: 138–57.

Hospers, John. 1962. The Ideal Aesthetic Observer, *British Journal of Aesthetics* 2/2: 99–111.

Huddleston, Andrew. 2012. In Defense of Artistic Value, *Philosophical Quarterly* 62/249: 705–14.

Hume, David. 1739. *A Treatise of Human Nature*. London: John Noon.

Hume, David. 1777. Of the Standard of Taste, *Four Dissertations*. London: Millar, pp. 227–49.

Hungerland, Isabel Creed. 1968. Once Again, Aesthetic and Non-Aesthetic, *Journal of Aesthetics and Art Criticism* 26/3: 285–95.

Hurka, Thomas. 2001. *Virtue, Vice, and Value*. Oxford: Oxford University Press.

Hurka, Thomas. 2006. Games and the Good, *Proceedings of the Aristotelian Society Supplementary Volume* 80: 217–35.
Hursthouse, Rosalind. 1999. *On Virtue Ethics*. Oxford: Oxford University Press.
Hutcheson, Francis. 1738. *An Inquiry into the Original of Our Ideas of Beauty and Virtue*, 4th edn. London.
Inglis, David. 2005. *The Sociology of Art: Ways of Seeing*, ed. David Inglis and John Hughson. London: Palgrave Macmillan, pp. 11–29.
Inglis, Matthew, and Andrew Aberdein. 2014. Beauty Is Not Simplicity: An Analysis of Mathematicians' Proof Appraisals, *Philosophia Mathematica* 23/1: 87–109.
Irvin, Sherri. 2007. Forgery and the Corruption of the Aesthetic Understanding, *Canadian Journal of Philosophy* 37/2: 283–303.
Irvin, Sherri. 2008a. Scratching an Itch, *Journal of Aesthetics and Art Criticism* 66/1: 25–35.
Irvin, Sherri. 2008b. The Pervasiveness of the Aesthetic in Ordinary Experience, *British Journal of Aesthetics* 48/1: 29–44.
Irvin, Sherri. 2014. Is Aesthetic Experience Possible? *Aesthetics and the Sciences of Mind*, ed. Gregory Currie, Matthew Kieran, Aaron Meskin, and Jon Robson. Oxford: Oxford University Press, pp. 37–51.
Irvin, Sherri, ed. 2016. *Body Aesthetics*. Oxford: Oxford University Press.
Irvin, Sherri. 2017. Resisting Body Oppression: An Aesthetic Approach, *Feminist Philosophy Quarterly* 3/4: 1–25.
Iseminger, Gary. 2004. *The Aesthetic Function of Art*. Ithaca, NY: Cornell University Press.
Isenberg, Arnold. 1949. Critical Communication, *Philosophical Review* 58/4: 330–44.
Jackson, Frank. 1998. *From Metaphysics to Ethics: A Defence of Conceptual Analysis*. Oxford: Oxford University Press.
Jacobson, Daniel. 1997. In Praise of Immoral Art, *Philosophical Topics* 25/1: 155–99.
James, Robin. 2013. Oppression, Privilege, and Aesthetics: The Use of the Aesthetic in Theories of Race, Gender, and Sexuality, and the Role of Race, Gender, and Sexuality in Philosophical Aesthetics, *Philosophy Compass* 8/2: 101–16.
Jekyll, Gertrude. 2009. *The Gardener's Essential Gertrude Jekyll*. Ludlow: Excellent Press.
Jenkins, Henry, Katie Clinton, Ravi Purushotma, Alice J. Robison, and Margaret Weigel. 2006. *Confronting the Challenges of Participatory Culture: Media Education for the 21st Century*. Chicago: MacArthur Foundation.
Johanson, Katya, Hilary Glow, and Anne Kershaw. 2014. New Modes of Arts Participation and the Limits of Cultural Indicators for Local Government, *Poetics* 43: 43–59.
Johansson, Petter. 2005. Failure to Detect Mismatches Between Intention and Outcome in a Simple Decision Task, *Science* 310/5745: 116–19.
Johansson, Petter, Lars Hall, Sverker Sikström, Betty Tärning, and Andreas Lind. 2006. How Something Can Be Said about Telling More Than We Can Know: On Choice Blindness and Introspection, *Consciousness and Cognition* 15/4: 673–92.
Johnston, Mark, 1998. Are Manifest Qualities Response-Dependent? *Monist* 81/1: 3–43.
Johnstone, Lesley, ed. 2007. *Hybrids: Reshaping the Contemporary Garden in Métis*. Vancouver: Blueimprint.
Jones, Robert. 1998. *Gender and the Formation of Taste*. Cambridge: Cambridge University Press.

Kaelin, E. F. 1989. *An Aesthetics for Art Educators*. New York: Teacher's College Press.
Kahneman, Daniel, and Gary Klein. 2009. Conditions for Intuitive Expertise: A Failure to Disagree, *American Psychologist* 64/6: 515–26.
Kant, Immanuel. 2000[1790]. *Critique of the Power of Judgement*, trans. Paul Guyer and Eric Matthews. Cambridge: Cambridge University Press.
Kemp, Gary. 1999. The Aesthetic Attitude, *British Journal of Aesthetics* 39/4: 392–9.
Kennedy, John M. 1993. *Drawing and the Blind: Pictures to Touch*. New Haven, CT: Yale University Press.
Kerr, Donna H. 1978. Aesthetic Policy, *Journal of Aesthetic Education* 12/1: 5–22.
Kidd, Dustin. 2012. Public Culture in America: A Review of Cultural Policy Debates, *Journal of Arts Management, Law, and Society* 42/1: 11–21.
Kieran, Matthew. 2001. In Defence of the Ethical Evaluation of Narrative Art, *British Journal of Aesthetics* 41/1: 26–38.
Kieran, Matthew. 2006. Art, Morality, and Ethics: On the (Im)moral Character of Art Works and Inter-Relations to Artistic Value, *Philosophy Compass* 1/2: 129–43.
Kieran, Matthew. 2008. Why Ideal Critics Are Not Ideal: Aesthetic Character, Motivation, and Value, *British Journal of Aesthetics* 48/3: 278–94.
Kieran, Matthew. 2009. The Vice of Snobbery: Aesthetic Knowledge, Justification, and Virtue in Art Appreciation, *Philosophical Quarterly* 60/239: 243–63.
King, Alex. forthcoming. The Amoralist and the Anaesthetic, *Pacific Philosophical Quarterly*.
Kitcher, Philip. 1993. *The Advancement of Science*. Oxford: Oxford University Press.
Kivy, Peter. 1975. What Makes "Aesthetic" Terms Aesthetic? *Philosophy and Phenomenological Research* 36/2: 197–211.
Kivy, Peter. 1980. A Failure of Aesthetic Emotivism, *Philosophical Studies* 38/4: 351–65.
Kivy, Peter. 2015. *De Gustibus: Arguing about Taste and Why We Do It*. Oxford: Oxford University Press.
Knight, Helen. 1967. The Use of "Good" in Aesthetic Judgements, *Aesthetic and Language*, ed. William Elton. Oxford: Blackwell, pp. 147–60.
Kölbel, Max. 2003. Faultless Disagreement, *Proceedings of the Aristotelian Society* 104: 53–73.
Kölbel, Max. 2004. Indexical Relativism Versus Genuine Relativism, *International Journal of Philosophical Studies* 12/3: 297–313.
Kölbel, Max. 2008. The Evidence for Relativism, *Synthese* 166/2: 375–95.
Kölbel, Max. 2016. Aesthetic Judge-Dependence and Expertise, *Inquiry* 59/6: 589–617.
Konigsberg, Amir. 2012. The Acquaintance Principle, Aesthetic Autonomy, and Aesthetic Appreciation, *British Journal of Aesthetics* 52/2: 153–68.
Konstan, David. 2014. *Beauty: The Fortunes of an Ancient Greek Idea*. Oxford: Oxford University Press.
Koopman, Constantijn. 2005. Art as Fulfilment: On the Justification of Education in the Arts, *Journal of Philosophy of Education* 39/1: 85–97.
Korsgaard, Christine M. 1983. Two Distinctions in Goodness, *Philosophical Review* 92/2: 169–95.
Korsgaard, Christine M. 1986. Skepticism about Practical Reason, *Journal of Philosophy* 83/1: 5–25.

Korsgaard, Christine M. 1996. *The Sources of Normativity*. Cambridge: Cambridge University Press.
Korsmeyer, Carolyn. 1998. Taste: Modern and Recent History, *Encyclopedia of Aesthetics*, ed. Michael Kelly. Oxford: Oxford University Press, vol. 4, pp. 360–3.
Korsmeyer, Carolyn. 1999. *Making Sense of Taste: Food and Philosophy*. Ithaca, NY: Cornell University Press.
Kristeller, P. O. 1951–2. The Modern System of the Arts, *Journal of the History of Ideas* 12/4: 496–527 and 13/1: 17–46.
Kulvicki, John. 2013. *Images*. London: Routledge.
Kushner, Roland J., and Randy Cohen. 2010. Measuring National-Level Cultural Capacity with the National Arts Index, *International Journal of Arts Management* 13/3: 20–40.
Laetz, Brian. 2008. A Modest Defense of Aesthetic Testimony, *Journal of Aesthetics and Art Criticism* 66/4: 355–63.
Laetz, Brian. 2010. Kendall Walton's "Categories of Art:" A Critical Commentary, *British Journal of Aesthetics* 50/3: 287–306.
Lamarque, Peter. 2008. *The Philosophy of Literature*. Oxford: Wiley–Blackwell.
Lamarque, Peter. 2010. Wittgenstein, Literature, and the Idea of a Practice, *British Journal of Aesthetics* 50/4: 375–88.
Lasersohn, Peter. 2005. Context Dependence, Disagreement, and Predicates of Personal Taste, *Linguistics and Philosophy* 28/6: 643–86.
Layton, Robert. 2011. Aesthetics: The Approach from Social Anthropology, *The Aesthetic Mind: Philosophy and Psychology*, ed. Elisabeth Schellekens and Peter Goldie. Oxford: Oxford University Press, pp. 208–22.
Lessig, Lawrence. 1995. The Regulation of Social Meaning, *University of Chicago Law Review* 62/3: 943–1045.
Levi, Albert William and Ralph A. Smith. 1991. *Art Education: A Critical Necessity*. Urbana, IL: University of Illinois Press.
Levinson, Jerrold. 1980. What a Musical Work Is, *Journal of Philosophy* 77/1: 5–28.
Levinson, Jerrold. 1984. Aesthetic Supervenience, *Southern Journal of Philosophy* 22/1: 93–110.
Levinson, Jerrold. 1992. Pleasure and the Value of Works of Art, *British Journal of Aesthetics* 32/4: 295–306.
Levinson, Jerrold. 1994. Being Realistic about Aesthetic Properties, *Journal of Aesthetics and Art Criticism* 51/3: 351–4.
Levinson, Jerrold. 2001. Aesthetic Properties, Evaluative Force, and Differences of Sensibility, *Aesthetic Concepts: Essays after Sibley*, ed. Emily Brady and Jerrold Levinson. Oxford: Oxford University Press, pp. 61–80.
Levinson, Jerrold. 2002. Hume's Standard of Taste: The Real Problem, *Journal of Aesthetics and Art Criticism* 60/3: 227–38.
Levinson, Jerrold. 2003. *Oxford Handbook of Aesthetics*. Oxford: Oxford University Press.
Levinson, Jerrold. 2005. Aesthetic Properties, *Aristotelian Society Supplementary Volume* 78: 211–27.
Levinson, Jerrold. 2010. Artistic Worth and Personal Taste, *Journal of Aesthetics and Art Criticism* 68/3: 225–33.

Levinson, Jerrold. 2011. Beauty Is Not One: The Irreducible Variety of Visual Beauty, *The Aesthetic Mind: Philosophy and Psychology*, ed. Elisabeth Schellekens and Peter Goldie. Oxford: Oxford University Press, pp. 190–207.
Levinson, Jerrold. 2016. Toward an Adequate Conception of Aesthetic Experience, *Aesthetic Pursuits*. Oxford: Oxford University Press, pp. 28–46.
Lewis, C. I. 1946. *An Analysis of Knowledge and Valuation*. La Salle, IL: Open Court.
Lewis, David K. 1969. *Convention: A Philosophical Study*. Cambridge, MA: Harvard University Press.
Lewis, David K. 1989. Dispositional Theories of Value, *Aristotelian Society Supplementary Volume* 63: 113–37.
Lifson, Ben. 1980. *Eugène Atget*. New York: Aperture.
Livingston, Paisley. 2003. On an Apparent Truism in Aesthetics, *British Journal of Aesthetics* 43/3: 260–78.
Lopes, Dominic McIver. 1996. *Understanding Pictures*. Oxford: Oxford University Press.
Lopes, Dominic McIver. 2000. From *Languages of Art* to Art in Mind, *Journal of Aesthetics and Art Criticism* 58/3: 227–31.
Lopes, Dominic McIver. 2002. Vision, Touch, and the Value of Pictures, *British Journal of Aesthetics* 42/2: 187–97.
Lopes, Dominic McIver. 2005. *Sight and Sensibility: Evaluating Pictures*. Oxford: Oxford University Press.
Lopes, Dominic McIver. 2008. Virtues of Art: Good Taste, *Aristotelian Society Supplementary Volume* 82: 197–211.
Lopes, Dominic McIver. 2009. *A Philosophy of Computer Art*. London: Routledge.
Lopes, Dominic McIver. 2014a. *Beyond Art*. Oxford: Oxford University Press.
Lopes, Dominic McIver. 2014b. Feckless Reason, *Aesthetics and the Sciences of Mind*, ed. Gregory Currie, Matthew Kieran, Aaron Meskin, and Jon Robson. Oxford: Oxford University Press, pp. 21–36.
Lopes, Dominic McIver. 2015. Aesthetic Experts, Guides to Value, *Journal of Aesthetics and Art Criticism* 73/3: 235–46.
Lopes, Dominic McIver. 2016a. *Four Arts of Photography: An Essay in Philosophy*. Oxford: Wiley-Blackwell.
Lopes, Dominic McIver. 2016b. In the Eye of the Beholder, *Art, Mind, and Narrative: Themes from the Work of Peter Goldie*, ed. Julian Dodd. Oxford: Oxford University Press, pp. 223–40.
Lopes, Dominic McIver. 2017a. Beauty, the Social Network, *Canadian Journal of Philosophy* 47/4: 437–53.
Lopes, Dominic McIver. 2017b. Disputing Taste, *Semantics of Aesthetic Judgement*, ed. James O. Young. Oxford: Oxford University Press, pp. 61–81.
Lopes, Dominic McIver. 2018. *Aesthetics on the Edge: Where Philosophy Meets the Human Sciences*. Oxford: Oxford University Press.
Lopes, Dominic McIver. forthcoming. Pictures: Their Power in Practice, *Pictorial Appreciation*, ed. Jérôme Pelletier and Alberto Voltolini. London: Routledge.
López de Sa, Dan. 2007. The Many Relativisms and the Question of Disagreement, *International Journal of Philosophical Studies* 15/2: 269–79.

McBrearty, Sally, and Alison S. Brooks. 2000. The Revolution That Wasn't: A New Interpretation of the Origin of Modern Human Behavior, *Journal of Human Evolution* 39/5: 453–563.
McDowell, John. 1979. Virtue and Reason, *Monist* 62/3: 331–50.
McDowell, John. 1983. Aesthetic Value, Objectivity, and the Fabric of the World, *Pleasure, Preference and Value*, ed. Eva Schaper. Cambridge: Cambridge University Press, pp. 1–16.
McDowell, John. 1985. Values and Secondary Qualities, *Morality and Objectivity*, ed. Ted Honderich. London: Routledge, pp. 110–29.
McEwan, Ian. 2012. *Sweet Tooth*. London: Random House.
MacFarlane, John. 2005. Making Sense of Relative Truth, *Proceedings of the Aristotelian Society* 105: 305–23.
McGonigal, Andrew. 2006. The Autonomy of Aesthetic Judgement, *British Journal of Aesthetics* 46/4: 331–48.
McGonigal, Andrew. 2010. Art, Value, and Character, *Philosophical Quarterly* 60/240: 545–66.
McGonigal, Andrew. 2017. Responding to Aesthetic Reasons, *Estetika* 54 10/1: 40–64.
McGonigal, Andrew. forthcoming. Aesthetic Reasons, *Oxford Handbook of Reasons and Normativity*, ed. Daniel Star. Oxford: Oxford University Press.
MacIntyre, Alasdair C. 1984. *After Virtue: A Study in Moral Theory*. Notre Dame: University of Notre Dame Press.
Mackie, J. L. 1977. *Ethics: Inventing Right and Wrong*. London: Penguin.
MacKinnon, John. 2001a. Aesthetic Supervenience: For and Against, *British Journal of Aesthetics* 41/1: 59–75.
MacKinnon, John. 2001b. Heroism and Reversal: Sibley on Aesthetic Supervenience, *Aesthetic Concepts: Essays after Sibley*, ed. Emily Brady and Jerrold Levinson. Oxford: Oxford University Press, pp. 81–99.
McLaughlin, Brian, and Karen Bennett. 2011. Supervenience, *Stanford Encyclopedia of Philosophy* <http://plato.stanford.edu>.
McNally, Louise, and Isidora Stojanovic. 2017. Aesthetic Adjectives. *Semantics of Aesthetic Judgement*, ed. James O. Young. Oxford: Oxford University Press, pp. 17–37.
Mag Uidhir, Christy, and Cameron Buckner. 2014. The Artist as Aesthetic Expert, *Aesthetics and the Sciences of Mind*, ed. Gregory Currie, Matthew Kieran, Aaron Meskin, and Jon Robson. Oxford: Oxford University Press, pp. 121–39.
Mason, Michelle. 1998. MacIntyre on Modernity and How It Has Marginalized the Virtues, *How Should One Live? Essays on the Virtues*, ed. Roger Crisp. Oxford: Oxford University Press, pp. 191–209.
Mason, Michelle. 2001. Moral Prejudice and Aesthetic Deformity: Rereading Hume's "Of the Standard of Taste," *Journal of Aesthetics and Art Criticism* 59/1: 59–71.
Masuda, Takahito, Richard Gonzalez, Letty Kwan, and Richard Nisbett. 2008. Culture and Aesthetic Preference: Comparing the Attention to Context of East Asians and Americans, *Personality and Social Psychology Bulletin* 34/9: 1260–75.
Matravers, Derek. 2010. Aesthetic Relativism, *Postgraduate Journal of Aesthetics* 7/1: 1–12.
Matthen, Mohan. 2015. Play, Skill, and the Origins of Perceptual Art, *British Journal of Aesthetics* 55/2: 173–97.

Matthen, Mohan. 2017. The Pleasure of Art, *Australasian Philosophical Review* 1/1: 6–28.
McBrearty, Sally, and Alison S. Brooks. 2000. The Revolution That Wasn't: A New Interpretation of the Origin of Modern Human Behavior, *Journal of Human Evolution* 39/5: 453–563.
McDowell, John. 1979. Virtue and Reason, *Monist* 62/3: 331–50.
McDowell, John. 1983. Aesthetic Value, Objectivity, and the Fabric of the World, *Pleasure, Preference and Value*, ed. Eva Schaper. Cambridge: Cambridge University Press, pp. 1–16.
McDowell, John. 1985. Values and Secondary Qualities, *Morality and Objectivity*, ed. Ted Honderich. London: Routledge, pp. 110–29.
McEwan, Ian. 2012. *Sweet Tooth*. London: Random House.
McGonigal, Andrew. 2006. The Autonomy of Aesthetic Judgement, *British Journal of Aesthetics* 46/4: 331–48.
McGonigal, Andrew. 2010. Art, Value, and Character, *Philosophical Quarterly* 60/240: 545–66.
McGonigal, Andrew. 2017. Responding to Aesthetic Reasons, *Estetika* 54 10/1: 40–64.
McGonigal, Andrew. forthcoming. Aesthetic Reasons, *Oxford Handbook of Reasons and Normativity*, ed. Daniel Star. Oxford: Oxford University Press.
McLaughlin, Brian, and Karen Bennett. 2011. Supervenience, *Stanford Encyclopedia of Philosophy* <http://plato.stanford.edu>.
McNally, Louise, and Isidora Stojanovic. 2017. Aesthetic Adjectives. *Semantics of Aesthetic Judgement*, ed. James O. Young. Oxford: Oxford University Press, pp. 17–37.
Meager, Ruby. 1985. Connoisseurship, *British Journal of Aesthetics* 25/2: 137–52.
Melchionne, Kevin. 2010. On the Old Saw "I Know Nothing about Art but I Know What I Like," *Journal of Aesthetics and Art Criticism* 68/2: 131–41.
Melchionne, Kevin. 2017. Art and Well-Being, *Estetika* 54 10/2: 189–211.
Meske, Eunice Boardman. 1987. Music in the Schools: A Rationale, *Journal of Aesthetic Education* 21/4: 41–9.
Meskin, Aaron. 2004. Aesthetic Testimony: What Can We Learn from Others about Beauty and Art? *Philosophy and Phenomenological Research* 69/1: 65–91.
Meskin, Aaron. 2006. Solving the Puzzle of Aesthetic Testimony, *Knowing Art: Essays in Epistemology and Aesthetics*, ed. Matthew Kieran and Dominic McIver Lopes. Dordrecht: Springer, pp. 109–24.
Millar, Alan. 2000. The Scope of Perceptual Knowledge, *Philosophy* 75/291: 73–88.
Miller, Richard W. 1998. Three Versions of Objectivity: Aesthetic, Moral, and Scientific, *Aesthetics and Ethics: Essays at the Intersection*, ed. Jerrold Levinson. Cambridge: Cambridge University Press, pp. 26–58.
Millikan, Ruth Garrett. 1984. *Language, Thought, and Other Biological Categories*. Cambridge, MA: MIT Press.
Mills, Charles W. 2005. "Ideal Theory" as Ideology, *Hypatia* 20/3: 165–84.
Mithen, Steven J. 1996. *The Prehistory of the Mind: A Search for the Origins of Art, Religion, and Science*. London: Thames and Hudson.
Mole, Christopher. 2016. Real Objective Beauty, *British Journal of Aesthetics* 56/4: 367–81.
Moore, G. E. 1903. *Principia Ethica*. Cambridge: Cambridge University Press.
Moran, Richard. 2012. Kant, Proust, and the Appeal of Beauty, *Critical Inquiry* 38/2: 298–329.

Morel, Gaëlle. 2012. *Berenice Abbott*, trans. James Gussen. Paris: Hazan.
Morton, Adam. 2012. *Bounded Thinking: Intellectual Virtues for Limited Agents*. Oxford: Oxford University Press.
Mothersill, Mary. 1984. *Beauty Restored*. Oxford: Oxford University Press.
Mothersill, Mary. 1989. Hume and the Paradox of Taste, *Aesthetics: A Critical Anthology*, ed. George Dickie, Richard Sclafani, and Ronald Roblin. New York: St Martin's, pp. 269–86.
Mothersill, Mary. 2004. Beauty and the Critic's Judgement, *Blackwell Guide to Aesthetics*, ed. Peter Kivy. Oxford: Wiley–Blackwell, pp. 152–66.
Myers, B. R. 2010. Smaller Than Life, *The Atlantic* 306/3: 114–20.
Nagel, Thomas. 1985. Public Support for the Arts, *Columbia Journal of Art and the Law* 9/208: 236–9.
Nanay, Bence. 2016. *Aesthetics as Philosophy of Perception*. Oxford: Oxford University Press.
Nehamas, Alexander. 2007. *Only a Promise of Happiness: The Place of Beauty in a World of Art*. Princeton, NJ: Princeton University Press.
Neufeld, Jonathan. 2015. Aesthetic Disobedience, *Journal of Aesthetics and Art Criticism* 73/2: 115–25.
Newall, Michael. 2016. The Crit: Toward a Theory of the Contemporary Art School, *Routledge Companion to Criticality in Art, Architecture, and Design*, ed. Chris Brisban and Myra Thiessen. London: Routledge.
Nguyen, C. Thi. 2017. Philosophy of Games, *Philosophy Compass* 12/8: 1–18.
Nichols, Shaun, and Trisha Folds-Bennett. 2003. Are Children Moral Objectivists? Children's Judgments about Moral and Response-Dependent Properties, *Cognition* 90/2: B23–32.
Nisbett, Richard. 2003. *The Geography of Thought: Why We Think the Way We Do*. New York: Simon and Schuster.
Nozick, Robert. 1981. *Philosophical Explanations*. Cambridge, MA: Harvard University Press.
Nozick, Robert. 1985. Public Support for the Arts, *Columbia Journal of Art and the Law* 9/208: 162–7.
Nussbaum, Martha C. 1990. *Love's Knowledge: Essays on Philosophy and Literature*. Oxford: Oxford University Press.
O'Hagan, John. 2016. Objectives of Arts Funding Agencies Often Do Not Map Well onto Societal Benefits, *Cultural Trends* 25/4: 249–62.
O'Neill, John. 1992. The Varieties of Intrinsic Value, *Monist* 75/2: 119–37.
Olsen, Stein Haugom. 1981. Literary Aesthetics and Literary Practice, *Mind* 90/360: 521–41.
Pahlka, Bill. 2012. Metaphors, Take Flight, *New York Times Book Review* (December 23): 31.
Pankratz, David B. 1983. Aesthetic Welfare, Government, and Educational Policy, *Journal of Aesthetic Education* 17/2: 97–110.
Parfit, Derek. 2011. *On What Matters*. Oxford: Oxford University Press. 2 vols.
Parsons, Glenn. 2008. *Aesthetics and Nature*. London: Continuum Press.
Parsons, Glenn. 2015. *The Philosophy of Design*. Oxford: Wiley-Blackwell.

Parsons, Glenn, and Allen Carlson. 2008. *Functional Beauty*. Oxford: Oxford University Press.

Patridge, Stephanie. 2016. The Many Faces of Appreciative Snobbery, Annual Meeting of the American Society for Aesthetics, November 23–6.

Paul, L. A. 2014. *Transformative Experience*. Oxford: Oxford University Press.

Pettit, Philip. 1983. The Possibility of Aesthetic Realism, *Pleasure, Preference, and Value*, ed. Eva Schaper. Cambridge: Cambridge University Press.

Pettit, Philip. 1991. Realism and Response-Dependence, *Mind* 100/4: 587–626.

Pollock, Sheldon. 2016. An Intellectual History of Rasa, *A Rasa Reader: Classical Indian Aesthetics*, trans and ed. Sheldon Pollock. New York: Columbia University Press, pp. 1–45.

Pratt, Henry John. 2012. Artistic Institutions, Valuable Experiences: Coming to Terms with Artistic Value, *Philosophia* 40/3: 591–606.

Prettejohn, Elizabeth. 2005. *Beauty and Art, 1750–2000*. Oxford: Oxford University Press.

Prinz, Jesse. 2006. Bad Taste, *Knowing Art: Essays in Epistemology and Aesthetics*, ed. Matthew Kieran and Dominic McIver Lopes. Dordrecht: Springer, pp. 95–107.

Pritchard, Duncan. 2010. Achievements, Luck, and Value. *Think* 9/25: 19–30.

Protasi, Sara. 2017. The Perfect Bikini Body: Can We All Really Have It? Loving Gaze as an Antioppressive Beauty Ideal, *Thought* 6/2: 93–101.

Quine. W. V. O. 1981. *Theories and Things*. Cambridge, MA: Harvard University Press.

Quinn, Warren. 1993. Rationality and the Human Good, *Morality and Action*. Cambridge: Cambridge University Press, pp. 210–17.

Radway, Janice A. 1997. *A Feeling for Books: The Book-of-the-Month Club, Literary Taste, and Middle-Class Desire*. Chapel Hill, NC: University of North Carolina Press.

Raffman, Diana. 2003. Is Twelve-Tone Music Artistically Defective? *Midwest Studies in Philosophy* 27: 69–87.

Railton, Peter. 1986. Moral Realism, *Philosophical Review* 95/2: 163–207.

Railton, Peter. 2000. Taste and Value, *Well-Being and Morality: Essays in Honour of James Griffin*, ed. Roger Crisp and Brad Hooker. Oxford: Oxford University Press, 53–74.

Railton, Peter. 2003. Aesthetic Value, Moral Value, and the Ambitions of Naturalism, *Facts, Values, and Norms: Essays Toward a Morality of Consequence*. Cambridge: Cambridge University Press, pp. 85–130.

Ransom, Madeleine. 2015. Aesthetic Expertise, High-Level Perceptual Content, and Non-Inferential Justification, Annual Meeting of the American Society for Aesthetics, November 11–14.

Ransom, Madeleine. 2017. Frauds, Posers and Sheep: A Virtue Theoretic Solution to the Acquaintance Debate, *Philosophy and Phenomenological Research*.

Rawls, John. 1971. *A Theory of Justice*. Cambridge, MA: Harvard University Press.

Raz, Joseph. 1991. Mixing Values, *Aristotelian Society Supplementary Volume* 65/1: 83–100.

Raz, Joseph. 1999a. *Engaging Reason: On the Theory of Value and Action*. Oxford: Oxford University Press.

Raz, Joseph. 1999b. Notes on Value and Objectivity, *Engaging Reason: On the Theory of Value and Action*. Oxford: Oxford University Press, pp. 118–60.

Raz, Joseph. 2003. *The Practice of Value*, ed. R. Jay Wallace. Oxford: Oxford University Press.

Reford, Alexander. 2001. *Reford Gardens*. Montréal: Fides.

Reford, Alexander. 2004. *Les Jardins de Métis: Le Paradis d'Elsie Reford*. Montréal: Éditions de l'Homme.

Reid, Louis Arnaud. 1948. The Nature and Justification of an "Arts" Education, *Higher Education Quarterly* 3/1: 427–516.

Ribeiro, Anna Christina. 2010. Aesthetic Attributions: The Case of Poetry, *Journal of Aesthetics and Art Criticism* 70/3: 293–302.

Richardson, Tim. 2009. *Great Gardens of America*. London: Frances Lincoln.

Riggle, Nicholas. 2013. Levinson on the Aesthetic Ideal, *Journal of Aesthetics and Art Criticism* 71/3: 277–81.

Riggle, Nicholas. 2015. On the Aesthetic Ideal, *British Journal of Aesthetics* 5/4: 433–47.

Riggle, Nicholas. 2016. On the Interest in Beauty and Disinterest, *Philosophers' Imprint* 16/9: 1–14.

Riggle, Nicholas. 2017. *On Being Awesome: A Unified Theory of How Not to Suck*. New York: Penguin.

Roberts, Tom. 2018. Aesthetic Virtues: Traits and Faculties, *Philosophical Studies* 175/2: 429–47.

Roelofs, Monique. 2005. Racialization as an Aesthetic Production: What Does the Aesthetic Do for Whiteness and Blackness and Vice Versa? *White on White/Black on Black*, ed. George Yancy. Lanham: Rowman and Littlefield, pp. 83–124.

Rooney, Kathleen. 2005. *Reading with Oprah: The Book Club That Changed America*. Fayetteville: University of Arkansas Press.

Rose, Sam. 2017. The Fear of Aesthetics in Art and Literary Theory, *New Literary History* 48/2: 223–44.

Rosen, Gideon. 1994. Objectivity and Modern Idealism: What Is the Question? *Philosophy in Mind*, ed. Michaelis Michael and John O'Leary-Hawthorne. Dordrecht: Kluwer, pp. 277–319.

Rosen, Gideon. 2010. Metaphysical Dependence: Grounding and Reduction, *Modality: Metaphysics, Logic, and Epistemology*, ed. Robert Hale and Aviv Hoffman. Oxford: Oxford University Press, pp. 109–36.

Ross, Stephanie. 2008. Humean Critics: Real or Ideal? *British Journal of Aesthetics* 48/1: 20–8.

Ross, Stephanie. 2011. Ideal Observer Theories in Aesthetics, *Philosophy Compass* 6/8: 513–22.

Ross, Stephanie. 2012. Comparing and Sharing Taste: Reflections on Critical Advice, *Journal of Aesthetics and Art Criticism* 70/4: 363–71.

Ross, Stephanie. 2014. When Critics Disagree: Prospects for Realism in Aesthetics, *Philosophical Quarterly* 64/257: 590–618.

Rushton, Michael. 2003. Cultural Diversity and Public Funding of the Arts: A View from Cultural Economics, *Journal of Arts Management, Law, and Society* 33/2: 85–97.

Ryle, Gilbert. 1954. Pleasure, *Aristotelian Society Supplementary Volume* 28: 135–46.

Saito, Yuriko. 2007. *Everyday Aesthetics*. Oxford: Oxford University Press.

Saito, Yuriko. 2015. Aesthetics of the Everyday, *Stanford Encyclopedia of Philosophy* <http://plato.stanford.edu>.

Santayana, George. 1896. *The Sense of Beauty*. New York: Scribner's.

Scanlon, T. M. 1985. Public Support for the Arts, *Columbia Journal of Art and the Law* 9/208: 167–71.

Scanlon, T. M. 1998a. The Status of Well-Being, *Tanner Lectures on Human Values* 19. Salt Lake City: University of Utah Press, pp. 91–143.

Scanlon, T. M. 1998b. *What We Owe to Each Other*. Cambridge, MA: Harvard University Press.

Scanlon, T. M. 2014. *Being Realistic about Reasons*. Oxford: Oxford University Press.

Scarry, Elaine. 2001. *On Beauty and Being Just*. Princeton, NJ: Princeton University Press.

Schaeffer, Jean-Marie. 2000. *Art of the Modern Age: Philosophy of Art from Kant to Heidegger*, trans. Steven Rendall. Princeton, NJ: Princeton University Press.

Schaeffer, Jean-Marie. 2015. *L'Expérience esthétique*. Paris: Gallimard.

Schaffer, Jonathan. 2009. On What Grounds What, *Metametaphysics: New Essays on the Foundations of Ontology*, ed. David Manley, David Chalmers, and Ryan Wasserman. Oxford: Oxford University Press, pp. 347–83.

Schellekens, Elisabeth. 2006. Towards a Reasonable Objectivism for Aesthetic Judgements, *British Journal of Aesthetics* 46/2: 163–77.

Schellekens, Elisabeth. 2017. Value Judgements and Standards of Normative Assessment, *Semantics of Aesthetic Judgement*, ed. James O. Young. Oxford: Oxford University Press, pp. 140–59.

Schelling, Thomas. 1960. *The Strategy of Conflict*. Cambridge, MA: Harvard University Press.

Schier, Flint. 1986. Hume and the Aesthetics of Agency, *Proceedings of the Aristotelian Society* 87: 121–35.

Schroeder, Mark. 2007. *Slaves of the Passions*. Oxford: Oxford University Press.

Schroeder, Timothy. 2004. *Three Faces of Desire*. Oxford: Oxford University Press.

Schwartz, David T. 1995. Can Intrinsic-Value Theorists Justify Subsidies for Contemporary Art? *Public Affairs Quarterly* 9/4: 331–43.

Scott, A. O. 2016. *Better Living Through Criticism: How to Think about Art, Pleasure, Beauty, and Truth*. New York: Penguin.

Searle, John R. 1995. *The Construction of Social Reality*. New York: Free Press.

Sewell, William, Jr. 1992. A Theory of Structure: Duality, Agency, and Transformation, *American Journal of Sociology* 98/1: 1–29.

Shafer-Landau, Russ. 2003. *Moral Realism: A Defence*. Oxford: Oxford University Press.

Shaftesbury, Anthony Ashley-Cooper, 3rd Earl of. 1999[1711]. *Characteristics of Men, Manners, Opinions, Times*, ed. Lawrence E. Klein. Cambridge: Cambridge University Press.

Sharpe, R. A. 2000. The Empiricist Theory of Artistic Value, *Journal of Aesthetics and Art Criticism* 58/4: 321–32.

Shelley, James. 2002. The Character and Role of Principles in the Evaluation of Art, *British Journal of Aesthetics* 42/1: 37–51.

Shelley, James. 2006. Critical Compatibilism, *Knowing Art: Essays in Epistemology and Aesthetics*, ed. Matthew Kieran and Dominic McIver Lopes. Dordrecht: Springer, pp. 125–36.

Shelley, James. 2010. Against Value Empiricism in Aesthetics, *Australasian Journal of Philosophy* 88/4: 707–20.

Shelley, James. 2011. Hume and the Value of the Beautiful, *British Journal of Aesthetics* 51/2: 213–22.
Shelley, James. 2013a. Hume and the Joint Verdict of True Judges, *Journal of Aesthetics and Art Criticism* 71/2: 146–53.
Shelley, James. 2013b. The Concept of the Aesthetic, *Stanford Encyclopedia of Philosophy* <http://plato.stanford.edu>.
Shimamura, Arthur, and Steven Palmer. 2011. *Aesthetic Science: Connecting Minds, Brains, and Experience*. Oxford: Oxford University Press.
Shiner, Larry. 2001. *The Invention of Art: A Cultural History*. Chicago, IL: University of Chicago Press.
Shusterman, Richard. 1989. Of the Scandal of Taste: Social Privilege as Nature in the Aesthetic Theories of Hume and Kant, *Philosophical Forum* 20/3: 211–29.
Sibley, Frank. 1959. Aesthetic Concepts, *Philosophical Review* 68/4: 421–50.
Sibley, Frank. 1965. Aesthetic and Nonaesthetic, *Philosophical Review* 74/2: 135–59.
Sibley, Frank. 1968. Objectivity and Aesthetics, *Aristotelian Society Supplementary Volume* 42: 31–54.
Sibley, Frank. 1974. Particularity, Art, and Evaluation, *Aristotelian Society Supplementary Volume* 48: 1–21.
Sibley, Frank. 2003a. General Criteria and Reasons in Aesthetics, *Approach to Aesthetics*, ed. John Benson, Betty Redfern, and Jeremy Roxbee Cox. Oxford: Oxford Unversity Press, pp. 104–18.
Sibley, Frank. 2003b. Taste, Smells, and Aesthetics, *Approach to Aesthetics*, ed. John Benson, Betty Redfern, and Jeremy Roxbee Cox. Oxford: Oxford Unversity Press, pp. 207–55.
Sidgwick, Henry. 1884. *The Methods of Ethics*, 3rd edn. Cambridge: Cambridge University Press.
Siebers, Tobin. 2011. *Disability Aesthetics*. Ann Arbor, MI: University of Michigan Press.
Silvia, Paul J. 2011. Human Emotions and Aesthetic Experience: An Overview of Empirical Aesthetics, *Aesthetic Science: Connecting Minds, Brains, and Experience*, ed. Arthur Shimamura and Steven Palmer. Oxford: Oxford University Press, pp. 250–75.
Simser, Bil. 2008. SimCity Source Code Released to the Wild! Let the Ports Begin, *Fear and Loathing* (January 10) <http://weblogs.asp.net/bsimser/simcity-source-code-released-to-the-wild-let-the-ports-begin>.
Skow, Bradford. 2016. *Reasons Why*. Oxford: Oxford University Press.
Slangard, Fabien. 2014. Reverse Engineering Strike Commander, *Fabien Slangard's Website* (January 22) <http://fabiensanglard.net/reverse_engineering_strike_commander>.
Slingerland, Edward G. 2014. *Trying Not to Try: The Art and Science of Spontaneity*. New York: Random House.
Slote, Michael A. 1971. The Rationality of Aesthetic Value Judgments, *Journal of Philosophy* 68/22: 821–39.
Smiley, David. 2001. Making the Modified Modern, *Perspecta* 32: 39–54.
Smith, Michael. 1987. The Humean Theory of Motivation, *Mind* 96/381: 36–61.
Smith, Michael. 1995. Internal Reasons, *Philosophy and Phenomenological Research* 55/1: 109–31.

Smith, Ralph A. 1975. Cultural Services, the Aesthetic Welfare, and Educational Research, *Studies in Art Education* 16/2: 5–11.
Smith, Ralph A. 1984. Formulating a Defensible Policy for Art Education, *Theory into Practice* 23/4: 273–9.
Smith, Ralph A., and Christina M. Smith. 1977. The Artworld and Aesthetic Skills: A Context for Research and Development, *Journal of Aesthetic Education* 11/2: 117–32.
Solomon-Godeau, Abigail. 1991. Canon Fodder: Authoring Eugène Atget, *Photography at the Dock: Essays on Photographic History, Institutions, and Practices*. Minneapolis, MN: University of Minnesota Press, pp. 28–51.
Sosa, Ernest. 2007. *A Virtue Epistemology: Apt Belief and Reflective Knowledge*. Oxford: Oxford University Press.
Sosa, Ernest. 2010. How Competence Matters in Epistemology, *Philosophical Perspectives* 24: 465–75.
Sosa, Ernest. 2011. *Knowing Full Well*. Princeton, NJ: Princeton University Press.
Sparshott, Francis. 1983. Why Artworks Have No Right to Have Rights, *Journal of Aesthetics and Art Criticism* 42/1: 5–15.
Spencer, Herbert. 1861. *Education: Intellectual, Moral, and Physical*. London: Manwaring.
Sperber, Dan. 1996. *Explaining Culture*. Oxford: Wiley-Blackwell.
Stang, Nicholas. 2012. Artworks Are Not Valuable for Their Own Sakes, *Journal of Aesthetics and Art Criticism* 70/3: 271–80.
Stecker, Robert. 1997. *Artworks: Definition, Meaning, Value*. University Park, PA: Penn State University Press.
Stecker, Robert. 2005. The Interaction of Ethical and Aesthetic Value, *British Journal of Aesthetics* 45/2: 138–50.
Stecker, Robert. 2006. Aesthetic Experience and Aesthetic Value, *Philosophy Compass* 1/1: 1–10.
Stecker, Robert. 2012. Artistic Value Defended, *Journal of Aesthetics and Art Criticism* 70/4: 355–62.
Steiner, Wendy. 2001. *Venus in Exile: The Rejection of Beauty in Twentieth-Century Art*. Riverside: Free Press.
Stephenson, Tamina. 2007. Judge Dependence, Epistemic Modals, and Predicates of Personal Taste, *Linguistics and Philosophy* 30/4: 487–525.
Stock, Kathleen, and Katherine Thomson-Jones. 2008. *New Waves in Aesthetics*. New York: Palgrave Macmillan.
Stokes, Dustin. 2014. Cognitive Penetration and the Perception of Art, *Dialectica* 68/1: 1–34.
Stokes, Dustin. 2018. Rich Perceptual Content and Aesthetic Properties, *Evaluative Perception*, ed. Anna Bergqvist and Robert Cowan. Oxford: Oxford University Press, pp. 19–41.
Strandberg, Caj. 2011. A Structural Disanalogy Between Aesthetic and Ethical Value Judgements, *British Journal of Aesthetics* 51/1: 51–67.
Strandberg, Caj. 2016. Aesthetic Internalism and Two Normative Puzzles, *Studi di estetica* 44/2: 23–70.
Suits, Bernard. 1978. *The Grasshopper: Games, Life, and Utopia*. Toronto: University of Toronto Press.

Sumner, Wayne. 1996. *Welfare, Happiness, and Ethics*. Oxford: Oxford University Press.
Sundell, Timothy. 2011. Disagreements about Taste, *Philosophical Studies* 155/2: 267–88.
Sundell, Timothy. 2017. Aesthetic Negotiation, *Semantics of Aesthetic Judgement*, ed. James O. Young. Oxford: Oxford University Press, pp. 82–105.
Swanton, Christine. 2005. *Virtue Ethics: A Pluralistic View*. Oxford: Oxford University Press.
Taliaferro, Charles. 1990. The Ideal Aesthetic Observer Revisited, *British Journal of Aesthetics* 30/1: 1–13.
Tanenhaus, Sam. 2010. Peace and War, *New York Times* (August 29): A1.
Tappolet, Christine. 2016. *Emotions, Value, and Agency*. Oxford: Oxford University Press.
Tavinor, Grant. 2009. *The Art of Videogames*. Oxford: Wiley-Blackwell.
Taylor, Charles. 1982. The Diversity of Goods, *Utilitarianism and Beyond*, ed. Amartya Sen and Bernard Williams. Cambridge: Cambridge University Press, pp. 129–44.
Taylor, Charles. 1989. *Sources of the Self: The Making of the Modern Identity*. Cambridge, MA: Harvard University Press.
Taylor, Paul C. 2016. *Black Is Beautiful: A Philosophy of Black Aesthetics*. Oxford: Wiley-Blackwell.
Taylor, Richard. 1970. *Good and Evil*. New York: Macmillan.
Tempest. 2008. Post to Atari Age (August 29, 2008) <https://atariage.com/forums/topic/130904-donkey-kong-source-code/page-3>.
Thomson, Judith Jarvis. 2008. *Normativity*. Chicago, IL: Open Court.
Todd, Cain Samuel. 2004. Quasi-Realism, Acquaintance, and the Normative Claims of Aesthetic Judgement, *British Journal of Aesthetics* 44/3: 277–96.
Toffler, Alvin. 1967. The Art of Measuring the Arts, *Annals of the American Academy of Political and Social Science* 373: 141–55.
Tormey, Alan. 1973a. Aesthetic Rights, *Journal of Aesthetics and Art Criticism* 32/2: 163–70.
Tormey, Alan. 1973b. Critical Judgments, *Theoria* 39/1–3: 35–49.
Townsend, Dabney. 2003. Thomas Reid and the Theory of Taste, *Journal of Aesthetics and Art Criticism* 61/4: 341–51.
Trottenberg, Arthur D. 1963. *A Vision of Paris: The Photographs of Eugène Atget, the Words of Marcel Proust*. New York: Macmillan.
Urmson, J. O. 1957. What Makes a Situation Aesthetic? *Proceedings of the Aristotelian Society* 31: 75–92.
Urmson, J. O. 1958. Saints and Heroes, *Essays in Moral Philosophy*, ed. A. I. Melden. Seattle: University of Washington Press, pp. 198–216.
Vaida, Iuliana Corina. 1998. The Quest for Objectivity: Secondary Qualities and Aesthetic Qualities, *Journal of Aesthetics and Art Criticism* 56/3: 283–97.
Vogt, Stine, and Svein Magnussen. 2007. Expertise in Pictorial Perception: Eye-Movement Patterns and Visual Memory in Artists and Laymen. *Perception* 36/1: 91–100.
Wallace, Jay. 2012. Duties of Love, *Aristotelian Society Supplementary Volume* 86: 175–98.
Walton, Kendall. 1970. Categories of Art, *Philosophical Review* 79/3: 334–67.
Walton, Kendall. 1993. How Marvelous! Towards a Theory of Aesthetic Value, *Journal of Aesthetics and Art Criticism* 51/3: 499–510.

Walton, Kendall. 2007. Aesthetics—What? Why? And Wherefore? *Journal of Aesthetics and Art Criticism* 65/2: 147–61.
Washburn, Dorothy Koster, ed. 1983. *Structure and Cognition in Art*. Cambridge: Cambridge University Press.
Watkins, Michael, and James Shelley. 2012. Response-Dependence about Aesthetic Value, *Pacific Philosophical Quarterly* 93/3: 338–52.
Wedgwood, Ralph. 2007. *The Nature of Normativity*. Oxford: Oxford University Press.
Wiggins, David. 1987a. A Sensible Subjectivism? *Needs, Values, Truth: Essays in the Philosophy of Value*. Oxford: Oxford University Press, pp. 185–211.
Wiggins, David. 1987b. Truth, Invention, and the Meaning of Life, *Needs, Values, Truth: Essays in the Philosophy of Value*. Oxford University Press, pp. 87–137.
Wiggins, David. 1990. Moral Cognitivism, Moral Relativism, and Motivating Moral Beliefs, *Proceedings of the Aristotelian Society* 91: 61–85.
Wiggins, David. 1998. Natural and Artificial Virtues: A Vindication of Hume's Scheme, *How Should One Live? Essays on the Virtues*, ed. Roger Crisp. Oxford: Oxford University Press, pp. 131–40.
Williams, Bernard. 1972. *Morality*. New York: Harper.
Williams, Bernard. 1973. A Critique of Utilitarianism, *Utilitarianism: For and Against*. Cambridge: Cambridge University Press, pp. 77–150.
Williams, Bernard. 1975. The Truth in Relativism, *Proceedings of the Aristotelian Society* 75: 215–28.
Williams, Bernard. 1981. Internal and External Reasons, *Moral Luck*. Cambridge: Cambridge University Press, pp. 101–13.
Williams, Bernard. 1985. *Ethics and the Limits of Philosophy*. Cambridge, MA: Harvard University Press.
Wilson, Daniel. 2017. *Lingua Aesthetica* <http://www.linguaaesthetica.com>.
Wilson, Jessica. 2017. Determinables and Determinates, *Stanford Encyclopedia of Philosophy* <http://plato.stanford.edu>.
Wilson, Timothy D., and Dana S. Dunn. 1985. Effects of Introspection on Attitude–Behavior Consistency: Analysing Reasons Versus Focusing on Feelings, *Journal of Experimental Social Psychology* 22/3: 249–63.
Wilson, Timothy D., and Jonathan W. Schooler. 1991. Thinking Too Much: Introspection Can Reduce the Quality of Preferences and Decisions, *Journal of Personality and Social Psychology* 60/2: 181–92.
Wilson, Timothy D., Dana S. Dunn, Jane A. Bybee, D. B. Hyman, and J. A. Rotondo. 1984. Effects of Analyzing Reasons on Attitude–Behavior Consistency, *Journal of Personality and Social Psychology* 47/1: 5–16.
Winner, Ellen, and Monica Cooper. 2000. Mute Those Claims: No Evidence (Yet) for a Causal Link Between Arts Study and Academic Achievement, *Journal of Aesthetic Education* 34/3–4: 11–75.
Winner, Ellen, and Lois Hetland, eds. 2000. The Arts and Academic Achievement: What the Evidence Shows, *Journal of Aesthetic Education* 34/3–4.
Witkin, Robert, and Tia DeNora. 1997. Aesthetic Materials and Aesthetic Agency, *Newsletter of the Sociology of Culture* 12/1: 1–6.

Wittgenstein, Ludwig. 1967. *Zettel*, ed. G. E. M. Anscombe and G. H. von Wright. Oxford: Blackwell.
Wolf, Susan. 1982. Moral Saints, *Journal of Philosophy* 79/8: 419–39.
Wolf, Susan. 2010. *Meaning in Life and Why It Matters*. Princeton, NJ: Princeton University Press.
Wolf, Susan. 2011. Good-for-Nothings, *Proceedings and Addresses of the American Philosophical Association* 85/2: 47–64.
Wollheim, Richard. 1980. *Art and Its Objects*, 2nd edn. Cambridge: Cambridge University Press.
Wollheim, Richard. 1985. Public Support for the Arts, *Columbia Journal of Art and the Law* 9/208: 179–86.
Wollheim, Richard. 1987. *Painting as an Art*. Princeton, NJ: Princeton University Press.
Wollheim, Richard. 1991. The Core of Aesthetics, *Journal of Aesthetic Education* 25/1: 37–45.
Wolterstorff, Nicholas. 2015. *Art Rethought: The Social Practices of Art*. Oxford: Oxford University Press.
Woodruff, David. 2001. A Virtue Theory of Aesthetics, *Journal of Aesthetic Education* 35/3: 23–36.
Worswick, Clark. 2002. *Berenice Abbott, Eugene Atget*. Santa Fe, NM: Arena.
Wright, Crispin. 1992. *Truth and Objectivity*. Cambridge, MA: Harvard University Press.
Wright, Sarah. 2010. Virtues, Social Roles, and Contextualism, *Metaphilosophy* 41/1: 95–114.
Yablo, Stephen. 1992. Mental Causation, *Philosophical Review* 101/2: 245–80.
Yancy, George. 2016. White Embodied Gazing, the Black Body as Disgust, and the Aesthetics of Un-Suturing, *Body Aesthetics*, ed. Sherri Irvin. Oxford: Oxford University Press, pp. 244–60.
Young, James O. 1997. Aesthetic Antirealism, *Southern Journal of Philosophy* 35/1: 119–34.
Young, James O., ed. 2017. *Semantics of Aesthetic Judgement*. Oxford: Oxford University Press.
Zagzebski, Linda Trinkaus. 1996. *Virtues of the Mind: An Inquiry into the Nature of Virtue and the Ethical Foundations of Knowledge*. Cambridge: Cambridge University Press.
Zangwill, Nick. 1992. Unkantian Notions of Disinterest, *British Journal of Aesthetics* 32/2: 149–52.
Zangwill, Nick. 1995. The Beautiful, the Dainty, and the Dumpy, *British Journal of Aesthetics* 35/4: 317–29.
Zangwill, Nick. 1998. Aesthetic/Sensory Dependence, *British Journal of Aesthetics* 38/1: 66–81.
Zangwill, Nick. 1999. Feasible Aesthetic Formalism, *Noûs* 33/4: 610–29.
Zangwill, Nick. 2000. In Defence of Moderate Aesthetic Formalism, *Philosophical Quarterly* 50/201: 476–93.
Ziff, Paul. 1966. Reasons in Art Criticism, *Philosophic Turnings*. Ithaca, NY: Cornell University Press, pp. 47–74.

Index

Abbott, Berenice 17–20
achievement 94, 97–8, 213
　normativity 107–8, 112–13, 133–42
　pleasurable 156–7
　see also competence; success
acts 94
acts, aesthetic 32–6, 49, 92
　aims of 95, 131–2
　appreciation model of 33, 45
　diversity of 16–24, 29
Addison, Joseph 6
advice 80–1, 152–3, 177–8
aesthetic profile 129–30, 170, 175, 179, 195
aesthetics
　aesthetic value in 7
　primitive question of 3, 8–9
　trends in 8
agency, aesthetic, *see* expertise, aesthetic
anaesthetes 202, 205
anchoring 195–8
Anderson, Elizabeth 68, 109
Anscombe, G. E. M. 40
anthropocentrism 198, 211
aptitude 114, 140
appreciation 29, 32–3, 35, 159–63
　competence in 160–3
　pleasurable 95, 160
　vs evaluation 35, 105–6, 160
approximation fallacy 78–9
Aristotle 156, 212
art 5–6
　theories of 7–8
arts, fine 122–3, 216
　concept of 7, 26, 45
attitudes, reactive 40
Archer, Alfred 40
Atget, Eugène 17–20
autonomy 233

Battaly, Heather 94
Baumgarten, Alexander 54–5
Baxandall, Michael 160–2
Beardsley, Monroe 4, 8, 43–4, 56, 131, 219–20, 222–3, 233
beautification 4–6
beauty, *see* value, aesthetic
beauty ideals 231–3
Becker, Howard 25, 121
Bishop, Michael 212–13

Blackburn, Simon 109, 143, 176
book clubs 20–1
Bourdieu, Pierre 26, 124–5
Braudel, Fernand 109
Budd, Malcolm 186

Cage, John 4
Carlson, Allen 158–9
Carroll, Noël 45
cognitivism 181
Cohen, Ted 82
Coleman, James 124–5
Collingwood, R. G. 7–8
communication, aesthetic 229–30
competence 96–7, 100, 112, 179–80, 185, 213
　counterfactual 101–3
　in evaluation 101–3
　path-dependent 179, 207–8, 222, 227–8
　perceptual 96–7, 102–3
　pleasurable 156–7
　see also metacompetence; virtue
Comte, Auguste 112
concepts, aesthetic 103, 129, 171–2
conflict 116–17, 124–5
confrontation 178–80
cooperation 114–15
coordination 115–16
connoisseurs 83, 86
Connor, Stephen 6
Cooper, Monica 2
Cormier, Claude 17
criticism, aesthetic 37, 67
criticism, personal 80–1, 152–3, 177–8
Cross, Anthony 40
Currie, Greg 179, 183–4

d'Alembert, Jean le Rond 7
Danto, Arthur 4–6, 8
De Clerq, Rafael 44, 46
deliberation 209–10
desires
　aesthetic 70, 84, 148–51
　hedonic 68–70, 84, 148, 157–8
　reason-given 148–9, 151
　reason-giving 69–70, 84–6
determinables and determinates 128, 192
Dewey, John 26–7
Dickie, George 8, 29
Diderot, Denis 7, 60

dignity 208
dilemmas 39–40
disagreement, aesthetic 8, 11, 166–7, 171–2
   faultless 167–9, 172
   objects of 168, 173–5
   persistent 168, 173–5
   pervasive 164–6
   purpose of 171–3, 176–8
   socially structured 167, 172–3, 175
   see also criticism, aesthetic; criticism, personal; semantics, aesthetic
disinterest 45
diversity, aesthetic 117–18, 141, 222–4, 229–33
Dworkin, Ronald 220

Eaton, Marcia 40, 54
education, aesthetic 2, 24, 123, 156–7, 178–80, 224–8
Egan, Andy 167, 172–3
Elgin, Catherine 226
Elster, John 85, 159
Epstein, Brian 193–4
eudaimonism 216
evaluation, aesthetic 34, 49, 92
   competence in 101–3, 112
   vs appreciation 35, 105–6, 160
experience, aesthetic 43–4
expertise 15, 25, 40–1, 92–3
expertise, aesthetic
   advice model of 80–1
   and achievement 98–9, 142–3
   demographics of 25–6, 72–3, 139–40
   education for 226–8
   hedonic 32, 59–61, 63, 65–7, 70, 72, 92–3
   imitation model of 78–9
   practice-relative 26–7, 73, 75, 140
   social dependencies of 73, 107–9, 151, 155, 159, 208–9, 231–3
   specialized 27–30, 73–5, 140–2
   stable 30–1, 75, 142–3
   value-tracking 35–6, 40–1, 101–3, 112
   see also achievement; competence; success; virtue
externalities 219

fakes and forgeries 134
Fine, Kit 188
Flickr 230
Fodor, Jerry 187
Foot, Philippa 168, 212, 216
Fried, Michael 85
function 158–9

Gallie, W. B. 164
games 159
Gaugin, Paul 3
gender 231–2

Goldie, Peter 216
Goldman, Alan 33
Gombrich, Ernst 149–50
good life 151, 208–10, 216
Goodman, Nelson 8
Greenberg, Clement 162
Griffin, James 212
grounding 187–8, 190, 193–5

happiness 211–13
Haslanger, Sally 110
hedonism 59
hedonism, aesthetic 9–11, 53–8, 77
   and appreciation 35, 95, 155
   and desire-based reasons 69–70, 85–6, 148
   and education 226
   and ordinal rankings 203–4
   naturalized 184–5
   see also motives; normativity, hedonic
Hegel, Georg Wilhelm Friedrich 7
Herrington, Susan 17
Hetland, Lois 2, 225–6
Hickey, Dave 1–2, 164–5
Hume, David 60–1, 63, 65, 136, 167
Hungerland, Isabel 165–6

integrity 208–9
Irvin, Sherri 134
Isenberg, Arnold 37

James, Henry 1
Jekyll, Gertrude 17
justice, social 213–16

Kahneman, Daniel 142
Kant, Immanuel 7, 26, 45, 60–1, 207
Kieran, Matthew 81, 153–5
Klein, Gary 142
Korsgaard, Christine 38, 68
Kristeller, P. O. 25
Kubala, Robbie 196

Lamb, Wally 21
language 112
Levinson, Jerrold 54, 62–7, 81–2, 189
Lewis, C. I. 8, 33, 57, 67

McDowell, John 198
McEwan, Ian 91
MacIntyre, Alasdair 142
MacOrlan, Pierre 19
masterpiece 64
masterwork 63–6, 76–7
Matthen, Mohan 156–7
Matravers, Derek 167
Meager, Ruby 83, 86
meaningful life 210–11

metacompetence 103–5
Miller, Mark 46
Mills, Charles 231–2
Moore, G. E. 8, 58, 184, 215
Morton, Adam 78–9, 99
Mothersill, Mary 3, 25, 33, 63–7, 97, 135–7, 202
motives 40–1, 49, 68, 86, 213
 aesthetic 149–55, 157–8
 careerist 150
 disinterested 45
 expert 150, 153–5
 snobbish 153–5
 social dependencies of 151–2, 154–5
music 163

Nagel, Thomas 221
naturalism 8, 182–3
 aesthetic value 185–6, 188–9, 191–2
 analytic 184, 186
 grounding 188–9
 normative 184–5
 reductive 183–4, 187
 substantive 185–6
Nehamas, Alexander 81, 101, 105–6, 165, 207–8
network theory 106–7, 119, 126–7, 134–5
Neufeld, Jonathan 177
nihilism 181–2
normativity 38–40, 42–3, 47–8, 124–5
 achievement 107–8, 112–13, 133–42
 hedonic 44–5, 48, 58–68, 78–81
 naturalized 184–5
 see also reasons; reasons, aesthetic
norms 120–1
 aesthetic 133–5
Nozick, Robert 7, 215, 220
Nussbaum, Martha 40

objectivism 8, 11, 182, 196–8, 211
opportunity, aesthetic 222–4, 227–8, 230, 232–3
Oprah Book Club 20–2
Oprah effect 20
original position, aesthetic 223
outsiders, aesthetic 202–4, 221–2

Paul, L. A. 54
Parfit, Derek 54, 196, 198
Parsons, Glenn 158–9
personality, aesthetic 81–3, 142, 207–10, 214, 216
photography 19, 123
pictures 122, 160–3
pleasure
 appreciative 95, 160

 as by-product 85, 159
 as public good 219–20
 disinterested 45
 facilitating 156–7
 finally valuable 55–6
 intellectual 54–5
 sensuous 5, 54–5
 snobbish 154–5
 variable 77–8
 see also normativity, hedonic
policy, aesthetic 2, 11, 217–18
 see also education, aesthetic; communication, aesthetic; justice, social; opportunity, aesthetic; public goods
positive psychology 212–13
practices, aesthetic 126–7, 139–43
 anchoring 195–6
 disagreement in 175
 dynamism of 143, 176–7
 hedonic 158–9, 213
 local 26, 30, 36, 136–8
 ranking of 27, 203–7
 see also aesthetic profile; norms; outsiders, aesthetic
practices, social 142
 anchoring 193–5
 and agency 110, 118, 155
 conflict 116–17, 124–5
 cooperation 114–15
 coordination 115–16
 explaining 110–11, 124–5
 norms of 120–1
 resources and schemas 120–3
 sanctions 127
 technology in 20–1, 122–3, 141
 trends in 116
Prettejohn, Elizabeth 54–5
primitive question 3–4, 201
Protasi, Sara 231–2
public goods 218–21

Quine, W. V. O. 183–4

race 231
Raffman, Diana 163
Railton, Peter 152
ranking
 impersonal 203–4
 agent-centred 206–7
Rawls, John 156
Raz, Joseph 27, 36, 143, 198
realism 181–2
reasons
 decisive 39
 factive 36
 practical 36–7
 theoretical 36

reasons, aesthetic 49, 91–2, 201, 203, 209
   achievement-based 112–13, 133–42, 148–9, 201–2, 205–6
   agent-centred 205–7, 225–6
   derived 206, 209, 227–8
   desire-based 68–70, 84–6, 148
   externalism 149–50
   internalism 68, 84–6
   path-dependent 179, 207–8, 222, 227–8
   practice-relative 205–6
   see also motives; normativity
Reford, Alexander 16–17
Reford, Elsie 15–17
relativism 177–80
response-dependence 59, 196–7
Riggle, Nick 82–3, 137
Rooney, Kathleen 20–2
Rosen, Gideon 188

sanctions 127
Santayana, George 2
Scanlon, Thomas 209–10, 220
Schaeffer, Jean-Marie 7
Scott, A. O. 5, 207
self-absorption 209–10
self-determination 233
semantics, aesthetic 166, 168–9
Sewell, William 120
Shafer-Landau, Russ 152–3
Shaftesbury 25
Shelley, James 77, 198, 204–5
Sibley, Frank 46, 103, 127–31, 186, 189, 192
Sidgwick, Henry 58
Sisyphus 201–11
skill 97, 156
Skow, Bradford 194–5
Slingerland, Edward 110
Smith, Michael 80
snobs 153–5
Socrates 3
Sosa, Ernie 94–6, 103, 131
specialization 113–14, 117–18
   see also expertise
spillovers, aesthetic 220–1
Stang, Nick 57
state of nature, aesthetic 111–12
structuralism 124–5
subjectivism 196, 211
success 94, 131–2, 138–9, 213

Sundell, Timothy 167
supervenience 189–90

Taylor, Charles 7
Taylor, Paul 231, 233
Taylor, Richard 201
Thomson, Judy Jarvis 92–3, 99
trends 116
true judges, *see* expertise, aesthetic

Urmson, J. O. 44

value
   final vs intrinsic 55–6
   fungible 56–7
   inherent 57–8
   positional 232
value, aesthetic
   attitude to 215
   demarcation of 42, 46–7
   determinable and determinate 127–9, 192
   pluralism 127–9, 204, 232–3
   reason-giving 38
   socially dependent 193, 197
   suspicion of 1, 4–6
   theory of 41–3, 47–8, 91–2
   valence of 130–3, 138–9
   see also beauty ideals, hedonism, aesthetic; naturalism, aesthetic value; network theory
video games 22–4, 159
virtue 30, 101, 153–5, 214–16
   see also expertise, aesthetic

Walton, Kendall 7, 108, 129, 134
Ware, Lauren 40
Watkins, Michael 198
well-being 212–13
Wiggins, David 196, 198, 211
Williams, Bernard 60, 68, 177–9
Winckelmann, Johann 55
Winfrey, Oprah 20–2
Winner, Ellen 2, 225–6
Wittgenstein, Ludwig 191–2
Wolf, Susan 210–11
Wollheim, Richard 8, 29–30, 33, 220

Xunzi 110

Zangwill, Nick 189

The manufacturer's authorised representative in the EU for product safety is Oxford University Press España S.A. of El Parque Empresarial San Fernando de Henares, Avenida de Castilla, 2 - 28830 Madrid (www.oup.es/en or product.safety@oup.com). OUP España S.A. also acts as importer into Spain of products made by the manufacturer.
Printed and bound by CPI Group (UK) Ltd, Croydon, CR0 4YY

22/04/2026

02094939-0002